THE GEOGRAPHY OF INJUSTICE

THE GEOGRAPHY OF INJUSTICE

EAST ASIA'S BATTLE BETWEEN MEMORY AND HISTORY

BARAK KUSHNER

CORNELL UNIVERSITY PRESS
Ithaca and London

First published 2024 by Cornell University Press

Library of Congress Cataloging-in-Publication Data

Names: Kushner, Barak, 1968– author.
Title: The geography of injustice : East Asia's battle between memory and history / Barak Kushner.
Other titles: East Asia's battle between memory and history
Description: Ithaca : Cornell University Press, 2024. | Includes bibliographical references and index.
Identifiers: LCCN 2023039445 (print) | LCCN 2023039446 (ebook) | ISBN 9781501774010 (hardcover) | ISBN 9781501774034 (epub) | ISBN 9781501774027 (pdf)
Subjects: LCSH: War crime trials—China—History—20th century. | War crime trials—Japan—History—20th century. | World War, 1939–1945—Influence. | Justice—History—20th century.
Classification: LCC DS842 .K87 2024 (print) | LCC DS842 (ebook) | DDC 940.53/5—dc23/eng/20230906
LC record available at https://lccn.loc.gov/2023039445
LC ebook record available at https://lccn.loc.gov/2023039446

To Oshō-san and Noriko, without your emotional warmth and embracing home my journey into East Asian history would never have begun. I owe it all and much more to your expansive hospitality and unflagging support over so many decades.

Contents

Acknowledgments

Investigating history around the world and then writing a book puts one in the debt of many. I would like to voice my deep appreciation to this global community because it takes a team to achieve this sort of expansive and expensive research. The kernel of the historical questions that galvanized my interest in pushing forward on this topic emerged from a six-year European Research Council (ERC) grant (2013–2019) that sponsored numerous workshops, international conferences, and travel funds to draw together an excellent cohort of scholars for the project "The Dissolution of the Japanese Empire and the Struggle for Legitimacy in Postwar East Asia, 1945–1965" (DOJSFL 313382). The sad fact that the UK decided to leave the warm embrace of the EU and the financial largesse that it offered scholars darkens my memories of that bright interlude. The subsequent edited volumes that grew from this collaboration were key for me and the group of postdocs who helped flesh out numerous ideas and the larger structures that undergird much of the effort behind this book.

The ERC administrative staff in Brussels were always professional, and Catherine Hirst was a great manager of the project. Matthew Funaiole made wonderful inventions with websites, and postdocs for the projects included Deokhyo Choi, Arnaud Doglia, Casper Wits, Sherzod Muminov, and Andrew Levidis, along with the eighty-five scholars who joined us for workshops at Cambridge and advanced our research over many years. Chen Hao continually kept up the good cheer with pointed questions as did other graduate students Mina Markovic, Ria Roy, Giulia Garbagni, Reyhan Silingar, Aiko Otsuka, Rashaad Eshack, Ko-hang Liao, Mariah Zhong, Rachel Williams, and many others whose names are too numerous to list. Students in my upper-level course on justice and reconciliation in East Asia, on whom I tested out some of the manuscript, offered critical and supportive comments. KJ Chen was a great research assistant, then my postdoc on a related digital humanities project, while remaining a Malbec enthusiast. Jonathan Yeung helped source crucial materials in Hong Kong.

In Cambridge, Nadya Mullen was instrumental in helping me with our auditors, as was Jen Goodwin, who took over the administrative reins after. Mickey Adolphson swooped in as chair of Japanese studies, and that made all the difference in establishing a firm platform from which to work. Freddie Semple has been a stable right hand as executive assistant for the chair. Ria Roy provided great cheer teaching us Korean, and Vicky Young always enthused with a good laugh and support, as did the staff of the FAMES admin office and other colleagues at the Faculty of Asian and Middle Eastern Studies. FAMES librarian Francoise Simmons, followed by Miki Jacobs and Japanese specialist librarian Kristin Williams, found important resources, as did Charles Aylmer for Chinese materials. The new Chinese specialist librarian Yan He and her husband Xin Fan have both been helpful with resources and support. The master of Corpus, Christopher Kelly and his partner Shawn, were very generous to celebrate my professorship. Jeff Kurashige provided inspiration sharing my office during his sabbatical. Joshua Batts taught me how to instruct text and translation classes in a whole new way and introduced the phrase "termly day of wonder," which I will continue to use.

The Japanese branch of my family, Watanabe Kiyoshi and Mizutori Michi, are elements who keep me grounded. Not to mention my partner in life Mami Mizutori, who journeys around the world flying the flag for the UN. In Japan, Wada Hideho remains a model. I have learned about the energy it takes to be a true scholar by following Kawashima Shin, Hosoya Yūichi, Asano Toyomi, among many others, as well as Takeda Kayoko, including the staff at her favorite bar near Rikkyo University. At Waseda University Umemori Naoyuki, Liu Jie, Tsuchiya Reiko, and others offered invited talks and constant feedback, as well as the opportunity to learn more about reconciliation in their massive Ministry of Education–supported research project. Suzuki Norio has been a sounding board for chats on Japan and East Asian history, and the Hitotsubashi University team has been instrumental as well. Over the years, discussions with the always intellectual Ono Hirohito were eye-opening. Ōnuma Yasuaki unfortunately passed away not long after I met him in person; I wish I could have gotten started on his book earlier to translate. Over the years I have learned much from Funabashi Yōichi, as well as from Naraoka Sōichi, Kishi Toshihiko, and Satō Takumi at Kyoto University, and of course Araragi Shinzō. At Osaka University, it was fun and educational to hang out with Rotem Kowner, as it was with Takahashi sensei, and the man who coordinates everyone, Sugita Yoneyuki.

Mike "Shi Chi" Lan is a pillar of support in Taiwan, and it was our conversations in 2011 that got the ball rolling with a number of projects that fed into what later became this book. Hsiao Hui-fen continues to find time to listen to my poor Chinese, and I continue to learn from the scholarship of Hsueh Hua-yuan, Huang Jen-Tzu, and Huang Tzu-chin. Fengjia University staff, He Jiawei and her team, assisted me over the long term with the creation of a related website. The "mole" copied so much in libraries for me as well.

In China, staff of the Shanghai Media Group with whom I filmed three episodes of a documentary series entitled *Asia-Pacific War Crimes Trials* taught me how to keep audiences interested. Directors Ao Xue, Dai Chengxian, and Xuan Furong, along with producer Chen Yinan, edited great film shots and organized an excellent array of interviews. These interactive moments in China stimulated further discussions into the nature of Sino-Japanese historical attitudes and memory. They were supported by the endearing company of cameraman Shen Jiajun, who was a master coordinator of choosing where to dine for every meal, and his colleague Zhang "Kung Fu Panda" Jun. The quiet but dependable lighting technician Huang Shanxiang kept us out of the shadows. Chang Chihyun, Hou Yanbo, Sun Yi, and Yan Haijian provided insights concerning my digital humanities websites and statistical calculations, while Liu Tong and Cheng Zhaoqi were munificent with their time and support at the Center for the Study of the Tokyo Trial at Shanghai Jiaotong University.

A shout-out to Haiyan Lee, Matthew Shores, Rana Mitter, and Yukiko Koga, among many others, for their comments and support. This includes my own father, who worked as assiduously on his autobiography while writing children's books into his nineties. Dad, you are a model for us all in how to reinvent yourself even decades after retirement. I received much feedback on early lackluster drafts and good advice from a number of people. Park Yuha, Sandra Wilson, James Llewelyn, and Robert Cribb shared their opinions, while Amy King, and Chuck Krauss from the Wilson Center, generously shared archives. Kerstin von Lingen has been exceptionally pointed in our discussions as we examine the issues from different angles. Sarah Kovner and Mickey Adolphson offered critical insights at draft stages, and David Chang saved me from numerous embarrassing blunders of fact. A lovely invitation to deliver a keynote in Israel was a highlight as were questions from Miki Bul, Nissim Otmazgim, and others. Reut Harari at Tel Aviv University and Danny Orbach at Hebrew University posed keen questions that got me thinking.

Tahirih Lee and Anika Culver at Florida State University offered a path into Chinese law. Jason Webb and Lori Meeks hosted a lovely evening at USC, while Jeremy Yellen invited me for a few days during which I was able to access the Center for China Studies at Chinese University Hong Kong, and offered a forum for a talk. Kelin Michael took scans of important archives at the libraries of Emory University for research purposes. An invitation to Stanford to discuss Carter Eckert's celebrated book on Park Chung-hee put me in contact with many scholars on the West Coast. Archival investigations but also joining a research project at the Hoover Institute with Ueda "Kay" Kaoru were key to shaping how this book opens and connects the prewar and postwar periods. Lin Hsiao-ting kindly invited me to join his group, which was sadly stymied by the pandemic. I did finally manage to make it to the Hoover archives, and we once again met in person.

The staff of the Swedish Collegium for Advanced Studies, where I was a visiting fellow from 2019 to 2020, was exceedingly supportive and permitted me the time and space to launch the writing of this book. The principal, Christina Garsten, went beyond the call of duty to support interaction. Hazem Kandil tried to explain how to write a trade book, at which I sadly failed. Ewan Jones is still the funniest Cambridge colleague, though I should not admit that in public. Merja Polvinen made us all fans of Finnish culture, while Boris Lanin was very adroit in regaling us with stories of his past. Unfortunately, the pandemic shortened these budding relationships, but the start was great indeed.

Numerous talks in many venues since early 2016 were constructive in helping me to sketch out my mental map of what I was digging into. I thank those many individuals who invited me and shared their time and banquet tables. There are many more who should be noted, but at some point I must open the starting chapters of the book and no longer delay. This includes my ever-expanding family of nieces and nephews, along with grand nieces and grand nephews, nieces-in-law and nephews-in-law in both Israel and the United States. Those who are not specifically mentioned still know they were of great assistance; we shall meet in the future once more since scholarship knows no end. I look forward to asking for support again as I embark on the next project.

Note on Transliteration

Japanese and Chinese names are written with the surname preceding the given name. All Chinese terms, except for the names of well-known figures and institutions such as Chiang Kai-shek, Sun Yat-sen, or the Japanese Kwantung Army, or terms directly cited from other works, are transcribed in the pinyin transliteration system. Japanese long vowels are indicated by a macron, except in well-known names such as Tokyo. All transliterations in parentheses throughout the text are Chinese/Japanese terms, which should be clear in context. A glossary of English for less commonly known Chinese and Japanese names, terms, and places is at the end of the book.

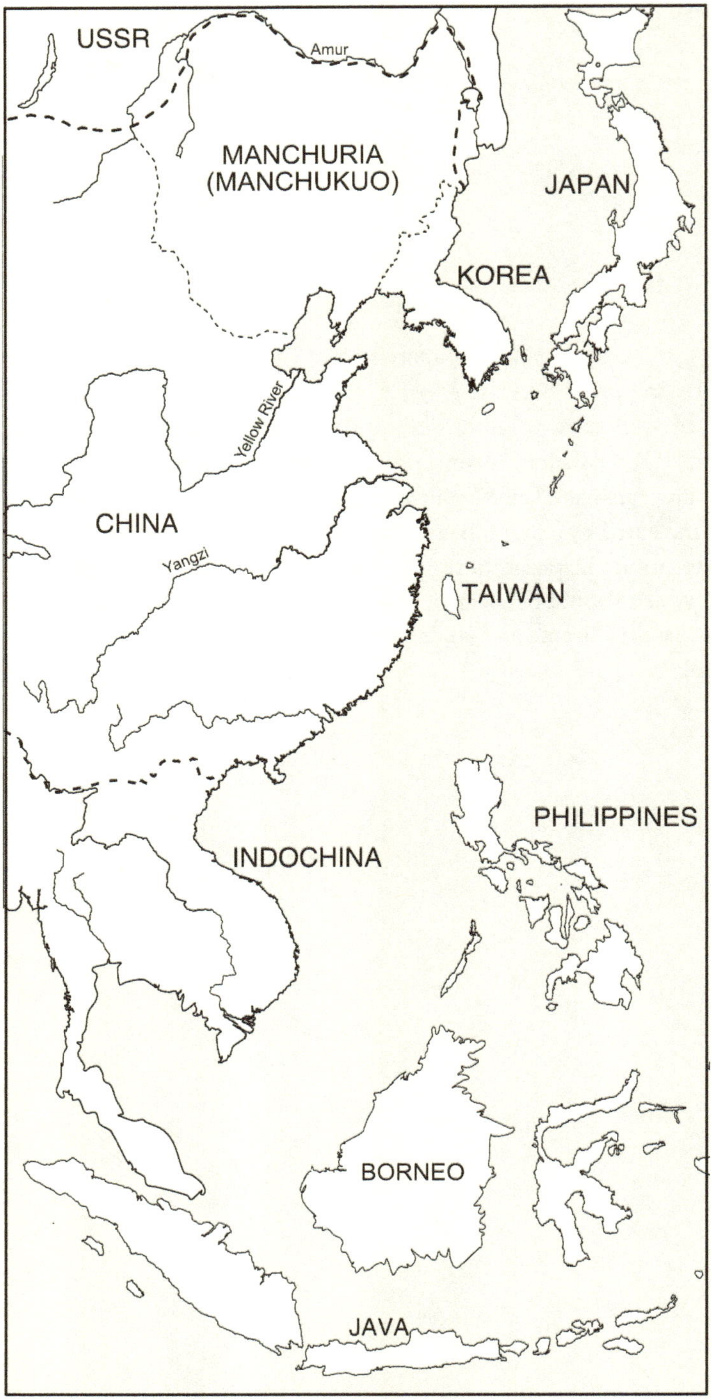

Map 1. Map of Northeast and Southeast Asia

MAP 2. Map of Northeast Asia

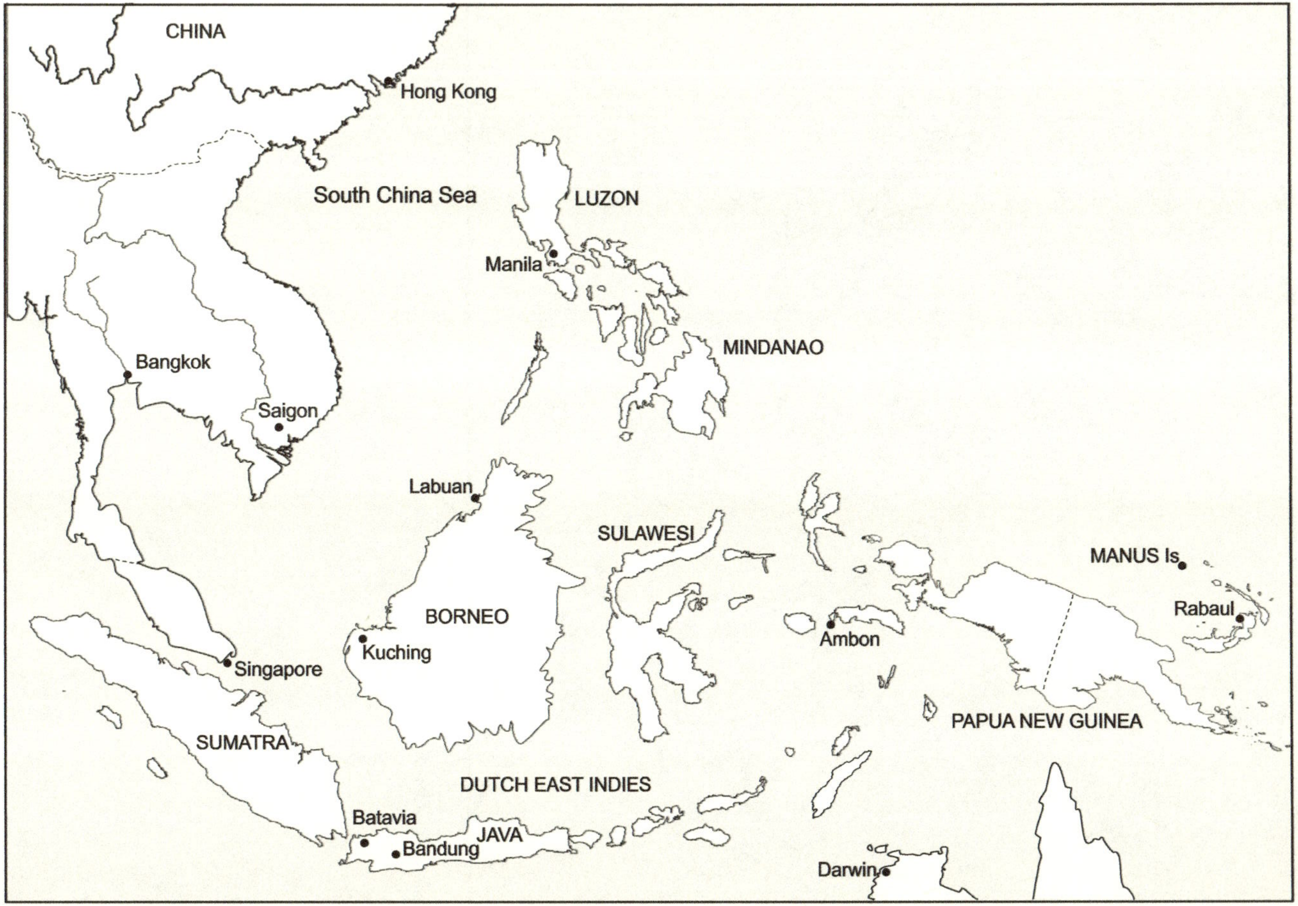

Map 3. Map of Southeast Asia

THE GEOGRAPHY OF INJUSTICE

Introduction
Making Bad Television

On a brutally hot day in late May 2019, sitting on an impossibly low sofa in an insignificant village in northern China, I failed. All I had to do was ask my guest a simple question on camera. Without a doubt, it was the worst interview of my life.

"Ask him," she said. The TV director pressed me. "Ask him what happened to his little sister." The director, who also served as translator when the Chinese dialect got the better of me, sat diagonally to my right, off camera. She kept urging me on, but I glanced at her and I knew. I realized at that moment the interview had taken an unexpected turn away from my control. It was too hot, and I was perspiring through my shirt. Rivulets of sweat dripped off my face; the room was airless and sticky. I was barely keeping it together, and I was supposed to be the one on camera leading the interview.

In the winter of the previous year I had been contacted by one of China's leading TV stations in Shanghai to see if I was interested in hosting a documentary series on Chinese war crimes trials in the aftermath of World War II.[1] Since I was the author of one of the few books on this topic, and since they were using my book as the template for some of the scripts, the choice seemed easy. However, I was reluctant. After all, the People's Republic of China (PRC) does not have a great record in open and trustworthy journalism. To put it more succinctly, the fourth estate has no role in China. Media is heavily censored, and there is no agency that is assigned the task to speak truth to power. And yet, I felt that by going to China and working with this team—an excellent group of young and enthusiastic Chinese journalists struggling with reservations similar to mine—I could learn about how history is written and conceived of in the PRC. In short, as a Japan specialist I could use this opportunity to travel around China and gain access to sites and people who would otherwise be off-limits. I would be able to observe how Chinese at the local level saw historical relations with Japan, and then also experience how this news was shaped and reported.

So, here I was in this dusty village in the middle of nowhere and not really doing my job well. How do you tactfully ask a man in his early nineties about the death of his family? I was unsuccessfully peppering this elderly Chinese peasant with questions regarding the intimate details of his family's demise during a wartime imperial Japanese military attack. It seemed grossly hypocritical to smile on camera and lean forward, attentive to his words, while he revealed the specifics of the singular horrible event that defined his life.

I started, but then suddenly I could not do it. For the first time in my life I failed to form words to pose a question. I was overcome with emotion; the moment was too intense. For years I had read accounts of Japanese imperial soldiers and the horrors they perpetrated on the Chinese, as well as Chinese recollections of these events. I had poured over transcripts of war crimes trials and read Japanese military field reports and diaries containing admissions of their crimes. I thought I was equipped. However, reading about such events and directly hearing it from the mouths of those who endured the experience are two completely different animals. It turns out that I was far from mentally or even academically prepared, so I sat and remained silent. All I could muster was the act of giving witness. I believe that when faced with a moment that defies understanding or challenges our vocabulary, one is obliged to sit and listen. The act of listening, of carefully hearing and providing human contact in the face of the unthinkable, is in my opinion a careful measurement of offering compassion.

The camera crew and I were in Beituan Village, Hebei Province, interviewing a number of Chinese peasants who were very young in 1942. In late May of that year an imperial Japanese army battalion stormed the village to eradicate Chinese communist resistance to Japanese rule. At the time, a young Li Qingxiang escaped the advancing assault by diving into one of the dark tunnels that honeycombed his village below ground. Japanese encroachment had worsened in 1938, prompting Chinese communists and locals to begin digging the passages. Short on weapons but strong on resistance, Communist Party members and others tunneled their way underground to defend themselves because they were so militarily outgunned and outmaneuvered by the Japanese imperial forces. Tunnel warfare became such a hallmark of Chinese communist resistance that popular Chinese films were later made about these campaigns, and remakes have been made as well. The Japanese flushed out this underground opposition by throwing poison gas cannisters into the tunnels. Those who chose to remain—often women and children—suffocated; those who came out were frequently rounded up at the entrances and sometimes summarily executed by the Japanese. In the terrifying and almost suffocating blackness of the tunnel, one was never sure of the direction—were you headed north and out of town or east toward another attack? Only when you dared to pop your head up in a hidden access hole could you maybe find safety. Li had fled with one of his sisters, and during the ensuing chaos in the maze-like subterrain, while they were both gasping for air, his grasp of his sister's hand loosened. When he finally surfaced, she was no longer next to him.[2] Li recounted the tragedy, and I instantly regretted that we had pushed him to grant us an interview: "My younger sister in my arms said that she couldn't move. She was just eight. It was too dark to see her. I don't really want to talk about this. I can't eat for days if I talk about it." His eyes swelled up with tears as he recalled the moment. "It wrenches my heart and makes me want to cry. My younger sister told me to go without her. I went out [he paused, having difficulty finishing the sentence] she died inside the tunnel."[3]

The room was suddenly drenched in silence, and I needed to ask the next question. But how do you follow up an interview when the person on the couch next to you is recalling a personal horror from the deep recesses of his mind? I was flummoxed. I wanted to reach out and hold his hand, to offer some form of comfort for a tragedy that took place in another time, long before I arrived on this earth, and which we had pushed him into recalling. There was nothing I could do, yet I was supposed to be in charge. I could not respond, because there was nothing to say. It was an infinitely horrible moment that seemed to drag on forever. Luckily, the director intervened and saved me from further shame. What is more, this was not making for good television. Previously, the directors had explained to me that on TV—in China or anywhere for that matter—things have to move; there has to be action. Turning the lens to Li might have been powerful, his eyes glistening as we pushed him to remember precisely what he was attempting to forget. But that would have been a cheap play. It was, in the end, a very difficult day.

Unfortunately, as emotionally entangling as Li's tragedy is, doubt remains. There are many problems with the history of Japanese war crimes and the trials that adjudicated justice in postwar East Asia. Discrepancies between fact and fiction, or facts that are able to be proved in a court of law, result in a situation that even today renders what actually happened in that small Chinese village and the war in Asia open to interpretation. More than seventy-five years after the war, these disagreements about whether justice was correctly pursued continue to feed political friction in the region. Japanese interpretations call into question the story of the Beituan massacre that Li survived. At least, this was according to the initial admissions of Japanese soldiers and officials. The KMT (Chinese Nationalist Party) never pursued justice for this atrocity. Not until 1956, fourteen years after the events, did the Chinese Communist Party (CCP) even bring charges to a tribunal of its own and gain confessions from the Japanese officers responsible. Unfortunately, within months these verdicts disappeared from mainland Chinese media, subsumed by the innumerable Chinese campaigns against their own counterrevolutionaries over the next few decades. These judgments were then also ignored by the rest of the world. The story of how this amnesia occurred and why will be explained in this book. Many Chinese who suffered Japanese war crimes would have to wait until the 1990s, but really the start of the twenty-first century, to resolve these injustices.

The legacy of war crimes trials in East Asia is an underexplored avenue for understanding the political divisions in the region today. This is because the trials tie the war and empire together in a set of competing narratives about modern history in East Asia. Obviously, Japan bears the brunt of responsibility for its actions, but the reasons why many individuals were not pursued after the war or put on trial, or not memorialized until decades later, is a topic that begs attention. Contrary to popular opinion, the failure to secure postwar justice in East Asia is not merely due to Japanese reluctance to apologize. The discord originates in the political and historical divisions that ensued over debates concerning the meaning of Japan's empire that emerged from war crimes trials. This is precisely the reason this book does not contain a singular definition of justice—in short because one does not exist. For vastly different ideological reasons, both Japanese and Chinese leaders aim to pursue such a utopian notion of justice. However, this goal cannot be enacted by fiat. I aver that it is because the notion of justice is arrived at through negotiated practices over the longer duration, that it becomes enmeshed (or negated) in the historical representations of the past.[4]

Distinctions within formulations of justice do, of course, exist. Haiyan Lee eloquently expands on notions of high and low justice in China. What serves the state interest is "high," while punishing the unfair treatment of individuals is "low."[5] But this orientation examines the ideas of justice within a sovereign nation, whereas my book investigates how the legacy of the pursuit of justice played a role in regional history and politics.[6] Transnational formulations of justice, I postulate, cannot be deemed solely by law; they emerge through convention and practice. Justice is mutually agreed upon by the aggrieved and perpetrating parties. Consequently, as much as politicians would like to call for an end to history so that justice can be declared, this is not possible. History has no end and is always evolving, as are our interpretations of the past. A declaration that history has arrived at its final terminus, that a complete consensus has been reached, is destined to disappoint and end in failure. In reconciliation, parties need to constantly engage, which is why justice and reconciliation are two different processes. Domestically, justice can be finite and have a declaration attached. This can be announced in a court of law but should not be confused with international historical interpretation. Beyond domestic boundaries, international reconciliation is without end and is based on present as well as future behavior. History never stops; we cannot put an end to discussions or debate.

To trace the paths of these national and international conversations about justice, I constructed this book in chapters that alternate between Japan and China to allow those who are neither East Asian specialists nor focused on either country to assess the history of war crimes trials as a regional juridical moment. The first several chapters trace the history of the end of World War II while looking back at the origins of imperial competition between China and Japan. Subsequent chapters delve into the constituent legal zones and efforts that formed East Asia's postwar search for justice and how Japan and China involved themselves in those often-competitive processes. Later chapters push the investigation beyond the conclusion of war crimes trials and examine how the verdicts evolved into blunter tools that both shaped foreign policy and generated industries of memory that further galvanize public opinion in contemporary East Asian society.

CHAPTER 1

The Kaleidoscope of Defeat in East Asia

World War II in Asia exploded because a young Japanese infantry soldier based just outside of Beijing temporarily went missing. He might have stopped to relieve himself or gotten lost on the road for a moment, depending on which account one believes. Tensions were running high between Japanese troops stationed very closely to Chinese Nationalist forces in northern China, and a series of blunders and misperceptions quickly escalated. The soldier soon returned to the ranks, but this change of circumstances was not reported up the chain of command. Add this to the random gunshots that evening, and that was pretext enough. An attack was under way, the Japanese forces claimed, and they needed to respond.[1] The Japanese military in northeast China, known as the Kwantung Army, was eager to bolster its puppet kingdom of Manchukuo and to create a buffer zone between Japanese holdings and the Chinese military presence south of their position. In the early morning of July 7, 1937, the Japanese unleashed a barrage of gunfire on a small village called Wanping. This unremarkable town fronted a key transportation hub, the Marco Polo Bridge, which forded a wide riverbed leading toward Beijing. The short skirmish sparked the beginning of an undeclared war that would last until late 1941, when China finally declared a state of war against Japan in December of that year. Zheng Fulai, now in his early nineties, was a young boy when Japanese troops clashed with Chinese soldiers at the bridge. Wanping is still a small town, but it bustles with tourists and caters to busloads of Chinese children and others who visit as part of countless trips to learn firsthand about World War II.

Zheng was a challenging interview because he maintained a certain patter to which he was wedded, having delivered the same spiel to Chinese schoolchildren over the years. Consequently, it was hard to divorce him from his set way of responding regardless of what was asked. He had grown up around the bridge on the other side of the river and remembered, he said, the day of the Japanese attack and subsequent escalation of Japanese troops in the area. But he more clearly remembered the arrival of Chinese communist troops in 1949 and relished recounting those moments. The CCP announced that "the Chinese people were the health of the country," he said with authority. "They instructed their soldiers not to steal the civilians' food or disturb them." Prudent Chinese communist military behavior, Zheng intimated, in terms of not requisitioning materials from the locals, made a lasting impression on the surrounding village populations. This was especially the case considering that the Chinese Nationalist troops did not care a wink about that, Zheng cheerfully explained.[2]

Not far from the Marco Polo Bridge is the museum of the war, the Chinese People's Anti-Japanese War Memorial Hall. It is a massive structure, replete with numerous banners reminding visitors, "Do not forget national humiliation." These rote quotations are suspended from the walls like visual prompts of Zheng's one-way monologue. Faced with my historical questions, Zheng never paused for reflection or took a moment to consider his response. His answers were no longer personal. His recollections were memorized and ended every few minutes with an anecdote that lauded the CCP and how it saved modern China. Little mention was devoted to the specifics of the war and the role of the Chinese Nationalists, who did the larger share of fighting. Listening to Zheng and visiting the war museum would cause one to think that the Chinese are vexed toward Japan because of World War II. This is not wrong, but in actuality, the push to not forget the humiliation of China's history runs much deeper. Sino-Japanese friction predates the battle at Marco Polo Bridge by almost half a century.

We need to step away from a Western understanding of Chinese attitudes in relation to Japan as centered on World War II because that was the West's first major military engagement with Japan. Instead, we need to reorient our view regarding an East Asian history—a regional moment. There are two major problems inherent in this duality of history. First, the Chinese responses to Japan in the postwar were not solely influenced by World War II experiences. Attitudes were shaped from the late Qing period in the 1890s until World War II. Second, we cannot omit how China resolved the war in the decades following Japan's surrender because this, too, guided the two countries' relationship. China's interaction with Japan involved armed conflict, but it also incorporated war crimes trials and a search for justice amid the rubble of war after 1945. Interviews like the one with Zheng, and personal memories of the war, are important for understanding an individual's take on what happened at the micro level, but we also need to be aware that such feelings often form part of a larger national story. Svetlana Alexievich, winner of the Nobel Prize for Literature, pointed to these discrepancies in her own work. She wrote that conducting interviews for her research on the tragic history of Chernobyl was, strangely, the easiest. Even though it was a calamity of epic proportions, it was not difficult for witnesses to reveal their intimate thoughts because they had not been instructed how to talk about it. By contrast, "For all of these other events and periods in Russian history, there were widely adopted narratives, habits of speaking that, Alexievich found, had a way of overshadowing actual personal experience and private memory."[3] This mirrors some of what I encountered in my interactions in China as well.

The weight of China's World War II history obscures a larger understanding of how we have arrived where we are today in the Sino-Japanese relationship, similar to Zheng's memorized script that he used with me. We need to start at the initial moments of discomfort in the modern era and then work forward through the postwar period. The wartime chronicle has generated industries of publishing and is fairly well memorized—both inside and outside of China. How the war was actually examined or imagined afterward has been shelved, replaced by more simplistic animations of the past. We should exit the echo chamber in which we have placed ourselves and venture outside the prescribed parameters of the bespoke historical narrative to get to the heart of the matter. And there is no better place to start than with a rusty set of large naval anchors that once adorned a park in central Tokyo.

Anchors of History

Outside of specialists in Japan and a handful of people in the West, few have heard, much less care, about the Qing-era *Dingyuan* and *Zhenyuan* warships. However, the history of the Qing dynasty's humiliation at the hands of imperial Japan is still vividly recalled, albeit most frequently in China's museums or on TV shows. But equally important is the evolution of this memory and how it has endured in China. The "national humiliation" of China began with the Qing dynasty's failure in the 1840s Opium Wars and continued in fits and starts through the 1890s. This escalated until the Chinese masses overthrew the ossified regime in the 1911 revolution. The subsequent government of the Republic of China shared this humiliation and then transplanted it to the KMT, or Chinese Nationalist Party, in the 1920–1930s. But the inherited humiliation did not cease. Even now, decades after the CCP's victory over the Chinese Nationalists in 1949, the CCP shoulders those same symbols of Qing dynasty shame as part of its own version of modern Chinese history.

The key moment of imperial competition with Japan in the early modern era can be traced to August 1886, when several naval vessels of the powerful Qing dynasty northern fleet pulled into the western Japanese port of Nagasaki. Japan was only twenty years into its Meiji project to renovate the nation, and the jury was still out whether it would be able to successfully modernize. Along with numerous other ships, the Qing fleet included several massive ironclad vessels, the prize of the squadron being the *Dingyuan* and the *Zhenyuan*. The *Dingyuan* was considered one of China's premier warships and dominated anything the Japanese maintained in their arsenal.[4] In the late summer of 1886, within a few days after docking during its tour of maritime East Asia, dozens of Qing sailors from the ships had a rollicking time in the Maruyama red-light section of Nagasaki. Riots with Japanese police and the public escalated to the point that local officials issued complaints and pleas for compensation to the Qing consulate. In the end, the disturbances left two Japanese and five Chinese sailors dead, and seventy-four injured.[5] The Nagasaki Incident, as it came to be known, created a notoriously bad image of Qing naval behavior on the archipelago.[6] In part, this friction unleashed a competition for supremacy in the region that would continue to feed behavior on both sides, pushing the Japanese to develop their subsequent imperial superiority.

Following the fracas in Nagasaki, the Japanese then encountered these same vessels eight years later in key naval battles during the Sino-Japanese War of 1894–1895. This was a war in which Japan sought dominion over the Korean peninsula and aimed to further influence the manner in which Korea would reform. In the ensuing years since the Nagasaki Incident, Japan had poured precious national funds into augmenting its naval strength. When the two clashed in the China Sea, world opinion assessed that the much larger and more powerful Qing forces would soon triumph over the more poorly equipped and outnumbered imperial Japanese sailors. However, corruption and inadequate military strategic command within the Chinese ranks opened up opportunities that the Japanese exploited. The Qing were routed. It was not a battle that immediately gained public attention, and most Chinese expected the Qing to be ultimately victorious. Chinese newspapers touted such conclusions to the public. The Chinese media referred to the Japanese as "dwarf pirates," a belittling but long-standing traditional epithet, and rarely reported the actual results of battles.[7]

Unfortunately, the Qing navy piled miscalculation on top of poor strategy on top of bad luck. On November 18, 1894, when the *Zhenyuan* left the port of Weihaiwei, it was seemingly damaged by sea mines that the navy had placed in its own harbor. It then beached.[8] In celebration of this major turning point, on December 9, 1894, the Tokyo city government staged an enormous celebration of a singular moment of victory. According to the program in the Japanese *Yomiuri Newspaper*, the main event was to be held from 5–7 p.m. on the banks of the Shinobazu Pond in Ueno Park.[9] The climax, celebrating Japan's successes in the war even before the final outcome was determined, was the reenactment of a fierce gun battle between Qing warships and the Japanese navy. Colossal plaster of paris models of the ships dramatized a naval encounter on the pond, complete with fireworks to replicate the actual mortars.[10] The "spectacle of battle" was employed in a propaganda orgy of self-congratulation to galvanize Japanese public opinion toward support for the military and imperial expansion.[11] One can only imagine the belated glee Japanese nationalists experienced in 1894 when they confronted these Qing ships after having been humiliated by them in 1886. The Qing losses in a major moment of the war prophesied its ultimate political demise, but the ensuing victory celebrations in Japan were unparalleled. Estimates of costs were way under as attendance ran high. The final bill came to more than 14,500 yen at the time (a budget of approximately $2.5 million in current US dollars).[12] It was a massive outlay for a victory party in the nation's capital, especially when the coffers were already virtually bare from wartime expenditures.

A few months later marked the end of Qing naval dominance and inaugurated imperial Japan's arrival on the world stage. By February 12, 1895, the second key port of northern China, Weihaiwei, had succumbed to Japanese naval attacks and the city was taken. The Japanese acquired the *Zhenyuan* as war booty, along with a whole host of other ships. In a barrage of international reporting the vessels were described as having been sunk or severely impaired by the imperial Japanese navy. In the end, while some were scuttled a bit below the water line and others were damaged in various states of disrepair, several were in semiworking condition.[13] The *Zhenyuan* was repaired and commandeered into the Japanese naval fleet. On its journey to Japan it steamed first back through Nagasaki and eventually to the Japanese naval port of Yokosuka, where cheering crowds greeted its arrival.[14] Japan's victory over the Qing was symbolized by two colossal Qing naval anchors on the edge of the

Shinobazu Pond in Ueno Park as a permanent display of war booty.[15] Elsewhere in the capital, enormous panoramas, which were constructed in entirely new buildings, allowed city dwellers to encounter aspects of famous battlefronts from numerous geographic angles. These 360-degree "experiences" offered a visual and sonorific immersion that also trumpeted Japan's victory.[16]

Peace talks eventually resulted in the acceptance of a humiliating military loss and forced the Qing empire to cede the island of Taiwan as reparation, although the Japanese were prevented by France, Germany, and Russia from taking over the Liaodong peninsula. The Japanese were euphoric with the triumph and fortune they received in indemnity payments. Japanese newspapers published advertisements for magic lantern shows that depicted the sinking of the Qing naval forces to show the public that the Qing empire had been subjugated.[17]

After Japan's conquest over the Qing, the anchors remained on a tiny outcrop of land in the middle of Ueno Park but gathered dust over the ensuing years. Japanese imperialism began to focus on pilfering other items from China's vast geographic storehouse of treasures. As the years piled up, the anchors' origin might have been forgotten, but they once again became fodder for patriotic propaganda in 1942, as Japan's naval front against the Western Allies expanded toward the Pacific in World War II. On May 28, 1942, the Japanese *Asahi Newspaper* notified the public that the Monument Dedication Ceremony of the anchors in Ueno Park had taken place the day before as part of National Imperial Navy Memorial Day.[18] Part of the reason, perhaps, the Qing anchors had been neglected amid the fog of war in Japan was that the country had escalated its celebratory war victories in other arenas. For example, in 1939, the fall of Wuhan (a major city in China) was honored with a massive war panorama model, which "completely filled a baseball field," built within the Nishinomiya Sports Stadium in Hyogo Prefecture in central Japan.[19]

Several years later in 1945, when Japan's imperial power had been vanquished, Chinese Nationalist forces began to negotiate with Japanese and US officials about returning the massive anchors. Theoretically, the KMT had no real legal claim to them since the booty had been part of the Qing empire. But the naval vessels represented the KMT's lineage as heir to the humiliation that the Qing had suffered. Restoring lost national pride would go a long way toward bolstering the image of the KMT to the Chinese public. KMT military attaché Lieutenant Commander Zhong Hanbo played a key role in this process. He was a naval officer sent as part of the Allied forces to represent China and assist in the occupation of Japan in the early years after World War II. In his memoirs he wrote that being able to occupy Japan after the war as one of the four victorious nations helped expunge China's hundred years of humiliation.[20] What was at stake for Zhong and others of his generation was a chronicle of national competition that predated the entire Western narrative about World War II. In the Western narrative Japan became an enemy in the late 1930s, more pointedly of course after December 1941. But in the Chinese view, like Zhong's, the desire for China to upstage Japan in the postwar era was a story that long predated World War II and had stronger links to the growth of the Japanese empire from the late nineteenth century, more than a half century prior.

The Chinese Mission in Japan, part of the occupation government but a force with few teeth since it had no power to dispatch any significant military to back its opinions, requested the anchors and leftover artillery shells because "they were part of war booty brought back by the Japanese at the conclusion of the Sino-Japanese War in 1895." "It is the belief of the Chinese Mission," they stated, "that public display of such objects should be at once discontinued and that the objects should be dismantled and brought back to China."[21] Initially, the Supreme Commander for the Allied Powers (SCAP), which oversaw the occupation of Japan essentially under US authority, cared little for this maneuver. SCAP indicated that incidents before 1937 were not in its purview. However, the Chinese Mission appears to have worn down US recalcitrance by suggesting that the objects glorified war and militarism and were in contravention of "educating the Japanese people in the fundamental principles of peace."[22] Ultimately, the KMT was able to procure the anchors and return the booty in a sort of reverse repatriation ceremony that attempted to publicly expunge the humiliation of the Qing empire's loss five decades prior.[23]

But the Chinese massage of the historical narrative was not yet complete.

A few years later in 1949, when mainland China switched hands to authority under the CCP, the anchors once again became an important part of national history under new management. Only this time the story needed to be linked to the communist version. Nowadays, the anchors are on display at the Military Museum of the Chinese People's Revolution in Beijing. This is not just any museum but one of the ten monumental buildings decreed by Premier Zhou Enlai to symbolize new China and completed in October 1959. The museum was expressly designed and constructed with the aim to "establish the hegemony of the interpretation of history by controlling both the retelling of the past and the means of representation."[24] Even though the history is seemingly unrelated, the Nanjing Massacre Museum (officially known as the Memorial Hall of the Victims in Nanjing Massacre by Japanese Invaders) also houses a picture of the sunken *Zhenyuan* warship with the obvious aim of establishing this moment as the true start of Japanese violent imperialism in

1894 and not solely with the 1937 massacre in Nanjing. Mainstream Chinese views of Japan maintain that there had been a single plan from that time, if not from the early 1870s with the military expedition to Taiwan, of Japanese military hegemony and imperial dominance in East Asia. The story continues today in more than one celebratory venue because the *Dingyuan* warship has been resurrected and is now a museum of sorts in Shandong Province. It forms part of a larger Sino-Japanese War Museum complex in Weihai City (renamed from Weihaiwei).

The memory of this history did not remain relegated to the Chinese mainland when the Chinese Nationalist Party fled after losing the civil war in 1949. Competition to control the historical narrative continues. In fact, the guardians of Chinese historical memory for China split into two—the communist People's Republic of China (PRC), with its capital in Beijing, and the Republic of China (ROC, later Taiwan), with what at that time was considered a temporary capital in Taipei. A few months before the repatriation of the anchors, a riot had erupted in the former Japanese colony of Taiwan, which evolved into a larger massacre beginning on February 28, 1947. I will detail this later in the book, but over the course of several months this social unrest led to the killing of tens of thousands of native Taiwanese. The unrest also impelled the shaky KMT rulers to implement martial law that, in fits and starts, eventually ruled Taiwan until the mid-1980s. Ironically, while the KMT was striving to expunge the humiliation for Qing-era mistakes, it was simultaneously trying to create a new political identity based on this heritage in the former Japanese colonial outpost of Taiwan.

These "anchors of history," as I describe the role of the warships in both the late nineteenth century and then the mid-twentieth century, demonstrate that friction in Sino-Japanese relations did not suddenly arise at the end of World War II.[25] Governments on the Chinese mainland chose to position themselves as though they were successors to the legacy of the Qing-era humiliation. This is paradoxical because both the KMT and the CCP governments declared that they were revolutionary and throwing off the shackles of the past.[26] Their subsequent search for justice and requests for the repatriation of war booty suggests, however, that long-standing feelings of what it meant to be Chinese in the face of Japanese aggression, regardless of the chronology, would play a serious political role. After the war, this incongruous nature of claiming a revolutionary break with the past but then providing continuity on the level of historical emotions will be a theme we encounter frequently as the book progresses. And a major element of this effort to overcome the humiliation of the past is linked to post-1945 war crimes trials of the Japanese.

A Short History of War Crimes Trials—Nuremberg versus Tokyo

Trying to find justice in the wake of wartime atrocities led the West to form the Nuremberg Principles, which have fundamentally taken hold of the political realm in many places around the world. Guided by the legal principles and international law ideology that emerged from the Nuremberg Trials of Nazi war criminals (1945–1946), the United Nations later helped to develop international criminal tribunals that served to adjudicate crimes in the former Yugoslavia and Rwanda. International law "represents an effort to impose a neutral restraint on power," and its offspring "international criminal law has, since the Second World War, been central to this project." The focus in the immediate postwar era aimed to ascertain "criminal accountability" with these new juridical tools, in a sense "promoting a world community under law."[27] In Europe and East Asia, Nuremberg is frequently invoked as a story of triumph—one that not only led Germany down the path of atonement and helped it gain reentry into the pantheon of civilized nations, but also created a blueprint for other post-catastrophe countries to help recover their dignity. Echoing the discussion above, "a central tenet of the Nuremberg legacy is that the International Military Tribunal (IMT) at Nuremberg helped construct the singular story that Germans tell regarding the violence of World War II. The legacy of the IMT is that 'truth' emerged from trials that individualized guilt. This liberal, individualist-humanist narrative supplanted the collective guilt accompanying the virulent nationalism that fueled Nazi atrocities."[28] Of course, not all agree. One of the deleterious effects of a narrative emerging from a system of war crimes trials is that the story becomes harder to adapt later. With Nuremberg the world prosecuted individuals and the Nazi Party for war crimes. However, in that quest the transaction costs have been great. We have grossly overlooked the financial and industrial structures that permitted such a genocide and atrocities to be carried out with impunity, all the while making a profit. The Germans created a new term for these individuals: "desk killers," those who murder through bureaucracy but never see the faces of their victims.[29]

This is similar to what happened at the Tokyo Trial; there, however, it was not individualized guilt but military culpability writ large. This verdict, which was not unanimous like the Nuremberg judgments, resulted in a pointed absence. The Tokyo Trial (1946–1948) and the lesser war crimes trials of former Japanese imperial soldiers throughout East and Southeast Asia never get mentioned with the same hushed tones of legal reverence as Nuremberg. Nor, importantly, was anyone able to apply the same potent legal salve to political and economic wounds in East Asia to help redress imperial Japan's wrongs. Most Japanese lawyers had been pro-war; few were purged in the postwar period. The main exception would have been Yokota Kisaburō, one of the vocal legal Japanese minds who promoted the pursuit of war crimes trials.[30] The story of what Nuremberg was for the Allies, compared with the goals of the Tokyo Trial and its aims, is encapsulated here. "In short, the narrative which the Nuremberg prosecution crafted was that of sedition from Western standards and values. This story of how Germany had deviated from the Western way promised to explain the unexplainable, and this very explanation would be the first transitional step back on the right path."[31] The story for Japan formulated differently.

Adjudicating justice for Japan's imperial aggression was not just about repatriating war booty. International pressure had grown during World War II to pursue entirely new categories of war crimes. And the narrative of justice linked to a similar sort of prewar competitive pursuit of those symbols of victory and humiliation—the anchors. Only now in the immediate post–World War II era, the anchors to historical interpretation turned into international tribunals that would define justice.

In Europe, war crimes trials were not divided into legal classes. However, in Asia, the trials were split between what were considered the leadership (Class A) and the "lesser" war crimes (Classes B and C). The three categories of war crimes—A, B, C—against Japanese defendants were, respectively, "crimes against peace," "conventional war crimes," and "crimes against humanity." Class A war criminals were the men who coordinated Japan's "aggressive" war but did not directly and physically commit crimes. There was only one Class A trial, and that was the Tokyo Trial (officially known as the International Military Tribunal for the Far East). There were two additional quasi–Class A trials, that of Lieutenant General Tamura Hiroshi and Admiral Toyoda Soemu, but they were not considered of the same magnitude.[32]

The lower classes of war crimes were labeled as BC. The B class was a holdover category from World War I for "conventional war crimes" (rape, murder, illegal incarceration, abusing prisoners of war [POWs], etc.). The C class was an entirely novel category of "crimes against humanity" (what essentially came to be known as genocide, though strictly speaking, genocide and crimes against humanity are legally different categories). The imperial Japanese armed forces were frequently brutal, as they were in Beituan Village, but they did not have a genocidal policy like the Nazis. Consequently, most lower-ranking Japanese defendants were charged as a combined category, "BC class."[33] One can think of the Class A war criminals as those who led the aggressor nation in its bid to conquer. BC class war criminals were the ones who came into direct contact with individuals, those who became the greater focus for the Chinese as we shall later see.

These BC class trials encompassed an enormous geographic space. Around 2,300 proceedings took place in approximately fifty locations throughout Asia and the Pacific. Australia, (Nationalist) China, France, the Netherlands, the Philippines, the United Kingdom, and the United States all convened various trials from 1945 until 1951. Some 5,700 imperial Japanese soldiers stood trial, and in the end just over 900 were executed.[34] The Soviets held a December 1949 trial at Khabarovsk, which has been relatively ignored, but given the fact that it was the sole tribunal to focus on Japan's bacteriological weapons, it merits attention.[35] The CCP, although not one of the wartime Allies, held its own investigations of approximately 1,000 Japanese prisoners. In 1956, it put forty-five of the "worst" offenders on trial but granted clemency to almost 960. Officially, along with the Soviet Union, the PRC was the only other postwar government not to execute a single Japanese prisoner, a fact that would come to play a large role in Chinese communist media pronouncements in the twenty-first century. There were, however, numerous unofficial so-called "people's trials" in the USSR and parts of China that remain either unrecorded or still buried in archival detritus. These were essentially summary executions after a sort of mock-up tribunal or mob revenge that might have taken the form of a tribunal. Estimates run in the thousands, but since evidence remains scant, there is only conjecture at this point. Chinese trials, both KMT and CCP, also muddy the statistics because many of those who might have been seen as war criminals, such as Chinese who engaged in actions for the Japanese side, were often instead indicted as traitors, *hanjian* in Chinese.[36] Essentially, only those soldiers with Japanese citizenship (which sometimes included Taiwanese and Koreans) were legally classed as war criminals. Those of other nationalities were frequently dealt with through local law.

For the Europeans there were a host of reasons for establishing tribunals to adjudicate Japanese war crimes, and the geographic range was wide. In Burma, for example, the British aimed at reasserting their colonial authority, but this was also the case for the Dutch in the Dutch East Indies (Indonesia), the French in Indochina, and the British in Hong Kong and Singapore. First, trials were commensurate with the overall goals of former European colonizers to reimpose colonial authority in former colonial holdings to regain prestige and resurrect their economies. The British Empire had racked up enormous bills in its efforts to bolster its faraway imperial defenses. At the time, this "soared to some three billion pounds—over a third of Britain's gross domestic product."[37] France was no better off. Defeat of Japanese rule meant little for former European imperial colonies "because liberation was a means to reestablish French greatness, not an end in itself."[38] Second, the trials helped discredit collaborators or interim leaders who had worked in concert with the Japanese. Importantly, some of these trials, including those in China, were held in former Japanese sites of authority or where prisoners had been incarcerated in former Japanese camps or prisons. Third, the trials were used as a form of propaganda to domestic audiences in the home country to inform them that the war had meant something and that the Europeans or other Allied powers were in a dominant position over the Japanese and had regained strength in the region. And fourth, the trials kept at bay the potential that the Japanese would militarily rise again by producing a record and memory of the atrocities they committed during their imperial era.[39] For some countries like France, which had been mostly occupied and partly managed by Nazi Germany during the war, the goal was also to make sure it could regain its international reputation, and this meant pushing for a judge's seat on the world's stage at the Tokyo Trial and putting Japanese on trial in Indochina. Most importantly, such trials offered an official record of proof that France had returned to being an ally and would be treated as such until the current day.[40]

War Crimes Trials Then and Now

In this maelstrom of postwar competition to control debates about the meaning of the war, the Japanese did not take the surrender lying down. Japanese officials of many stripes attempted to initially manage their own trials. Later they tried to secure the records of the war crimes trials to investigate the charges but encountered persistent resistance from the Allies. These impediments convinced many Japanese and others that the trials were a form of victor's justice and that the Allies were hiding their mistakes. The unbridled confidence that Japan was always working with East Asia's best interest in mind remains a conservative mainstay political belief in contemporary Japan. Today's conservative groups in Japan undergird this assertion by opposing the historical pronouncements concerning those who were "damned" by the Tokyo War Crimes Trial and other war crimes tribunal verdicts. Numerous monuments around Japan laud the martyrdom, as it is termed, of those war criminals, but few try to delve into the issue of the war crimes themselves.

Mainland China, by contrast, is a one-party state and so does not allow for competing historical views within either government or society. There is no competition for public opinion about history in China. However, it is important to note how these histories were neglected for so long on the mainland but then suddenly reinvigorated more than seven decades after the end of

World War II. This renovation of wartime and postwar history now supports the Chinese state in its drive to codify what it labels as "proper historical understanding." The CCP strives to depict its postwar benevolence and how it stemmed revenge toward those Japanese who were "damned" in war crimes tribunals for their actions while imperial soldiers.[41]

The competition over notions of "correct history" and justice that emerged from the military tribunals of those "damned" war criminals remains hotly contested long after the embers of battle have cooled. The furor surrounding efforts to massage the history of Japan's military actions shows a lack of consensus among the Japanese public, officialdom, and Japanese academics, who are the international vanguard for uncovering this uncomfortable history.[42] It is a history known well in some circles in Japan, but outside of the country such activities receive weak international attention. What does receive rousing headlines in the international media is what makes front-page news—Japanese official denials.

The Difficulty of Implementing War Crimes Trials and Controlling Their Legacy

International criminal law is not sufficient to render justice all the time, particularly when the scale is so large or based on state-sponsored violence. To pose this issue crudely, did the hanging of seven Japanese leaders bring about adequate closure to the end of World War II in East Asia?

Regardless of the potential of enlightened goals, these sorts of trials harbor a litany of stumbling blocks. Martti Koskenniemi, a professor of law and eminent philosopher about the complexity of war crimes trials, makes a cogent point about the slippery nature of these trials:

> The reasons that make "show trials"—that is to say, trials of only few political leaders—acceptable, even beneficial, at the national level, while others are granted amnesty, are not present when criminal justice is conducted at the international plane. When trials are conducted by a foreign prosecutor, and before foreign judges, no moral community is being affirmed beyond the elusive and self-congratulatory "international community." Every failure to prosecute is a scandal, every judgement too little to restore the dignity of the victims, and no symbolism persuasive enough to justify the drawing of the thick line between the past and the future.[43]

It is precisely at a war crimes trial where the creation of history and an anti-history narrative emerge. The crucial distinction here lies between legal and historical truth. To avoid the pretext of having a predetermined outcome, judges must allow defendants room to speak and to mount a defense. More importantly, the court needs to take such utterances seriously, however repugnant or removed from reality they may be. But this format creates a subsequent problem. Through recording their defense at court, defendants are able to propose a counternarrative to the history being presented in the same venue by the prosecutor.[44] It is at this intersection that legal trials and history come into conflict. While the prosecution is attempting to interpret law to gain a conviction, defendants are thinking of posterity and their personal construction of history. This competition between prosecutor and defense sets up a power play at trial. Judges want to base a historical verdict on evidence. Lawyers for the victims need to ensure that a courtroom can also serve as a surrogate emotional stage on which to mourn the memory of those who perished.

The competition for the domestic and international audiences first involves public acceptance of the necessity for war crimes trials, which was not a guarantee after the end of World War II, or even now for that matter.[45] Regardless of all the merits of implementing war crimes trials, detractors point out that the accused will try to protect himself (usually male) or his view of history within the context of which the whole trial is taking place. French lawyer Jacques Vergès, colloquially referred to as "the devil's advocate," once defended Algerian independence activists that the French government labeled as terrorists. In Vergès's opinion, the real battle was not in attaining a client's freedom. The key, he wrote, revolved around creating a historical rupture. At that moment, "the goal for the defense is not so much to get the accused released but rather to get his ideas out for public consumption."[46] In Vergès's strategy, war crimes tribunals were fundamentally sites of historical contention. The power play, in the same vein as British prime minister Margaret Thatcher argued when facing those critical of her, was to control "the oxygen of publicity" to win the day.

When the historical narrative is reconstructed by the defense, these sorts of large trials about state violence can end up being show trials but not in the strict Soviet sense from the Stalinist 1930s. Because of the limits of what the law imposes, these trials remain venues for the accused to manipulate historical narratives and gain adherents. Koskenniemi says there are great risks in trying to establish "'sacred facts' through the banality of the legal process."[47] This caution that war crimes trials have their limits strongly reverberates. Viet Thanh Nguyen, a Pulitzer Prize winner for literature, wrote about his personal insights on "just memory" concerning the Vietnam War and the United States. As Nguyen explains, we face a need outside of the courts and public venues of commoditized memory packaging in films and books to consider a past that does not lean on nationalistic tendencies. As he sees it, "A just memory opposes this kind of identity politics by recalling the weak, the subjugated, the different, the enemy, and the forgotten. A just memory says that ethically recalling our own is not enough to work through the past." Nguyen ends by reminding us that the key to "just memory" is making sure our history is precisely one not only composed of memories that can be abused by those in power.[48] Specialists would label this "competitive victimhood" and underline that "groups who compete over their share of victimhood are more motivated to establish their in-group's suffering than to let go of the painful past."[49] The parallel phenomenon is also a tendency to oppose a historical story "that can be seen as 'winner justice,' a narrative forced by outsiders."[50] I think positioning the issues in this way, to show how trials create a powerful engine for national memory, sums up many of the conflicts that plague Sino-Japanese relations, as we will see in subsequent chapters.

This list of ever-expanding problems we hope the law will resolve also goes to the heart of the problem. Such considerations are not limited to problems with war crimes trials but stretch further toward the larger interaction between the realm of politics and the law. Judges, the law, and the courts help order society. Theoretically, therefore, the same should be true for war crimes tribunals. They should, in the best of all worlds, lead to a transition of peace. But society's overreliance on the law has formed what the former chief of the Supreme Court of the United Kingdom, Lord Jonathan Sumption, describes as a situation where we are ruled by an "empire of law." Societies are too dependent on the law, while courts are too frequently the sole venue to consider resolutions and create reconciliation in their pursuit of what they deem as justice. Sumption argues that the use of the law as a panacea for resolution has shoved significant political processes to the sidelines.[51] This diversion comes into greater relief when we look at Japan's bilateral relations. Chinese and Japanese consistently try to resolve imperial-era crimes in the courts but less in political discussions or at the level of popular dialogue. Unfortunately, the record of success continues to be dismal. Yukiko Koga has analyzed the numerous failed legal proceedings brought by Chinese against the Japanese government and corporations. She arrives at a conclusion similar to Sumption's but emphasizes that this sort of case "positions the plaintiffs not *before the law* but *between the law* by declaring the Law's irrelevance in belatedly accounting for historical violence."[52] Other scholars assess that the insistence to include the offense of crimes against peace for any defendant charged in the Tokyo Trial shifted the historical focus to "examining less *the way* Japan had conducted the war but more *the reasons* why Japan had conducted it."[53]

Many on both sides of the Japan Sea and across the Taiwan Strait to a lesser extent believe, ironically, that these war crimes tribunals did not resolve the problems because not *enough* law was applied. We need stronger courts and more trials to make things right, goes their reasoning. The fundamental question, then, follows: Did East Asian war crimes lend themselves to being resolved through legal channels? Can the history of empire be something resolved outside of the courtroom?

War Crimes Trials and Supposedly Impugning Japanese Dignity

A secondary problem that has developed over the years, reflecting this growing competitive divergence between Japan and China, is the lived legacy of the war crimes trials. Many of the KMT-managed trials in China during the second half of the 1940s had been rushed, relied on dubious evidence, or lacked proper translators. This became a constant refrain in numerous Japanese memoirs of these tribunals. The situation was depicted as far from always legally dependable. In the ensuing chaos of rebuilding East Asia, many of these deficiencies were forgotten, only to reemerge in the twenty-first century after the rise of China, the bursting of Japan's economic bubble in the 1990s, and the democratization of Taiwan and South Korea. The lost memories of war crimes trials, combined with a renewed effort to build political relations on the backs of the trial judgments, caused deep fractures to develop between Japan and its closest geographic neighbors. The history of war crimes trials is now deeply entwined with the postwar political history of both China and Japan and at times virtually inseparable from national identity.

A prime example that combines all these issues would be the grisly "hundred-man killing contest." The gist of this episode emerged from an infamous wartime Japanese newspaper article that detailed a hideous competition between two Japanese soldiers to see who could lop off more heads of Chinese peasants on the imperial army's march to conquer Nanjing in December 1937. The competition became a celebrated story in postwar China, and the news article was used as evidence for the subsequent war crimes trial of the two Japanese officers, who were eventually executed. The trial and aftermath serve to link past and present, which has unfortunately grown into a malignant tumor that continues to enflame contemporary political relations. The story was most likely a Japanese wartime propaganda fabrication, but because the evidence and the record of the trial are enshrined in an internationally recognized war crimes trial verdict, the Chinese mainland government consistently uses the case to recall imperial Japanese barbarity.[54]

Japanese conservatives, in turn, employ the same trial to demonstrate in their eyes the lack of Chinese understanding of international law and the absence of rational thought in historical analysis. A standoff has ensued, but the case lives on. In 2003, the families of the executed Japanese soldiers sued the Japanese *Mainichi Newspaper* and related publishers for defamation over their coverage of the events.[55] The case was eventually dismissed, but the idea of injustice to Japanese domestic pride drew the attention of top Japanese leaders lending their names to the cause of "defending Japan's national honor."[56] One such champion was Inada Tomomi. She rose to fame within Japan's majority political party as the lawyer who pushed the defamation case and wrote a book about it.[57] She served as defense minister in 2016, among other key roles. Inada is also a prominent player in one of Japan's most powerful political lobbying groups, the Nippon Kaigi (Japan Conference). The Japan Conference is the leading political pressure group for Japan's main political party, the Liberal Democratic Party (LDP). The Conference is a consistent critic of the Tokyo Trial and other Japanese war crimes trials of having perverted the real pursuit of justice and tarring Japan with a negative historical brush.[58] While not wholly incorrect in the assertion that the war crimes trials contained many defects, the Conference is incapable of reflecting on Japanese imperial behavior and seeks only to glorify itself as a victim of Western or Chinese international malfeasance.

Finding justice for Japanese war crimes, or creating injustice where crimes were not committed, is just one example of the weighty emotional baggage that infects East Asia and shapes the current political landscape. The legacy of war crimes trials casts a long shadow on the present, but we need to look at the situation from both the Chinese and the Japanese sides to understand how this seemingly insurmountable structure was erected over time. Initial euphoria to manage justice in East Asia quickly gave way to other concerns, and these dominated the situation until recently. In this way, authorities in the region did not get a chance to reconcile the excesses of war until the present day. In part, this language explains why now in the twenty-first century we see a tendency to lean on emotional opprobrium, whereas a seeming calm about the past is thought to be more the norm in Western Europe. We should be wary, however, of painting too rosy a picture of reconciliation in Europe, noting with care that "the overall records of justice were poor on both sides of the Iron Curtain."[59]

In the West, Europe coalesced ostensibly in a bid to rebuild and avoid the frictions that would potentially lead to a third world war. At the same time, and facing similar pressures, East Asia never united around anything more than a continual focus on blaming Japan and keeping that emotional catalyst alive, even as the war grew more distant with each subsequent generation. Why did justice seemingly fail in East Asia when theoretically the same international law was pursued on both sides of the globe? Why has the evolution of seeking justice given birth to two such divergent postwar forms in the East and West? Put another way, even with all of the legal and political problems Nuremberg divulged, its legal moment bequeathed an academy to carry forth into the next generation the Nuremberg Principles. By contrast, what happened in Tokyo that rendered it legally impotent?[60] I am not making a normative statement that justice was found only in the West. Rather, I aim to investigate the constellation of structures and policies that pushed parallel legal attempts across the globe to seemingly opposite conclusions.

The question concerning how this apparent significant construction and implementation of international law and its by-products took root in the West and produced a countereffect, spurring further separation among countries in the Far East, is potent to the twenty-first century. By looking at the geography and distribution of what was perceived as unjust—under what circumstances local and national officials brought Japanese war crimes to justice and then

FIGURE 1.1. Beituan Village in 2019. The slogan on the wall reads: "Study the Spirit of Beituan Village's War of Resistance, Xicheng Township Is on the Move."

memorialized that story—we can chart the disassembly of the Japanese empire and then analyze the causes behind why justice was believed lost.

Let's return briefly to Beituan Village and the issue of law, justice, and history. What are we to make of an atrocity that is revered as an indisputable historical fact in a small village in central China, but where inhabitants were forced to forget the massacre for so many of the subsequent decades? Beituan is a village that now, once again, remembers this tragedy as a single defining feature of its existence. Even today, almost eighty years after this brutal attack, political slogans painted on village walls exhort Chinese citizens to remember the valor of those who resisted Japan. What we are dealing with here is history on two levels. First is the history of justice lost in East Asia—the sort that Chinese peasants might have expected but missed out on during the lengthy restructuring of the political order across the Chinese mainland that I detail in this book. Moreover, the war crimes trials themselves and the story of justice gained or lost are only one plotline. The secondary thread is the life of the memory and commemoration of, or absence of, these trials in East Asia. Because the main protagonists involved in this contestation over the meaning and impact of these trials are mainly Japan and China, I will spend most of the time focused on their histories.

Chapter 2

The Shape of Justice

Creating New Symbols of International Stature

Postwar East Asian efforts to control the history of Japanese war crimes trials are evidence that governments were deeply concerned with the need to manage how their domestic populations understood the meaning of World War II and the significance of Japan's imperial loss. Japan was looking to salvage what it could and aimed to deflect, to the extent possible, the intrusion of the Great Powers, which seemed set on once again ruling the world stage. Managing the postwar conversation about "justice" demonstrated the importance both the Allies and the Japanese attributed to being able to define the war. The situation in East Asia saw a collection of crumbling imperial spheres—Japan's and those of former European hegemons—competing within a narrowing space while two newly forming superpowers (the USSR and the United States) vied for dominance. China was able to gain a seat at the international table of elites for the first time at the tail end of World War II, but its ascent to world power did not really begin until the start of the twenty-first century.

Currently, the CCP wishes to treasure the Nuremberg and Tokyo Trials, retaining the master narrative from the previous era. Unfortunately, that is no longer truly reflective of international reality. While accepting the historical need for the Tokyo Trial, scholarship over the years has grown equally critical of its implementation. One of the real ironies is that the CCP has appropriated for its own use Chinese participation in the Tokyo Trial even though the

CCP was never part of it and the law used was not even communist. In fact, for years the Chinese communists were critical of the Tokyo Trial. The mouthpiece of the Shanghai branch of the CCP, the *Liberation Daily*, published a contemptuous editorial in late July 1946:

> The strange drama unfolding at the International Tribunal for the Far East symbolizes Chiang Kai-shek government's loss of authority, national humiliation and decay. On the world stage not only can they not represent the Chinese people's will, each day they manage to increasingly lose respect for our nation. If this situation continues, the honor we have gained as one of the four major allies through our sacrifice of the Chinese people's blood in this struggle risks being completely lost.[1]

Getting to the Legal Stage

Chinese and Japanese leaders were cognizant of the fact that war crimes trials were on the horizon at the end of World War II. This was a move that propelled the Chinese Nationalists to move with speed. However, China was in a bind because fundamentally the world did not highly estimate Chinese law; thus, many of its own elites constantly felt the need to trumpet that China actually had a rule of law and was not despotic. In 1932, the man who would serve as the Republic of China's judge at the Tokyo Trial, Mei Ruao, penned a short piece in which he tried to defend Chinese law. The traditional notions of *li* and *fa*, the carrot-and-stick approach, he wrote, were much like natural law and positive law in the West. This was a brief attempt in a respected Western academic journal to deflect naysayers who believed that China had no history of legal affairs.[2] Much of this probably fell on deaf ears. The view that the system of Chinese law was somehow incapable of becoming modern did not only emanate from foreigners. One of China's late Qing jurists, Ju Zheng, who later became eminent during the Republican era, also opined that Chinese law had a deep and broad history. Ju had studied law in Japan and over the years served in key posts in the KMT Party and government, including head of the Judicial Council (*sifa yuan*) in the early 1930s and then as minister of justice in 1934.[3]

But Ju also believed that in earlier times Confucian ideology had virtually subsumed law. This devolution ossified legal thinking through the ensuing dynasties. Ju Zheng assessed that the development of Chinese jurisprudence had stopped with the entry of the Great Powers into China. They created hybrid legal cities that, in Ju's estimation, broke China's system. The biggest culprit, which in the end destabilized Chinese law, was the law of extraterritoriality and the consular system of trials. The problem after the mid-nineteenth century, he estimated, was that whenever there was discord or disagreement with foreign merchants, they did not wish to resolve their problems in a Chinese court (although the Chinese thought this was a good idea at the time). And so, Chinese sovereignty took a blow. Officials in the late Qing era tried to change this, but it was only window dressing and not fundamental enough.[4]

Chinese pundits and scholars at the time may differ in their position and point to the issue that it was, in fact, Western bias that prohibited the late Qing dynasty from adapting to international change just as the West was implementing this iteration of new legal ideas. Ju Zheng estimated that foreign consular courts took away from China the opportunity to change its own system because there was no room for legal intellectual revision. There was no way for the system or professionals to adapt to social changes. Because Chinese legal practice mostly followed "formalities," any attempts were usually made pointless by the changing circumstances. At the same time, the Chinese also could not just suddenly adopt Western law, to which they were not acclimatized.[5] In the end, Ju Zheng's idea was that China needed to reformat and rebuild its legal system to adapt to modernity. This entailed fomenting a revolution to establish new legislation and overcoming historical problems. The impediments were precisely defined as the ritualization of law and tradition that had taken over law, eliminating the real distinction between public and private law.[6]

Ju Zheng believed that extraterritoriality was the "alien" element of the Chinese legal system and that it hampered the independence and completion of a modern Chinese legal system. Because of this impediment, he asserted, China could not become an independent country.[7] It was obvious to many that the abolition of extraterritoriality in 1943, and the potential for war crimes trials against the Japanese, was a moment ripe for the Chinese to fully implement an updated system of law. It also served as a way to prove to both the domestic and international populations that China was due the respect as a victorious ally in World War II, alongside the USSR, the United States, and the UK. Yang Zhaolong, another key jurist from the Republican era with a doctorate in law from abroad, was concerned about legal education in China. Yang assessed that prewar China faced two kinds of problems concerning legal education: the schools and the students. The management of schools was not sufficient, and there was no proper planning for the education students received, he complained.[8]

The war had pulverized China. Its judicial system existed but was sclerotic and neither adequately robust nor effective in many regions.[9] China had not yet fully developed its own homogenous legal environment and was thus split into two competing schools for reform. On one side was the "*yingmei* (Anglo-American)" group, which was "represented foremost by the Soochow School of Comparative Law." On the other side was a "rival legal culture, promoted by at least six law schools in Shanghai, [and] commonly known as *deri* (German-Japanese)."[10] Soochow University (Dongwu University) was fundamental in China's moves to seek justice against the Japanese because it supplied virtually the entirety of the Chinese legal staff employed for the Tokyo War Crimes Trial.[11] The albatross of competing legal philosophies, along with the additional burden of small numbers of staff within an enormous country dotted with innumerable sites of Japanese atrocities, created a problem. Chinese leaders from all political stripes wanted to upgrade their legal systems, show their prowess, and recover from the war to claim international victory.

What Emerges from Juridical Competition?

Societies do not automatically embark on a path to seek justice in the aftermath of war or social revolution. There has to be a specific domestic push, or calculation, that urges forward this sort of action. Or the international community has to exert an influence. Previous conceptions of justice do not explain, however, even with all this effort, why a belief emerged that justice was not satisfactory concerning the war crimes trials in East Asia. Rather, we need to forge another idea, one where the notion of *competitive justice* reigned, to consider this judicial imbalance.

This competition in East Asia has a long genesis that influenced the evolution of the trials because these courtroom dramas were part of a much larger international trend. The Allies, or United Nations as they called themselves, responded to the horrors committed by the Axis nations in World War II in two ways. First, they encouraged states to commit themselves to international law. Second, with the Holocaust atrocities in mind, they established a legal system to punish these newly defined crimes. This practice was initially managed through the auspices of a new body based in London with a subcommittee in Chongqing, China, the United Nations War Crimes Commission (UNWCC). In a way, 1945 created an international juridical moment and a shared set of legal beliefs that using courts to mediate war crimes was the preferred process to end a state of war. This new strategy of using international law was a formula to transcend the obstacles of national law and forge new legal methods to pursue an individual for a crime that the international community assessed as heinous but that required a novel set of legal tools to bring to justice. We could use different language to discuss the same idea and see these trials as part of an international "economy of justice," where countries gained legitimacy or the currency of being recognized as civilized by promoting their use of international law. This economy of justice was propped up through various legal transactions including the circulation of the objects of justice, namely Japanese soldiers, or the movement of legal staff that traded Japanese prisoners or information, oftentimes reluctantly. This pursuit of justice and the act of sharing memory and history have not stopped, so the trials and their verdicts retain a certain value within contemporary regional geopolitics.[12]

The issue of competitive justice is twofold. First, in the initial years after the war ended, officials and laymen involved with war crimes trials debated the question of the fairness of the trials (lopsided pursuit of victor's justice or a quest for the truth?). It was a moment so pregnant with importance that the United States ignored the fact that extraterritoriality had been abolished in China in 1943. Infringing on Chinese sovereignty and even before China had initiated its own trials, the US quickly implemented a series of ten different war crimes trials in Shanghai against close to fifty Japanese who had abused or executed downed US airmen.[13] The trials all took place in a special section within Shanghai's Ward Road Jail from January to September 1946. All the prosecutors, judges, legal clerks, defense attorneys, and so on were appointed by the US military.[14] This jail later served as the site where the KMT pursued its Shanghai war crimes trials.

So keen were the Americans on moving quickly that the War Crimes Branch Office for the China Theater was already established in April 1945, and after V-J Day judge advocates were sent to Japanese POW camps in Mukden (now known as Shenyang), Beijing, Shanghai, Canton, Hong Kong, and later Taiwan. Former allied POWs were questioned and Japanese camp guards placed in custody.[15] The men at these camps must have been eager to tell the story of their harrowing experiences. US general Jonathan Wainwright explained why. "Apparently it [Mukden POW camp] was built on the presumption that Japan would not only win the war but would keep many prisoners at work for years to come." The men sent to that camp were told that if they behaved and worked diligently for the next "ten to twenty years," after that "relatives from America would be permitted to visit them!"[16]

The rancor within American public opinion concerning the news of downed US airmen being unjustly executed should not be underestimated. Regardless, a US commission's review of the Shanghai Trials was not overly convinced of the legality of the proceedings, or at least seemed skeptical of the pursuit of justice against lower-ranking Japanese officers.[17] Controlling the postwar conversation about "justice" in newly minted military tribunals became a paramount policy for all the Allies to balance emotion and evidence. The same was true for needing to show the public which government could then, in turn, actually implement this justice. This sort of internal and external pressure to bring war crimes trials to the forefront of the public's attention was palpable in East Asia and throughout the West.

For Japan, the war concerned two historical issues: empire and the military battle for supremacy of East Asia. Maintaining success in that war of words continued to be important even after defeat. The competition was also on the information front. The Americans concealed data about some Japanese biological and chemical weapons war crimes to keep what they believed were vital military secrets for themselves during the start of the Cold War. The USSR, by contrast, opened one of the only trials on biological warfare in 1949, but the Americans denigrated it as "propaganda" in a bid to discredit it. The competition over justice spread to the trials and even the prevention of the dissemination of some trial records.[18]

An additional element of competitive justice centers on its significance. This is a conversation about justice received or denied, which never abated and continues to this day. East Asian authorities' persistent attention to this problem demonstrates the emphasis the Allies (including the Chinese), former colonial subjects in East Asia, and the Japanese themselves attribute to being able to define the meaning of Japan's empire and World War II. This historical moment has deep and contemporary political ramifications. Had the war been, as the Japanese propaganda emphasized, for the "liberation" of Asia? Had it been a war of liberty versus fascism as defined by the Chinese? Or was it more about colonial oppression as the Koreans later argued?

Bringing anyone to court in the chaotic symphony of postwar East Asia was far from easy, but the Western Allies did not hold out much hope to elicit justice in any form except in their own trials. Each government competed with the others in the region to prove its political legitimacy through the use of such trials. William Hamilton, an official at the Australian embassy at Nanjing, recalled in his memoirs "that all evidence about atrocities during the Nanking Incident would need to be provided by Europeans" because the Chinese exaggerated. A colleague of Hamilton's, somewhat oblivious to the international changes since the start of the war, assessed that "the Chinese would be quite uninterested in war criminals; and that many Chinese did not dislike the Japanese any more or less than other foreigners."[19]

The British concurred with the generally low Western opinion of Chinese legal savvy but were also wary that the Americans had already made brisk moves to pursue their own war crimes trials in China, as evidenced in Shanghai. The British were worried not only about the decline of their imperial holdings but also about their extensive imperial assets in both Southeast Asia and China, which were sorely needed as the postwar British economy foundered. Feeling the same pressure to bring forward their own trials, British officials made it clear in a confidential internal memo that they wanted to "uphold" British prestige in East Asia, and this meant holding war crimes trials even though they were not fully ready. The British aimed to do so by publicizing throughout China and the region "reports of all trials in Hong Kong of war crimes committed against British subjects there."[20] From the early days of the postwar period, the pursuit of justice in East Asia served a range of stakeholders for a variety of competing national interests.

The popular notion of transitional justice revolves around gaining legal closure within a unified territory, among the same people who share a common language and relatively the same political outlook or at least future-oriented goals. When we zoom out to examine history more regionally, this framework does not fit.[21] There were too many trials over a very large geographic space, which created very different dynamics among the numerous ruling agencies. War criminals were moved back and forth to testify, sometimes at several different trials. For example, former Manchukuo "last emperor" Pu Yi was put on the stand—as a loan from the Soviets where he was sequestered—for the longest of any witness at the Tokyo Trial. Several years later in December 1949, the Soviets again employed his testimony at their trial at Khabarovsk. He was finally trotted out for the cameras in 1956 by the Chinese communists in their last trials of Japanese war criminals in Shenyang, after the Soviets handed him over to the CCP in the summer of 1950. Sejima Ryūzō, a high-ranking Japanese officer of the Imperial General Headquarters, was also brought forward by the Soviets for legal display at the Tokyo Trial and then detained for eleven years at Khabarovsk in the USSR. Other witnesses and defendants showed up here and there, as did legal staff and a few judges. William Webb, the Australian chief of the Tokyo Trial, had led a team to investigate Japanese war crimes against Australian POWs in the last years of the war. The Chinese judge at the Tokyo Trial, Mei Ruao, later served as a consultant for the CCP investigations and trials in the 1950s, and many of the Japanese legal defense teams at Tokyo played important roles in the committee that analyzed redrafting Japan's constitution in the 1960s.

Locating the Nexus of Justice in East Asia

In contemporary East Asia a fierce battle between memory and history has solidified political camps on all sides of the debate. In part, this cementing of national opinion was paradoxically caused by war crimes trials. The courtroom is a place where documents and testimony are presented with the legal aim of establishing a factual base in veracity and then assigning blame. But public or even personal memory may not be something that can be authoritatively fixed by this process. In short, out of a mass inventory of details surrounding something that occurred, we select a limited supply of evidence and employ this in court. But hatred, forgetfulness, and other emotions are supposedly not at work in a legal tribunal as they are in the form of memory. Consequently, history and memory work in opposition on the legal stage. Moreover, trials do not conclude with the incarceration or execution of the guilty prisoners. Tribunals continue on as experience remembered by those who participated in the process. In fact, while the pursuit of justice may have truly begun with the trials, the ramifications endure long after.

While it is challenging to holistically analyze the similarities and differences among the several thousand trials of Japanese war crimes across half the globe, we can make a few generalizations. The charges of the USSR against the Japanese remain somewhat ambiguous given the lack of archival access but were mostly focused on the killing of civilians, which is also in part what the CCP trials were about. US trials focused on the abuse of POWs in detention centers and similar atrocities on the battlefields. KMT and the Filipino courts centered on abuses of prisoners and the massacres of civilians who opposed Japan; the British, Australian, French, and Dutch trials, meanwhile, mainly pursued abuses of those in POW camps and the abuse of civilians.[22] When the trials are looked at geographically we can see similarities but also differences depending on where in the former empire any given Japanese soldier was arrested. An examination of these colonial to postcolonial and competitive connections reveals the web of legal information and technology that also made the evolution of the trials possible. These flows are observable in the movement of internationally educated judges who took part in more than one war crimes trial, as well as the prosecutors who shared information, including the interpersonal relationships and layers of employment of legal staff, defendants, and witnesses among the countries involved. For example, in one surreal moment in 1946, after the Tokyo Trial had begun, Judge Mei Ruao invited to dinner members of the prosecution investigation team who were also in Shanghai gathering evidence. The Chinese lead prosecutor from the trial, Xiang Zhejun, joined the meal, compounding what was an unusual rendezvous because it contravened most legal practices where judges normally separate themselves from trial staff.[23] Countries could not fully operate trials on their own and needed to share data and prisoners behind the scenes to implement actionable justice. The fact that this information network later lent itself to the construction of commemorative symbols and sites of memorialization is intimately tied into regional politics owing to the legacy of the trials and the relationship among locations that meted out justice. All these elements have a large impact on today's East Asian societies.

Our overemphasis on national history and its connection to justice has blinded us to what was happening regionally, and we need to acknowledge that victors are not the only ones who write history. The history of justice reminds us of how we have ignored the centrality of the history of defeat in East Asia. The trials of Japanese war criminals from 1945 to 1956, the legal precedents set by such trials, and the political forces that then created and reinforced this memory through public ceremonies and popular culture demonstrate that the manner in which law resolved Japanese imperial responsibility continues to exert a deep force on contemporary political relations.[24]

In some measure the trials did pursue the truth about the nature of Japan's imperial reign. But they were also certainly employed to demonstrate which authority was now back in power. When examining the postwar trials of Japanese war criminals, we should keep in mind that legal proceedings served several simultaneous goals but also bestowed a set of memories enshrined in legal verdicts onto a variety of national histories—Korean, Taiwanese, Chinese, French, British, and so forth—and, of course, Japanese national memory.

The memoirs of Kaya Okinori, Japanese wartime minister of finance, convicted Class A war criminal, and postwar minister of justice, reveal how justice and the memory of empire remain intertwined. In his reminiscences, Kaya wrote that he believed he bore no legal responsibility for war crimes but was burdened with the weight of political morality. Kaya admitted he felt most responsible for the start of the war, which he meant as Japan's official war with the West from December 1941. He seemed oblivious to the issues of empire and thus ignored the long years of Japanese aggression in China that predated 1941. This occlusion allowed him to avoid taking into full account the poison gas warfare issue or many atrocities against Chinese peasants because it remained outside of his narrow window of liability. In its defeat, Japan suffered greatly, Kaya recalled, and the people endured sacrifice and tragedy. That is the responsibility he felt. What he failed to acknowledge, however, were the larger legal issues concerning what the Japanese did to others under the guise of empire.[25]

Kaya was a high-ranking member of the Japanese leadership involved in the liaison conferences between the wartime imperial military and the government. Even though he was adamantly against the war with the United States, he was still in a position to have stopped it. He failed and thus felt responsible, he claimed. He asked his readers: How should that responsibility be dealt with? Should I have committed suicide in atonement? "No, I would return to be a normal citizen and work hard for the country," he penned.[26] Kaya never set out to elaborate more clearly how that responsibility would be dealt with and only commented on how the West harshly adjudicated Japan in war tribunals, never China or the other aggrieved Asian countries. He was indignant that the charge of "war of aggression" was never defined to his satisfaction. Were the Allies the ones to sit in judgment? he asked. The implied answer was no. According to Kaya's logic, the UK, France, and the Netherlands all previously used their militaries to take colonial lands, so what were their qualifications to judge Japan? It is not an invalid historical question, but it is also not a legal defense that lets Japan off the hook. One of the infuriating realizations with this sort of benign plea of mea culpa is that Kaya and those who followed him never really get around to explaining who was responsible for Japan's innumerable atrocities committed in the name of empire and war. In a sense, Kaya remained focused on issues that dealt with leaders who led Japan to war, Class A crimes. He appears incapable of considering the long list of Japanese BC class war crimes and thinking about either their origin or impact in the empire and during the war.

Framing history in this way allowed Japanese in a variety of leadership positions to avoid discussing atrocities in Asia. Instead, they drew their inspiration from wartime propaganda that grew more potent after 1941 when Japan supposedly could no longer avoid a war that had become in their words "inevitable."[27] Harold Isaacs, a longtime American journalist in East Asia who reported from many corners of the region during the 1930s and 1940s, noted this. In his assessment, immediate postwar Japan really had not been forced to change much. In 1947, he wrote, "Imperial Japan survived its defeat. The empire was lost, industries crippled, cities laid waste, but the social regime still stood. No groundswell rose from amongst the people to topple it. No anger rising among its millions of victims at home shook its foundations."[28] How did this come about? he asked. In a slightly acerbic tone, Isaacs observed that the US occupation forces required change but not too much. Japanese financiers, politicians, and bureaucrats were at first scared of what they would have to do to satisfy the American conquerors but quickly understood that the new world order needed Japan. "After their first fright and uncertainty, they soon realized that the results would not be as ruinous as they had feared. In the realm of political power they had to clip a little of the divinity off the edges of the imperial myth, but otherwise they could preserve the essence of their social and political system."[29]

Kaya admitted that the real pity was that Japan did not conduct its own war crimes trials. This was precisely one of the potential flaws in the postwar adjudication of justice. The former minister for justice rightly noted that true war responsibility could not merely be dealt with by managing a series of tribunals, and his postwar life is evidence of this.

The Weaponization of History and the Memory of the Empire in Japan

Insight into the war and its resolution can be grasped by envisaging how the Allies required Japan to restructure and fit into a new and shifting international order in which the failed Japanese empire was no longer dominant. The Allies monopolized the investigations into the causes behind World War II and the tracking of the legal routes of inquiry to punish those they held responsible. The Japanese, too, fought to influence the outcome of these international war crimes trials. In September 1945, the first postwar Japanese Cabinet called for Japan to hold its own trials. Japanese officials were keen to prove to the world that their nation had suddenly changed from a month prior. On September 15, 1945, the *Manchester Guardian* reported Japan's first postwar prime minister, Higashikuni Naruhiko, pleading with the United States to "forget Pearl Harbor," because "the Japanese people now intend to be entirely peaceful."[30] A byproduct that cleaved the Japanese away from thinking about their own war crimes was the manner in which the Allied occupation shaped Japan, allowing Emperor Hirohito to serve as a figurehead, defanged of any sort of power, but nonetheless remaining on the mantle of leadership as a symbol of the state. The emperor faced a personal struggle in dealing with the concept of war criminals since at its roots the war had been fought in his name. On December 10, 1945, he voiced to his confidantes that while from the American point of view they might be seen as war criminals, for "our country they were individuals who rendered distinguished service" to the empire.[31] He would ultimately grow to regret this statement, and decades later he vowed to no longer make official visits to the Yasukuni Shrine after war criminals were enshrined there.

The emperor's role in Japan's defeat vexed many nationalists, like Tokutomi Sohō. Tokutomi's life and career mirrored the rise and fall of Japan's imperial era from 1863 to 1957. He had begun as an angry young turk of the Meiji era who pushed Japan to modernize. A prolific and influential journalist, by the 1920s Tokutomi's tone had grown strident as an imperial nationalist. Having long supported the military aims with deep ties to the imperial leadership, Tokutomi initially considered suicide after surrender, afraid of being arrested as a war criminal. While waiting for his expected demise, he simultaneously decided to examine the origins of Japan's defeat. In his personal diaries he was extremely critical of the lack of leadership, particularly from the emperor, and an absence of clear goals from the military.[32] Tokutomi's concerns about the defeat did not go unnoticed. Nakasone Yasuhiro, one of Japan's postwar conservative leaders who rose in the ranks of politics from the 1950s, visited Tokutomi several times in the early postwar period to hear his thoughts on Japan's imperial failure and its future.[33]

Nakasone was not a run-of-the-mill conservative. In his memoirs, aptly subtitled "as a defendant in the court of history," Nakasone assessed that Japan's war against the West should be differentiated from its war in Asia. The former was a war of self-defense, the latter a war of aggression. This, in turn, colored his perception of the Tokyo Trial as improper because it did not distinguish between these events.[34]

While Tokutomi and others voiced disappointment toward the emperor, some saw a moment to retake the throne amid the tectonic political shifts. During those uncertain times, everything was up for grabs, including the role of emperor. In what was a very popular story at the time, many believed the position was essentially democratized because the emperor had renounced his divinity, or at least the palace was open to being challenged given the emperor's failure to protect the nation. This meant others could potentially lay claim to it. Over the next few years, about nineteen pseudo emperors announced in the Japanese media, "I am the true emperor." Most were crackpots, some had interesting historical claims, and others were confused by differing interpretations of what democratizing Japan signified.[35]

We can see a situation where, until the nation surrendered, the Japanese had written their own war history. Suddenly, with the imperial fall, Japan's war history was forced to undergo a massive revision to be retold and explained to the population in an entirely different format by the victorious occupiers. Toward the end of the war, printing supplies and paper had dwindled to such short supply that newspapers were limited to two sheets with poor ink quality at that. As the Americans took over, the situation changed abruptly. On December 8, 1945, Japanese newspapers began to publish much longer four-page exposés of the war at the behest of SCAP, the occupation authority under the United States. New radio shows appeared as well, informing the population of a new "truth" about what had happened during the war.[36] However, this news in the Japanese media was clearly identified as American produced. It was denoted as a foreign interpretation of Japan's war, which helps explain why the newer historical interpretation was not believed. In addition, the new war history ran counter to the daily hardships of millions of Japanese. The gap was never more apparent than in the grand narrative the Tokyo Trial tried to reveal of the larger war but which did not fit with the more personal experiences of people on the ground. Japanese recalled sending family members to the front, or children and families escaping from the cities to the countryside as US air raids grew and fear of the bombing increased. In the end, the US version of the Pacific War did not mesh with Japanese recollections and experiences. Japan seemed incapable in the early years of prioritizing the experience of others in the way that Nguyen described as "just memory."[37]

Frequently, even the archival records of the trials turned into political footballs, bandied back and forth by nations eager to use them as blunt instruments when drafting new peace treaties and trade stipulations with postwar Japan. The Japanese side tried to secure the records of the war crimes trials initially after they took place but encountered persistent resistance from the Allies. These impediments later convinced the Japanese that the trials were a clear form of victor's justice and that the Allies were hiding something nefarious. Australia, perhaps the most egregious holdout, continually balked and did not publicly release the archives of its war crimes trials against the Japanese until years later. Ostensibly, this was because it feared feeding the frenzy of "victor's justice" baiting in Japan. The Australian government was anxious because "almost all of the trials of 'B' and 'C' class criminals have elements appearing on the face of the records which would provide a hostile reader with anti-Australian ammunition." Australian officials worried that "we should therefore be wary of providing adverse propaganda against ourselves."[38]

End of Empire and the Competition to Recolonize and Decolonize

The fall of the Japanese empire was the initial trigger for the start of the reordering of the world order in East Asia, what has been deemed the Cold War in the West. The structure of the war crimes trials and the narrative they offered subsequent generations shaped the story of how the war ended and where war responsibility was located. It was the end of Japan's dominance across the regions that also lit the initial fuse of imperial destruction for the European colonial powers in East and Southeast Asia. Japan's end of empire was not just about a military defeat but also about a dual structure of decolonization. To offer just one example, this imperial downfall meant that France would spend nearly a decade trying to regain Indochina (composed of Vietnam, Laos, and Cambodia), leading to a whole series of destabilizing wars that successive historians have labeled the first and second Indochina wars. These battles between the French and the Vietnamese continued until 1954 when the Geneva Conference paved the way toward new accords and a plan for a peace treaty. However, even this war over independence from France did not cease with the French withdrawal, because the United States had become increasingly involved. The key feature is to consider how long the impact of Japanese colonization in Southeast Asia led to the conflicts we continue to see in the region today.

We need to examine how imperial violence and World War II slid into the subsequent civil wars all throughout the region where the Japanese empire reigned supreme. Accordingly, the legacy of that imperial control wielded an immeasurable influence on the following decades. But while the facade of empire had crumbled, the remnants of the old networks of power and political legitimacy took a while to be reestablished and reconstructed.[39] We are dealing with the consequences of violent alteration of both the physical environment and geographical boundaries, but the thick continuities associated with colonialism, migration, industrialization, and technology also complicate the relationship between imperialism and subsequent decolonization. Japan's surrender involved all sorts of administrative and military machinations among the various authorities to ensure their upper hand in the initial power vacuum.

The Cold War paradigm in East Asia is problematic because it does not mimic the situation in Western Europe. The Cold War is a topic of great debate—when did it start, has it ended, and what exactly was it are topics of deep concern to many historians, politicians, policymakers, and military leaders. Some define it as the moment when the US military presence grew dominant as the new postwar superpower. Others see it as a legacy of communist versus capitalist camps within Europe as the Marshall Plan went into effect to save Western Europe from potentially falling into post–World War II economic ruin. A few researchers believe the Cold War to have started the moment the United States dropped the first atomic bomb on Hiroshima, not in a bid merely to conquer Japan but as a stern message of warning to the Soviet Union. This book does not attempt to provide a definitive answer to this conundrum. Instead, I offer an alternative way of conceiving how the Cold War took shape in East Asia. More importantly, I suggest that to really grasp what the Cold War was in the Asian region of the globe, we need to place the end of the Japanese empire at the center of it and analyze what happened in light of that failure. Ian Buruma paints 1945 as an international Year Zero, when the world emerged from the "wreckage" of World War II. He depicts the ensuing battle against hunger, revenge, and repatriation in what he calls "draining the poison" of demilitarization.[40] That aspect may be accurate, but I believe continuities remained strong from wartime to post-surrender East Asia owing to Japan's imperial legacy, and these structures set the regional postwar history apart from the Europe story.

The great irony of the postwar period in East Asia (defined as Japan, China, Taiwan, and North and South Korea) is that Japan's surrender brought peace to its home islands but little to the rest of its former empire. One way to unbraid the tangle of political relations, or the forging of new ones, is to accept the idea that "a chronology that prioritizes the cold war is a partial one and explains little about non-geopolitical aspects of international relations or about transnational movements."[41] A lingering question concerns the Eurocentric paradigm of the Cold War and trying to use it to understand East Asia. The West has become *the* standard model to examine history, defined essentially as two ideologically opposed nuclear superpowers in a standoff. This was mirrored in the alliances, both political and economic, of the subparties that attached themselves to their master states. However, in Asia that system never held. Parties outside of these liberal or Marxist-Leninist camps have always existed—for example, the PRC. Initially, China said it was "leaning to one side" and joining the Soviet bloc, but that adherence was fairly short-lived and ended in military acrimony between the former allies. In addition, in East Asia the liberal-capitalist camp versus the Marxist-Leninist camp as a divided world order never really held.

East and Southeast Asian countries after the end of World War II were busy shedding their imperial colonial heritage and forming their countries independently for the first time. These countries did not toe either ideological line, with the exception of Japan. When we think of North and South Korea, or Taiwan, none of them were democratic but rather built on state-led development under an autocratic leader. It was the same in Southeast Asia with Indonesia and Vietnam. Western Europe was already industrially advanced, whereas most of Asia was not, apart from Japan. The vast imbalance in East Asia between an already industrialized and international Japan and its partners in the region, which were neither, was a yawning chasm. We do not see such imbalances in Europe, unless we move from Western to Eastern Europe, where this gap was also very apparent.[42] In fact, "large parts of Northeast Asia, in particular, including the People's Republic of China (PRC), the Russian Far East, and North Korea, remain decisively *outside* the American imperium, and have *never* been part of it."[43]

At the same time, division in East Asia has not ended, which then calls into question Western pronouncements that the Cold War has ended. North Korea remains isolated with only a few international countries willing to host diplomatic relations—importantly *not* among them are South Korea and Japan. Moreover, the Korean peninsula remains split, in part, owing to the legacy of Japan's colonial rule and Chinese / Soviet support of the north. The Korean minority issue of citizenship in Japan remains unresolved, as do many border issues within East Asia. These divisions are the result of quickly managed occupation policies that strove to repatriate specific ethnicities from across the wide expanse of the former Japanese empire.[44] The sediments of time remain in place more than seventy years after the end of World War II, not to mention the issue of Taiwan and its tense relationship with mainland China—is it a renegade province or an independent country? The legacy of Japan's empire in East Asia ran deep and laid extensive roots into the various societies it touched. In East and Southeast Asia the transformation was palpable with the creation of a whole panoply of decolonized states after Japan's fall.

Postimperial Changes

Three crucial transformations in East Asia, which occurred after August 1945, help us grasp the political dynamics that prevented war crimes trials from forming a base for reconciliation in the region. This narrative aids a larger understanding behind the meaning of how and why justice was stymied in postwar East Asia. First, Japan ceased to be an empire but crumbled and needed to be dismantled. This "un-building" of empire was a process fraught with difficulty and came at the same time when other nations were forming or struggling with reasserting themselves against reimposed European colonial rule and the impositions of what became the Cold War in the West. For Japan and its former occupied lands, this transformation entailed all the intricacies of reverse engineering empire—taking apart in a very short time what had previously been under Japanese control. The small geographic space of Japan now had to absorb back into itself all the expansion of empire that it had created and decide what to discard. Who would it protect, and which elements would it sacrifice for the nation?[45] Second, the use of legal court decisions about the Japanese past, produced in China and elsewhere in war crimes trials, would come to represent the various national set of memories on which foreign policy was built. However, these legal precedents were produced by a China that was relatively new to international proceedings and opposed by a Japan that had a much deeper, albeit somewhat ambivalent, understanding of international law. How the legacy of these trials evolved—including their omission from history for more than thirty years in China and Taiwan, and a Japanese government reluctant to reflect on its own past—has left deep scars on the present state of affairs and political relations in East Asia. Third, the manner in which the war was lost was uneven throughout East Asia and was quickly supplanted by colonial goals of the European powers, so the interaction of the trials on a regional level is necessary to consider. We cannot understand East Asia only by looking at the Tokyo Trial, nor can we figure out what went wrong only by examining, for example, lesser-ranked trials conducted by the British in Hong Kong or the French in Saigon. What we need is a more holistic overview of how these trials exerted pressure within a common and connected international system to shape the current state of conflicting political views.

These points might seem insignificant, but they are not. In fact, one's political stance on the Tokyo Trial defines a whole generation in Japan, pits leaders against Japan on the Korean peninsula, and is the basis of how the CCP on mainland China generates a major source of its contemporary legitimacy. Understanding the legacy of war crimes trials in East Asia is a crucial conduit through which we can come to understand how and why the region is politically divided as it is today and what the origin of the historical friction is that continues to cause discontent. The situation in East Asia was about both empire and war and shaped the postwar search for justice in a very different manner from the European continent.

CHAPTER 3

When the Hero of Your Story Is the Villain of Another

While anchored to the past through the physical form of captured naval vessels and war booty, China was also tethered to an outmoded tradition in its legal arena. This proved to be a major obstacle in its attempts to uphold international goals of justice given the constraints. Even though the Chinese faced an uphill battle in terms of both staffing and creating the actual sites for war crimes tribunals, they had slowly pushed ahead during the war at least with a nod to the future and what might be legally within reach.[1] As the international community began to pay more attention to Nazi atrocities in Europe, China's role in interacting with the UNWCC and the development of war crimes processes advanced but was not always a well-coordinated activity.[2] Chiang Kai-shek had told his men: confiscate enemy property, do not collude with those who were collaborators, disarm Japanese and prepare them for repatriation, and ensure as little disruption as possible to commerce and public services.[3]

The rule of law existed, but at the dawn of its victory over Japan, the Republic of China was feeling anything but triumphant. Its population never had a chance to enjoy the spoils of victory, if any were to be had, nor did the Japanese still stationed in China really believe in the empire's defeat. One of the last directors of Japan's Cabinet Information Bureau, Minister Shimomura Kainan (Hiroshi), wrote in his memoirs that the Japanese military in China remained without enemies. He assessed that Japan had never succumbed to the Chinese and that defeat was only due to the American intervention. Shimomura quoted KMT general He Yingqin as saying that China had not won the war by itself but with the assistance of the Allies.[4] And regardless of the supposed victory, China was in dire straits. Millions were starving in Hunan Province, and the prognosis of further massive food shortages was evident for Sichuan, Guangxi, and Guangdong Provinces as well. This was followed by "a tidal wave of confiscation throughout the once-occupied regions. Confiscation technically referred only to enemy and *hanjian* [traitor] property, but it quickly degenerated into general looting."[5]

Just before the opening of the Tokyo Trial, Chinese legal consultant Ni Zhengyu journeyed to the United States to deepen Chinese understanding of international law procedures. One of his key consultants was Roscoe Pound, a renowned professor of law at Harvard University and postwar legal consultant to the KMT.[6] Pound had already been involved in the curriculum and teaching of law at Soochow University in 1935 and 1937. He was seventy-seven when he retired from Harvard and made his way to China after the war to teach and serve as an adviser in 1946. Ni went by the English name of "Judson Nyi," and on January 5, 1946, he, once again, opened correspondence with Pound. In his letter to the Harvard professor, Ni told him that he had been a judge for twelve years in Shanghai and Chongqing and recently was a counselor to the Ministry of Justice. But the letter was mostly to press Pound to accept and make plans to teach and advise on law in China. On February 16, 1946, Ni wrote to Pound, saying that he enjoyed their meeting and requested several introductions to legal scholars in the UK "who can explain to me some of the salient features of judicial administration there. In the meantime I would also like to meet some professor with whom I can discuss a few problems in connection with court system [*sic*], procedure, etc."[7] Ni was introduced to at least two scholars at Cambridge University—Sir Percy Henry Winfield and Henry Arthur Hollond, both scholars of law—and Arthur Lehman Goodhart, an American-born British academic who was professor of jurisprudence at the University of Oxford. In addition, Ni met with Lord Wright of Durley (Robert Wright), who was then serving as chair of the UNWCC.

Ni wrote back to Pound on April 19, 1946, thanking him for the introductions in England and saying that he had met with Lord Wright and was himself going to Tokyo to observe the war crimes trial. Ni visited London courts and a prison in the UK. He also toured Scotland Yard "to see how they investigate criminal cases before they are prosecuted in courts. The kind of liason [*sic*] between the police and the courts is very much needed in China."[8] It is interesting, and perhaps a bit of a window into the problems of cronyism that continually plagued the KMT, to see several appeals from Hsia Ch'in, president of the

Supreme Court of the Republic of China, to Pound. Hsia wrote directly to Pound in a bid to get his son into Harvard. "Would you be so kind as to help him get his admission and a tuition scholarship if possible," Hsia wrote.[9]

The Chinese faced difficulties at the Tokyo Trial and were caught off guard—Judge Mei Ruao, legal consultant Ni Zhengyu, and head of the KMT War Crimes Investigation Committee and witness at the Tokyo Trial, Qin Dechun, all mentioned this in their memoirs.[10] In Ni's estimation, the Chinese were not completely familiar with the system of evidence procurement, and this demonstrated the paradox of Chinese law at the time.[11] The Chinese were fundamentally unprepared for trial, and when Japan declared surrender, Ni Zhengyu was in the United States. He heard the surprising news about the extensive damage caused by the two atomic bombs. Tokyo Trial Chinese prosecutor Xiang Zhejun was dispatched to Tokyo several months later and handed the US legal team a list of eleven names of war criminals for prosecution. The Allied prosecution team was stunned that the Chinese had arrived with such a short list and that they were not prepared to prosecute in open court. The Chinese were also flummoxed; they had not been told to bring materials or evidence, or really to prepare anything. They had not collected evidence or prepared much in advance because they believed the guilt of Japanese war criminals was "plainly obvious," as Ni Zhengyu wrote in his memoirs.[12] Only when they arrived in Japan did they realize the Tokyo Trial would not be using continental law but English/US law. In Ni Zhengyu's understanding, the US and UK legal systems employed a direct confrontation system, where both sides battled it out equally in the court, taking care with evidence but asking the questions. The continental system, the one Chinese lawyers were theoretically used to at home even if many of them trained in American law at Soochow, used the interrogative system, where the judges posed the questions and managed the trial process.[13]

At one point in the prosecution's presentation of evidence for the Nanjing Massacre section of the Tokyo Trial, the Chinese got into trouble. They did not offer the court much in the way of what was expected, and this drew Chief Justice William Webb's sharp criticism. "Most of them [witness statements] were formulaically written, single-page statements of offense that contained bare minimum information about dates, locations, types of offense, and victims involved. In a word, there was not much substance in them." This lackluster showing pushed Webb to remark, "There is hardly evidence. There are no details. What court could act on evidence like that?" Webb felt the Chinese were using slim material to put forward their prima facie case, but that had only a very limited application.[14]

The phenomenon of the "obviousness" of the crimes could also be seen in the Nanjing and Shanghai BC class war crimes courtrooms, where the bones of victims were placed on the judge's dais in open court. It seemed normal to the Chinese at the time to set up their courts with such displays because they believed Japanese guilt was self-evident. But it was certainly a legally suspect move. While the nature of the war crimes might have been easily discernible, the speed of justice was not. The Tokyo Trial advanced at a glacial pace, with each statement translated from English into Japanese and back again, announcing to defendants each charge and asking whether he was guilty. The process bogged down. The Chinese, and others, continually commented on the interminable slog.[15] Prosecutor Xiang and his staff realized they also needed stronger evidence to stand up to this sort of prolonged scrutiny, so they quickly returned to China and asked for an increase in staff. They interviewed witnesses and shuttled through war-torn areas but had a hard time amassing concrete proof in the budding civil war. In Nanjing, Yang Zhaolong, who was now Ministry of Justice Criminal Division chief, assisted Xiang in looking through Nanjing Massacre files. American prosecutor Joseph Keenan used up part of his budget and sent subordinates to China, while permitting Xiang to hire five more assistants.[16] This tiny Chinese team was dwarfed by the platoon of legal staff the Soviets originally wanted to send of seventy men, which the Allied coordinators negotiated down to thirty.

The Imposition of War Crimes Trials

The move to use international law to stem postimperial violence in East Asia after Japan's surrender emerged first from Europe and the various exiled governments in London that pushed the world to think about how to prosecute the Nazis for crimes over which law had not yet ably defined its jurisdiction. While the Chinese were keen to pursue war crimes against the Japanese, they were also noticeably circumspect in how they went about doing it. Both parties—the KMT and the CCP—took a stance on what they termed "to repay hatred with kindness" at the time of Japan's surrender. Generalissimo Chiang Kai-shek broadcast a radio message to the nation clearly enunciating that China held the Japanese military clique as the enemy and not the Japanese people. Chiang emphasized that the Chinese wanted to hold the military leadership responsible but did not seek revenge on the innocent, nor wish to add to their suffering. It is worth mentioning that Chiang never actually employed the phrase "to repay hatred with kindness," but the slogan came to symbolize

KMT strategy.[17] Many criticized the KMT as the war ended, even though Chiang Kai-shek said he would take back in those who had worked for other administrations—meaning those who had saddled up to Wang Jingwei's government in Nanjing that accommodated the Japanese, as well as those who took positions in the Japanese-managed Manchukuo administration. There was also much criticism that Chiang was doing this just to gain financial support. In the parlance of the day, "Those with money get consideration, those without will not see the light of day."[18]

The issue of adjudicating legal responsibility for war crimes and collaboration became a long-term struggle for legitimacy between the Chinese Nationalists and the Communists. The CCP touched on the idea of benevolence, as Chiang Kai-shek had, but pushed harder on the issue of pursuing war criminals. In part this was a calculated political move to show the Chinese populace that the CCP believed the KMT was reneging on its pledge to arrest Japanese war criminals, but it was also a move to force the matter into the media spotlight. Contestation over the administration of postwar China and Taiwan remained a pitched battle between two main competitors—the KMT and the CCP—and sometimes the remaining Japanese. Precisely how Japan responded is investigated in the next chapter.

Chinese POWs and the Legacy of Trials

The tales and trials of Japanese who abused or killed Allied POWs were a mainstay of news stories during and in the immediate aftermath of the war. For obvious reasons the pursuit of justice against those crimes was a crucial focal point for the United States and European former colonial powers. However, one of the great contradictions when examining Japan's war from the Asian context is the absence of parallel trials for Chinese POWs. While a grand number of Allied trials concern abused or murdered western POWs, during the war imperial Japanese forces also no doubt killed and captured tens of thousands of Chinese soldiers. But their records are scarce. With the exception of some select examples, mostly in Australia trials, they remain outside the grand narrative. Consequently, trials of Chinese POW abuse and their legacy do not follow the same trajectory as the history in the West. But the story is vastly more complicated because while the "Japanese authorities claimed to have had in their possession scores of thousands of Western prisoners, they acknowledged having only fifty-six Chinese prisoners of war."[19] The Chinese were unable to organize tribunals around Chinese prisoners owing to this lacuna, and such an absence would also therefore dictate the sort of war crimes that later became foundations of China's postwar history of the war of resistance against Japan.

Part of the reason that the numbers of Chinese POWs disappeared from the story of World War II is that various agencies within the Japanese government did not open their archival treasures to public scrutiny, failed to collate adequate information, and often were just remiss in doing due diligence.[20] There was also great ambiguity concerning who was a soldier, who was Chinese, or what was actually happening. An example of this can be seen during an incident described by Yamada Fūtarō, a young student at the Tokyo Medical Higher School, who was transferred to the countryside of Nagano Prefecture to avoid the increasing US air raids. Yamada wrote in his diary that the aisles and all the seats of the train were packed. The train departed Shinjuku Station in Tokyo in the morning and arrived at the central mountainous area at Tatsuno Station at 5 p.m. All the students disembarked and waited two hours for a connecting ride on another line toward their destination. While they were waiting they observed what was happening at the rail station. Yamada spied a motley crew of forty to fifty young, middle-aged, and old soldiers in formation in front of the station. They were speaking Chinese to each other, and two or three were being carried by stretcher. Were they POWs? he wondered. Commands in Japanese were yelled at them, and they took off marching down the street, singing "March of the Beloved Horse," a peppy Japanese military tune.[21]

At the end of 1942, the Japanese wartime cabinet under General Tōjō Hideki recognized that Japan was facing labor shortages owing to more manpower being drained to the front. In an effort to sustain domestic industrial and agricultural production, the cabinet passed a November 27, 1942, decision to "move Chinese laborers to Japan's interior." Kaya Okinori was the finance minister and Kishi Nobusuke was minister of commerce and industry at the time. The law allowed the government to "transport" Chinese laborers into positions within what were considered key industries of mining, production, or construction projects for national defense.[22]

Yamada was not sure whether these men were Chinese forced laborers or soldiers taken as POWs and put to work. He believed, however, that it was possible they were the ones taken to construct what he had heard rumors about—the Matsushiro Underground Imperial Headquarters in Nagano Prefecture.[23] This massive complex, for which unknown tunnels were still being discovered in the 1990s, was built by the Kajima and Nishimatsu construction companies. Labor was provided mainly by about seven thousand Koreans, although the true size and composition of the labor teams are not fully known.[24]

Although the specifics of how many Chinese were taken prisoner were never truly clear, what was known was the high death toll and the fact that

Chinese POWs and forced labor did exist. Key to this knowledge was a five-volume set of investigations that the Japanese Ministry of Foreign Affairs (MOFA) conducted in the immediate postwar and then "lost."[25] The ministry wanted all places of employment to inform it of the conditions of Chinese forced laborers, their contracts and status of employment, deaths, numbers, salaries, and so forth. In all likelihood this was done to avoid being charged with war crimes.[26] Many Japanese officials knew of the existence of these records, or had heard about them, but no one could find them. Sadly, they appeared either adrift in the wreckage of war or deliberately destroyed after their commission.[27] For over five decades these investigations were mentioned in parliament, but whenever the topic was broached, MOFA confirmed that it could no longer locate the documents. They ended up being known as the "phantom Ministry of Foreign Affairs reports." This remained the situation until 1993, when Japan's public broadcasting corporation, NHK, filmed a documentary of the reports finally being located after almost a half century of enforced obscurity.[28] This revelation about forced labor resulted in a whole new set of contemporary legal trials, which links back to my point that war crimes trials did not resolve the entirety of the war.[29]

MOFA's use of the term "laborer" for Chinese workers demonstrates its concerted effort to show that Japanese were hiding the fact that they forced Chinese civilians and soldiers to work—it was not always voluntary. Included in the five volumes was the file "Top Secret: Record of Committee Countermeasure Activities concerning Chinese and Korean Laborers." It discussed ways of dealing with the postwar compensation demands that would inevitably arise from these workers and how to avoid future legal trials. This document also talked about investigating what happened with this forced labor with the potential for dealing with future war crimes trials in mind. Japanese officials wanted to collect information concerning what happened at various companies regarding the forced labor of Chinese, including POWs, to stem any legal problems. There was tellingly much less Japanese interest in investigating for the sake of actually seeking justice. In March 1946, while the government was still fumbling around with deliberating its own war responsibility, MOFA dispatched sixteen investigators to every single one of the sites where Japanese companies used forced labor. A number of these companies continue to exist today.[30] Many of the companies do not reveal their past abuse of forced Chinese labor, let alone offer financial redress. In many ways they remain hidden behind the cloak of the law.[31] But here we find injustice once again because "the Japanese government repurposed these records to determine the allocation of compensation to 135 corporate offices, which amounted to approximately 57 million Japanese yen." In short, the

Chinese were denied compensation, but the actual Japanese industrial culprits profited with "tacit US approval."[32]

Over the last few years of the war, in those 135 locations within Japan, approximately forty thousand Chinese had been dragooned into forced servitude. In theory they were supposed to have been paid and treated as workers. In reality, most were often treated like slaves or worse. About seven thousand died.[33] One site, the Hanaoka Mine in Akita Prefecture, operated under the Kajima Corporation, had been particularly brutal in its treatment of Chinese laborers. They eventually rose up and rioted in protest during the late summer of 1945. Of the close to one thousand Chinese forced laborers who worked at Hanaoka, about four hundred had died by the end of the war.[34] After the uprising, the local and military police went into the mountains to search for escaped Chinese laborers. They dragged many back and kept them tied up for several days in the town square.[35] During that time, the two police forces tortured and killed about one hundred Chinese laborers in a building off the main square.[36]

It was not just domestically that Japan used a wide range of dragooned labor, clouding the issue of civilian and military prisoners. Across its oceanic empire on remote islands in the Pacific at the fringes of Japanese power, a mix of Chinese civilians and military men found themselves in varying formats of forced labor. In Australian war crimes trials at Rabaul, in what are currently the domestic frontiers of Papua New Guinea, Chinese military officers provided testimony of having been taken as POWs from China, then relocated an ocean away to serve the Japanese empire in a forced labor capacity.

Forced labor during World War II was a complicated affair for several reasons. First, these Chinese were from several layers of society when pressed into servitude. Taiwanese laborers of various stripes, military and civilian, had also been dispatched in the spring of 1943 to build what would become fortifications of key Japanese military outposts on Rabaul. Because Taiwan was a colony under Japanese imperial control, hiring these men as war labor would not be considered a war crime. However, some of the first Chinese POWs brought to Rabaul for forced labor were Chinese Nationalist troops taken prisoner during the late 1937 Sihang Warehouse Battle of Shanghai. This was before Japan had declared official war on China, so these men were never legally defined as POWs.[37] Forced labor from captured or surrendered Indian forces who had made up portions of British troops in Southeast Asia was much larger in number than the Chinese. They were transferred throughout the empire after their capture in early 1942 when Southeast Asia fell to the Japanese onslaught. Like the Taiwanese, they, too, fell through the cracks in the postwar period concerning their lack of access to legal redress. Their stories compelled one historian to label them "the men who never were."[38]

The captured Chinese soldiers from the Sihang Warehouse Battle were first taken to a Nanjing POW camp, but the several hundred soldiers taken from that conflict were fiercely opposed to Japan and Japanese authorities feared an uprising among them. Japanese officers separated the group over several sites for labor. In late 1942, about fifty-seven men were taken as laborers to what became the land known as Papua New Guinea, where many died due to harsh conditions.[39] Eventually, through various battles with both KMT and "guerilla troops," which sometimes referred to CCP soldiers, POW detention sites in Nanjing and Shanghai expanded. From there about fifteen hundred Chinese forced laborers ended up in Rabaul by the end of World War II. There they mixed with local populations and Indian coolies also compelled into forced labor or indentured in other kinds of labor.[40] One former Chinese soldier, Li Weixun, who was taken and detained in the Nanjing concentration camp, said that the detention center was so well known as a source of forced labor for the Japanese empire that it became colloquially referred to as the "Coolie Dispatch Center."[41] Lu Xinfang from Zhejiang Province had been taken prisoner during the Quzhou Battle, in western Zhejiang Province. The ship that transported him to Australia gave him a small bunk but lacked adequate water and food and took about a month to make the journey across the ocean. After arrival, the prisoners were put to work digging air raid shelters underground. Lu managed to get back to Shanghai in 1947, and then in 1950 he followed the KMT military to Taiwan.[42]

KMT lieutenant Colonel Woo Yian featured as a prominent member of the forced POW labor group and showed up in several war crimes trials, testifying against the Japanese. He appears in numerous photos as well, documenting his situation. Woo stated that the POWs were from the KMT military and included some Chinese guerrilla fighters as well.[43] Confounding the situation were Chinese from mainland China already living in the region, having arrived years earlier to work as coolie laborers. They were not necessarily integrated into Australian life in the Rabaul area but had been around since the 1920s.[44]

Regardless of the makeup of the Chinese POWs held in Rabaul, the Japanese were found responsible for war crimes against some of them. Matsushima Tozaburō was charged with other Japanese soldiers and seven "other Formosans," as they were labeled in the Australian court record. Matsushima was on trial for having taken part in the killing of numerous Chinese POWs, some of whom had been KMT soldiers. In the cross-examination of one Chinese officer, Captain Liu Wei Pao, the issue of relations between the Formosans and the Japanese was called into question. Liu replied, "In my opinion the Japanese treated these Formosans on an equal level and they certainly were vested with a great deal of power. We regarded these particular Formosans as not being true to type of their country but were very pro-Japanese and as they treated us most brutally it is rather difficult to explain just how we regarded them."[45] The "Formosans," for the most part, tried to paint themselves as pawns of the Japanese, hapless victims of circumstance who were not military at all and mere laborers in the empire. To a man, they all submitted petitions to the court protesting that the Chinese "hated" them because of their own wartime situation and that "false charges" were being made against them. They all wrote at the end of their petitions that they had come from Taiwan as "laborers" and had family waiting for them back home in Taiwan.[46]

At the trial of Hirota Akira, held in Rabaul, KMT lieutenant colonel Woo Yian offered testimony in a related case of Chinese POW murders. He declared that he "was captured by the Japanese at the end of May 1942." Along with about five hundred Chinese military POWs taken in various places, their party was joined by a thousand Chinese POWs made up of guerrilla forces. "All the Chinese troops brought to Rabaul were made to work as labourers," he explained. The Chinese military POWs showed up in Rabaul still in their uniforms, but "after we had been in Rabaul for two or three months the Japanese took our uniforms and issued us with Japanese style uniforms without badges or rank."[47] However, other POWs had different experiences. Major Chen Kwok Leong said that he was "a guerrilla leader of the Chinese National Army fighting against the Japanese in China." He was taken prisoner, and then with a thousand others, as Woo had mentioned, shipped from Shanghai to Rabaul. At Rabaul, these "guerrilla fighters" were paid for the first ten months. But his section was the only one paid for the first ten months because the Japanese officer in charge "was well disposed to the Chinese," Chen said. But, Chen emphasized, their loyalty never wavered, and they did not lose their status as POWs just because they were laborers.[48]

The trial of the wartime Japanese commander of the area, General Imamura Hitoshi, fuzzied the issue of POW or laborer because the Japanese officers serving under the general did not seem to fully grasp the illegality of forcing a prisoner to be a laborer for an enemy force. Hosoda Hiromu, who had been a staff officer of the Imperial General Headquarters, at one point said in his testimony at the Imamura trial that although there were extant regulations that covered what a military could and could not do in terms of employing labor, he had a different view of what happened in the Rabaul area: "The staff of the Imperial GHQ in Japan recognized and knew that the Japanese soldiers and the Third Nationals, that is, labourers, were working together in harmony. This is not only the opinion in Imperial GHQ but also the general public, and even at this present day this is still thought. The reason for that is Gen Imamura's good character, his wide international and public fame, and his endearing efforts that is his life for his subordinates, and their supervision and direction, and I am strongly of this opinion."[49]

The importance of these trials, and the earnestness of those being prosecuted, did nothing to impede the problems faced at other trials of the Japanese—namely, language issues that added to the torpor of getting justice. The humid and sticky weather at many Southeast Asian tropical venues created at times what can only have been moments of farcical levity. At one point during his own trial, not only did General Imamura fall asleep, but the military police officer assigned to guard him also dozed. The president of the court had to wake both.[50]

And yet, this was the same Imamura who was very keen not to let his soldiers get haphazardly caught up in war crimes trials. Before anyone in Tokyo had gotten their act together—or perhaps in coordination (the record is not clear)—Imamura took matters into his own command and counseled his men on how to respond to war criminal allegations:

> *Top Secret: Burn after reading*
> *Re: concerning those suspected of being war criminals*
>
> *From Japanese Commander in Charge, General Imamura Hitoshi*
> *December 4, 1945, Rabaul*
>
> *This instruction is for Japanese soldiers who are now under criminal investigation by the Allied army, particularly for those who have had their photographs taken and soldiers who are under suspicion. The commanding officer must educate them in detail concerning the following measures.*
>
> *Area Army Chief of Staff: Katō Rinpei*
>
> *In prior wars atrocities such as robbery, looting and other violence inflicted on innocent civilians by military soldiers were adjudicated in their own military's court martial tribunals. Now, however, these trials are being managed by the enemy's side after the conclusion of the war. In this way because there are no precedents, under the label of a war crime they obstinately select each individual action as fodder for their indictments. They say that doing things in this manner will extinguish all possibility of war erupting again in the future.*
>
> *But their true nature masks nothing more than deep feelings of enmity and hatred toward the Japanese and Germanic races. As the Commander in charge in Rabaul, I, upon reflection believe that because you men have maintained good military discipline there are not so many war criminals. It is likely the Australian*

forces have the same opinion, but following the demands of their home government, even if it is political, it appears they are obliged to open courts in this region. The result of this is that when such courts are established I will enumerate below how you must answer them and this is most important to remember.

First: Regardless of the category of your act, I, as the commander in chief, feel deeply responsible in leading you and this moves me to great sympathy. Shameful offences, or crimes, as reflected in our military law, are not permitted. Moreover, as Japanese we should be embarrassed by such issues. For example, during the heat of the moment in a fierce air raid should you inflict violence on a powerless POW, who had no connection to the incident, this contravenes the Japanese spirit which sanctifies helping the weak. However, I suppose problems related to the treatment of POWs emerges from battlefield exigencies and were based on actions thrust upon you. You have no reason to feel shame about this. Rather, as a Japanese who loyally performed his duties, you should be praised.

Second: Do not disgrace samurai honor

As mentioned above, if you can regain the calmness of spirit, there is no need to fear the investigating officers of the Allied forces. You must not posture a sulky attitude toward their demands. However, behaving in ways that you think will be perceived in a lofty and heroic manner shows the differences in how the East and West see the world. They will most definitely not accept your responses in this way. You must take care when answering and ensure that there are no discrepancies in what you say before and after. Speak calmly and ensure your expressions are clear. A good example of this can be found in the Tokugawa Era. Even when facing the threat of drawn swords in the hands of forceful samurai guards of the Shogun, Banzuin Chōbei responded in a calm and courteous demeanor without bringing shame to the "Edokko" [those who lived in early modern Tokyo].[51] *This is the reason why his story is still told even now in the tales of our traditions as a man among men, the symbol of manliness.*

On one hand, we all want to call on a friend when we cannot bear the burden alone. "It was not my idea to do this, it was a command," or "my fellow corpsmen also committed such and such." Such a response will result in causing problems for many others. If a situation comes to this it will be troublesome and it will be impossible to avoid being labeled as a coward. The fact is in military courts martial at the New Guinea front because this sort of behavior was present the spirit of bushido was sullied. These stories were picked up in the enemies' newspapers, becoming the object of derision and gaining a bad reputation as the actions of the "mean and cowardly." In these times I recall the story of "Sakura Sōgorō," one of the most famous martyrs in our country.[52] *To carry out his mission he sacrificed himself and even his family, without getting any of his fellow villagers wrapped up in the matter. It is precisely due to these actions that he is now enshrined as a "just imperial subject."*

Third: It is of the utmost importance to painstakingly prepare for answering clearly and in good order. Of course, in court you must say that affairs are uncertain when they are, but if there may be an act for which the enemies deem you to be guilty, you must explain in detail that during a severe air-raid the extreme stupidity of the actions of the Indian military prisoners was, as it were, as if they had committed suicide. It is advisable to explain that there was no other way besides soundly rebuking them. To this end we slapped them with our bare hands and during the chaos due to instances of burglary we could not help but mete out further punishments to preserve order. This unfortunate turn of events was due to problems in communication and such which rendered the situation even more confusing. You should maintain high spirits in the knowledge that these were special circumstances of your duty.

Fourth: Think about your fellow soldiers who are also under suspicion and imprisoned. "To the victor go the spoils." Allied force front line camps are already incarcerating several thousand of our countrymen in detention centers and calling them war criminals. In our motherland many of our high officials, ministers, high ranking military officers, nobles and even the princes of our imperial families who had direct concerns with this great war, have been detained and sent to the same interned lives as you now face. When you feel unease and loneliness of spirit, remind yourselves that your sacrifice is the cornerstone of our great nation and that among your fellow detainees are the elderly with grey hair aged more than seventy to eighty. For example, Tokutomi Sohō, the famous statesman aged eighty-two, is now still solemnly facing a moment in court. As such, deepen your resolve, and use your utmost effort to avoid embarrassing yourselves as true Japanese.[53]

Six months later Imamura was less sure of his stance, or at least less pleased with the prospect of life imprisonment. He first tried to commit suicide in July 1946 by taking poison, but it proved ineffective and only left him sick. He also tried to cut his own throat but missed the main artery and was unsuccessful a second time. Ultimately, he went on to live a long life in postwar Japan and wrote about his time as a war criminal under Australian oversight.[54]

Japan's Other Role in the Region as Innovator

Certainly Japan's dubious efforts to dragoon labor to feed its war machine, even as victory petered out, needed to be adjudicated in some measure. However, for many in the region, Japan was not one solely defined by its military actions. The Japanese empire and its imperial legacy meant that for those living in East Asia, their experience would be very different from those of Americans or Europeans who were coming into contact with the Japanese only through battle. Our singular and mostly nationalistic approach to investigating history has obscured large arenas. I am not arguing that we have missed the historical record of Japanese atrocities, but I would agree with Timothy Snyder's assessment that we should consider a supranational and more regional approach to cut across nationalist histories that overly emphasize a Western-centered approach.[55] Europe "works as a silent referent in historical knowledge," and we should try to recenter our thinking so that when we talk about war crimes and guilt it is not merely from the standpoint of overemphasizing the role of Nuremberg.[56] Nuremberg is, of course, central to the evolution of international law, but war crimes trials in East Asia birthed a historical industry of its own that also requires analysis on its own terms.

This is especially the case in both Japan and East Asia, where national suffering or victory is remembered and sanctified above all else, creating a very easy to digest yet overly simplistic version of history that essentially smooths out the complex and uneven seams. Hiroshima is certainly foremost in the minds of many Japanese as a memory of the end of war, a recollection that feeds a victimhood mentality, while that is not the case outside the main Japanese islands. We need to pit more of the domestic history against a regional and international backdrop to ascertain the larger context of war crimes trials, as well as postimperial violence pertaining to de-imperialization in Taiwan, Korea, and China. This will reveal a more accurate picture of how the rule of law and new political bodies were able to be reconstructed after the war.

East Asia, for the reasons that I detail in this book, was a vastly different historical landscape in comparison with Europe. We need to recall that the region of East Asia frequently held two conflicting opinions concerning Japan, and these attitudes colored the pursuit of justice. Even acknowledging the horrific impact of World War II initiated by Japan's imperial expansion, key leaders throughout the East also remembered the other side of Japan's influence. This aspect is worth reiterating to balance our historical assessments of what sort of legacy these trials pursued. This is not revisionist. I merely propose to include in our equation why some war crimes might have been pursued differently in various geographic settings.

One of the obstacles created by the memory of war crimes trials and the legal precedents they set is the potential tendency to overemphasize Japan's aggression to the neglect of the rest of its lengthy imperial legacy. Consider the differences in the way those who interacted with Japan in the East shared contrasting perspectives from their European or American interlocutors. This is manifest in three examples that I briefly illustrate below. Most specifically, these attitudes come into relief when postwar PRC Korean, and Republic of China leaders expressed their opinions on Japan's Meiji Restoration, in their eyes a seminal moment not to be ignored.

Guo Moruo, Chinese literary giant and head of the Chinese Academy of Social Sciences, had studied for decades in prewar Japan and only returned to China on the eve of Japan's more aggressive stature for war in 1937. He made an important set of comments in a wide-ranging discussion with a Japanese colleague of the literary world, Tanizaki Jun'ichirō. In the mid-1950s Guo was on a trip to Japan as part of mainland China's attempts to entertain more civilian diplomatic relations. At a roundtable promoting bilateral exchange, he remarked that Western scholars said that the "Meiji Restoration was the 'miracle of the Far East.' In that same vein, the changes in our new China are, if we can call it such, 'the second miracle of the Far East.'" According to the newspaper, Guo grew more excited as he made this comparison, and his voice began to rise.[57] It might not seem like much to us now, but Guo was a man very close to the Chinese center of power, including Premier Zhou Enlai. For Guo to remark that he still valued much of what the previous generation in Japan had developed as a model of modernity was a remarkable statement. That Guo left his Japanese wife and five children in Japan when he returned to China in 1937 and then remarried and had another family on the mainland is not often included in biographic descriptions of him in China. He believed that he remained indebted to Japanese publishing magnate Iwanami Shigeo, who had paid for some of his Japanese children's education during that interim. In 1955 during his trip to Japan, Guo visited Iwanami's grave to thank him.[58]

South Korean autocrat Park Chung-hee, who received his formative education and ideas about economic development under Japanese colonialism in an imperial Japanese military academy, reformed Korea in the 1970s along the lines of the Meiji Restoration. While Park's interpretation of renovation had eerie overtones reminiscent of Japan's imperial leaders, he specifically chose to name it Yushin (Revitalizing Reform), employing the exact same Chinese characters as Japan's Meiji reformers had chosen.[59] There is no equivocation. Park, like Guo, assessed that Japan had modernized, and Korea, like Japan, needed to follow a similar pattern for its society to progress. Even after World War II, Japan and its advancement remained the template for the region. When Harvard historian Carter Eckert interviewed Park's former close comrades about the most formative moment in Park's life, they all answered in unison: "Japanese army officer education" at the Manchukuo Military Academy.[60]

At the graduation of the first class of the KMT's military officer training school in the mountains north of Taipei city, Taiwan, on June 27, 1950, Chiang Kai-shek told his students to listen to their new Japanese instructors. (Former Japanese imperial officers had secretly and in contravention to existing surrender treaties at the time been smuggled in as part of Generalissimo Chiang's efforts to reform his party and military for their planned "retake" of mainland China.[61]) Chiang admonished the military trainees to pay attention to the six important characteristics that Japanese instructors embodied: "feelings of responsibility, attention to commands, spirit of service, spirit of sacrifice, power of imagination, and respect for the law."[62] It was the Meiji Restoration that had created the conditions necessary, Chiang believed, for that small country of Japan on the edge of East Asia to renovate and within a few short decades make itself great. Japan understood, Chiang said years later, how to marry "knowledge and action" in a way that the Chinese Nationalist top leader so ardently wished he could implement for his own people.[63]

The postwar period in East Asia was a mix of these conflicting sentiments: Japan as imperial success story, and Japan as wartime military aggressor. How the war crimes trials and subsequent historical debates balanced both of these elements was at the heart of this conundrum.

CHAPTER 4

Laying Blame for Japan's War Responsibility

Early postwar East Asia was chaotic, and within weeks of Japan's surrender most areas had fallen into social and economic turmoil. The United States orchestrated the occupation of Japan with spasmodic assistance from the other Allies. The KMT claimed it would send troops but was unable to because of its own fight for survival on the Chinese mainland. The rest of the former empire was confused and anxious. The UK and Australia sent some troops to specific regions in Japan but were limited by the United States. The USSR, eager to gain a foothold, was kept completely at arm's length except for elite positions on committees. Fearful of Japan's potential to remilitarize, the US military took over Okinawa and did not return it to Japan until decades later.

Americans had been drafting plans for years before Japan's surrender concerning how to deal with the envisioned defeat. The term "postimperial" was not employed, because no decision had officially been forthcoming regarding the imperial institution itself. Rumors abounded. Many Japanese were stupefied when they heard Emperor Hirohito's radio appeal that they should lay down their arms. Few fully understood the broadcast, and most had to wait for the explanation that followed since it was crafted in archaic speech. In certain parts of the empire where defeat was not predicted, like Beijing, many Japanese swore they heard that the Japanese government was going to dispatch ships to pick them up and help them repatriate. Nothing was further from the truth. In fact, the Japanese MOFA drafted initial plans not to protect Japanese colonials stranded abroad as "helpless victims" but to leave the imperial settlers alone. The war had brought the Japanese empire to its financial, economic, and political knees. The government initially judged it too much of a logistical and psychological burden on the home islands to accept the millions who would return and require assistance.

We should not forget that on the morning of August 9, 1945, Japanese newspapers spoke of the American "new bomb," which the media labeled as "inhumane." This prepped the scene for the victimization of Japan. Some articles discussed the bomb dropped on the 6th on Hiroshima even though news companies and the government did not acknowledge either the nature of the new weapon or its exact damage. The *Asahi Newspaper* criticized that the "enemy espouses 'justice and humanity' but it bombs innocent civilians."[1]

Other Japanese, depending on their locale, took the defeat more to heart. Although most high-ranking imperial military officers did not commit suicide, an interesting omission since they had long been instructed that surrender was not an option, several tried. General Tōjō Hideki, wartime prime minister and promoter of the attack on Pearl Harbor in December 1941, orchestrated one of the less successful attempts. On the day US military police arrested him as a Class A war criminal suspect in September 1945, he tried to shoot himself in the heart but failed. The population initially mocked him for his carelessness to carry out this final mission. Japanese imperial army general Anami Korechika had been resolute until the end that Japan should not surrender as he believed his men were fighting a holy war to defend the land of the gods. He disputed Emperor Hirohito's recommendation to accept the July 1945 Potsdam Declaration even though Anami still accepted the decision with the rest of the cabinet. On the morning of August 15, Anami took his own life by ritually stabbing himself in the gut. In a more traditional *seppuku* ceremony, the offender would plunge the dagger in or merely draw blood and then be decapitated by his second, who would be standing behind with a long sword at the ready. In Anami's case, he suffered for several hours before he finally succumbed.[2] Some high-ranking Japanese officers, such as Adachi Hatazō in Rabaul (then New Guinea), took responsibility for the failings of those they had commanded and the crimes their soldiers had committed. Adachi waited to commit suicide until his trial under Australian management was over and he had received his sentence of life in prison. Some saw this decision as a form of atonement. Others perceived his choice as the means to avoid responsibility.[3]

The end of war involved not just military men in Tokyo but children of the crumbling empire as well. Norimura Kaneko grew up as a colonial Japanese girl in a family residing in what was then the small town of Andong, China (now the city of Dandong), on the border with North Korea along the Yalu River. She had been born in China and never set foot in Japan until 1958, when she finally repatriated. When the war ended, she was young and not too cognizant of what was happening. Her mother was quite aware, however, and had heard rumors that the Americans would soon be landing nearby. In preparation for such doom, Kaneko's mother showed her children a kitchen knife and said, "I will kill you with this, then hopefully kill one or two of the enemy, and I plan on using it on myself in the end."[4] As the bell tolled for the end of Japan's might in Asia, former colonists were now fearful of any number of enemies: the Chinese Communist Eighth Route Army, the Chinese Nationalists, the Soviets who had declared war on Japan on August 9, 1945, or the American marines who were streaming into China as well.

Death plays a feature role in many first-person accounts of the disorder following Japan's imperial collapse but so do descriptions of willful disregard for others. With millions of people in transit—dislocated families, small children, young wives and boyfriends, even soldiers—bedding down each night in a secure location created difficulties. Relieving oneself the following morning proved a monumental task of hygiene. With little to no preparation for defeat, this meant that tens of thousands of people on the move were not too particular about where and when they evacuated their bowels.[5] The sudden collapse of empire meant that imperial migration was dirty, dangerous, and very poorly managed at the initial stages. In particular, in the early months a lack of certitude about anything on the Chinese mainland caused great anguish among those suddenly thrust to the lower rungs of the world order.

Japan's surrender also symbolized the rudderlessness of the European imperial powers' efforts to regain control of East and Southeast Asian colonies they had lost years before. "Japan's defeat would ignite a scramble for control of the areas formerly held by imperial troops."[6] British leaders believed that a strong France was key for a return to security in Europe, and Britain's first postwar prime minister, Clement Atlee, went so far as to try to stabilize the situation in Indochina until the French could properly muster their military there after Japanese surrender. This move ignored the fact that the Marshal Philippe Pétain-led collaborationist Vichy French regime had colluded with the Nazis and the Vichy authority actually ruled under the Japanese in Indochina from the autumn of 1940 to March 1945. British soldiers essentially "held" Vietnam for France's return and were deployed from the SEAC military command, which was lampooned during the war as the "Supreme Example of Allied Confusion."[7] In actuality, the term signified South East Asian Command. The situation was more complex as Britain did not have enough soldiers on hand, so the Chinese Nationalists accepted the proposal to maintain order north of Vietnam's 16th parallel, while the UK organized the southern region.[8] In total, close to one hundred thousand Japanese soldiers were used as key police and troops to maintain order in areas where Allied troop presence was initially low. These Japanese prisoners were labeled with a new term, "surrendered personnel," in a bid to avoid granting them status as POWs under the Geneva Convention, which would have forbade their use as guardians of postwar law and order.[9]

European imperial leaders attempted to resume the prewar status quo as if neither a war nor their previous defeat mattered. Just after September 2, 1945, the day Tokyo signed the formal surrender on the USS *Missouri* in Tokyo Bay, British lieutenant general Arthur Percival returned to Singapore to accept surrender from Japanese general Yamashita Tomoyuki. Four years earlier Yamashita had faced the battered British military leader across the table in a humiliating defeat for the British. Under European management, a "whole series of events was carefully choreographed to impress on the peoples of Asia that Japan had been defeated by force of arms, and to erase the memory of the earlier Allied capitulations."[10] British major general Eric Hayes had rushed from Chongqing, China, the moment the defeat was announced to witness Japan's surrender in Nanjing on September 9, 1945. Soon after, he cajoled his way onto a train to Shanghai. There he dined and chatted with seventy prominent members of the British community. Astonishingly, he "found a remarkable lack of realization of the implications of the abolition of extra-territoriality and of the fact that from now on Shanghai will be essentially a Chinese city." He felt he had to be frank with them in order to disabuse them of their "unjustifiable illusions."[11]

The Allied goals of de-Nazification and stabilizing a Europe that was in social and economic freefall greatly diverged from the same international reordering of political power in East Asia. From the outset, stemming postwar violence in East Asia and aiding the growing alliances were galvanized by two Allied motivations: (1) to corral Japan out of power in the region and de-imperialize it and (2) to reestablish European dominance and prevent decolonization.

Within Japan a dizzying array of domestic attitudes reflected the hierarchy and duplicity of wartime Japanese society and authority. Because Japanese held competing views of the war—as "just" against encroachment from the West or as the "liberation" of Asia from white colonial rule—they did not always see American attempts to democratize the former Axis nation as positive. Officially, Japan did not conceive of surrender as defeat but lexically as *shūsen*, literally the "end of war." This was an ambiguous label, as was the emperor's verbal mastery to not actually use the word "surrender" in his famous broadcast. The term "surrender," of course, was used in the West and in other Asian countries but

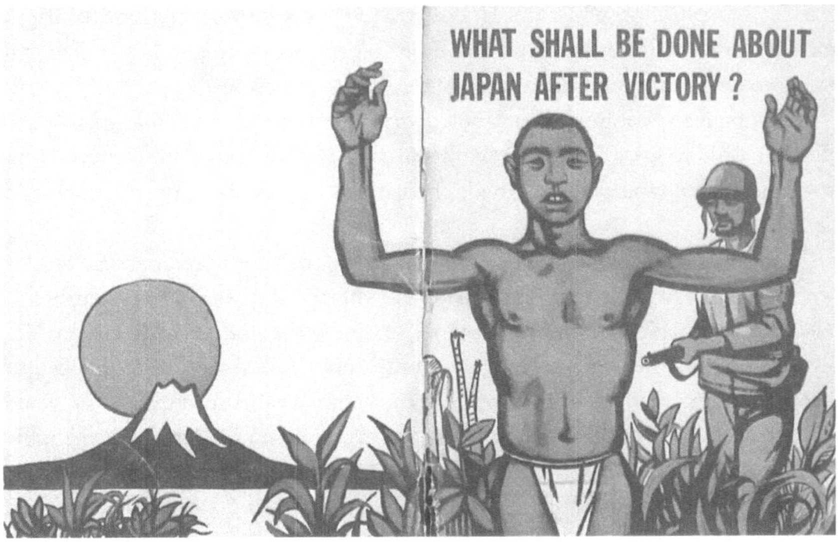

FIGURE 4.1. US pamphlet for GIs, "What shall be done about Japan after victory?" American Historical Association. Historical Service Board (1945). *What shall be done about Japan after victory?* This pamphlet was part of a series produced by the War Department under the title GI Roundtable.

not among officials in Japan. Consequently, in Japan the war (and empire over which it had seemingly been fought) suddenly became a nontopic because it was over. The new focus of discussion quickly turned to how to rebuild the stricken nation. Examining the damage Japan caused was a subject left relatively untouched at first. Meting out responsibility in oblique discussions was more the norm. Part of this was a legacy of how the US-led occupation shaped Japan, not charging the emperor with war crimes and allowing him to remain as a "symbol" of a reconstructed Japan. Continual media censorship, now managed by the American overlords, also further impeded new discussions on responsibility from arising. Moreover, those who retained power in Japan, including many former wartime bureaucrats and politicians, were mostly the same as before, with the exception of the reemergence of the Japanese communists.

Japan Creates the War Responsibility Council

Once Japan lost the war, all layers of society, the political world, and the military had to come to terms with it. The ensuing national discussion in the parliament but also in the editing rooms of newspapers and among officials was,

"What happened and who was responsible?" Various conflicting trauma narratives vied for superiority within the complex landscape of cultural memory in postwar Japan. These emotions derived from how the Japanese conceived of their human failures or in how they depicted the moral character of their heroes and victims. In short, they pivoted on the moral interpretations of defeat and the course they charted for national recovery. The notion of "just war" is a very prevalent idea in the West. For Japan it was a "sacred war"—a propaganda slogan to be sure but one that also thoroughly resounded among certain strata of society. War crimes trials, both the development of their implementation and then their lived legacies, combine, in many ways, all these narratives.

These steps were not seamless and often in contradiction.[12] Even months after the defeat, speculation abounded about how the transition to peace would develop. One Japanese POW in the Philippines, Komatsu Shinichi, recalled that many believed the rumor following General Yamashita Tomoyuki's execution by the Americans. Yamashita had returned alive, was taken to the United States, and was working with the Americans on military strategy against the Soviets. This was part of Japan's "heroes never die" mythology.[13]

Disputes about the causes of the war and Japan's ultimate defeat reflect long-standing imperial-era loggerheads within Japan itself. Deep political divisions and a lack of trust between the people and the nation's leaders had existed since the 1868 Meiji Restoration. The imperial army and navy held each other in mutual contempt and competed for a share of the national budget, pressuring the already hard-pressed populace to accept what each saw as good for the nation.[14] The end of war almost seemed up for grabs—an albeit short-lived military coup saw an attempt to steal the recorded radio broadcast of the emperor communicating the fact of surrender to his people. This act reflected, in part, a lack of consensus about responsibility for the war. In Japanese, the term "war responsibility" (*sensō sekinin*) is vague, and few were talking about justice at this point.[15] Did responsibility mean the decisions for launching the war in general, against China in the 1930s, or later against the Western Allies; for continuing the war when it was clearly already bringing the country to ruin; or for losing the war? At times various postwar Japanese agencies, including MOFA and the imperial army and navy, postured to monopolize control, and at other times they shared authority. However, more often than not these groups did not cooperate and chose instead to protect themselves and their ruling cliques from whatever backlash the imperial defeat would create.

It may be worth noting the gap in ability of the Allied leadership assigned to the West and East. For the Nuremberg Trial, US planners dispatched eminent lawyer Robert Jackson, while Joseph Keenan was pushed on Tokyo. The difference was stark. In early June 1946, at which point the Tokyo Trial would have already begun, the British prosecutors at the Canadian Legation hosted a party. The lead prosecutor for the Tokyo Trial, Joseph Keenan, showed up unexpectedly just before dinner. "He was exceedingly drunk, dressed in sports clothes and only in the mood for flying his arms around the necks of those present, and boasting, in a quite disgusting way, about his intimacy with President Truman and other great men." Things quieted down and they found a seat for him at dinner. But, as Macmahon Ball, the Australian representative to the Allied Council of Japan, recalled, "Soon after dinner it became clear he was losing control of his limbs and he was half helped and half carried off to his car." The hosts were angry and humiliated. This was not the first time such a situation had arisen. Two weeks prior, Keenan had joined Lord Wright (head of the UNWCC) for dinner and "arrived so drunk that he was unable to go in to dinner at all, but had to be first taken to the lavatory and then carried to a spare bedroom and put to bed." Ball was incredulous that Keenan could have been chosen for such an important task as the Tokyo Trial.[16] Japanese, in response, must have been somewhat confused concerning how the pursuit of war criminals would turn out.

We know that there was no *one* Japanese response to the sudden dissolution of empire and the war crimes trials that most people knew defeat would bring in its wake. A spectrum of attitudes reflected and reproduced the hierarchy and duplicity of wartime Japanese society and authority. Fundamentally, Japan's reactions break down into six layers of stakeholders: (1) the civilian government, (2) the emperor, (3) the imperial army, (4) the imperial navy (both army and navy had their own ministries and demobilization bureaus, which pursued separate, if not competing, goals), (5) the Japanese media, and (6) the Japanese Communist Party. Each group, with the exception of the communists, had managed elements of wartime Japanese society and held their own ideologies concerning how to deal with or respond to the Allied calls for war crimes trials. These divisions demonstrate the fractured nature of authority and rule in both wartime and immediate postwar Japan. This "deeply divided leadership, replete with rivalry, factionalism, and competition," was a dilemma for the Tokyo Trial because the charge of conspiracy "was accepted by the majority judges even though their judgment implicitly reveals just the division and conflicts alluded to by [Chief Prosecutor Joseph] Keenan."[17]

Space does not permit a full illumination of each layer, but it is clear that each Japanese institution wished to mitigate its own losses, lessen the responsibility that it would be seen to hold for the war, and press for continued privileges. In many ways, postwar Japan reflected the same disparate notion of state and authority that had plagued it prewar. In fact, what was apparent in the cacophony of voices surrounding the surrender was how little agreement existed within Japan concerning the issue of responsibility—both responsibility for launching the war and then for losing it. The two issues were essentially rolled up in the same public and private debates.

Exactly who was responsible for the resounding defeat that saw the majority of Japan's urban areas flattened with bombs in the last year of the war? The question was an important one because it was linked to the fate and future of the nation. The Japanese government had calibrated that "the war in its entirety destroyed one quarter of the nation's wealth."[18] This does not take into account the loss of Japanese lives as well as those of non-Japanese who inhabited the empire. Chinese estimates were of millions killed and tens of millions left as refugees as a result of Japan's war of aggression. Further, the significance of the defeat depended almost entirely on the subgroup to which one belonged. The imperial army might feel able to bask in the self-deluding satisfaction of unshackling East Asian and Southeast Asian countries from the bonds of European colonialism. But at what cost? The imperial navy found false pride in the illusion that its sailors had at least conducted themselves better than their supposedly crueler and intractable army brethren. But neither group really managed to come to terms with the destruction that their imperial "liberation" had wrought, either domestically or internationally.

The announcement of Japan's defeat left many people dazed with shock, even highly educated elites.[19] The cabinet had a plan, but it did not always have access to international intelligence. MOFA knew what was going on in Europe with the Nazis and others because it retained access to the outside world and was served by incoming intelligence reporting. Extraordinarily, MOFA had already prepared a dossier for the 87th Imperial parliament (June 1945) on the question of how the Allies were pursuing war criminals and what was happening within the UNWCC.[20]

How Japan dealt with the Allied push for war crimes adjudication is significant because within this process lies the key for understanding how Japan defined the war and its own imperial behavior. If the nation could remove the stain of war guilt, then wartime propaganda and claims of keeping "Asia for the Asiatics," and removing the shackles of colonialism from Asia could shine that much brighter for the exhausted and impoverished Japanese, brought to their knees by their own war. If war crimes trials proved otherwise, then the war would have been fought in vain and the nation might collapse, give in to its own humiliation, or, worse yet, be taken over by the expanding forces of communism, it was believed. While smoke was still rising from the ashes, Japanese officialdom was busily trying to shore up its positions. Before they were disbanded in December 1945 to form two bureaus for demobilization, the army and navy ministries moved with the greatest alacrity, wanting to ensure that the Allied occupation did not take a stance that contradicted Japan's own interests or the military's. That meant defining the terms of what the war had meant, that it had been "inevitable" and necessary to push back against Western colonialism. Such military efforts show that the Japanese civilian government was still not in control of the country, because it did not fully manage the immediate postwar period. One major reason that Japan ended up in the position it is in today, reluctant to engage fully with the legacy of the war, is that divided civilian and military opinion about the war competed with vested interests concerning discussions about war responsibility.

On the hot and cloudy day of September 5, 1945, in the 88th session of the lower house of the imperial parliament, representative Ashida Hitoshi put forth a proposal "to make clear the reasons and locus of responsibility which led to the disadvantageous results of the Greater East Asian War." Ashida had been a long-serving member of the Foreign Ministry in the early part of the twentieth century and was elected to parliament eleven times, at one point briefly serving as prime minister in 1948. In parliament he laid out a multipoint set of questions to the government concerning war responsibility. Why had it gone to war with more than forty countries when it knew it lacked the manpower, technical ability, and political structures to carry it out? These are complex matters, he reasoned, and "therefore, it goes without saying that responsibility for the defeat is not something that can merely be placed on the shoulders of two or three war leaders."[21] Prime Minister Higashikuni Naruhiko agreed and said there "was value in looking into" Ashida's query. While agreeing with Ashida's aims superficially, the prime minister's response was also a paragon of vacillation and pretty verbiage. Higashikuni thanked other countries in the Greater East Asian League—never specifically named—for their efforts, but now a historic time in Japan's three-thousand-year history had arrived with the US occupation on Japan's shores. Japan will move forward and will have open and free discussions based on freedom of speech, which is the basis of liberty, he said. The Diet erupted in applause.[22]

Lower House Delegate Tōgō Minoru then took the floor and spoke. He assessed that Japan needed to be honest with the aims of the occupation and the analysis of what happened during the war to properly rebuild for the future and for peace. He concluded that the occupation authorities were also on trial for their actions if they were to judge Japan on the scales of international justice. Thus, it was only fair that Japan at the same time talk about the dropping of the atomic bomb by the United States and its ramifications.[23] In his memoirs, the country's first postwar prime minister, Higashikuni, noted, "We need to deeply consider the circumstances that brought our country to this defeat." If Japan did not do this, he cautioned, then the country was doomed. However, rather than telling the Japanese people to admit defeat, the emperor called on the Japanese to "pave the way for a grand peace for all the generations to come by enduring the unendurable and suffering what is insufferable."[24] Society at the upper levels looked at war responsibility as a means of figuring out how Japan lost and renovating quickly with an eye toward the future. Little attention was paid to identifying the significance of the defeat or crimes committed during the war, a specific focus for the Allies.

In its September 11, 1945, report "Research on problems related to punishing war criminals," the Treaty Bureau of the Ministry of Foreign Affairs expressed surprise at the jumble of responsibility and authority within the higher levels of the Japanese government and officialdom. A MOFA report ventured into a discussion of war crimes trials and suggested that they would probably be implemented not only against those who abused POWs but also against those who bore political responsibility for the war. Japanese officials were aware of how their leadership structure differed from that of Nazi Germany, and the document lucidly contrasted how the Nazis had clearly delineated layers of authority while the Japanese did not. This made the full pursuit of responsibility difficult, to say the least. Structurally, Japanese civilian government was not designed to allow for individuals to be seen as "responsible" for decisions.[25]

On September 12, 1945, Prime Minister Higashikuni, Foreign Minister Shigemitsu Mamoru, Minister of the Army Shimomura Sadamu, Minister of the Navy Yonai Mitsumasa, Chief of the Army General Staff Umezu Yoshijirō, Chief of the Navy General Staff Admiral Toyoda Soemu, Minister of State Konoe Fumimaro, and Minister of Justice Iwata Chūzō met at the Council for Dealing with the End of the War (established on August 22) to discuss putting together investigation boards to examine Japanese war crimes. The group announced that in accordance with Allied demands and legal jurisprudence Japan would try those who had been listed by the occupiers as criminals or those who had committed war crimes.[26] A postwar Japanese government summary of Japan's early policies toward war crimes trials states that at the September 12 meeting the group decided that even if the Allies were to put Japanese in the dock, Japan should move first to investigate war crimes and conduct trials of major individuals and of those responsible. This policy was taken as the means to "clarify the merits of the cases the report noted.[27] Japanese officials wanted to take these countermeasures so that the Allies could not conduct adjudications unilaterally. After making their decision, Kido Kōichi, the Lord Keeper of the Privy Seal, presented the council's argument to Emperor Hirohito. The emperor responded: "While these individuals have been designated as war criminals by the Allied Nations, from the imperial [my royal] point of view these are loyal subjects, and furthermore include some, I believe, who have achieved great success for the nation. It is very difficult to accept that they will be criminally punished for having fought in my name." Kido brought the imperial utterance back to the council and they re-debated it, given the emperor's hesitation. But the group was adamant about what it had decided in the morning and believed that such a decision was appropriate. The summary added that the prime minister, minister of foreign affairs, and minister of justice all went to see the emperor again.[28] Kido and the group received imperial dispensation to push forward on domestic war crimes trials with the rationale that this could guarantee the trials were kept "proper" or "just." The summary also cautioned that handing over those who had been named as war crimes suspects unconditionally would "go against the traditional precepts of *bushidō*."[29]

The final move, on September 18, was Higashikuni's press conference with foreign correspondents, held in the afternoon with approximately one hundred journalists in attendance. This was an epic moment since Japan had been essentially closed off to foreign media for years. Most of the journalists asked about the executions of downed pilots who had flown in the 1942 Doolittle raids or the mistreatment of Allied POWs. One directly asked if the emperor had war responsibility, and Higashikuni replied emphatically "absolutely not."[30] According to some sources, a few trials did indeed take place on the Japanese side; others list only one. Tanaka Hiromi suggests that because records of these trials cannot be found, they are "phantom trials."[31] The draft English text of the cabinet decision to mete out domestic justice was never officially released even though it had been recorded.[32]

The Japanese government and army pursued and investigated a selection of war crimes, but eventually in March 1946 SCAP ordered such investigations to be dropped, according to one source.[33] In the end, Japan was only permitted to collect data for trials, and the only confirmed case of someone being brought to trial was that of General Honma Masaharu.[34] Honma was deemed responsible for atrocities such as the Bataan Death March in 1942; as punishment, his pay was docked. During this forced march in the Philippines, thousands of US and Filipino soldiers were mistreated and many died. By this point, Prime Minister Higashikuni had already made an announcement that the entire Japanese nation regretted the war—"*ichioku sō zange*"—a public and collective admission of guilt or at least national contrition. Such a statement neatly avoided any mention of individual responsibility and thus conveniently sidestepped the issue of apology.

It is telling that no mention was made of atrocities or issues regarding the abusive and exploitative manner in which Japan's empire was managed in these early domestic discussions. Plans were seemingly organized with a view to countering war crimes trials. The Japanese were concerned about the causes of the war in general and about the failure of the empire. But then they immediately turned to how to rebuild and the need to strengthen people's relationship with the emperor. Most officials aimed to implement new education programs and to build transport while providing jobs for veterans to the extent possible. Japanese leaders of all colors were seemingly already thinking about the future, even as the nation suffered in its new predicament. Unfortunately, pausing to reflect on the harm that Japan caused at the fringes of the empire did not arise in the same manner. The intersection of Japan's concern for itself and the destruction it caused abroad remains a nonexistent feature of Japan's official policies toward war crimes trials to this day.[35]

Japan's military also had to very quickly deal with the potential for further violence within its own ranks due to nihilism. Suddenly facing defeat, many soldiers questioned the very meaning of their existence and pondered what purpose their sacrifices had served. For example, naval captain Okino Matao noted in his diary that he was deeply ashamed of repatriating after being a POW.[36] Okino's plane en route over China had run into problems and crash landed. Initially taken prisoner by the Chinese Nationalist forces, he suffered a leg wound that turned gangrenous and he underwent a partial amputation. He was one of the few high-level Japanese POWs, so the Americans took a keen interest and eventually he was clandestinely flown to Washington, DC, during the war. There he divulged much about Japan's imperial military structure and ideology to his interrogators at a secret intelligence camp, Fort Hunt.[37] How could he return to Japan? he wondered. Luckily, just after the end of the war, the emperor released former soldiers taken as POWs from their state of mental anguish. Imperial Army Order No. 1385 on August 18, 1945, announced: "Imperial military armed forces or those belonging to the army who are under the authority of the enemy's military are not considered prisoners of war upon the implementation of this imperial edict. To quickly caution against rash acts at all levels of subordinates and with the aim to assist our imperial country's prosperous future, we must very thoroughly implement this order with patience and prudence." The navy released an order of similar magnitude the following day.[38] This sort of military order was initially drafted by the Imperial General Headquarters. The chief of staff submitted it as a memorial to the throne, and once it gained imperial acquiescence it was transmitted to the armed forces as an imperial edict with all of that weight behind it. While it might appear cosmetic to outsiders, it held tremendous force. Okino and others believed the imperial order relieved soldiers of the undue guilt of having become a prisoner. The aim was to avoid any further problems in the postwar period, either where the soldiers were stationed or when they eventually repatriated.

Pressure to investigate the reasons behind Japan's defeat was also emerging from former high-level military officials. Imperial Japanese Army lieutenant general Ishiwara Kanji, one of the masterminds behind the 1931 Manchurian Incident, which led Japan further into aggression in China, initially wrote about the reasons for Japan's loss toward the end of August 1945 in the *Mainichi Newspaper*. This involved, "prior to being embarrassingly exposed naked before others, the need for Japan to remove the cloak under which it hoodwinked itself, peel off its skin and squeeze out the cancer of defeat."[39] Ishiwara believed one of the main reasons for defeat was the "moral decay" of the people. He later held rallies and demonstrated that Japan lost the war "because our false leaders took us into a war for which we were not ready. They betrayed the emperor, as they betrayed the land." Ishiwara expounded that Japan needed to rebuild a new Asiatic Co-Prosperity Sphere and ensure its future by making friends, not by using force. Mark Gayn, a Russian-born US journalist who had covered Asia for years, was less taken with the message and wrote that "Japan was getting more than a new Messiah. She was also receiving a happy explanation of the causes of defeat."[40]

As the military moved to ease the psychological pressure on its soldiers who only weeks before would have been shamed as POWs, the government moved forward regarding how to deal with the further fallout from defeat and all that surrender would entail. On October 23, 1945, the Council for Dealing with the End of the War laid out more of its policy for proceeding with potential war crimes trials. The pursuit of justice appeared secondary to the aim of mitigating any blemish on the imperial prestige of Japan—seemingly unsullied even with the unconditional surrender. The goal was to minimize to the extent possible damage to both individuals and "the empire" as it was termed in the Japanese plan. In some ways this move mirrored the imperial government and military's goal to protect that vaguely defined "national polity," or *kokutai*. The primary argument hinged on the claim that on the level of international law the pursuit of so-called war criminals was irrational. Second, officials insisted that the emperor was an entity, separate from the evolution of the war, and that he stood above the imperial constitution. The third element of the report argued that the pressures of the international situation during the 1930s had forced the nation into a corner and that Japan had no choice other than to wage war or face annihilation.[41] There was another plan that never saw the light of day, entitled "Urgent Imperial Decree to Stabilize the People's Mind and Establish the Independent Popular Morality Necessary to Maintain National Order."[42] This strategy depicted the war as a "tragic perversion" of the emperor's trust. "Loser's justice, like victor's justice, ultimately would have entailed arguing that Japan had been led into 'aggressive militarism' by a small cabal of irresponsible militaristic leaders."[43] A postwar summary examining the problem with A-class war criminals had three aims:

1. Do not touch on anything related to the emperor's responsibility
2. Protect the nation
3. Within the framework of the first two points and to the extent possible, defend individuals[44]

Shidehara Kijūrō had taken over as prime minister on October 9, 1945, and he wanted to examine precisely what had brought Japan to its knees. Only by building on this knowledge, he explained, could they rebuild Japan. On October 30, 1945, a cabinet decision discussed the reasons for defeat and the establishment of an investigation body to examine the issues. The decision read as follows: "To clarify the real facts and reasons for defeat in the Greater East Asian War and to ensure that these mistakes are not repeated in the future, it is believed to be necessary to establish an investigation office in the Cabinet that will thoroughly investigate these issues across the broad range of political, military, economic, thought and cultural fields."[45] The five sections were chaired by a host of key politicians, elite journalists, philosophy professors, industrialists, and military officers, among others.[46]

On November 20 this body became an official government agency.[47] Initially the bureau was known as the Greater East Asia War Investigation Council (Daitōa sensō chōsakai), but in January 1946 it changed its name to simply the War Investigation Council (Sensō chōsakai). Shidehara Kijūrō headed the organ, after he took over as prime minister in October 1945, but the Allies were suspicious that it was a group designed to aid the rise of Japan's military again, and the council did not last long before being ordered to dissolve.[48] Aoki Tokuzō, who was made chief secretary of the council, recalled that the emperor had spoken with Higashikuni about needing to look into the war and its origins so that Japan did not make the same mistake twice. It was eventually disbanded on September 30, 1946, after completing an initial set of investigations that recorded early postwar Japanese attitudes about defeat and responsibility.[49] The picture was confused, to say the least.

In discussions in the upper house of parliament concerning the investigation council, Prime Minister Shidehara provided rather vague responses regarding what exactly was meant by war responsibility (*sensō sekinin*). From a December 2, 1945, record, Shidehara responded to a question from Matsumura Giichi. Matsumura had been a onetime official in the Home Ministry, but as a politician he was now calling for pursuit of those who had war responsibility. Shidehara answered that Japan was precisely in its current predicament because of its loss in the Greater East Asian War. There was some "public sentiment" toward those who started this war, he averred, but many also wanted to pursue them. In this vein, Shidehara admitted, he could not help but agree in part with Matsumura. But if Japan put those individuals on trial, there were many things the country needed to consider, Shidehara cautioned, underscoring the seriousness of these matters. In addition, those responsible for the war may have committed mistakes, but they did not sell out the country or commit action with that in mind, he said. Plus, Shidehara concluded, could Japan create a law now and make it retroactive to prosecute those men? If Japan followed such a path it would do so at its own peril because the nation would become quite unstable, Shidehara articulated. Moreover, pursuing this line against those Japan deemed as responsible had the potential to set up a tendency to allow difficulties to occur in the political realm where the winner could pursue the loser in future elections. Shidehara said that punishing those responsible for the war would only occur so rarely that it would not prove to be any impediment, but creating retroactive laws also contravened the spirit of democracy. It is interesting to see how the idea or shield of democracy was now employed by Japanese leaders to avoid war crimes tribunals. In response to Matsumura's query, Shidehara said that Japan must in some measure wait for public opinion. The country should use its own commission to suss out the truth of the war and then naturally the Japanese themselves will find those responsible, Shidehara opined.[50]

On December 4, Shidehara stated that Japan needed to assess the reasons for and truth about the war, determining whether the result of the Pacific War was the outgrowth of militarism. On December 6, he explained that if Japan conducted this investigation on its own, it would be able to find, once the efforts were complete, where the locus of responsibility was and mete out either political or criminal judgments. On that same day, in a budget meeting, the prime minister remarked that he did not accept the Allied basis for choosing who was responsible for the war and that only the Japanese could ascertain who or what had caused their loss. On the 12th, Shidehara said in a lower house meeting that the investigation was to make sure that the Japanese understood the reasons behind the war and did not make the same mistakes again. Public opinion was already posing difficult questions about war responsibility, he said, and reprimands from the media were growing harsh.[51]

It was apparent that momentum had begun to build for the Japanese public to question the nature of itself and what had led it down the road to war. A popular column in the *Asahi Newspaper* on January 9, 1946, clarified: "It is indeed irritating that the Government has not the will to punish war criminals by itself, but it also may be that it is unable to do so because there is no proper law in Japan which covers the situation. It is very natural for criminal law to have no provisions for the punishment of war criminals because no one thought of such a thing when the law code was made. The Government should enact a new law for this purpose. The people will never oppose it. It is deplorable that the officials were proud of their desk plans during the war and are now too cowardly to manage the new state of affairs."[52]

A few months later at the second all-hands meeting for the investigation council on April 4, 1946, held in the prime minister's residence, Shidehara laid out the goals and methods. In the discussion the prime minister said that the leaders had a duty to tell the people what happened. They could not hold back on the investigation, he implored. Shidehara told those gathered that the goal was not the pursuit of war responsibility but rather to look internally at Japan and find blame to pursue. While the pursuit of war responsibility might not be a goal, he said, the council should still find out where it lay, with its expansive investigation. The council would examine memos and question the government, but it would also need to query the military, especially the army. This was all necessary to understand the internal conditions and ideas behind what happened. At one point Shidehara intoned, "We are being watched by the Allies and the world so choose your words carefully because they are paying attention and these comments will impact back on Japan. These proceedings are not a courtroom where we judge; we will analyze and look at problems."[53]

In response to Shidehara, Baba Tsunego, CEO of the *Yomiuri Newspaper* and member of the upper house of the Diet, spoke up. Baba said that if council members were going to talk about the aims of this council and look first into the reasons for the nation's defeat, they should also keep in mind the future constitution and outlawing war in it. If members truly investigated the defeat, was it, he asked, because Japan began a war it should not have started? It was lost from the outset, he remarked. Baba informed members that a better goal would be to start with a new draft of the constitution, outlawing war and weapons. In this way the council would not be pursuing individual responsibility but looking at how the act of war itself was a mistake. It was wrong for Japan to have initiated that war. The council could arrive at the conclusion that war itself should be outlawed, and promote such ideas in a new constitution. What Japan should be examining, Baba suggested, is whether war has value. Shidehara retorted that the council was investigating the issue of how Japan arrived at its defeat so that it could paint an accurate picture for future generations. War was exceedingly difficult to eradicate, and if one looked at what foreigners had written, they have discussed this a bit, he added. Their conclusion, Shidehara said, was that war pulls against the middle, meaning that in the end it does not pay for the victors or the losers.[54]

These discussions were pregnant with great potential for a national conversation about war responsibility. Sadly, such moves only faced retrenchment of opinions from most quarters.[55] It was not only the Americans who ultimately stopped the council's investigation; pushback emerged from the Soviet Union as well. Lieutenant General Kuzma Nikolaevich Derevyanko, who had signed for the Soviet Union on the USS *Missouri* at the surrender ceremony, was adamant about the nefarious nature of the investigation council. General Douglas MacArthur did not respect the Russians and supposedly treated Derevyanko "like a piece of furniture," ignoring him completely.[56] At the 11th Far Eastern Commission (FEC) meeting on August 7, 1946, Derevyanko spoke up concerning the war investigation council. He believed the research group aimed to collect experience from all angles—political, economic, military, technical—and this contravened the demilitarization of Japan. "We should thus disband it," he suggested, as one could see there were many military men listed in its rosters and that was evidence enough for him.[57] Derevyanko continued to voice his displeasure. At the 16th FEC meeting on October 10, 1946, he claimed the use of so many military officers and examination of their experiences in battle was obviously to prepare effectively for Japan's next military misadventure. At the meeting Derevyanko said he now heard that the council had been disbanded, and he wanted to emphasize that it had been illegal in the first place.[58]

We can sense the push for answers about war responsibility coming from various directions within Japan's civilian leadership. One diplomat, Nakamura Toyoichi, early on believed it important to think about Japan's strategy toward the war crimes trials. On November 20, 1945, Nakamura proposed a strategy for Japan's response to the war crimes trial process. Nakamura's proposal was rejected out of hand, in part because the Japanese government wanted a unity of opinion to show its opposition to the Allied pursuit of its own justice and to demonstrate government unanimity.[59] Eventually, however, this goal was abandoned, and each agency mostly pursued policies to the greater benefit of its own members.

Yoshida Shigeru, as foreign minister in the Shidehara cabinet (he had already taken over from Shigemitsu Mamoru in mid-September 1945 because SCAP pursued Shigemitsu as a Class A war criminal), was not a fan of his own government's attempt to unify its stance on war crimes. Yoshida believed that twisting the truth and hiding facts to get individuals absolved was not in Japan's long-term interest (and it seems Yoshida might have won that argument for the government side of things but could not convince the military). But then MOFA could not sit by and do nothing. So, in a sense both sides compromised as a way not to directly guide defense lawyers but to assist them. Yoshida, together with University of Tokyo professor of law Takayanagi Kenzō, formed the Judicial Affairs Deliberation Office (*Hōmu shinsa-shitsu*). This office was similar in effect to what Nakamura Toyoichi had proposed, and it was established in December 1945, under the aegis of the Foreign Ministry, providing materials to the court. Sone Eki was put in charge, and on December 14 the heads of various ministries were called to the prime minister's residence for a colloquium in which Okazaki Katsuo, who was working directly for the foreign minister, informed them that the plan to take a unified stance on Allied war crimes trials was being scrapped and that the emperor bore no war responsibility. In effect, this meant that Japan would follow orders from the American occupation authorities when dealing with the war crimes trials but that officials should not think about blaming the emperor.[60]

Shimoda Takezsō, a Japanese diplomat and later ambassador to the United States, reported that Yoshida Shigeru had opined to MOFA officials when he returned to political power in the immediate postwar period that this was the first time in Japan's history that the country had been vanquished. It was a defeated nation. Consequently, Japan was now "on the chopping board like a dead fish," he said. This meant that Japan faced a hopeless situation and needed to buck up and deal with it. By pushing a strategy for rebuilding Japan, using the Allied trials as the means to purge Japanese society of those who had brought it to defeat, Yoshida tried to craft a new postwar orientation. In fact, Yoshida refused to sign a petition in support of wartime Foreign Minister Tōgō Shigenori because Tōgō had been minister at the start of the Pacific War and Yoshida believed he should have taken responsibility and stepped down after negotiations with the United States failed.[61]

While the Japanese government did not issue a unified official directive toward war crimes trials, unofficially each agency or administrative unit did internally. MOFA did not oppose the indictments publicly but subjected them to analysis and was not at all conciliatory. The office within MOFA that managed war crimes issues was the End of War Liaison Bureau War Crimes Office First Section (*Shūren daiichibu no senpan jimushitsu*). It took care of all war criminal administrative matters, including providing assistance, offering documents, and answering lawyers' questions. There was also an organ called the Domestic and Foreign Legal and Political Study Group (*Naigai hōsei kenkyūkai*, more commonly known as the *Hōsei*), which was like a prep team for the trials. On the heels of a push from Nakamura, and with some support from the financial world, this organization was established. Officially appearing in February 1946, it was a private entity not linked with the government and was set up to offer assistance and analysis for war crimes trial defense. It was staffed by the very best of Japan's legal minds. These men produced high-level legal scholarship on questions of war responsibility.[62]

What is fascinating is the extent to which the Japanese government kept veterans far away from the investigations. Not that all former Japanese soldiers would have been swayed communist, or antigovernment, but it is striking to examine soldiers' diaries for their opinions. The men on the ground who supposedly knew what they were fighting for do not make much of an appearance in high-level government commissions, where deliberations seemingly tried to analyze what Japan's war had been about. Komatsu Shinichi had been an officer in the war in the Philippines and witnessed it all—the success, then the encroaching failure, lack of supplies, the cruelty to Allied POWs, the cannibalism, and being taken as a POW at the end. In his diary he listed twenty-one reasons for Japan's loss in the war. Obviously, supply lines and poor military strategic decision making were nagging problems. The lack of scientific knowledge, training, and materiel, in particular, when compared with that of the United States, which is always how the loss is portrayed, was also itemized. Most of the other reasons can be imagined, but Komatsu underscored that "Japanese conviction in their own greatness meant they had little empathy with others," that "they have a tendency to not think plans through to the end," and that "people got tired of the fighting." He also noted, as other contemporary Japanese military historians have remarked, "Japanese treated life without much care; Americans treated life as sacrosanct."[63] Komatsu reasoned that these reasons inexorably lead one to conclude that "the Japanese did not have the power or a culture suited to politically manage East Asia."[64]

It is possible that Komatsu was also influenced by Japanese general Yamashita Tomoyuki and his reflections before his February 1946 execution in the Philippines, as told to a Buddhist cleric at the prison:

> In a free society, you should nurture your own ability to make moral judgments in order to carry out your duties. Duties can only be carried out correctly by a socially mature person with an independent mind and with culture and dignity. The fundamental reason why the world has lost confidence in our nation, and why we have so many war-crime suspects who left ugly scars on our history, was this lack of morals. I would like you to cultivate and accept the common moral judgment of the world, and become a people who fulfill duties on your own responsibility. You are expected to be independent and carve out your own future. No one can avoid this responsibility and choose an easy way. Only through that path can eternal peace be attained in the world.[65]

And yet at the same time, even given all this elite analysis above, we should heed the evaluation of historian Duan Ruicong. Duan notes, "Generally speaking in the postwar, the biggest problem within the war investigation council, ministry of foreign affairs, and army and navy ministries was the absence of the point of view of those who suffered from the war. In other words, all of these groups reflected on the causes of Japan's loss, but lacked introspection toward the invasive war itself."[66]

Chapter 5

The Tyranny of Tiny Decisions

The Failure of the Japanese Left

One of the mainstays of antagonism toward war criminals that drove calls to pursue justice within Japan emerged from a group that had been pushed underground during Japan's imperial rise. In the immediate postwar period, the Japanese Communist Party (JCP) tried to rebuild after years of forced inactivity. During the war, Japanese government officials and police had all but eviscerated the communists with imprisonment, along with threats and efforts to cajole them into abandoning their policies. The start of the occupation had not changed their situation much. The immediate postwar Japanese government had retained the force of the imperial Peace Preservation Law, which suppressed public criticism of the imperial house and strove to uphold the national polity (*kokutai*).[1] The persistence of this law and the authority it bestowed to detain political prisoners, even after Japan's surrender, demonstrated the reluctance of Japanese leaders to finally face the winds of change.

To be sure, the imperial authorities who had dragged Japan into war and were trying to salvage their own power were not keen on seeing it all swept away by enthusiastic communists. The release of Japanese political prisoners and initial official recalcitrance to allow the Peace Preservation Law to lapse ultimately pulled down the Higashikuni cabinet. Ministers had opposed these measures and the changes that the lapse would force in Japan's imperial system. In fact, in the initial moments after Japan's surrender from late August to September 1945 the Home Ministry closely monitored the movements of the left wing. One report stated that about 7,700 or so individuals, particularly communists, needed to be surveilled as they believed in Japan's defeat. They were being relatively quiet, police noted, but officials should monitor their activities and prepare to immediately arrest them if the need arises during this "new situation," referring to Japan's surrender, the internal assessment suggested.[2] The word "surrender" was never used in these documents. Sometimes "defeat" was mentioned, but often in these early days the applied term was Japan's "new situation." Later in September, Ministry of Home Affairs' reports estimated that it was only a matter of time before the communists "take advantage of unemployment, inflation, starvation, and other social problems among the vast litany of social chaos issues that will probably arise." If that happens and they coalesce their power, the authorities must get ready to sow dissent and factionalize, another report concluded.[3]

French journalist Robert Guillain, a long-term Asia hand who lived in Japan during the war, was one of a group of foreign journalists who broke the story that the Japanese government had not released its political prisoners after surrender. Guillain discovered that the Japanese government was keeping the JCP vanguard imprisoned. Along with Harold Isaacs from *Newsweek* and a few others, on October 1, 1945, Guillain traveled to Fuchū Prison on the edge of Tokyo to find out what was happening.

Guillain recalled, years later, that he had heard communists were still being held but did not know in which prison. He decided that he could easily drive to the massive Fuchū Prison complex on the outskirts of the city, and so Guillain and his colleagues dressed as US officers and drove an American Jeep there. The prison head initially denied that any communists were incarcerated. At first, the Western journalists, closely watched by the guards, found no sign of the communists in the prison. Then, in a move that seems straight out of a bad comedy movie, Guillain wrote that they pushed the prison guard to one side and took off in the opposite direction of where he was trying to lead them. They eventually pressed deeper into the heart of the prison against the guards' remonstrations and came to an enormous door at the end of the hallway. "Open it," they demanded. The guard reluctantly took out a key and, with great effort, opened the heavy door. What Guillain saw, he wrote, he would never forget. "In the middle of this enormous cell was a small group of people all wearing khaki colored clothing. Their heads were all shaved as monks and they were sitting on benches." The room fell silent as both groups looked at each other in astonishment. "I heard English spoken in a trembling voice. 'We are communist party members. I am Tokuda.' Two guys with Korean features got on top of the bench and sang the *Internationale* [communist anthem].

Another prisoner with a thin face walked over and started speaking English. 'Finally, you came to get us. We have been waiting for weeks.' That was Shiga [Yoshio]."[4] Japanese Domei news reporter Kay Tateishi, a Nissei from the United States, was also there. He wrote that when the Japanese were initially arrested, along with several Korean prisoners, they were "beaten with baseball bats and tortured with burning incense sticks forced under their fingernails."[5] The foreign journalists ended up interviewing Tokuda Kyūichi, Shiga Yoshio, and Kim Ch'on-hae, a Korean communist activist. That Japanese communists were still being detained weeks after Japan surrendered shocked the Allies.

Tokuda was a fascinating character, a stalwart communist who could not back down when he saw injustice. In part, this might have started in his early childhood, given the extreme poverty in which he grew up on the fringes of the Japanese empire in Okinawa. His father was the illegitimate offspring of a union between an itinerant marine salesman from Kagoshima and one of his Okinawan mistresses. At this time, many men who traveled between Okinawa and mainland Japan to trade goods had a family in each port. This was not morally unacceptable in Japan, but the circumstances meant that Tokuda grew up penniless and on the bottom rungs of Okinawan society, already at the low end of the social and political hierarchy within the Japanese empire. His maternal grandmother was a loan shark of sorts, lending small sums for extortionate interest rates.[6] He detested her. His mother had been born into a family in such dire straits that two of the three daughters had been sold into prostitution.[7] One gets a feeling of Tokuda's born leadership ability and his goal to constantly better himself, perhaps based on the constant opposition he encountered. Discrimination against Okinawans was rampant in mainland Japan at that time. When he traveled to Tokyo to study, a distant relative with whom he stayed would not allow him to eat with the family or use the family's bathing tub. Tokuda was forced to use the public baths.[8]

He was a founding member of the JCP in 1922. He wrote that to extricate himself from poverty and ignorance, he woke every morning at five to study, usually for several hours until nine or so. Every day. Maybe this was due, he says, to his long incarceration or age. He would read voraciously and then write letters and manuscripts.[9]

Tokuda's eighteen years of imprisonment had been harsh. He was first incarcerated with Shiga Yoshio, a fellow communist leader, in a Hokkaido prison. It was not unusual for outside temperatures to drop to thirty degrees below zero. Even inside rooms with heaters the temperature might rise to only minus eight or nine degrees. One's breath at night often caused small icicles to form on the walls. Tokuda wrote that the chill never really left one's body. "God it was cold! This was the sort of cold that took away the ability to speak and cut to the core of your bones. The memory even now of the cold six years living at Abashiri Prison freezes me."[10] Suicide was not uncommon in such severe conditions. To counter this, the prison had a rule that inmates could not envelop their entire bodies inside their futons; this way, the guards could constantly monitor them. Detainees ignored this rule, Tokuda said, due to the frigid temperatures inside their cells. Tokuda recalled that prisoners would wrap their whole bodies and tuck their heads inside their futons at night, or they risked getting frostbite on their lips if they directly breathed the outside air. Even getting ready for bed was a challenge. Prisoners would normally splash ice water on their bodies before getting into their pajamas, which were normally frozen stiff. If you put on the freezing nightgown without preparing your body, you would instantly catch a chill and risked getting pneumonia, he recalled.[11] Years later, Tokuda and Shiga were transferred to the Fuchū Prison outside of Tokyo, where it was not as cold as Japan's deep north. But such conditions took their toll. Tokuda died relatively young in 1953 after only an eight-year political life following his release. Shiga, however, lived into his late eighties. He was deaf in one ear because prison guards had continually slapped him, and his eyesight was poor due to malnutrition during his long imprisonment.[12]

The foreign news reporters' announcement to the world that Japan was continuing to incarcerate political prisoners galvanized US occupation officials into action. John Emmerson, longtime China hand diplomat who was posted to Japan in the early postwar period, wrote in his memoirs that he was having drinks with Harold Isaacs, the *Newsweek* correspondent, in the Dai-Ichi hotel. Isaacs had interviewed some of the communists at Fuchū, along with the French reporter Guillain, and said that SCAP should send someone to chat with them since they would be future political activists. Emmerson was friendly with the Canadian diplomat and Japan expert E. H. Norman, so on October 5 they drove to the prison. Emmerson penned that the Fuchū warden "looks like a pig-literally." He has a "bullet shaped head, small eyes, sadistic face!" Tokuda got together in a room with many others and they all chatted. Tokuda and several others "spoke volubly, with the pent-up flood of nearly two decades of isolation." Shiga was less showy, Emmerson detailed, having graduated from Tokyo Imperial University, and spoke decent English.[13]

On October 7, 1945, Emmerson and Norman drove Tokuda, Shiga, and Kim to the SCAP headquarters in Tokyo for more careful discussions. Emmerson said Tokuda was "fiery" and a "spellbinder," very different from the quiet JCP leader in western China, Nosaka Sanzō, whom Emmerson had met in Yenan during the war. Nosaka had also grown up poor but managed to graduate from the elite Keiō University and studied at the London School of Economics under

Clement Attlee for several years, before being expelled from Great Britain for political agitation following the end of World War I.[14] Emmerson noted that Tokuda wanted to overthrow Japan's imperial system. Nosaka had a different and more careful approach. He aimed to make the party lovable to gain more members, not just rally for revolution like Tokuda initially wanted.[15] This interrogation of the JCP members had a long political propaganda life in the 1950s and later set off an extended conspiracy hunt for communist agents within the US State Department, reaching its apex during the McCarthy hearings. General Charles Willoughby, essentially MacArthur's second in command within the occupation leadership, had a deep-seated fear of the supposed communist world conspiracy. His writings and the false beliefs of many others in the higher chains of the US command pointed to Emmerson's interaction with the JCP as evidence that the American occupiers were aiding the Japanese communists and giving them succor.[16]

Whatever the case, the American occupiers quickly called the Japanese out on their torpor to release those deemed politically unsavory. But what had also set off quivers of anxiety was that only a week earlier, on September 26, famed Marxist philosopher Miki Kiyoshi died in Toyotama Prison from an entirely preventable death of "malnutrition, scabies, and kidney failure."[17] This news spurred the occupation forces to command the Japanese to release or produce all political prisoners, something the Japanese leaders were initially very reluctant to implement. Eventually, Japanese officials relented, and this was when the Americans realized that, for change to occur, much of it, like the eventual new Japanese Constitution, would have to be foisted on the Japanese from above and could not initially spring forth from below.

Not long after, on October 10, 1945, heir apparent to the communist leadership throne in Japan, Tokuda, was feted at a massive event. Upon release, Tokuda Kyūichi and Shiga Yoshio, among others, immediately joined a rally hosted by the JCP and left wing, "The People's Rally to Celebrate the Warriors Release from Prison." Red flags stood tall around the hall and banners with slogans such as "Punish All of the War Criminals!" were draped on the walls.[18] About two thousand people attended the event, and the Japanese newspapers noted, in what was a first for such gatherings since they had previously been banned, that even a few women joined. This was a key moment for the rebirth of the JCP. Before the war, it never mustered more than a thousand souls on the party roster, but by 1950 it would gain about one million.[19] After the master of ceremonies Fuse Tatsuji gave opening remarks, a few more rousing speeches followed and the participants all went outside to demonstrate.[20] Fuse was a top-flight lawyer who had long assisted Koreans in imperial Japan in their struggles for equality and justice. He also openly criticized the imperial system in a publicly produced pamphlet and called for a public debate on whether the imperial throne should be preserved.[21] As part of its occupation plan, SCAP authorities invited Tokuda Kyūichi to debate Kiyose Ichirō in a US-sponsored radio roundtable on Japan's imperial system that was broadcast on November 21, 1945. This was also later produced into a newsreel for public consumption in cinemas. Such shows generated immense debate within Japan regarding the emperor, his responsibility, and his role in postwar society.[22] Although communist sympathies were growing at this time, a *Yomiuri Newspaper* public opinion poll revealed in December 1945 that a majority of Japanese still supported the imperial institution.[23]

Zainichi Issues

The Korean issue in Japan was intimately tied to the problem of imperial and colonial responsibility as well as the resurrection of Japan's left-wing political force. Many Koreans were communist, and some had worked side by side with Tokuda and Shiga. Many had faced years of discrimination within Japan's empire, but thousands had also joined the Japanese imperial armed forces in some capacity. Korean attitudes toward war crimes trials have not been well examined, but in the initial years of the occupation they were vocal and it was a topic of great interest.[24]

Koreans were quickly booted from the bosom of Japan's empire, so they had to create their own organizations to assist livelihoods in the new post-downfall social setting. Early on, with JCP support, alliances quickly formed. These organizations, numbering almost three hundred throughout Japan, coalesced toward the end of August 1945. Their main focus was on helping Koreans living in Japan and resolving other problems, including health and welfare, and repatriation. There were, of course, different groups of Koreans—communists, pro-Japanese, and nationalists. These various associations reflected differing political and social orientations among the Koreans who remained in Japan after the war and were known as *Zainichi*, which in Japanese literally means "to be in Japan." But these associations sprouted up in individual cities, so a move was quickly afoot to push them into a national coalition.[25] Facing grave issues of feeding families and discrimination in the aftermath of a crumbling empire, a splinter group of individuals broke off and formed a more cohesive unit: the League of Korean Residents in Japan (*Zainihon chōsenjin renmei, Chōren* for short in Japanese).[26] Interestingly, the left-leaning Korean organization *Chōren* came into a financial windfall that was used to restart the JCP. Hundreds of *Zainichi* Koreans had yelled *mansei* (all hail!) when Tokuda and Kim exited the Fuchū prison on October 10, 1945. Before the war, the JCP was the only political party that had opposed the colonialization of Korea. And because Kim had been chosen within the JCP's leading committee soon after its resurrection, start-up money to the JCP came from the *Chōren*'s coffers as a thank-you.[27]

At the Korean League's inaugural October 15–16 convention, Kim Ch'on-hae delivered a speech on punishing pro-Japanese Korean traitors and called for the establishment of people's trials.[28] *Chōren* publicly announced in its manifesto that it aimed to "eliminate the remnants of Japanese imperialism," among other goals.[29] Members worked closely with the various elements of leftist Japanese political parties. However, JCP and Korean ideologues such as Kim increasingly pushed the *Chōren* toward more left-leaning ideological visions and alienated many. One can understand why this group had difficulty initially steering its own path, because it was attended by both pro-Japanese Koreans and Korean communists. The communists tried to push out the pro-Japan faction and those who they felt were not upholding Korean nationalism, now labeled as "ethnic traitors." The shift in how Koreans in Japan dealt with Japanese imperialism relates, in part, to how they were being treated by the postwar Japanese administration. In one sense, the pendulum had swung from one direction of Koreans as a "liberated people" to now being considered more as an "enemy people." In 1949 the occupation authorities ordered *Chōren* to disband as fears over the threat of communism rose in Japan. The vestiges of the *Chōren* later reformulated and by 1955 emerged as the General Federation of Resident Koreans in Japan (*Zainihon chōsenjin sōren gōkai*, *Sōren* in Japanese, *Chongryun* in Korean).

Similar to Shiga and Tokuda, Korean political activists were also sometimes imprisoned for lengthy terms in prewar Japan. Korean anarchist Park Yeol was released from Akita Prison in October 1945. In 1923, Park had been implicated with his wife, Kaneko Fumiko, in an alleged plot to assassinate the Crown Prince (later Emperor Hirohito).[30] Their trial in 1926 handed down a death sentence to both, although this was later commuted to life in prison. Kaneko died by suicide not long after. After release in October 1945, Park helped form and lead a competing nonleftist Korean ethnic association that assisted with repatriation and support during the tumultuous time of transition.

The reappearance of Park Yeol, after more than twenty years in an Akita prison and much of it in solitary confinement, galvanized sections of the Korean community in Japan. He had been young when first incarcerated, but that did not dull his innate charisma when he exited prison. Park took a bit of time to acclimate to life out of jail, and in December 1945 he made his way south to Tokyo. On December 7, a grand welcoming home party was held in

Tokyo's Hibiya Park in his honor.[31] Park, along with a select coterie of supporters, chafed at the Korean communists' approach. He asserted that Koreans in Japan needed a different organization to represent their interests. In 1946, they organized a more nationalist Korean group. Park and others wanted it to be an association that would have the people, democracy, and the people's livelihoods at its core. In February 1946, they established the New Korea Constructive Alliance. They opposed the administration of a political trust imposed on Korea by the Allies to manage the country until the international community deemed Koreans "mature enough" to rule themselves.[32]

Within several years, Korean associations further developed, and in 1948 a new and more forceful group emerged, naming itself the Community of Resident South Koreans in Japan (*Zainihon daikanminkoku kyoryū mindan*, abbreviated as *Mindan*). Park Yeol was its first leader, in part because he was already widely known owing to media exposure during the circus of his mid-1920s trial and his efforts to push against the Korean communists. However, by the 1950s a paradox had emerged within the *Zainichi* Korean community. Even though most hailed originally from locales in South Korea, ideologically at this point more identified with the North through the *Sōren* organization.[33]

To maintain the upper hand on their political leverage during the breakdown of imperial authority, the old guard took several steps. On November 5, 1945, the Shidehara government handed down a cabinet decision that confirmed the absence of the emperor's war responsibility. In a word salad revealing enormous textual flexibility and prehensile groping, the announcement deprived the emperor of any agency or indeed the ability to have altered the course of history. With such a move, the immediate postwar Japanese government leaders also played into the hands of the similar judgment later revealed by the Tokyo Trial verdict that the military were the main culprits. In rather archaic language reserved for referring only to the imperial sovereign, the decision's first section significantly related to the emperor. The cabinet-level decision explaining the war focused mainly on issues relating to Japan's military engagement with the West and avoided mentioning China, or Japanese actions before 1941, and nothing in general concerning the extent of Japanese atrocities.[34]

In November 1945, the left-wing *People's Newspaper* came out with its first issue. This newspaper was a sort-of sister news journal following the postwar restart of the JCP main newspaper, *Red Flag* (*Akahata*). The inaugural issue editorial, penned by Sunama Ichirō, called for "opposing the ideas of the leadership class who are war criminals."[35] This was reflected in its headline: "Let's Start a Mass Movement to Punish the War Criminals."[36] The paper reiterated what Tokuda Kyūichi had first raised in his public speech a few weeks prior.[37]

Not long after, a tiny article at the bottom of the morning edition of the *Asahi Newspaper* noted that on December 8, 1945, the JCP would hold a "people's rally to pursue the war criminals" in Tokyo, Osaka, Kyoto, Kobe, Yokohama, Sapporo, Fukushima, and elsewhere around Japan to memorialize the day the war began.[38] (While December 7 is remembered in the United States as the "day of infamy," it was already a day later in Japan, so for the Japanese the official start of the war is December 8.) Of course, this decision reflected a bias toward the West in defining Japan's war, whereas Japan's imperial army forays into China had already started in 1937 with years of an undeclared war. Regardless, one node of the event, held in the Kyoritsu Hall in Tokyo, was electric and very well attended. The journalist Mark Gayn was there. He wrote that the venue was packed and "hummed with impatience."[39] Shiga was in a "more fiery mood on the stage." Poised in front of the large audience, he began to name individually all the leaders and businessmen who had mistakenly led Japan to war. He came to the last name—the emperor—and paused for dramatic effect.[40] The impact on those watching was palpable. "The crowd cheered and stamped its feet. The whole cavernous darkness of the hall was now filled with sound and with fury, and they beat against the stage and the thin figure behind the pulpit."[41]

Shiga told those gathered that unless the imperial system was destroyed, militarism would return. The JCP then handed out its central committee decision from a few days prior. The course of action called out the emperor and other royal members and said the party would be announcing a list of who should be put on trial. The decision stated "the fact is and without a doubt . . . all elements of the ruling elite, starting namely with the emperor, his ministers, the military clique, bureaucrats of the legal administration, landlords who cooperated with the financial clique's war, members of the upper and lower houses, thuggish reactionary groups, and others are the leaders and organizers of this criminally aggressive war."[42] A few days later, on December 11, JCP Central Committee chair Kuroki Shigenori visited the government's chief cabinet secretary Tsugita Daizaburō and a member of the US occupation leadership to hand them the party's list of more than one thousand names concerning which Japanese should be prosecuted as war criminals.[43]

All of this occurred at a frantic pace and before the grandfather of Japanese communists, Nosaka Sanzō, had even returned from his self-enforced exile in China. Nosaka withstood the war from the outside, having found refuge first in Moscow, where he was close to Stalin, and then later with Mao in western China. Nosaka was instrumental at the CCP refuge in Yenan, the seat of the CCP, and assisted the Chinese Eighth Route Army in managing the surrender of and reeducation of Japanese imperial soldiers during the war. His repatriation was big news. On January 26, 1946, Nosaka's triumphant return received a grand reception in Hibiya Park, just down the road from the imperial palace in Tokyo. The event, called the "National People's Gathering to Welcome Home Returning Nosaka Sanzō," was attended by tens of thousands of eager supporters who braved the rain on a winter's day.[44]

Prince Higashikuni, the first Japanese postwar prime minister, had not been far off the mark in terms of assessing the larger issue of wartime responsibility, and his comments were repeated in early 1945 by the JCP. By this time the Japanese communists had regrouped and were fully flexing their political muscles in opposition to what they felt was a government and leadership that merely wished to drag their feet and bide their time until the US occupiers left. The communist pressure on the war crimes issue increased and soon published another call to arms in a short pamphlet, *A People's Court to Try War Criminals*. It was an intriguing document that demonstrated one aspect of how the discussion of war crimes trials developed in Japan during the early months of the occupation. "The exploitative and cruel war is over and the Allies are democratizing Japan," the pamphlet joyously announced. However, the JCP told its followers, what awaited them was deprivation, unemployment, sickness, and poverty at never-before-seen levels. This was the result of a war labeled as "the liberation of the Asian peoples" and the "establishment of the new world order."[45]

What the JCP called for, to right those past wrongs, was a social revolution. Where were the war criminals and who should pursue them? the JCP queried. What the communists realized and proclaimed to the Japanese public was that, chillingly, war criminals were everywhere—they were "in every factory, every hamlet, every organization, within every managerial group . . . within villages and towns and within schools."[46] Who was going to conduct the trials of these criminals? they asked. Was it going to be the upper house of parliament, those who guarded their special class privileges, and "who applauded the budget for the war, who strengthened for the worse the 1938 Peace Preservation Law?" Or should they expect justice to emerge from the lower house of the Diet, from those "who pushed forward the decision to pursue the holy war with a standing ovation?" "It is obvious," the pamphlet concluded, that "these groups do not have one iota of qualification to stand at the forefront of a democratic movement."[47] The manifesto ended by touching on the issue of war responsibility and the emperor, asking: Who announced the start of the war? And in whose name were those who opposed the war thrown into prison? For the Japanese communists, anyone who had been in power or linked to the wartime administrations, which meant everyone in authority in the early days of the postwar period, was suspect.

While the individual strategies may have shifted, the situation continued to escalate even further. On May 1, 1946, responding to a worsening situation with both rations and the economy, left-wing groups staged an enormous rally in front of the imperial palace. Calls to "pursue and root out all war criminals" were part of the slogans, while forums with such goals in mind were held all over the country. The Tokyo event was enormous, with tens of thousands massing into the gathering. Blurry pictures of it were published in the *Asahi Newspaper* under the headline "Historic May Day Adds Our Voice to the World."[48]

But no one listened.

The JCP certainly had the ear of popular opinion at the time, so what happened? In short, as we will see in later chapters, the JCP and the left wing in general soon fell into a long period of internecine warfare. One faction aligned itself with the Soviets and called for a full revolution, or a partial one. The JCP and other vanguard political groups, after once again being given a seat in the theater of power, squandered their efforts instead by trying to upend each other rather than focusing on the task at hand—reforming the nation.[49]

At the moment of surrender and immediately thereafter, the JCP struggled with its political orientation. Should it cleave close to its elder brother the Soviet Union and follow calls for outright violent revolution as the locus of change? Such appeals left many cold. Or should they, as Nosaka opined, promote the idea that the JCP should create a likable party and talk about abolishing the imperial system when democracy in Japan evolved to a point that the whole nation could discuss it?[50] The JCP had not really been popular before the war; its membership was dismal. This change of tack was a grand transformation but also pitted Nosaka's orientation against others. His main rival would soon turn out to be Itō Ritsu, another long-standing member of the JCP. Itō was assistant editor of the JCP main organ, *Red Flag*, and had not fled to the mainland, eking out a living throughout the war in country. Although beginning in 1940 he was imprisoned for several years.

Further undermining JCP support was the belief that the party was responsible for a series of train-related mishaps in 1949. The first president of the Japanese National Rail was assassinated and the culprit never found, in what was called the Shimoyama Incident. Two rail accidents in the summer of 1949, the Mitaka Incident and the Matsukawa Incident, were publicly perceived as violent acts by a disruptive JCP. Was this part of a battle between the lovable and violent factional split in the JCP? It is hard to ascertain the truth, but blame was squarely placed on communist elements. By January 1950, the Cominform (Information Bureau of the Communist and Workers' Parties, but essentially a political organization under Soviet rule to maintain a Stalinist political orientation in communist countries) was criticizing Nosaka's ideas, saying that his notion of reform through parliamentary procedure was not tenable.[51] At the same time, it was somewhat embarrassing for the JCP that it could not orchestrate the return of hundreds of thousands of Japanese POWs from the USSR.[52]

Even though they initially proclaimed the US military to be their liberators, within a few years JCP members openly condemned the same occupation on the Diet floor. As a consequence, on February 24, 1950, Major General Courtney Whitney of SCAP's Chief of Government Section summoned lower house member Sunama Ichirō and reprimanded him. Sunama had written the editorial in the *People's Newspaper* calling for war crimes trials. The reprimand read in part: "You, your leaders, and hundreds of your fellows were released from prison where you have long been incarcerated by the Civil Liberties Directive issued by the Supreme Commander immediately following the surrender. Since then, the Supreme Commander has fed you, clothed you and your families and protected your right to organize as a lawful political party in Japan. He has literally saved Japan from the brink of impending disaster. Have you no intelligence or gratitude?"[53] By this point SCAP was wary of the JCP and, more importantly, anxious about its actual and supposed links with the Soviet Union to foment an international conspiracy. Nowhere was this more evident than with General Charles Willoughby, MacArthur's "lovable fascist" and head of SCAP's counterintelligence bureau. After the occupation, Willoughby wrote a book about this supposed international communist conspiracy. General Douglas MacArthur penned the preface. The former head of Japan's occupation believed that Willoughby's book was gravely important because it "presents a clear delineation of a world-wide pattern of communist sabotage and betrayal which is still being practiced today."[54] Willoughby saw conspiracies everywhere, even within SCAP. He called Beate Sirota Gordon, the only woman on the team that had redrafted the Japanese constitution and a key figure owing to her fluent Japanese, "'childish,' 'almost psychopathic,' 'stateless jewess' [*sic*] with imagined family connections to Richard Sorge, a German communist spy who had relayed intelligence from Tokyo to the Soviet Union in the Second World War."[55]

To learn why MacArthur and his number two assessed that Japan played a role in this international communist conspiracy, we need to go back in time to the war and the Sorge spy ring. Sorge, a double agent who posed as a Nazi but who gave important intelligence to the Soviets, along with his Japanese counterpart, Ozaki Hotsumi, was executed in the midst of the war. The Japanese Ministry of Justice had published some intelligence about the events publicly in 1942, but mostly the story was unknown and kept out of the Japanese media because of concerns about national security. But the whole secretive affair turned into something very different after the war was over. This was because "the case was of interest to the public: Ozaki had been executed as a traitor to the very system they were in the process of dismantling." From the immediate postwar standpoint, was Ozaki not therefore a patriot?[56] He had never been a member of the Communist Party, but, nonetheless, the JCP wanted to paint him as a martyr and say that he was one of them. This would help support the movement as it tried to reestablish a political voice from its oppressed membership that had barely survived the war. As the JCP developed a deepened interest in the case in the hopes of creating a party hero for the postwar period, SCAP suffered growing anxiety about the same case. By early February 1949, SCAP released a report, "The Sorge Spy Ring: A Case Study in International Espionage in the Far East." The report named JCP stalwart Itō Ritsu as an "unwitting Judas" whose confession had eventually led to Sorge's arrest.[57] The party publicly claimed that it had examined all charges against Itō and found him blameless. However, he disappeared in June 1950 and seemingly so did the whole JCP leadership. By 1953, Itō was purged from the party and formally expelled in 1955, though at the time no one could say where he had gone or what happened to him. It was as if he had vanished from the face of the earth. The mystery of his whereabouts and the JCP's machinations would not come to light until 1980, and even then they disavowed any connection.[58]

SCAP and MacArthur's men, and later the CIA in Japan, frequently saw communist fire even where there was no smoke.[59] For Willoughby and the American public devouring his theories about communist aims to dominate the world in the early 1950s, the Sorge spy ring was indicative of an international conspiracy. This fear was building at precisely the time when the United States considered that it had "lost" China to the Chinese communists and that the USSR and its bloc would soon threaten the world. Willoughby wrote, "Shanghai was the vineyard of communism. Here were sown the dragon's teeth that ripened into the Red Harvest of today, and the farm labor was done by men and women of many nationalities who had no personal stakes in China other than an inexplicable fanaticism for an alien cause, the 'Communist *jehad*' for the subjugation of the Western world."[60] Through Willoughby's mind-set of fear concerning the Sorge case and what it symbolized for America's future, we can see why the JCP had such difficulty gaining traction for its cause of pursuing war crimes within Japan. Willoughby concluded his bestseller: "The purpose of the Tokyo investigations can hardly be stated more clearly. The thefts of our atom secrets—the fruits of American technical ingenuity—were made possible by naïve tolerance of Communists and their front organization, of the saccharine vagaries of fellow travellers and prostituted liberals, and, unless we learn the art of self-defense in international terms, we will have the suicide of Western civilization on our conscience."[61] A US congressional subcommittee debate on US security issues related to the activities and fears of communist moves even mentioned Tokuda and Shiga's eighteen years in prison. This reflected fears in the United States about the potential destabilizing power of the Japanese communists.[62]

Not all communists were as adamant about the war crimes trials, and the conversion of some reflected the intense pressure prewar Japanese society had exerted on the left wing. A few years after the war, famed communist turned nationalist Nabeyama Sadachika helped usher this new era forward. After defeat, Japan switched its ideological project from being imperialist to aligning with neighbors to defeat communism in Asia. "As it was recast into an ideology of its own, anti-communism partially replaced prewar imperial ideology," and this helped provide a new platform on which "new connections could be forged" both domestically and internationally.[63] Former Japanese communists and imperialists established new alliances across former lines of enmity to create alternate bogeymen—the PRC, the USSR, among others. Nabeyama even went as far as to serve as an informant for the Chinese Nationalists in postwar China before the end of its civil war. He became the darling of postwar Japanese defense and police agencies, such as the Public Security Investigation Bureau, and gave talks on anticommunism and loyalty. Tokuda Kyūichi despised him. Nabeyama joined forces with Yabe Teiji and assisted on the Japanese side in linking with the Asian People's Anti-Communist League, launched by Chiang Kai-shek in Taiwan and Synghman Rhee in South Korea.[64] Yabe was a political scientist and had been a member of the short-lived yet influential wartime Showa Research Association. A Chinese Nationalist author at the time explaining the situation suggested that the fate of Japan to resist communism was linked to similar KMT objectives owing to their shared predicament of having to remake themselves after defeat. Japan regained its sovereignty but "still stands in the chaotic battleground of rebuilding its nationalistic spirit and reshaping its intellectual world." The KMT "well understands Japan's struggle to impede the flood of communism from the outside." To achieve a common goal, Japan needed to first strengthen its own "cultural traditions" and use those to restore itself. This shift required a strong anticommunist policy and the need for improved defense forces, the author wrote. Japan also needed to deepen ties with fellow democratic and free nations (like the ROC, Taiwan). This was not just a goal for Japan alone, the author exerted, but something that needed to be done together across Asia.[65]

Imperial Interference

The JCP was clear about its aim to remove the emperor and the Japanese imperial throne from power. But there were also other plans proposed from different sectors of society concerning what the emperor should do following surrender: abdicate, persist, or become a Buddhist monk and retreat from society. And these were only a few of the recommended strategies. There was even a secret plan to reinstate the imperial system when possible, and the team that espoused that objective did not formally disband until the 1980s.[66]

While it is possible that the emperor in his talks with MacArthur in the late summer and early autumn of 1945 pleaded for general leniency and attempted to take some responsibility for the war upon the throne, the result never bore fruit.[67] Little more than a year later, the emperor took a much more proactive stance. The public clamor to limit the areas placed under judicial scrutiny concerning war responsibility soon led to a large portion of Japanese society being forgiven. On November 3, 1946, Emperor Hirohito bestowed a "great amnesty" to the Japanese people. Ironically, this was the same day of the announcement of Japan's new constitution, imposed by the United States. In fact, Hirohito's decree ended prison for many charged with crimes during the war, such as those convicted of lèse-majesté, thought crimes, and political crimes. At the same time, the imperial fiat also granted amnesty to soldiers who had gone AWOL, those who had been convicted in courts-martial, those who had not followed orders of a superior officer during the war, and, more importantly, members of the imperial navy and army who had committed crimes against POWs or other crimes abroad.[68] The *Asahi Newspaper* labeled this scope "unprecedented." The imperial measure also contained a clause that stipulated that such amnesty was not applicable to those who committed crimes "against the goals of the occupation."[69] In some ways, Hirohito's imperial pronouncement offered an imperial pardon for the very type of war crimes that the Allies were starting to pursue against the Japanese, though it remains unclear whether the edict had any legal teeth. Regardless, it certainly set the moral contours for the internal debate on war crimes soon after Japan's surrender.

Japanese newspapers wrote of seven types of crimes being pardoned, which led to 330,000 suspects being granted amnesty.[70] That this imperial benevolence extended to improper wartime laws, which had terrorized Japanese liberals, as well as laws that related to war crimes and crimes against non-Japanese, would serve to dampen even further Japanese postwar interest in the need to address the legacy of war crimes. With the "Great Amnesty," as it was termed, the emperor appeared to have essentially delivered his own imperial verdict on the war. However, even this was not exactly as it initially seemed because we now know that the emperor was deeply conflicted. According to newly disclosed diaries of those close to the emperor, Hirohito actually toyed with the idea of being allowed to abdicate or at least to face the public and talk openly about war responsibility not long after surrender. Ironically, it was his new office—democratized and now symbolic—that constrained him from doing so. What kept the emperor quiet was that Japan's new constitution denied him a political role, and Prime Minister Yoshida Shigeru told him not to make public statements. Japan's own postwar government wanted to focus on rebuilding the nation, not imperial soul-searching. The postwar imperial emperor seemingly wanted change, but the democratic administration did not wish to allow him to play a role in it.[71]

The Imperial Military Response

As previously discussed, Japan's imperial forces never saw eye to eye and further divided their own internal power into small subgroups that vied for ascendancy at any one time: the imperial Japanese army and imperial navy ministers each held a cabinet post, which were in charge of administrative matters. The armed forces also retained the Chief of the Imperial Army General Staff (*Sanbō sōchō*) and Chief of the Imperial Navy General Staff (*Gunreibu*), who dealt with operational and battle strategy matters and were consultative offices directly under the aegis of the emperor, separate from the government. The navy had already moved on September 10 to establish a section that would carefully manage and arrange matters dealing with POWs and international law. The army had responded on September 17 with its own "plan concerning a summary of responses to Allied investigations of treatment of POWs," which it sent to all its troops. This plan admitted that previous orders to burn documents left the army with little evidence to defend its own actions, so each unit needed to organize and forward all the materials that it could to the Army Ministry. To prove that POWs were not maltreated, the committee amassed details about the items served for POW meals, though the death statistics released thereafter would contradict that data.[72]

In short, Japanese military officials took diverging strategies toward war crimes trials depending on the geography of the venue. Men like army lieutenant general Tanaka Hisakazu, charged in China for war crimes, were contemptuous in internal reports about the meaning and value of their trials. Tanaka wrote to military headquarters complaining about Chinese war crimes trial procedures, stating that he could accept Chinese attempts to charge his underlings with crimes, but they needed to do it lawfully and bear in mind the burden of proof. Tanaka claimed that he was not trying to avoid responsibility, but the courts could not sit idly by and rely on Chinese oral testimony or newspaper articles because these materials were too flimsy for the purposes of an indictment.[73] The navy was even more diligent in its long-term efforts to keep its men out of war crimes trials.

These postwar efforts continued for decades even after the war crimes trials were finished, demonstrating that long-term Japanese postwar military anxiety about its image did not cease with defeat.[74] It is important to note that in all these discussions few voices were heard that castigated the military for having caused so many Japanese young men to die a death that should not be considered a sacrifice. The eminent Japanese historian Fujiwara Akira, who wrote on a personal level about his own experiences in the war, questioned many of the dubious tactics used by the Japanese imperial forces. He said that even as an old man he still dreamt about having to feed his men on the battlefields of China. The Japanese army had made little provision to supply its soldiers.[75] Fujiwara penned a very poignant article concerning the issue of dying a "dog's death"—that is, a death with no meaning. Fujiwara explained that he could understand why many believed using this term against former "brothers in arms" or fellow fallen soldiers might be considered blasphemous. But, he cautioned, we should remember that Japan's invasion was nothing more than an unmitigated aggressive imperial war. We are not permitted to "glorify" those who died in this unjust and immoral war at Yasukuni Shrine. Their deaths were without value and thus a "dog's death," he asserted. Fujiwara admitted that many involved in the war or part of survivor families might not be able to accept his views. But let us look at their deaths, he suggests. Many were due to starvation, not actual warfare. In short, the imperial Japanese army did not look after its own and did not care about supplies. These were *unnecessary* sacrifices. Most men killed in Japan's war died in conflict during the last year. As victory grew ever more distant and less certain, the Japanese high command insisted on sending more and more young men to their deaths, cognizant of its uselessness.[76] Fujiwara concluded his observations on a cold note, that the Japanese military did not value life.[77]

Japanese public intellectual Oda Makoto took a slightly different stance. For him, these were "meaningless deaths" but important because they reflected a moment devoid of significance. Oda exhorted his readers not to look to the last day of the war and kamikaze pilots to find some beauty in sacrifice. Instead, look to the day before, August 14, and the air raid on Osaka, he suggested. Is there not anything more pitiful than the people who died on that day, he asked, those in the armaments factory that was completely destroyed? They had managed to survive and the war was already confirmed over, so their deaths "were the most meaningless of all were they not?" Oda recalled that he "lived near the factory and passed that hellish afternoon shaking in the air raid shelter. Afterward, I picked up leaflets dropped from the sky which said things like 'Your country's government has surrendered, the war is over.'" Oda questioned this sort of death. It was not gallant or glorious; it was a waste, he averred. It was a death "devoid of meaning" because, within a day, sacrifice for the emperor and the ideals of the Greater East Asia Co-Prosperity Sphere became laughable notions.[78] Oda analyzed that the growing gap between the public situation, where the war was described as inevitable and a holy war, and an individual's personal circumstances, where their rights were increasingly deprived and men were being sent off to die in distant battlefields, grew untenable. To bridge this divide, people tried to bestow a deeper meaning on death, even though it actually had served no purpose.[79]

Chapter 6

The Violence of Imperial Dissolution at the Periphery

Just after Japan's surrender in China, Wang Lin organized a group of one hundred or so Japanese POWs to fix the local roads that the imperial military had destroyed. Wang was a head schoolmaster in Shangbai Village, Zhejiang Province, slightly northwest of the city of Hangzhou. During this activity in August 1945, Wang recalls that he got to know some of the prisoners well, after spending about ten days interacting with them on the site.

There were five Japanese officers among the POWs, and they understood basic English. In addition, their ability to read and write Chinese characters, along with frequent gestures, allowed the Japanese prisoners and their Chinese guards to have "chats" and converse in a manner of sorts. Not all was tranquil, however. Wang remembered, "These five officers were quite arrogant and demonstrated they were not pleased to have lost the war. Among them was Second Lieutenant Okamoto Masano. He was from Nagasaki and because the atom bomb had completely wiped out his whole family he was dejected and dispirited. I spoke with him the most and the most frequently." Part of their conversation was so memorable for Wang that he wrote about it forty years later in a brief recollection. Asked why he came to China in the first place, Okamoto responded that his school textbooks said that China was vast, and if Japan could master the continent, Japanese could live out their days easily. Okamoto said he had wanted the war to end but could not have imagined

Japan's defeat. Things grew more interesting toward the end of their conversation.

> WANG: After going through this war, do you think your country Japan can rebuild?
> OKAMOTO: (confidently in tone) Yes it can.
> WANG: We Chinese will also be able to revive.
> OKAMOTO: (after thinking, smiles) With effort.

For years Wang pondered this conversation and what Okamoto meant. He was not sure if Okamoto was being prescient about the problems China would face or the insurmountable obstacles that he believed Japan could easily overcome because it had already modernized. What is remarkable is Wang's positive attitude and absence of hatred. China suffered a great calamity, he wrote, but the Chinese needed to think deeply about the lessons of history and the war for the future.[1]

For the first several years following Japan's downfall, the Allies' goal was to restrain and demobilize Japan. However, the situation turned potentially unstable with the threat of a growing communist bloc in Japan linking with a surging movement in China and the Soviet Union. Consequently, US occupation officials changed their tack and began what is called the "reverse course." This shift in policy marked the time when the United States actively started to rebuild Japan and include it as a burgeoning new ally in East Asia. This reversal, of course, angered other parties in the region, and by 1949 North Korean leader Kim Il Sung saw America's support for Japan and the push to rearm it as part of a clear path toward Japanese remilitarization. Mao estimated that North Korea believed that if US troops left the peninsula, South Korea would then join in cahoots with former Japanese troops to reunite the Korean peninsula. The irony of the end of World War II was that Japan, the country responsible for much of the destruction and ultimate destabilization of the region, was arguably "the least volatile" and essentially retained the structure of its national government and borders, along with the majority of its internal population.[2] Japan lost its sovereignty under the occupation of six and a half years until April 1952, but for all intents and purposes it also kept much of its internal political networks, social norms, and for many the dream of reestablishing itself as leader of sorts in the region.

We should recall that although Japan initiated the war, and ultimately failed in its objectives, it was still the most technologically educated and advanced industrial power in East Asia. Even with all the social mobilization during World War II in East Asia, most regions were still agricultural and industrially poor. Japan had invested heavily in northern Korea and Manchuria, known to prewar leaders as the "cockpit of Asia." In the immediate aftermath of the surrender, this region saw law and order disintegrate, devolving into mass atrocities even involving communist troops.[3] The end of empire left many in awkward positions with little preparation, not just former Japanese colonists. "Koreans in Manchuria were not only saddled with past participation in the failed experiment of Manchukuo and rejected as collaborators by the Chinese Nationalist Party (Guomindang), they were often unable to return to ancestral locales on the Korean peninsula."[4] Some Chinese even referred to the large numbers of Koreans living in the border region between northeast China and Korea, on the edge of the Soviet Union, as "secondary devils," in supporting roles to the main "Japanese devils."[5] Japanese rule left a trail of tears as well as a legacy of infrastructure in those areas, which meant it would be an important site for contestation of control after the war.[6] Japan's former puppet kingdom of Manchukuo produced "more than a third of China's total industrial output in 1949, and this rose to over a half by 1952."[7]

While lone stragglers on the plains of northern Manchuria could sometimes find comfort in the arms of others, there was no normal situation anywhere. Life was up for grabs, completely dependent on one's environment.

And it was not all about enmity, of course. Yamaguchi Mitsufumi faced Japan's defeat after being a member of the Manchuria-Mongolia Pioneer Youth Volunteer Army for less than a year. Caught by the invading Soviet army, he was marched across the vast and empty plains of northern Manchuria as a prisoner to the Yanji Detention Center, in the Korean Autonomous zone, not far from the North Korean border. Struck with fierce dysentery and a fever, Yamaguchi had to relieve himself every fifty meters or so. However, the increasing intervals of explosive diarrhea ensured that the young man could not keep pace with the other detainees. In an effort to move more quickly, he wrote, he ended up "wearing my trousers around my shoulders and walking with my butt out in a sort of crab walk" to avoid the agony of soiling himself. Eventually his anus prolapsed owing to the pressure from the constant diarrhea and walking. He also had to keep swatting away the flies that were swarming around his enflamed and sensitive rectal area.[8] Not long after Yamaguchi lost sight of his group a kindly old Korean woman saw him and took pity on his lamentable state, inviting him to come inside to rest. She warmed some water and helped him wash his bottom. As soon as the "warm water hit my rectum a feeling like I had gone to heaven enveloped me from head to toe. My anus was pushed back up and returned to its original position and the great pain suddenly dissipated as if it had never happened." The family had a box of medicine and from it they took out a few precious *seirogan* pills, used to treat dysentery.[9] They put Yamaguchi to bed, gave him a few more doses of medicine, and arguably saved his life.

Resolving Disunity on the Chinese Mainland

We should not read the end of war as solely a moment of liberation—or in Yamaguchi's case, salvation—because the regional inhabitants did not know exactly what they were returning to and were often quite frustrated.[10] Unlike Western Europe, which saw many of its governments go into exile and thus have some sort of elastic authoritative body to repatriate and rule following the defeat of the Nazis, East Asia could not rely on similar institutions. Moreover, many regions had numerous hurdles to overcome. Korea never held formal war crimes trials of Japanese because it was not in a state of war with the metropole, but it did implement some domestic tribunals for those deemed as collaborators. But then again, Korea was not in control of its own fate since it had been a formal colony of Japan and remained in a dubious position as a "trust" under Allied leadership in the initial years after Japan's surrender. US troops "performed" the defeat of Japan on the Korean peninsula.[11] China also faced multiple and competing issues, not only restoring or establishing Chinese authority in areas but also deciding precisely the boundaries of this management. The Chinese needed to disband two main puppet governments that had maintained their own armies during the era of Japanese aggression. The first was the Nanjing Provisional Government, which until his premature death in late 1944 had been under the leadership of Wang Jingwei, a defector from the KMT government in Chongqing. The second was the Manchukuo administration, based out of Changchun in the north; although it was run mainly by the Japanese, it still had thousands of Chinese bureaucrats and a strong contingent of weaponized forces in the form of the Manchukuo Imperial Army.

The fate of the Manchukuo army was a sensitive enough topic that it garnered division among high-ranking KMT military leaders. Chiang Kai-shek believed it necessary to reincorporate "traitor" soldiers into the fold, while his number two, General Chen Cheng, did not think they were useful.[12] General Chen believed KMT forces should not mix with Japanese and former Manchukuo forces because that would dilute the Chinese Nationalist fighting force. Chen wrote, "We are a victorious nation, we absolutely do not need to incorporate Japanese and Manchukuo forces to beat the Communist Party; we have battalions that are equipped with American arms which is enough to decimate the communists."[13] Chen was also perhaps overly optimistic about

KMT military strength. KMT generals He Yingqin and Bai Chongxi were of the opposite opinion and chose to fold Manchukuo platoons into their own ranks.

One of the elements behind Chiang's reasoning was that in the summer of 1945, KMT forces were stationed mostly in their home-front areas of China's southwest. They had been essentially pushed there by Japan's massive assault known as Operation Ichigō. This final major confrontation on the continent was a colossal setback for the Chinese. About half a million battle-ready Japanese soldiers mobilized in a supreme last-ditch effort in one of the war's biggest operations. The aim was to link Manchukuo, Korea, and China since Japan was facing enormous setbacks in the Pacific and losing its naval fleet. A secondary Japanese goal was to destroy US bases in China, which were used to pummel Japan from the sky with all too frequent air raids. Chiang felt Ichigō was his worst humiliation and China's greatest source of suffering in a series of battles that lasted eight months. KMT forces encountered enormous logistical problems. Many Chinese soldiers were too malnourished to be of use. While they might have been tough and disciplined, 90 percent of the recruits were also illiterate, which made training and maneuvers difficult.[14]

Estimates vary according to KMT sources or wartime Japanese generals, but the consensus was that the Manchukuo Army at the end of war mustered about six hundred thousand soldiers, including local forces. When those were extracted, and when the police and the others that were poorly equipped were removed, the KMT took in on the order of about four hundred thousand soldiers from the Manchukuo military. These troops were renamed and then woven into nationalist troops as the means to defeat the CCP.[15] In all likelihood they had little impact on the outcome of the Chinese civil war, which the KMT lost.

The Violence of Imperial Dissolution at the Fringes of Empire

Three crucial historical episodes give us insight into the manner in which the end of empire and impediments to finding justice complicated the beginning of the postwar period. Because Japan was not merely a country at the time of its defeat, "the history of imperial memory was not a Japanese affair alone, but must be situated within larger processes and transformations of the postwar order in East Asia."[16] To investigate the failure of justice and the emergence of post-surrender violence requires conducting an autopsy of the 1946 Shibuya Incident in Tokyo, Japan; the February 28, 1947, Incident in Taiwan; and the 1948 Jeju Island Incident in Korea. After all, the course of justice was intimately affected by numerous events around the former empire. Violence that spewed forth at the end of empire was not always directed at the Japanese and thus the form justice took was also not monochromatic. Different allegiances and former networks of power affected how it evolved. In fact, these archetypal incidents—in Japan, Taiwan, and Korea—spotlight the difficulty of demobilized but weaponized societies where youths were recently disenfranchised from the empire. No Asian victory in World War II—Chinese, Korean, or Taiwanese—followed the path the early modern European theorist of war Carl von Clausewitz outlined.[17] Triumph did not allow the victor, the Chinese Nationalist Party, to assert its dominance or its version of a new world order on the conquered party—in this case, Japan. The early postwar period in East Asia was disorganized and violent, though often the fracases were within the same ethnic groups where various cliques were vying for power. All three of these moments geographically relate to Japan's crumbling empire, although historiographically they have normally been treated within their own national histories and rarely been viewed from a more regional perspective, linked specifically with the disintegration of Japan's empire.

In fact, what these violent encounters tell us is that we have not yet crafted a suitable vocabulary for the interim between the failure of war, the twilight of empire, and the arrival of peace. It certainly does not happen overnight.[18] The shift from defeat to finding justice is a process that requires years. What is the difference between "defeat" and "the end of war"? When does a postwar period begin, and do these terms come with a finite beginning and end? This is a period for which we currently have no real, adequate linguistic phrase. We have not yet sufficiently discussed these issues, because until recently history was preternaturally focused on the outbreak and denouement of war but not its conclusion or when fighting is brought to a close. A further historiographical problem is that we tend to discuss defeat as just the small sliver of time during which the formalities of military combat and the ceremony of surrender occur. We then quickly move on to the idea of the postwar period. However, this speed pushes us too easily to dismiss significant changes in circumstances.

Shibuya Incident, Tokyo, 1946

Japanese authorities were anxious about the immediate aftermath of the war. The empire and home islands teemed with malcontents nursing a variety of grievances. A Japanese report of unknown provenance detailing the situation of Taiwanese and Koreans stated that because of the change of circumstances, Japanese authorities were most worried about potential incidents at places where many Korean and Taiwanese workers were stationed. In Akita Prefecture there was an incident at a mine where a dozen or so Korean workers were drinking on August 15 and yelled at their Japanese supervisors, "Japan lost the war so now we will make you work in the mines!" Then they destroyed items in their dormitory and ran amok. It took fifty police officers and others to suppress the conflict. There were other incidents at various mines and at a naval facility in Kanagawa where about seven thousand Taiwanese labored. On August 23 they stopped work and food at the facilities quickly diminished. The incensed Taiwanese saw female employees and cafeteria workers absconding with supplies and accosted them. The dispatch of several hundred Japanese military police to the area was required to restore order.[19] The Japanese MOFA investigated that for many expat Japanese living on Taiwan there had not been too great a change in lifestyle toward the end of the war, so things appeared relatively stable after the war. However, no one could sell their assets and with prices rising due to stricter rationing, it grew harder to make ends meet and the situation grew more precarious.[20]

The Shibuya Incident in Tokyo was essentially a riot in July 1946 during which several hundred Taiwanese black marketeers fought with Japanese gangsters in pitched battles over turf. This was a time of penurious economic conditions brought about just after the conclusion of the war. Japan's economy had virtually come to a standstill, and to eke out a living, those already at the bottom rungs of Japanese imperial society—the Taiwanese, Chinese, Koreans, and other "lesser Asians," as they were often deemed—competed for profit among the forty-five thousand open-air stalls in Tokyo. In the end, six Taiwanese and a Japanese police officer were killed. Approximately forty Taiwanese were arrested and eventually put on trial in a specially established US military court because Chinese/Taiwanese were exempt from being pursued under Japanese domestic law. Non-Japanese were no longer legally Japanese with the signing of the surrender document. On the Chinese mainland the incident upset Chinese attitudes toward the Americans, whom the left wing increasingly viewed as eager to prop up militant Japanese regrowth.

The Japanese public closely observed the trial of the Shibuya Incident because it was one of the first test cases that showed the new postwar limits of Japanese law to resolve postimperial problems. The Chinese Mission in Japan also carefully supervised the trial to ensure that the Taiwanese (now newly enfranchised citizens of the Republic of China) were allowed access to proper legal representation.[21] The overseas Chinese association assiduously followed the tribunal. The Americans tried the Taiwanese in a US military tribunal but ultimately allowed a Chinese judge to join the court. This was Henry Qiu (Qiu Shaoheng), who had initially been brought in as a secretary and interpreter for

Chinese prosecutor Xiang Zhejun to assist in the Tokyo Trial. (As we will see, Qiu was also instrumental decades later in the Gang of Four trial in Beijing.)

Yorkson Shen (Shen Jinding), acting chief of the Chinese Mission, kept up pressure on General MacArthur. Shen felt the Americans occupying Japan were preferential to the Japanese and needed to take the incident more seriously and note its potential ramifications. The Mission assessed that the Taiwanese were "defenseless victims" upon whom the Japanese police had aggressively fired.[22] In short, the "Shibuya Incident of 1946 was illustrative of China's attempts to influence US policy in postwar Japan, and the ultimate frustration of those attempts."[23]

The trial started on September 30, 1946, and lasted until December 10 within a courtroom in the Tokyo Metropolitan Police Bureau. The Taiwanese were charged with crimes against the goals of the occupation. Of the formally indicted forty-one Taiwanese, two were released as not guilty, and the remaining thirty-nine were sentenced. One was given three years of hard labor, and the other thirty-eight were given two years of hard labor. Yorkson Shen dissented against the court's decision to little avail.[24] The verdict chafed against Chinese official opinion, which many viewed as "Japan's perceived unrepentant attitude toward China."[25] Already from the outset of the end of empire, Taiwanese could see that they would be treated differently and that their former loyalty to the Japanese empire suddenly meant very little. For Japanese, while the war might have been about defending the empire, such propaganda slogans would now ring very hollow for the empire's peripheral subjects so easily jettisoned after surrender.

February 28 Incident, Taiwan

Riots lit by the discontent of formerly militarily indoctrinated youths were endemic to immediate postwar imperial Japan. Like the young Taiwanese men who had to come to terms with the failure of the Japanese empire on the Japanese home islands, Taiwanese now under the heel of the KMT authorities on the island of Taiwan also had to deal with equally complex issues. By the late years of the war, slightly more than two hundred thousand Taiwanese men were mobilized in some capacity for Japan's imperial military juggernaut. Some were soldiers, and others served as camp guards who were sent far away to remote islands in Southeast Asia. Many labored merely as support staff or low-level workers in camps. Some found this empowering or at least a positive experience. They did not necessarily see themselves as Japanese but nonetheless did consider themselves high on the imperial hierarchy.

During the last stage of the war, US planners were researching how to invade and then rule Taiwan to prepare for an eventual Chinese takeover. The United States estimated that the KMT military was weak and did not have the expertise to properly administer Taiwan. US officials believed that the UK was also not properly staffed militarily but maybe could join with the KMT to occupy and manage Taiwan together.[26] Fundamentally, there was discord between the Chinese vision of a sudden takeover following Japan's defeat and the opinions of the other Allies. It was not clear in the initial handover who would have final authority. It is interesting to note that Chinese Nationalist leaders believed or acted as if Taiwan was or always had been part of China even though fifty years had passed since the island had been separated from Qing dynasty control, when the KMT had not even existed. Because the KMT could devote only a small force to occupy Taiwan, US authorities agreed to take control at first. This alacrity was also how the Americans were able to quickly procure the Japanese soldiers they wanted for trials in Shanghai of atrocities against downed American pilots.[27]

Taiwan sits uncomfortably at the intersection of the history of decolonization and global history. Its story is not a happy and uplifting one, because it confronts difficult moments of the past. What the conflict revealed, in part, was the unbridled hostility of those who had grown up under Japanese colonial rule and were now suddenly constrained by Chinese authority. KMT leaders were baffled at the opposition, believing that all Chinese held the same political distaste for imperial Japan. The aftermath of the uproar showed the gap between native-born Taiwanese under Japanese rule, *benshengren* in Chinese, and those born on the mainland who arrived after Japan's defeat, *waishengren* in Chinese. This chasm widened and remained a fairly constant source of political friction between the two societies arguably until at least the early twenty-first century.

The KMT was so disorganized concerning the takeover on Taiwan that it sent only a small number of soldiers and not its elite forces, which caused great consternation. We should recall that the KMT was militarily weak, not only on mainland China but particularly in Taiwan. It could not fully restore order, so it incorporated local paramilitary groups into its own police troops. This move clearly shows how there was no seamless shift from war to peace.[28] Kamisago Shōshichi had been a military police officer in Taiwan for thirty years. He remembered that in early October about 150 Chinese military police arrived in grand style at Danshui (Tamsui) port, all dressed to the hilt with new equipment, and parading on the quay in a way that puzzled as much as impressed the Taiwanese who watched from the shore.[29] But he added that even though the Chinese troops looked well prepared, the Taiwanese afterward said, "As we thought . . . the Japanese military is better."[30] Kamisago recalled that the initial Taiwanese response to the Chinese military landing was to send their daughters away and shut their houses.[31] A Japanese military report from Taiwan high command to Tokyo in late October 1945 detailed that immediately after the surrender the situation remained calm on the island but then picked up and was marred by a rise in theft and acts against the police. The Japanese military had not yet handed over its weapons, but the Japanese administration was quite concerned about the future of social stability in Taiwan. The Japanese military command also noted that there were thousands of demilitarized individuals in Taiwan, including naval laborers, soldiers, student workers who were employed by the military, injured soldiers, and others, all of whom were now in a predicament. There were also many Taiwanese families arriving at the Japanese military headquarters to request that the Japanese government repatriate their loved ones. The headquarters in Taiwan was forced to get in touch with offices in the Philippines, Indonesia, and other Southeast Asian locales where Taiwanese were frequently dispatched to find out what had happened since news from Tokyo was scarce.[32]

Peng Ming-min recalled his initial reaction to the KMT. Peng came from a wealthy Taiwanese family and was educated in the Japanese language in Taiwan, later traveling to Japan for further study at Tokyo Imperial University. He returned toward the end of the war by way of Nagasaki, where he witnessed the atomic bomb being dropped. Peng was contemptuous of the KMT, perhaps reflective of his Japanese attitudes? He wrote, "Public officials from China proved incompetent and incredibly corrupt, and the rag-tag conscript Nationalist troops were petty thieves, becoming a rabble of scavengers as soon as they came off the ships."[33] In his memoirs he described the terror he felt once order crumbled, hiding with his family, and the lack of certitude about the future.[34] Other KMT officials would criticize the party leaders in similar ways, but Peng reserved his deepest opprobrium for Taiwan's secondary invaders. The world of high-ranking KMT officials, he wrote, was filled with loyalties or enmity based solely on personal relations with "no room for individual dedication to abstract causes as ephemeral as democracy and human rights."[35] Many Taiwanese were also dissatisfied with their continual treatment as second-class citizens after the KMT arrival. KMT party individuals often took over jobs at the top of the food chain, with salaries higher than those of their Taiwanese counterparts.[36]

Regardless of the inner mechanisms of the party, its fractured nature in part probably led to mistaken plans to take over Taiwan.[37] On October 25, 1945, more than two months after Japan's formal surrender, General Chen Yi announced the "return" of Taiwan. Taiwan was being restored to the motherland

and would be administered as a province of China, in some ways reverting back to its Qing dynasty status. The US role in underwriting this return orchestrating the removal of the Japanese was glossed over or ignored.[38]

All of this tension among the various social and political layers had been brewing internally and found a pretext to explode just after February 27, 1947. That evening a Taiwanese widow was selling black market tobacco on the streets of Taipei. Thuggish agents of the Monopoly Bureau discovered her illegal activities and beat her. Passersby formed an angry mob into which an agent fired a warning shot, which killed an onlooker. Fleeing the scene, the agents took shelter in a nearby police station while the mob bayed for justice against the culprits.[39] The next day, things grew worse. The widow was reported to have died. The violent treatment incensed locals, and several thousand converged on the Monopoly Bureau demanding justice in the form of dismissal of the director. Unemployment in the former colony was running at very high levels, and many were struggling to buy food and find work. As the crowd crossed town, a soldier manning a machine gun perched on a government building let loose a volley, killing at least four in the melee.[40] Fighting and looting broke out in Taipei, where martial law was enacted in the afternoon of February 28, as the killings and riots spread across the island. Governor General Chen Yi made a radio appeal, which merely added fuel to the fire. One broadcast said that US diplomats witnessed armed forces killing unarmed civilians in Taipei.[41] The situation continued to escalate, and demands of the government to release those being held pushed forward. On March 9, more Chinese Nationalist troops from the mainland arrived, and the killings continued to spiral upward.[42] One problem stemmed from the KMT's initial overly lax attitude toward the potential for difficulty in administrating Taiwan. Chiang Kai-shek, of course, wanted to keep as many troops as possible on the mainland to bring the civil war to an end. Initially, military leaders dispatched slightly more than five thousand KMT soldiers to the island to keep order, and they were thinly spread out. This was Chen Yi's first miscalculation. The incident had taken him completely by surprise, and by early March he was requesting more troops.[43]

US reports downplayed the potential for the rise of communism in Taiwan because the island had been schooled under Japanese colonialism. US analysts believed that as long as living standards remained high there was little support on the island for communist ideas.[44] However, the KMT, following a pattern South Korean leaders would employ when dealing with internal unrest, blamed a communist insurgency for the incident. George Kerr, a US diplomat in Taipei at the time, said, "Formosan enthusiasm for 'liberation' lasted about six weeks," after which they started calling the KMT governor general a "fat pig."[45]

Widespread looting and a lack of respect from the KMT, the Taiwanese considered, for their private property and belongings quickly led to more friction.

The February 28 Incident might have started out as popular local discontent with KMT brutality against those seen as vulnerable—an old woman selling tobacco in a bad economy. But it quickly transformed into a backlash of deep-seated social discontent with KMT planning and policy. At one point, with the takeover of a radio station, broadcasts were made not in Chinese, a new language for many, but Japanese. The announcements called for everyone to protect themselves and their community. It was, effectively, a call to arms against the KMT. It is hard to determine whether this was done as an appeal to continue the riots, but that would not necessarily have been completely out of context.[46] The movement may have escalated because it allowed Taiwanese young men to feel energized, after the demasculinization of defeat, which they were also not allowed to wallow in or celebrate.[47] The KMT and US authorities believed some of the rumors and news, panicking that there were actual Japanese soldiers in Taiwan helping out.[48] In all likelihood, the February 28 Incident was the result of a tremendous underestimation of the ability of a colonized island to suddenly be retaken by a foreign power with whom the local population had no experience. Hundreds were soon arrested and charged, which meant by 1948 that Taipei Prison was "in part seriously overcrowded with inmates convicted of 'rebellion.'"[49]

Discord and economic riots were not unknown to the KMT, and in other areas of China, unrest was suppressed. On November 30, 1946, an enormous melee erupted in Shanghai between street stall vendors and the police. About seven hundred to eight hundred individuals were arrested, and a violent opposition to the police action grew. This was only slightly before what happened in Taiwan, so what allowed the KMT to regain control relatively more easily in Shanghai than in Taiwan? First, KMT leaders believed or at least espoused the idea that what was happening in Taiwan was a conspiracy of communist agents. The second problem was that in Taiwan the army took over, whereas in Shanghai the mayor did not permit the military police to take action. Consequently, KMT suppression against Taiwanese was more violent and brutal, in part because mainland Chinese forces saw the Taiwanese as individuals who had been supposedly indoctrinated with Japanese imperial education and were thus different.[50]

The Republic of China (ROC) was attempting to take over territory within the former Japanese empire with little preparation. Taiwanese, as colonial subjects within Japan's empire, had spread around East and Southeast Asia by choice and also due to military mobilization. They had taken up positions as guards in POW camps, as doctors, and as administrators in Manchukuo and in south

China. As the empire crumbled, so did their prestige and qualifications to work. Following the outbreak of the February 28 Incident, the ROC government mandated that all Taiwanese who had served in administrative positions in Manchuria would not be eligible for work in official Taiwanese positions, nor would they be eligible to sit for national exams. It was therefore necessary to hide this experience if one sought employment or a new qualification.[51] The British consul in Taiwan, G. R. Tingle, stationed at Danshui (Tamsui), noted that Chinese officials in Taiwan "appear to have been exploiting the island in a high-handed way and to have excluded native Formosans from all higher branches of the administration." This bred deep discontent, Tingle concluded.[52]

The February 28 Incident opened a Pandora's box of excessive KMT responses to a perceived (though sometimes credible) communist threat within Taiwan's borders. This was the tragic situation in Luku Village, a settlement in the northern mountains of Taiwan, midway between Taipei and Keelung City.[53] From December 1952 to March 1953, about ten thousand KMT soldiers surrounded this small village and crushed it for being a communist hive. About 183 villagers were arrested in the Luku Incident. Most were illiterate and worked in very poor conditions in the local coal mines. "In total 36 villagers were executed. A further 97 villagers (including 19 teenagers) were sentenced and imprisoned for a total of 871 years."[54]

KMT general Sun Li-jen was an early supporter of Generalissimo Chiang Kai-shek, but he soon saw the writing on the wall and quickly came to grasp how poorly prepared the KMT was to take over the former colony. Sun had studied at the Virginia Military Institute and spoke excellent English. He was by all accounts a successful military leader during the Chinese civil war, and at one point he was approached by the Americans to depose Chiang. Originally one of Chiang's right-hand men, he grew increasingly depressed about the downward political spiral in Taiwan by the early 1950s. He explained what he saw as a steep decline in the future of the Chinese Nationalist ability to rule: "There is no freedom of speech or press, or rule of law; any deviation from the Party line of thought expressed in any way—brings swift punishment. The Secret Police pick up people without warrant, and they are often shot without trial."[55]

Dealing with Postwar Colonies: Victim or Perpetrator?

The war crimes issue within the ranks of former colonial subjects cuts to the heart of two problems central to identity: Were these young men Taiwanese first, or imperial Japanese? One question that lurks behind the weaponized discontent in the immediate postwar period ties into their confusion concerning how we should consider this mixed colonial past and postwar period.[56]

Hayashi Miki, like many young Taiwanese of his generation, became a POW camp guard. Hayashi completed his training at the Shirakawa Training Grounds. Like many other Taiwanese guards, Hayashi was eventually sent to north Borneo (which had been a British colonial territory), to the Kuching detention camp. Camp guards had duties to keep detainees working or deter them from escaping. The camp eventually moved farther into the jungle as the war worsened, and only when they came back to the village for supplies did they hear news of Japan's surrender. Upon hearing the announcement, his whole body went numb, Hayashi recalled.[57] After the war, he was given a fifteen-year sentence in an Australia war crimes tribunal for maltreating POWs. Often Taiwanese arrested as war criminals saw themselves as double victims—of colonialism and then being tried for participating in imperialism.

What Hayashi did not talk about more explicitly was his role in empire at the Shirakawa camp, which also housed a notoriously brutal Japanese imperial POW camp.[58] Many foreign POWs recalled being shipped through Taiwan to other camps. Taiwan was a vital central depot within the Japanese empire. One glance at a map of imperial oceanic transport demonstrates the importance of Taiwan to Japan's functioning as an empire. Taiwanese guards, and the location of Taiwan as a POW transport hub and the site of numerous labor camps, tell us this.[59]

Jack Edwards, a British POW, spent a hellacious three years in Japanese-owned mines in Taiwan, particularly at Kinkaseki (*Jinguashi* in Chinese), under the management of the Nippon Mining Company. In intimate detail, he described the beatings and the Japanese officers' disinterest in human life.[60] When US troops liberated the camp, Edwards weighed a mere eighty-five pounds. He went back to Asia after liberation and recuperation because he felt it was his duty to testify at court about his maltreatment.[61] Edwards claimed that when he returned to Taiwan after the war to investigate war crimes, he found plans at the Kinkaseki mine. These records, which he included in a translated version in his autobiography, had not been completely burned and instructed the leaders of the camp to kill all the POWs before Japan's surrender. These documents were also presented at the war crimes trial in Hong Kong of the men who had controlled the POW camp. Edwards asserted that he found the only document that was also produced at the Tokyo Trial, which revealed the order to kill POWs at the end of the war.[62]

A problem with the memories of someone who has been victimized is that they do not always correspond to the scene on the ground, regardless of how much we wish it were so. After more careful investigation, the order that Jack Edwards claimed to have found in the burned-out remnants of Kinkaseki in Taiwan was most likely a Japanese imperial military response to a hypothetical situation that was recorded in a journal. It was *not* an official order. There were seemingly orders of a similar kind, often thoughts on paper, but no overall order emanating from imperial headquarters.[63] The masterful collator of the Tokyo Trial records, John Pritchard, is dubious. Pritchard takes a calculated and distanced approach. As he sees it, the problem is one of both provenance of the order and misunderstanding it. He admits that there was a cultural policy of deviance toward POWs, so wanting them dead was easily read into any Japanese document that revealed elements of such a cruel plan. Sadly, Edwards's conspiracy was never supported by volumes of other data, rendering his smoking-gun testimony lukewarm.[64]

However, the issue is complicated by the fact that the murder of Allied POWs did sometimes occur following superior orders. It just was not done necessarily in accordance with a centralized directive and thus was not evidence of a larger Japanese imperial conspiracy. Taiwanese guards, compelled to be the sharp end of imperial punishment at camps throughout Southeast Asia and the South Pacific, recall similar situations. For example, Ke Jingxing was an impoverished young Taiwanese man who joined the Japanese military out of economic need. He trained at the Shirakawa Training Ground in Taiwan and was later sent to Kuching in north Borneo (now the state of Sarawak in Malaysia) as a POW camp guard in 1942.[65] Ke was dispatched to several different work/POW camps and ended up in Labuan, where he oversaw work on an airfield. Toward the end of the war, the teams were split as the war took a turn for the worse, and Ke, along with a small coterie of guards and prisoners, retreated to a place called Miri. In June 1945 they learned that the Allies had come ashore in north Borneo, and their commanding officer gave the order to kill the prisoners. The Taiwanese guards were forced to take arms and shoot the prisoners, or, as Ke recalled, they themselves would surely have been killed. Ke never knew whether the order to shoot the prisoners came from central command or was solely the decision of the local commander. After the war, Ke was charged with war crimes and only returned to Taiwan in 1953.[66] In the face of this oral testimony, no one can deny the atrocities coordinated against Allied POWs. But doubt remains strong against the idea of conspiracy.[67] Japanese businesses did make a profit from POW suffering, and the fact that those conglomerates received postwar compensation, while the POWs were left out in the cold, was a travesty of justice. But, unfortunately, that part of the story does not mean that at the root level of the central government and military a conspiracy existed that gave the imperial order to kill all POWs at war's end.

Aftermath of the Trials

Not only did the KMT continually waffle in its own internal policies toward Taiwanese war criminals, but the Japanese government did too. Tokyo made halfhearted attempts in December 1952 to educate society about creating rest homes for Korean and Taiwanese war criminals—places for these individuals to reside while they waited for transit back to their "own" countries. The idea of empire had now been virtually erased in Japan.[68] There were several rest homes established in Tokyo and at least one in Saitama Prefecture, which was the largest, but all were merely stopgap measures to help the men transit through Japan to their final destination.[69] There was public awareness but less direct public empathy in Japan for those who had fallen into the holes of history.

Where the Japanese public actively clamored for more input was ironically for Taiwanese stories of suffering in war crimes trials at the hands of the Allies. As the Taiwanese transited through Tokyo, copies of the last wills and final words of executed war criminals were folded into the collection of the Japanese bestseller *Last Wills and Testaments of the Century*, published in the early 1950s. This edited volume was a collection of the final declarations written by Japanese soldiers who were executed BC class war criminals. The collection was by no means exhaustive, but it did indicate that many former Taiwanese soldiers believed in themselves as imperial Japanese subjects and did not want to have died in vain. Many of their last writings were included, and Japanese readers snapped up copies. Lin Jinlong was a Taiwanese military laborer who was tried by the United States in Manila and executed on July 17, 1946. He wrote that it was the destiny of young Taiwanese to die on the field of battle, proclaiming, "I have sacrificed myself for imperial Japan and now go to heaven." He wrote to his friends in an April 1946 letter, just after being handed his sentence, that although their assistance had been futile, he appreciated their efforts.[70] Li An, a Taiwanese military laborer from Jiayi, was tried in Guangdong. Li penned a will to his father and said rather stoically, "I swear that I have not broken any national laws. I have a wife and child, no debts. Even though I will be executed, please make sure no one seeks revenge for my death."[71]

Like many of the Taiwanese rounded up in Southeast Asia, Lin Jiangshan was a Taiwanese military laborer executed at Rabaul by an Australian court.

Lin thanked his friends and then wrote that he had given his youth to the nation and his body was destined to be spread on the fields of Rabaul. Then, in a measure out of character with many of the Taiwanese last testaments, Lin followed with a separate message in the Chinese language where he thanked his friends for sending flowers. Their fragrant smell lessened my loneliness, he wrote. "People are like flowers in that no two are alike, at their peak they blossom and then fall to the ground in slumber."[72] Yasuda Muneharu was one of the Taiwanese military laborers put to death by the British at Changi Prison in Singapore. Yasuda had been posted to Malaya and elsewhere since 1942 and was arrested by the Allies on suspicion of having committed torture. "The fact that my destiny has been decided in this way means that I have become a victim of having carried out my duties," Yasuda wrote. He informed his family about his bank account in a Shimonoseki branch back in Japan and asked that they please take out the money. Yasuda also asked his brother to carry on the family name.[73] The fact that these men's final writings were included in a postwar Japanese book to promote sympathy for Japan's lost empire, while failing to investigate the issues of responsibility within the larger population itself, speaks volumes about the manner in which the details of imperial sacrifice were massaged depending on the geography of the postwar narrative.[74]

Jeju, Korea: When Imperial Struggles Bleed into Cold War Conflict

The third incident in the chain of events demonstrating how the fall of Japan imperiled ideas of postwar justice surrounds the manner in which Koreans accepted and took on the mantle of independence. This moment concerns the dark terrain of violence on Jeju Island from April 1948 to May 1949. During this time and after an estimated thirty thousand Koreans were slaughtered by Korean police forces, who believed the island had become a hotbed of communist agitation.[75] Ultimately lasting for seven years, the massacre had harrowing consequences: "one out of every two households in the island became victims of rape, torture or murder."[76]

Jeju Island (sometimes Cheju in English) is now celebrated as the locale of many resorts and the site of international conferences owing to its fine hotels and beaches. But in the middle of the last century it was a poor island off the southwestern tip of the Korean peninsula. This small island saw its population double in size to three hundred thousand people in the immediate period after the end of World War II.[77] Many Koreans were choosing to move back after leaving for employment elsewhere, and others were trying to get away from difficulties on the peninsula, where the looming clouds of civil war kept growing. The situation on Jeju Island was similar to that of Taiwan, where young men had been mobilized and weaponized for imperial war, but after the war they were left hanging with nothing to do and no nation for which to fight. In the interim years after Japan's sudden surrender, fear and discontent mounted. Both the KMT and South Korean forces (along with the Americans) were wary that these incidents might have been the work of fifth column communists, and so they tried to crush such uprisings with a strong and demonstrative military hand. Starting around early April 1948, people rose up in protest against the US-sponsored elections in South Korea and were met with a heavy police presence. Tens of thousands, about one-fifth of the island population, were killed, but as many as forty thousand had fled to Japan and half of the villages on the island had been destroyed. We likely need to use a different word than "incident," because this term downplays the severity of what was at its core a seven-year guerrilla war with counterinsurgency battles.

The number of people killed between October 1948 and February 1949 accounted for a bit more than 60 percent of all deaths. This included children being shot, beheadings, and whole families being wiped out.[78] The US occupation of South Korea generally relied on the police to keep order and deemed homegrown local grassroots groups illegal. This decision was not popular since the police in Korea were seen as a symbol of collaboration with the imperial Japanese. As the Americans began taking measures against the JCP in Japan, they also began crushing the left wing in Korea.[79]

Depending on one's assessment, the Jeju Island Incident was a democratic movement, a popular uprising, a massacre, a riot, or even an anti-American struggle.[80] We must remember that Jeju, like Taiwan, was a demilitarized zone of the former Japanese imperial periphery, and many young men had been trained, had access to weapons, and were suddenly left rootless with the end of empire. Indeed, the Jeju Incident was not inevitable but rather an unfortunate outgrowth of the process of de-imperialization. Those involved had put forward little preparation for different former imperial elements coming into contact with each other.

In response, a general strike against police violence was called. As with post-imperial violence in Taiwan, there was a cultural and psychological divide on Jeju between native islanders and more recent arrivals from the Korean peninsula. The majority of the police force was from the Korean mainland, and the islanders kept themselves distant. The Communist Party was present and did inspire protests, so it was not a fiction as the KMT had tried to pretend in Taiwan. In May 1948, the UN managed the first free elections in South Korea. Less than half a year later, in November, South Korean president Synghman

Rhee declared martial law on Jeju Island and deployed a large number of Korean military forces to restore order.

Until the late 1980s, the Jeju Incident, like the February 28 Incident in Taiwan, was mainly depicted as a communist rebellion. However, since the democratization of South Korea in 1987, Jeju is now conceived as more of a popular uprising. More responsibility is put on Korean and US misrule and oppression. In parallel with the subsequent decades-long amnesia of similar events in Taiwan, South Koreans placed initial blame on President Rhee, who greatly relied on those who had collaborated with imperial Japan–aligned individuals for stability and support of his administration. In 1948, a special Korean court was established to investigate Japanese collaboration, and within several months the tribunal had opened 682 cases. Rhee said the court was pro-communist and used this label elsewhere and a fear of communism to suppress these sorts of investigations. A brief moment of light appeared in 1960 when students wished to pursue the truth, but the 1961 Park Chung-hee coup and his rule until his assassination in 1978 meant that repression and historical amnesia reigned until the later 1980s. Again, almost coterminous with Taiwanese historical redressing of past wrongs, it is only in the twenty-first century that South Korea has come face to face with its domestic litany of repression and atrocities.[81]

Postimperial Violence: What Does It Signify?

In all three incidents in Japan, Taiwan, and Korea newly enfranchised forces were bent on putting down what were essentially partially demobilized societies that until recently had contained large bands of young and weaponized Japanese imperial youths. Sometimes these groups had been connected to the imperial military but not necessarily. It is, perhaps, a gross oversimplification, but the example of South Korean autocrat Park Chung-hee helps fill in many gaps for this era. A young member of the Japanese empire, Park studied Japanese imperial military science, joined the ranks, and then rose through the staff of the South Korean military. Park's most recent biographer in English noted the difficulty in assessing Park's legacy in relation to contemporary attitudes in East Asia. "That a Korean young man in the 1940s could find his 'true self' in the IJA [Imperial Japanese Army] or Manchurian officer corps does not rest well today with Korean nationalist sentiment that tends to equate being true to one's Korean self at the time with being anti-Japanese, and joining the imperial officer corps equivalent to betraying the Korean nation."[82]

Regardless of how they positioned themselves after the war, toward the end of World War II both Korean and Taiwanese men were being drafted and trained for the imperial Japanese armed forces. These incidents tell us that far from being suddenly over, the postwar period within East Asia and throughout areas that Japan previously controlled was affected by two major issues. First, the primary problem of how to expel the Japanese from various colonized or occupied lands remained a conundrum since this was either accomplished through violence or dependent on assistance from former colonial powers, such as the case with Indochina. The second major obstacle was how to establish independent and sovereign rule in the frequent absence of experience or ability. The question of how to repatriate the Japanese from their entrenched positions as imperial leaders was also far from easy, especially given that many of the former European colonial powers wished to gain a quick upper hand in "restoring" order, and many of those internal leaders retained connections with their own imperial past, or defined themselves by their opposition to it.

Even with the economic rise and growing importance of contemporary China, the region's understanding of its own past and its internal dynamics remain deeply rooted in the contours of the manner in which World War II ended. These narratives became exceedingly important to the rise of numerous leaders and served as ballast for their authority. While the KMT and other political parties in East Asia did not necessarily maintain a sharp focus on their 1945 victory over the Japanese military as propaganda fodder for their contemporary political ideology, for many groups it is still an element of their founding ethos. These stories are often linked to the process of how Japanese imperial rule was dismantled at the local level, often by those who had opposed Japan but also by collaborators. Japan's sudden surrender in no way signified that the country would immediately disavow its extensive imperial ideology. The same could be said for former Japanese occupied lands, which suffered as much trauma in trying to recover their claims to political authority as they did while pursuing justice against their former Japanese overlords and those they defined as national "traitors."

The Korean War Interlude and Prisoner Repatriation

The Jeju Incident was not the end of violence on the Korean peninsula that was related to the end of empire. This continuation of instability in the wake of Japanese imperial dissolution would cast a long shadow on Korea, mainland Chinese society, and Taiwan for years to come. Within a few years of the start of the Korean War in the summer of 1950, a nearby island would face extremes of military violence, only this time between feuding bands of Chinese POWs.[83] Koje Island (Geoje) was smaller and closer to the Korean coast than its larger brother island Jeju. It was also the site of deep discord among captured Chinese prisoners and was representative of political fissures the Japanese empire had unleashed but never reconciled. The distinguished Japanese scholar Wada Haruki called the Korean War "unfinished," and part of the triggering mechanism was linked to the fall of the Japanese empire. When Japan's empire crumbled, the moment for reconciliation with Korea as a former colony was ripe. Unfortunately, Japan did little and ignored the potential problems. As Wada carefully notes, the end of the Japanese empire, sadly, did not bring peace to Asia, though strangely it did bring more stability to the Japanese islands where the military had ceased engagement with the world since 1945.[84] Hirano Ryūji goes further, suggesting that the origins of the Korean War can more likely be traced back to divisions within Korean armed forces—between those that were trained in Japanese and Manchukuo military academies and those who were educated by the communists as partisans against Japan's imperial project. After 1945, they merely relocated their geographic struggle from Manchuria to the Korean peninsula.[85] The Korean War has also been understood as a proxy war between the USSR and the United States, a civil war, and "a northeast Asia war."[86] Regardless of how we define this war, Japan's demise ushered in this shift to a new regional order. In short, for many inhabitants of East Asia—Chinese, Taiwanese, Koreans across the peninsula and Japanese abroad—"news of Japan's surrender marked only a momentary hiatus in their continuing experience of war."[87]

In the summer of 1950, under the leadership of Kim Il Sung, North Korea invaded the south and set off a vicious civil war that further engulfed the peninsula for three years. The Chinese had been prepped for the situation, and "on October 8, 1950, Mao ordered the formation of the Chinese People's Volunteers Army (CPV)." The name was a misnomer because the Chinese "troops consisted of PLA [People's Liberation Army] veterans, 'liberated' former Nationalist troops, and some new recruits."[88] Within a matter of months an enormous deployment of slightly more than twenty-one thousand Chinese communist "voluntary" soldiers had surrendered, been vanquished, or just caved in to the United Nations' forces.[89]

Very soon thereafter, Koje Island became a fierce battleground surrounding the destiny of these Chinese POWs. Both sides—the United States and the PRC—dug in their heels concerning the right of POWs to choose their preferred country of repatriation. The PRC wanted all Chinese prisoners returned to the Chinese mainland. Representing "free China" or the Chinese Nationalists' interest, the United States wanted to allow the Chinese soldiers to choose the ROC (the island of Taiwan) if they wished. So contentious was this issue that negotiations were one of the main stumbling blocks in reaching an armistice and arguably delayed the end of violence for close to two years. Both the United States and China inclined to employ POW repatriation for their own political ends, and neither was willing to concede. Admiral C. Turner Joy, who fronted efforts for the United States with PLA officials during the Korean War negotiations, noted that the Chinese communists had a hatred of Chiang Kaishek "so intense as to border on psychotic."[90]

Ultimately, two-thirds of the approximately twenty-one thousand Chinese POWs detained during the Korean War chose to "repatriate" to Taiwan even if most had not originated from there. Huang Tiancai, a Taiwanese interpreter who worked at the front lines and in the POW camps during the Korean War, recalled the stories of numerous Chinese prisoners he interrogated. Many related sad tales of originally being Chinese Nationalist soldiers but later being folded into the PRC volunteer army after the KMT's defeat. In actuality, both sides intimated that they constantly faced discrimination within prisoner ranks.[91]

This larger group of Chinese prisoners, who chose Taiwan over the PRC, was a public relations coup for the United States and "free China," as the ROC would now emphasize. The ones who returned to the ROC were called anticommunist heroes, and nationalist Chinese celebrated the return of soldiers who had never before set foot in the new "motherland."[92] In late January 1954, the *People's Daily*, the mouthpiece of the CCP, published an angry article that ranted against the supposed US perversion of justice of allowing the prisoners to go where they wanted. The newspaper criticized the exploitation of POWs in this way and added that this "allows the world to clearly see that the US uses the fresh blood of prisoners of war to dress up its signage that America stands for a belief in human rights."[93] Appealing to ideas of international justice and recalling the "court of justice" that had pursued the "German fascists" after World War II, the newspaper was adamant that the world would see through this supposed US propaganda effort and not permit it to go unanswered.[94]

By contrast, POW repatriates on the mainland did not receive the same hospitality from Chinese communists. While the PRC castigated the US and ROC plan to repatriate the larger share of Chinese prisoners, the seven thousand or so soldiers who chose repatriation to communist China faced unforeseen difficulties. Their fate was ironically similar to what their defeated former enemy Japanese forces had met with on their return to the home islands of Japan. The PRC leadership was fully capable of maintaining two contradictory policies toward its domestic prisoners. One policy was aimed at the KMT officers already in its prisons. The other was a massive reeducation and active propaganda strategy it implemented against returning Chinese POWs from the Korean War. The policies were by no means always in opposition, but neither were they unified. When the former POWs returned to China from Korea, instead of being welcomed with celebratory parades for their war sacrifices, "they faced a disheartening situation. Forced confession, persecution, punishment, and humiliation turned the former 'war heroes' into enemies of the state."[95] The major problem surrounded the fact that regardless of all the rhetoric, at its core the Chinese communist military did not believe that captured soldiers remained loyal. These prisoners were considered suspect and needed to prove themselves to reenter PRC society.[96]

China's POW policy in the Korean War was important because the PRC was a newly minted country, and so how it managed its POW policy would have a direct impact on the international image of the nation.[97] The war was the frontier between old China and the potential new China—if it could eke out a victory, or at least claim it. And, all this was taking place at the same time as investigation offices in Fushun and Taiyuan were digging into Japanese war crimes and considering what to do with the KMT POWs. The new Chinese People's Volunteer Army had slightly reworked the PLA military pledge into something resembling the Japanese imperial credo. The new code stated that soldiers "would rather die than become a POW."[98] When these Chinese POWs returned from Korea, they were first debriefed under a new agency, the Repatriates Management Agency. The released prisoners stayed in this repatriation camp for three months, educating themselves and writing up confessions. In some ways, their treatment mirrored similar processes forced on KMT prisoners after the Chinese civil war and the investigations that had been undertaken for Japanese war criminals to assess their guilt. The Repatriates Management Agency implemented procedures that "went through four phases of study sessions: political verification and education, confession, reassessment, and reassignment."[99] He Ming, a repatriated POW, noted the negative Chinese social attitudes toward former prisoners from the Korean War. "Many people believed that if you were not injured, or if you did not resist and just raised your hands that this was all a form of surrender. Many colleagues even said in their own confessions to the investigation committees that they 'selfishly clung to life and feared death so were taken prisoner and surrendered.'"[100] Those sorts of ideas were prevalent. Antipathy within postwar Chinese society toward Korean War vets ran deep enough that even though these men were eventually allowed to reenter society, most still could not join the party and were discriminated against in job prospects. It was not until the 1980s, along with the reinstatement of the rule of law in China, that many were rehabilitated to full pensions and rights.

Chapter 7

The Geography of Power

Producing Political Legitimacy in Republican China

On a partially cloudy summer day on June 17, 1947, a massive Chinese crowd in Shanghai surged forward to witness the executions of two Japanese former imperial officers: Captain Yonemura Haruki and Sergeant Shimota Jirō. Yonemura was known as the "wolf of Changshu," a city in the vicinity of Suzhou, Jiangsu Province. Chinese newspapers and the foreign press labeled Shimota the "tiger of Jiangyin," a city in the same region. The two men's arms were tied tightly behind their bodies, and long, thin wooden signboards pinched their shoulders back and forced their bodies awkwardly upright. Each sign, written by hand in black ink Chinese characters, jutted upward several feet above their heads and detailed the soldier's crimes and the military order that they were to be executed by pistol. The two detainees departed from the Chinese prison, located in the former run-down Jewish refugee sector of the city, in an open-bed military truck, provided by the US government. The large truck, crammed with guards, lazily led the prisoners in a sort of tragic parade from Ward Road Jail, through the city streets, and to the outskirts of town, finally stopping at the execution grounds. This was a conscious choice of political and propaganda expediency because the Ward Road Jail had its own internal execution grounds. These two Japanese officers, however, were specifically taken outside of city limits and publicly executed as a moment of cathartic theater for the masses. Nearly five years earlier, the Japanese imperial army had used these same Kiangwan (Jiangwan in contemporary Chinese transliteration) grounds to execute a handful of US soldiers who had been crew members in the famous 1942 Doolittle air raid on Tokyo.

In the 1930s Ward Road was the largest prison in the world. It was notorious for not allowing those incarcerated to speak, and disease and desperation ran rampant. No one had ever escaped from Ward Road. Following the end of World War II, the jail was managed briefly by the Americans and used to incarcerate Japanese and other war criminals. Later, the Chinese Nationalists recouped it to house more suspected Japanese war criminals and Chinese communists who were already fomenting trouble as a Chinese civil war loomed. Finally, after 1949, when the Chinese communists took over leadership of mainland China, the communists used the jail to incarcerate those they labeled as counterrevolutionaries. More often than not these individuals were the previous Chinese Nationalist administrators, along with others. Grumbling over the capitalist name of the former foreign jail, communist leader Mao Zedong finally renamed the prison Tilanqiao Prison (Basket Bridge Prison), based on its location.[1]

At the time of the executions, World War II in East Asia had been over for almost two years, but the mob in arguably one of China's most important former international cities, Shanghai, wanted blood. Men dressed in their daily garb of a long outer coat and Western-style hat jostled with police officers and peasant women, all sporting smiles. The *West Australian* newspaper described the crowds as "jeering" and wrote that "some spat and even threw garbage," straining forward to see the delivery of capital punishment and baying as they followed former imperial officers to their end.[2] Some Japanese captives chose to receive a tranquilizer before the moment of execution; others were more stoic.[3] Yonemura had ordered the live burial of more than one hundred Chinese. Shimota was charged with murdering several Chinese on the day of surrender. After both men were shot, Chinese newspapers pressed graphic photos of their executed corpses dripping with blood.

The war crimes trials and subsequent executions of these two men were big news in immediate postwar China and reverberated somewhat in Japan, but they mostly went ignored elsewhere and certainly few paid attention in the West. News teletype wires twitched more excitedly with the events of seven executions more than a year later, near Christmas Day 1948. On that day, the main imperial Japanese military leaders and one former prime minister were held responsible for Japan's aggressive war in Asia. In Sugamo Prison, Tokyo, their sentence was death by hanging.

The executions of these seven Japanese leaders in Tokyo were of such importance that the full Tokyo Trial judgment, all 1,200 lengthy and legally cumbersome pages of it, was read in open court November 4–12, 1948, in what naval officer William Sebald, political adviser to General MacArthur during the occupation of Japan, called a "wearisome ceremony."[4] The death sentences were handed down on November 12, 1948, but the date for the execution was decided in secret and delayed until a few days before its final implementation in late December. The US occupiers wanted to avoid any public rallies or demonstrations of support for the accused Japanese. On December 23, 1948, in a much less public manner than the Chinese chaos of justice that was pursued in Shanghai, the Americans executed the leaders the Tokyo Trial charged with Class A war crimes, or "crimes against peace." For their evening meal prior to execution, the prisoners dined simply on rice, miso soup, and grilled fish. General Tōjō Hideki and three others were escorted downstairs to the ground floor at 11:30 p.m.

William Sebald was officially present at the executions, having been ordered to stand as a witness, and reminisced that at 11:50 p.m. the Allied observers entered a well-lit room and "faced a long wooden platform, over which were suspended five ropes, each ending in a noose." Sebald said that outside the door he could hear "banzai," what he described as the traditional ceremonial Japanese yell "used to express triumph, joy, sorrow or resignation."[5] Hanayama Shinshō, chief Buddhist priest of the Sugamo Prison, recalled that the men proclaimed three times in a loud chorus "Long live the Emperor" and "Long live the Japanese Empire!" Then he gave each prisoner a sip of wine and offered them a biscuit. All but General Matsui Iwane declined because they had already removed their various dental fittings.[6] The first four men entered seconds after midnight, all muttering what Sebald suspected were Buddhist prayers. All the prisoners were wearing US military clothing that was sizes too big and devoid of any insignia. "It helped to make them all look old, very old, helpless, pitiful, and tragic," Sebald said.[7] The accused mounted the platform, nooses were placed around their necks, and black hoods were fitted over their heads. One word, "proceed," was given, and all the prisoners simultaneously dropped through the trap doors below their feet.

Hanayama Shinshō recollected the moment of execution walking from the death chamber back to his cleric's office, from which he had ushered the condemned men. "I heard a banging sound behind me and when I looked at my watch it was one minute past midnight," he wrote.[8] The second group of three prisoners soon followed suit and were executed at twenty past midnight. A doctor attended to the prisoners quickly, using a stethoscope to listen to their hearts, and officially declared them deceased. As Sebald wrote, the prisoners' bodies, which included men who only a few years prior had been at the apex of power in the Japanese empire, were cremated and their ashes were distributed to an undisclosed location so that they could not become martyrs later on, even though that did occur to a certain extent. The US officer Sebald, who had spent time in Japan in the 1920s and 1930s, only to depart during the uptick in militarization in 1939, observed that he was humbled by the Tokyo executions. The somber scene in Tokyo was quite different from the cacophonous executions in Shanghai. Sebald detailed, "These men, who had wielded such enormous power and influence, died secretly and alone, surrounded by former enemies. There was something inexorable in this finale, for the mode of death, not the fact of death, was impressive to fatalistic Japanese."[9]

But even as the Tokyo Trial came to completion, the US occupiers were closing up shop on further war crimes trials, and this irritated their Chinese colleagues. On December 25, 1948, the KMT-led *Shenbao* newspaper castigated General MacArthur's decision to release nineteen not-yet-charged Class A war criminals.[10] Several days later, Tokyo Trial judge Mei Ruao announced his displeasure at the release of these suspected Class A war criminals, which included former foreign minister Amō Eiji, Minister of Munitions Kishi Nobusuke, founding member of the ultranationalist Black Dragon Society Kuzuu Yoshihisa, and others. Mei said that these men had committed crimes against the Chinese and had been arrested, so they should be handed over to China. The USSR also opposed the release of these Class A war criminals and opined this was the beginning of the end of Allied cooperation on high-level war crimes trials.[11]

The postwar adjudication of wartime responsibility did not see all Japanese trussed up, paraded in front of execution grounds, or even put to death in somewhat secretive locations as the clock struck midnight. Many key figures of Japan's imperial and collaborationist administrations both in Japan and throughout the former empire managed to evade capture and punishment altogether. For these individuals, the end of war evolved into a story not about an execution but about continuity from the war to the postwar. This third category tells us as much about the pursuit or failure of finding justice at the end of the war as it does about serendipity and being in the right place at the right time. According to most accounts, Japanese colonel Tsuji Masanobu, although monomaniacal and convinced of his own military greatness, was responsible for countless atrocities in Singapore and elsewhere in Southeast Asia. He should have been arrested and put on trial for war crimes. However, Tsuji was a master spy, and at the moment of Japan's surrender, he dropped his imperial Japanese military kit, donned the saffron robe of a Thai Buddhist priest, and slipped into the shadows of a religious pilgrim. He remained essentially untouched and unrecognized until his reappearance in Japan later. He returned to Japan before the end of the US occupation in 1952 but remained incognito, relying on the help of friends, right-wing financial backers, and his own cunning. Tsuji had fled China at the end of the war and journeyed around Southeast Asia to arrive back in Japan, where he published a self-aggrandizing account of the exciting details of his adventures and his attempts to supposedly help East and Southeast nationalist groups push for independence against European recolonization in the immediate postwar period. In 1950, these exploits were published in *My Long Underground Escape*, which quickly became a bestseller in Japan.[12] Advertisements in Japanese newspapers at the time trumpeted the electrifying details one would learn from Tsuji's journey of escape and eagerly proclaimed, "Looking death in the face 7 times while crossing 4 frontiers—the thrilling and tumultuous secret story of the defeat."[13]

Unlike other high-ranking officers who were executed on a damp field outside of Shanghai or alone in a bright cell in Tokyo, Tsuji evaded capture and then mesmerized the Japanese public with his alleged insights gained while on his lengthy quest to repatriate undetected. It was too late for the occupation authorities to charge him, even if evidence could have been procured, but Tsuji also banked on his notoriety for later success. In 1952, he was elected as a representative to Japan's lower house and later the upper house. He obviously managed to dupe many, and for a time even the CIA tried to reel him in as an intelligence agent. However, according to their own analysis, they realized that "Tsuji is the type of man who, given the chance, would start World War III without any misgivings."[14] In August 1952, addressing a large crowd in Kanazawa, Tsuji announced "Truman is the number one war criminal and Stalin the number two war criminal."[15] Apropos of war crimes, he was also quoted as saying, "Although America may find it hard to forget Pearl Harbor, Japan finds it more difficult to forget Hiroshima and Nagasaki."[16] He died under mysterious circumstances while on a personal trip to meet Ho Chi Minh in Vietnam in 1961.

The globalization of law and the internationalization of norms advanced quickly in the early 1940s, mainly in London, which centered on discussions among exiled governments fleeing Nazi oppression. China was part of these debates. This global moment, in part, also emerged from parallel debates around the world, all slowly propping up the ideal that law could resolve political debacles. This was not only a point made among liberal democracies and their representatives in London, but a global set of new opinions.[17]

This global conversation about jurisprudence and the laws of war was not limited to the West. The USSR produced key players who pushed at the edges of redefining the idea of crimes against peace. A well-known Soviet legal theorist and judge, Aron Trainin, produced the doctrine of complicity and helped formulate the concept of crimes against peace. Soviet prosecutor Andrey Vyshinsky, the man responsible for Stalin's great purge trials of the 1930s, promoted new ideals of Soviet legal doctrine. This could be considered doubly ironic since it was likely that some of Vyshinsky's ideas about justice were dubious to say the least. But, concerning the issue of war and international law, Soviet legal minds early on pressed the idea that aggressive war should be considered a Class A war crime. The result of this international groundswell of opinion about war crimes was the establishment of the United Nations War Crimes Commission on October 20, 1943. The committee comprised seventeen of the Allied nations, including the Chinese, and eventually also created a subcommittee in Chongqing, China (the wartime capital of the Chinese Nationalist Party), to track Japanese war crimes. Essentially, the UNWCC managed an international discussion that widened the purview of not only what could be defined as a war crime but also what would be pursued in a court of law. "Until 1939, legal theory maintained that war crimes must be dealt with in military courts, or in civilian courts applying the laws of war—a line the British Foreign Office still adhered to during the 1940s—and could only involve cases which had been committed within a state's own territory or against its nationals." Obviously, the establishment of the UNWCC demonstrated a significant change in international thinking and greatly expanded the idea of borders in which legal jurisdiction could be applied.[18]

One of the main differences between the Class A Tokyo Trial and its sister trials around the region was tedium. The Tokyo Trial dragged on for two and a half years, and to echo the words of famed journalist Rebecca West, who covered the Nuremberg Trial, "the courtroom was a citadel of boredom."[19] BC class war crimes trials, by contrast, were generally short, and sometimes they were held in the very venues where only months before Allied soldiers had been incarcerated or abused, and so theirs were the sites of legal retribution. But despite being dull, the trials still galvanized Japanese public opinion, and the Chinese needed to consider this. Take, for example, what happened after the executions of the Class A Japanese war criminals. On the afternoon of December 24, 1948, a Buddhist ceremony of remembrance was supposed to be held at the Aoyama Funeral Home. Hanayama Shinshō, who had been the main cleric at Sugamo Prison and had ministered to the seven guilty men in their last moments, had planned to preside at this public event.

The *Yomiuri Newspaper* announced on the morning of December 24 that a remembrance ceremony would be held.[20] The newspaper reported that the event would be led by Hanayama and that the widow of Tōjō Hideki and other surviving family members would be in attendance. At the last moment, occupation authorities canceled the event, but people started to gather anyway.

By 2:30 that afternoon more than one thousand people had gathered, some traveling from afar to pay their respects. An *Asahi Newspaper* car pulled up with Hanayama inside, and he told some of those gathered that SCAP had canceled the day's events. Then, perhaps to disperse the crowd, Hanayama wrangled up a few priests, and together they performed a brief ceremony and placed the deceased spirit tablets with the executed leaders' posthumous names on them at the site. Relatives of General Doihara Kenji had also shown up so they all went to a coffee shop and chatted. Policeman in plainclothes were present but did not directly intervene. About 4.30pm the whole event finished and everyone departed.[21]

KMT War Crimes Trials, 1946–1949

As the Tokyo Trial was getting under way, the Chinese domestic adjudication of hundreds of their own Japanese prisoners was also unfolding. The latter, however, followed a different set of political goals. Even before General Okamura Yasuji, the Japanese imperial army's last commander in China, met with his Chinese counterparts and laid down his arms, Chinese Nationalist Party leader Generalissimo Chiang Kai-shek's radio broadcast in August 1945 had ordered the Chinese people to be benevolent toward the Japanese and not seek retribution. Chiang exhorted his countrymen to repay malevolence with benevolence. His mix of Confucian ethics, Christian teachings, and political savvy made for a very effective policy toward the recently defeated Japanese.

The Chinese trials of Japanese war crimes were at worst a microcosm reflecting the horrors of the Japanese empire and at best a record of how the stated aims of the war were actually experienced at the local level. Consequently, Chinese adjudication of Japanese soldiers demonstrates two facets of the postwar period: First, it reveals how the Japanese behaved during their imperial reign, because the trials recorded a trail of atrocities that came to light. Second, the trials signified the manner in which China attempted to appropriate power in the aftermath of surrender, to the extent possible, by following the model of using law and order to gain international respect from the other Allies.

We need to think about the difference between the aims of the Tokyo Trial and what the KMT was doing. The Tokyo Trial was led mostly by the United States, and thus its sights were focused on POWs and how the war with the West was on a different timeline than what happened in China. This was a key reason China tried to use the charge of crimes against peace against several defendants in the beginning, because the nature of the war in China was different from how Japan's war against the West evolved. In China, it was mostly midlevel Japanese imperial officers whose careers were centered on China who plotted and commanded the series of assassinations and incidents that developed organically over a period of years as Japan slowly gobbled up China beginning in the early 1930s. Against the United States, Japan's policy to go to war was a cabinet-level decision of government and the highest-ranking officers, so that is who the United States pursued for war responsibility. However, for China, those who designed the invasion and "conspiracy" against China were a different class. China was also now independent after the war. So, what to do? China would allow the United States to take the yeoman's share of Class A glory, and then it would try to push its own interpretation of who was responsible for the war. This plan demonstrates the difficulty of trying to let the Tokyo Trial stand for the closure of several war theaters that were of an entirely different nature. There were key differences among the Chinese trials as well. Nanjing was the seat of postwar KMT power once the capital returned there in May 1946, so it was important to have trials with more public impact there. Most defendants for trials in Nanjing were transferred from other sites or Japan, but in other cases, adjudication of justice took place in venues that were closer to where the war criminal was originally captured or arrested.[22]

A Republic of China committee meeting concerning how to deal with Japanese war criminals discussed the aims of war crimes trial procedures for the KMT. Present at the October 25, 1946, meeting, among others, were Bai Chongxi, head of the Ministry of Defense; Yang Zhaolong, head of the criminal section of the Ministry of Justice; and Wang Shijie, who represented the Foreign Ministry. The meeting pushed the idea of how to showcase the spirit of Chinese benevolence toward the Japanese war criminals. Those gathered at the meeting acknowledged that China, at the time, was short on legal expertise in international law, so the goal needed to center on "preventing trials that would be judged poorly by international standards." A secondary goal was speed to further highlight the goal of benevolence through all the trials. The aim was to conduct the investigations and finalize charges within a year. But if this could not be achieved, then a decision would be made not to indict and to release those prisoners to repatriate. The KMT wanted to avoid requesting that those being tried in the Tokyo Trial stand trial a second time. The pay for most clerks at these trials was very low, the report noted, and had a great influence on the work done. Thus, there was a dire need to find a way to improve salaries. The committee also observed that those imprisoned were not in good health, likely due to cold or sickness, and the conditions in the prisons needed to improve.[23]

At the outset, Chinese jurisdiction for the trials was shared among a number of competing government sections, and there was little uniformity. This sort of legal game of *Go*, in which lawyers, defendants, prosecutors, and diplomats moved around a geographic area, was a complex matrix of events, ideas, locations, and people. Various authorities around East Asia vied to arrest and prosecute the same Japanese war criminal, at times even sharing information and collaborating. At the same time, particularly in many cases that took place within Japan's home islands, key figures also obstructed the pursuit of justice for more nationalist aims. These linkages among the trials in the form of the movement of ideas and people had a major influence on exactly what sort of postwar cases arrived in courts all throughout East Asia.

When Justice Gets Misplaced

As mentioned in chapter 1, the "hundred-man killing contest," the archetype of a heinous Japanese war crime against the Chinese, involved a Japanese newspaper touting the supposed December 1937 actions of two Japanese low-ranking officers, Mukai Toshiaki and Noda Tsuyoshi. The wartime Japanese media broadcast the story that the two concocted a competition to see who could slay one hundred Chinese on the military campaign toward the city of Nanjing. Whether the incident actually happened remains dubious for several reasons, including the disputed details, the language used in the Japanese news articles, the actual rank of the two men in the imperial army, the fact that Japanese military swords do not have the tensile strength to kill that many people in one stroke, and numerous other unsavory reasons.[24] The Japanese press at the time was far from honest, and the "media's fixation on kill-counts both dehumanized the enemy into an abstract numerical figure and transformed battlefield violence into a modern game with outcomes easy for readers to compare, classify, and track."[25] In a sense, Japan was drunk on its propaganda euphoria regarding its expanding military might. The late November to early December 1937 siege of Nanjing witnessed a Japanese media whirlwind of exaggerated exploits by individual soldiers highlighted as propaganda. These came to symbolize aggressive Japanese imperial warfare tactics and a hatred of the Chinese.

The hundred-man killing contest has led a vibrant, if not checkered, historical life as a war crimes trial. The trial was closely linked with the Nanjing Massacre in general and has the patina of legal precedent because the two Japanese were found guilty at a postwar Nanjing court in 1947, regardless of the contrived nature of the evidence. Because this event received prominent press at the time, it was sanctified as a legal fact in a Chinese court. The "contest" has gained stature as a pillar of modern Chinese history in the war against Japanese aggression, as it is termed on the mainland.[26] By contrast, Japanese textbooks usually do not discuss the incident in any fashion, either real or imagined. While this incident remains burned into the memories of Chinese schoolchildren, because of the education system, it also enflames public passion in Japan in a contrary way. In the early 1970s, Japanese journalist Honda Katsuichi brought the "killing contest" story back to life in postwar Japan with his interviews of Chinese who had supposedly been at the scene.[27] In 2003, descendants of the two Japanese soldiers executed for the "contest" sued several publishers along with Honda for defamation of character. In 2006, a Japanese court rejected the plaintiff's argument and pronounced that even if they were uncomfortable with their families' history, they could not prove the incident did not occur. Many now believe that the event was at least a partial fabrication by Japanese news companies at the time. This was a fairly confusing decision but turned on the fact that what the Japanese court was analyzing was not the veracity of the historical atrocity but whether any narrative of it was libelous to the reputations of the two executed Japanese soldiers.[28]

On December 18, 1947, the Nanjing military tribunal opened against Noda and Mukai. The KMT government blanketed the city of Nanjing with large posters of the verdict on January 27, 1948. The government announced that the men had been found guilty of killing Chinese POWs and unarmed civilians, according to evidence provided in court. At noon on January 28 the sentence of death would be carried out at the Yuhuatai execution site, on the outskirts of Nanjing.[29] Today, Yuhuatai is a national park that houses memorials for Chinese communists executed there during the KMT purges of communists and those who died during the civil war. No mention is made about the same grounds being used to execute Japanese war criminals in the immediate postwar period. At this large public site outside of Nanjing, the supremacy of CCP victimhood trumps the desire to discuss or memorialize Japanese war crimes—the historical thread there has been severed, unlike with the courtroom museum of CCP trials up north in Shenyang or the Lijixiang comfort women museum in Nanjing.

Another reason this story regained traction in China was because of the wall-to-wall coverage of Gao Wenbin as one of the few remaining legal staff members of the Tokyo Trial. When historical analyses of the Tokyo Trial were reinvigorated in China after 2011, Gao was the go-to interviewee until he passed away in 2020 at the ripe age of ninety-nine. He had been sent in May 1946 to provide English translation at the Tokyo Trial. In the postwar period, contrary to our assumption that the hundred-man killing contest must have repulsed Chinese in and around Nanjing and thus aroused passions for justice, Gao's recollection suggests otherwise. The pursuit of these defendants appears much more happenstance and due to his intervention and the chance that he came across this story while in Japan looking for evidence of Japanese atrocities during the Tokyo Trial. He found, ironically, what he was looking for in Japanese newspapers.[30] Was the pursuit of Chinese justice really this haphazard, or was it more methodical, as others have tried to suggest? For example, Gao Wenbin first served as a translator and then later as an assistant to the Chinese prosecutor at the Tokyo Trial, Xiang Zhejun. Gao's placement was significant but serendipitous for the evolution of what came to be a symbolic war crimes trial in China. His story helps us understand the linkages between the Class A trial in Tokyo and the BC class cases that were managed on the Chinese mainland. Gao, in several postwar revelations and in a story that has gained attention over the past decade in the Chinese press, claims that he was the catalyst for uncovering the hundred-man killing contest after reading the Japanese newspaper article about it during the immediate postwar period.[31]

War Responsibility and War Crimes Trials—the Search for Justice

The problem with war and war crimes is that nationality and the action of the crime do not heed state boundaries. Not only did the US military dispatch war crimes investigation teams to China—to pursue the Shanghai war crimes trials against those who had harmed US military soldiers, and arguably US interests—but so did the British. Letters from the British embassy in Nanjing on August 1, 1946, informed the Chinese about the British war crimes investigation groups. Some of those on the team were police officers who had worked in Shanghai before the war when it was an international city. They asked for Chinese understanding and assistance, particularly when trying to gain access to former Japanese military police agents, *kempeitai*.[32] Of particular interest to the British was what happened at Bridge House, in Shanghai. The British authorities wanted a list of Japanese who had worked at this prison so that they could be judged.[33] The British Foreign Office requested Chinese assistance, and in Shanghai the British established the 9th War Crimes Investigation Team.[34]

To get a personal feel for how nationalist China competed in this milieu, I interviewed Li Zhiqun, daughter of Shanghai military tribunal clerk Li Yechu. She was very energetic and talkative, telling us a lot about her father's life and how he had taken part in the trials of two infamous Japanese war criminals, Yonemura Haruki and Shimota Jirō (whose executions were detailed at the beginning of this chapter). Li Zhiqun explained that her father had recounted to her the details of the parade of the two Japanese officers around town in the truck on the way to their execution. The vehicle was surrounded by such large crowds that Li Yechu had to keep slapping the side of the truck, loudly yelling at people to let the vehicle pass. His daughter said that on their way through the city the mob threw all sorts of things at the Japanese prisoners. It was certainly not "civilized," she said, and her dad had to continually remonstrate the crowds. Li Zhiqun quoted her father as saying, "I told everyone to control their emotions. I slammed the door with my hand, and my watch eventually broke."[35] The parade of the prisoners had departed at 3:15 p.m. from the prison and they arrived at the execution site at 4:45 p.m., according to the *Zhonghua ribao* newspaper.[36]

Li Yechu tried to assume some of the blame for having created a public disturbance where throngs of unruly Chinese witnessed the condemned Japanese on their way to the execution grounds. Li Yechu had been the clerk for Li Liang, a well-known civil law expert. Li Yechu explained that initially Judge Li Liang had held a meeting with court officers, telling them to be prudent and vigilant on the day of the execution. Li Yechu asked the judge to change the plans because, after being occupied by such a vicious Japanese overlord for years, seeing the condemned Japanese would help the downtrodden Chinese to once again "feel proud." The judge agreed but the mob-like behavior surrounding the execution created an unforeseen international backlash. About a month after the execution fiasco, a package from China's Ministry of Defense arrived at the court. When Li Yechu opened it, he found international news clippings critical of the treatment of the Japanese prisoners on the way to the execution site. Li Yechu summarized the enclosed official letter, which informed the court that "our allies are dissatisfied" with the way China was running things. Li Yechu drafted a response letter in which he admitted that the parade was his idea and showed it to Judge Li Liang. The judge looked at the response and then changed it to read, "It was this court's opinion for the parade to take place," allowing Li Yechu off the hook. Judge Li Liang took full responsibility and was eventually dismissed, seemingly due to complaints from the US government and others.[37]

Li Yechu reflected on the trial:

> "I took the team to Changshu on October 5, 1946 and informed the newspapers *Shenbao* and *Xinwenbao* to send reporters along with us." The locals from the area angrily told us: "Yonemura killed people like it was

> a child's game. . . ." One of the locals showed Li Yechu and his team where bodies were buried. Li continued: "I remember coming to a mound above the ground level at Tiantaigang. The folks immediately used shovels and started digging. After a few spadefulls, I heard a 'cachaw' sound, and the ground opened to expose a few white bones. The crew dug further and soon found the bones of several corpses. Some were on their sides, some were standing, some were headless. . . . I packed a few bags up of the corpses as evidence, and reporters promptly took photos to publish in the newspapers. During the time of the formal trial, Judge Li took out the bones and put them on the dais. The hundreds of spectators packing the court to capacity seethed with anger, tears dripping down their faces."[38]

Li Liang served as the chief of the civil court in the Shanghai High Court before the war of resistance against Japan. After the fall of Shanghai, the Japanese army forcibly occupied the courts, hoping that Li Liang and several other members of the Shanghai judicial community would work for the Japanese side. Li Liang was arrested and imprisoned because he was unwilling to work for the Japanese. In his autobiography, entitled *National Difficulties*, Li Liang describes his experience in the Japanese prison. "The prison was connected with the toilet; there was no distinction between men and women, all were packed in a messy room. We sit and sleep on the floor, forbidden from chatting. We were fed three times a day with porridge and rice. There was no salt and chopsticks. I suffered for my nation, and the food was hard to swallow."[39]

In a separate interview, Judge Li Liang's daughter, Li Jiajing, intimated to the director of one episode of our documentary, "After my father was arrested and imprisoned, my mother was frightened and tortured by the Japanese and eventually developed a psychosis so she could no longer take care of herself. My elder and younger brother both starved to death because of our poor family condition, or else they'd still be alive." After victory, in July 1946, the forty-eight-year-old Li Liang received his new appointment as head of the Shanghai Military Tribunal and was awarded the rank of major general.[40]

Li Zhiqun was very nice and talked to us at length, but sadly she would not let me copy her father's diary, which I am sure contained much more than the news articles I could see poking out from between the handwritten pages. After the interview, in a situation that would become familiar in other interviews I conducted for the documentary, Li Zhiqun followed me downstairs to the tiny alley and spoke to me alone. With everyone else out of earshot, she wanted to tell me what happened to her father after the KMT trials. Someone in Li Yechu's neighborhood had informed on him, and he was called to the police station in the mid-1950s. After a cursory trial of sorts he was handed an eight-year sentence; he had been branded a counterrevolutionary for seemingly having taken part in the KMT's war crimes trials of the Japanese or a related trumped-up charge. The former law clerk who had assisted in Chinese Nationalist war crimes trials against the Japanese was soon sent to remote Qinghai Province, where he served out his communist sentence of prison labor. In the mid-1960s, when he was about to be released, the party once again labeled Li Yechu a counterrevolutionary and made him wear a dunce cap. In the end, Li did not return to Shanghai until 1980, his daughter told me. This was not an unknown story; it had happened to many in China.

A similar interview in Taiyuan, Shanxi Province with Liu Linsheng brought home this issue of the postwar maltreatment of those connected to the Japanese imperial war machine but in very different ways. Liu was a professor and is the author of a book about a Japanese prison camp in the city of Taiyuan where Chinese were previously detained. The book is titled *China's Auschwitz: A True Record of the Japanese and the Taiyuan Detention Camp.*[41] Aside from the obvious problems of trying to compare what happened in China to the Holocaust, his book is informative. With the exception of a POW camp in Shenyang, which was mainly for Western military prisoners, the one that Professor Liu helped research and ultimately managed to turn into a cultural heritage site remains one of the few extant examples in China.[42] As I discussed briefly in chapter one, there is scant research on Chinese POWs incarcerated by the Japanese imperial armed forces.

In the city of Taiyuan the facility where the Chinese prisoners were kept was medieval. Years later, improved conditions were created for the Japanese prisoners when they were confined in the same place for the Taiyuan war crimes investigations and trials. Liu informed me that he used his own money to buy a stone monument in the shape of Shanxi Province and erect it as a memorial in front of one of the former detention sites. Liu's father had been a prisoner of the Japanese during the war and detained in one of the buildings. Against the city planners who preferred to use the site for industrial expansion, Liu managed to raise funds to restore the prison buildings. But Liu also explained that his own father never told him anything. It was only after his father died and Liu read his father's memoirs that he learned about his time as a prisoner in Taiyuan.

One of the situations that always seems to develop in China, and perhaps more so when you are a foreigner dealing with Japanese war crimes in a country to which you are not native, is that your interviewees also like to intimate details to you they do not wish broadcast within China. Liu explained to me, after we had wrapped up filming and put the cameras away, that he had also done an interview with the *Guardian* newspaper a few years prior. In that interview with a foreign journalist Liu noted that while his father was imprisoned by the Japanese he then escaped. Ironically, his father was then actually imprisoned longer by the CCP postwar, during the Cultural Revolution, something Liu did not mention in the Chinese TV interview. I pointed this out to the directors. They noted the discrepancy and the lack of criticism but said we could not include Liu's dual historiography because it would just get the documentary into trouble with censors. *The Guardian* had published:

> Liu's father, who had been imprisoned from December 1940 to June 1941, was packed off to a labour camp in Inner Mongolia during the 60s and returned a broken man. "My father always said, 'The Japanese kept me in jail for seven months while the Communist party kept me in jail for seven years,'" he said.[43]

The fascinating part is that Liu himself was motivated to find the locations of the detention site because of a visit from two former Japanese war criminals who returned to Taiyuan and wanted to pay their respects and apologize. The city had to help these former Japanese soldiers figure out where the buildings were, and that is also what started Liu on his research journey.

Both Li and Liu's stories of postwar injustice to those already caught up in the Chinese legal system gave me pause. This was, interestingly, because while they did not wish to broadcast news of their fathers' double incarcerations too volubly their stories were already known. For Liu it was in his admission to a foreign journalist and for Li it was a small byline on an article her father had written in 1989, which explained, "Li Yechu [. . .] after liberation was unjustly charged and for a long time sent down to Qinghai Province. In 1982, he was finally formally re-instated."[44]

Judging Justice with the KMT

The Number Two Archives in Nanjing, in concert with the Center for the Tokyo Trial Studies at Shanghai Jiaotong University, published many of the records related to the KMT trials against Japanese war criminals. In his introduction to this new archival record, the director of the Number Two Archives, Ma Zhendu, is a bit disingenuous when he writes that one of the limitations that previously pushed against releasing these materials was Chinese anxiety over responses from Japan's right wing, which denies atrocities.[45] Rather, it was Chinese politics that slowed the opening of these important archives to the public. After all, I had asked for them twelve years earlier and was rebuffed!

Liu Tong, a researcher into the KMT trials at the center, offered his own assessment of the KMT trials.[46] While they were a good attempt at pursuing justice under difficult legal and international circumstances, he admits, such tribunals were not without their problems. In some ways this view correlates with my previous findings, but Liu's extensive archival research advanced further conclusions. He postulates a major lacuna that prevented the KMT from implementing a greater number of and more important trials domestically derived from a paucity of evidence. This absence of corroborative evidence was due to several contributing factors. By comparing Japanese and US statistics with Chinese numbers of individuals eventually brought to trial, Liu tabulated that out of around 2,259 arrested individuals, only 38 percent were eventually convicted in some form in Chinese military tribunals. Approximately 41 percent of the Japanese prisoners were found not guilty or were never charged and brought to court.[47] The cause for this gap between plan and action was a lack of evidence, and it was one issue that ate away at the core of the KMT's ability to bring justice to Japanese war crimes. This is also one reason that evidence was more in supply for trials against Japanese *kempeitai* forces or special intelligence services stationed in cities. There, Chinese citizens could bring their own statements based on personal experience to serve as evidence. There was, in contrast, much less personally related evidence with which to charge and then convict higher-ranking Japanese officers accused of larger-scale atrocities. There were other problems as well, which concerned the difficulty in procuring solid evidence overall. Chinese who were involved, or at least who frequently knew about such crimes, were potentially considered as collaborators and thus did not wish to divulge what they knew, to avoid getting wrapped up in further postwar complications.[48]

KMT trials of the Japanese military machine followed a format very different from a normal situation where a victorious power judges the vanquished. The KMT had side motives of reestablishing a postwar peace deal with Japan that, in part, guided its war crimes trial policy. It is for this reason that Yan Haijian suggests that the KMT pursuit of justice was both benevolent *and* overly lenient. The magnanimity of KMT trials allowed the ROC to secure an early peace treaty with Japan, but the sometimes insufficient sternness of this justice later permitted some quarters within Japan too much leeway to harbor ambivalent ideas about actual Japanese war crimes. Such ambiguity, in the end, also hampered Sino-Japanese relations and the process of reestablishing diplomatic relations in the region.[49] This duality mirrored the international stature of China. The KMT was eager to demonstrate through such trials that it was collaborating with international efforts to secure justice in the immediate postwar period as one of the four main victorious allies. But at the same time, Chinese Nationalist leaders at many levels also realized they were far from being powerful enough to branch out on their own on a path that diverged too much from what the other Allied powers were doing. Aside from the focus that the Nanjing Massacre received at the Tokyo Trial, China, internationally, failed to emphasize how Japan's war in and against China had been unique and thus worthy of a different set of trials of Japanese imperial aggression than occurred elsewhere. In this regard, the KMT failed to extend justice to its citizens.[50]

Even with all the Chinese attention to detail and budgetary limitations to pursue Japanese war crimes, soon after the KMT wrapped up its proceedings in 1949, the Korean War exploded in the summer of 1950. This new battleground shifted the sands on which the world order would be restructured once again and propelled the West to turn away from war crimes trials because it appeared they were not helping the situation. Seemingly, all parties struggled with the meaning and significance of why they had held war crimes trials—it was not merely a Chinese difficulty.

CHAPTER 8

Creating a Theater of Law in Mao's China

In late 1949, Mao Zedong announced the establishment of the People's Republic of China and simultaneously annulled all the Chinese Nationalist laws. Once Mao and his party dominated China politically, it was also time to align the new international partnerships. Soon after he would depart on first trip abroad, to the Soviet Union, where he met with his communist patron Joseph Stalin. The rendezvous had been stalled for years, and the moment was not all cozy. Mao informed a TASS reporter that his sojourn might last several weeks to iron out the problems in the bilateral relationship.[1]

Mao recalled his first visit years later: "When I came to Moscow [in December 1949], he [Stalin] did not want to conclude a treaty of friendship with us and did not want to annul the old treaty with the Guomindang [Kuomintang]. I recall that [Soviet interpreter Nikolai] Fedorenko and [Stalin's emissary to the PRC Ivan] Kovalev passed me his [Stalin's] advice to take a trip around the country, to look around. But I told them that I have only three tasks: eat, sleep and shit. I did not come to Moscow only to congratulate Stalin on his birthday. Therefore I said that if you do not want to conclude a treaty of friendship, so be it. I will fulfill my three tasks."[2]

Mao was annoyed that Mongolia had been split off in the ROC-USSR 1945 treaty, but Stalin would not budge on undoing its independence. The February 14, 1950, PRC-USSR treaty ultimately offered the Chinese fairly benign terms—except it did include $300 million in military aid over five years and the Soviets relinquished their territorial concessions, including the port of Dalian. Since China was losing its Japanese technicians, it was in need of numerous consultants to help it industrialize, and the USSR promised thousands of Soviet advisers who were to be guaranteed high salaries, not dissimilar to treaty concessions of years past. And even though the West had abrogated extraterritoriality with China in 1943, the new treaty stipulated that USSR advisers would not be subject to Chinese law.

Given all the problems that new China faced as it took over the country in the autumn of 1949, a vexing conundrum remains. Why did the CCP believe it necessary to launch its own trials of Japanese war criminals in the midst of running a counterrevolutionary campaign just after a major civil war? The roots of this policy tie back to the goal of pursuing international legitimacy by demonstrating the application of competitive justice to Japanese war crimes. There was obvious dissatisfaction in China on many levels, including the legacy of the Tokyo Trial, which the Chinese believed had not taught the appropriate lessons about justice to the US occupiers of Japan. Mei Ruao, the former Tokyo Trial judge, voiced such discontent in March 1950 in the CCP's flagship newspaper, the *People's Daily*. Mei wrote, "MacArthur's release of Japanese war criminals contravenes the Chinese peoples' interest." Mei was emphatic that MacArthur's "arbitrary decision" had no basis in law and went against international accords. By the end of 1949, occupation authorities in Japan had started to reconsider incarcerating all the Japanese prisoners for the duration of their sentences. In March 1950, the United States created a parole system for Sugamo inmates. The new edict established that "all war criminals would be eligible for a remission of one-third of their sentences for good behaviour in prison."[3] This move was particularly vexing for the Chinese because it occurred just after the USSR had prosecuted Japanese bacteriological weapons war crimes in the city of Khabarovsk in December 1949.[4]

It appears that Soviet foreign minister Vyshinsky first broached the topic of "gifting" to the CCP about one thousand carefully selected Japanese POWs the Soviets had detained in Siberia. (The Soviets had illegally detained more than half a million Japanese soldiers and some bureaucrats from Japan's former puppet kingdom Manchukuo immediately following Japan's surrender.) It is not clear precisely what the Soviets hoped to achieve with this transfer of Japanese prisoners, but Vyshinsky's comments suggest that the USSR might have hoped that China would follow Soviet socialist legal precedent and hold its own show trials.[5] In his secret diary Vyshinsky wrote on January 6, 1950:

> 1) In general, there is no doubt that the Japanese military criminals must be transferred to China to stand trial. 2) However, the Chinese

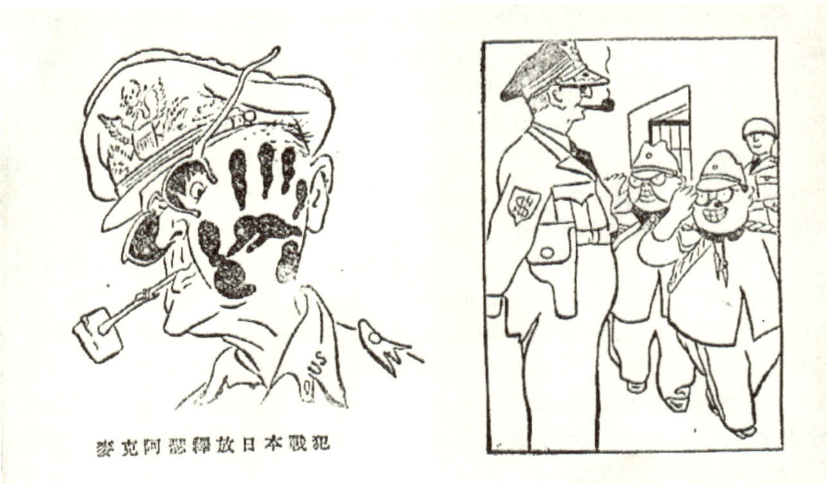

FIGURE 8.1. CCP cartoons critical of MacArthur's decision to release Japanese war criminals. "Zhanfan Maikease," *Xuanchuanhua cankao ziliao*, di 1ji, Renmin meishu chubanshe, 6. (It is unclear exactly when this propaganda collection was produced, but it seems likely it was during the Korean War.)

> Government intends to put the Japanese military criminals on trial at the same time as the Guomindang [Chinese Nationalists] military criminals. The organization of such a trial process is planned to take place approximately during the first or second half of 1951. Therefore, it would be desirable for the Soviet Government to agree temporarily to keep the aforementioned Japanese military criminals in the Soviet Union, roughly until the second half of 1950. I noted that, since the Soviet Union is bound by corresponding obligations—to repatriate all Japanese military prisoners by January of 1950, perhaps it would be more expedient to agree on formally considering the Japanese military criminals as having been transferred to China, but in fact to temporarily leave them on the Soviet territory. Mao said that this is the exact formula he considers to be the most expedient.[6]

Casting about for what to do with Japanese war criminals, all the while terminating China's KMT-era legal structure, was a complex affair. It might be a relatively simple task at the tail end of a revolution to abolish former political frameworks, and this policy was mightily popular at first. Mao preached that the dictatorship of the people should rule the country, and that the courts, along with the military and police, had been "tools for one class to oppress another class" and thus should be dismantled. In many ways he was deadly serious, but less so when it came to Japanese war criminals.[7] What both the KMT and then the CCP wanted, which never wavered from the beginning of the war to the end, even through a massive regime change, was equality on the level of international law.[8]

Fundamentally, Communist ideology conceives of itself essentially as pursuing what the Soviets termed "people's justice." This emphasis stressed the class nature of law, which was at the same time deemed secondary to political goals.[9] Law is not independent of the state.[10] Vyshinsky, legal counselor and onetime Soviet foreign minister, was a key socialist legal theorist whose works were influential in like-minded states. In his magnum opus on Soviet jurisprudence, *Law of the Soviet State*, Vyshinsky details that new socialist law was designed to keep the exploited from being controlled by the exploiters.[11] On the surface this sounds wonderfully utopian, but a sinister element lurks below. Socialist law fundamentally pivots on propping up the state and has little time for discussion of rights and "the rule of law" as understood in liberal democracies. Vyshinsky is angry in his turgid book on this form of law, but it is illustrative of how this legal ideology would operate in the socialist paradise: "Bourgeois theories of state and law—irrespective of the subjective aspirations and wishes of those who created those theories—serve the cause of exploitation. To expose their real nature is the first and most important problem of Soviet knowledge, dedicated, as it is, to the development of a theory of state and law."[12] A later US assessment of the aims of Chinese socialist law defined it as a way to organize and manage a revolutionary society by focusing on the worst offenders as those who tried to subvert the new socialist system. The real aim of this law was to "consolidate the people's democratic dictatorship." A Chinese assessment of its own law noted: "The tasks of our criminal law are thus to struggle against all traitors, counter-revolutionaries and other criminals with penal methods in order to keep the people's democratic system and social order from being offended, to educate the citizens to observe law self-consciously, and thereby to protect and promote the successful accomplishment of the state's socialist construction and socialist transformation."[13] In short, socialist law is used for state political goals and has less to do with deeper issues of truth or justice.

New China aimed to gain the stature to celebrate international equality of law, but the nation's leaders also wanted to demonstrate that the PRC was a country that belonged among the realm of civilized nations. On January 4, 1950, Shen Junru delivered the opening remarks to a gathering of more than three hundred legal specialists at China University of Political Science and Law to reform their thinking and establish an institute of research for "new law." Shen had studied law in early twentieth-century Tokyo and later became chief

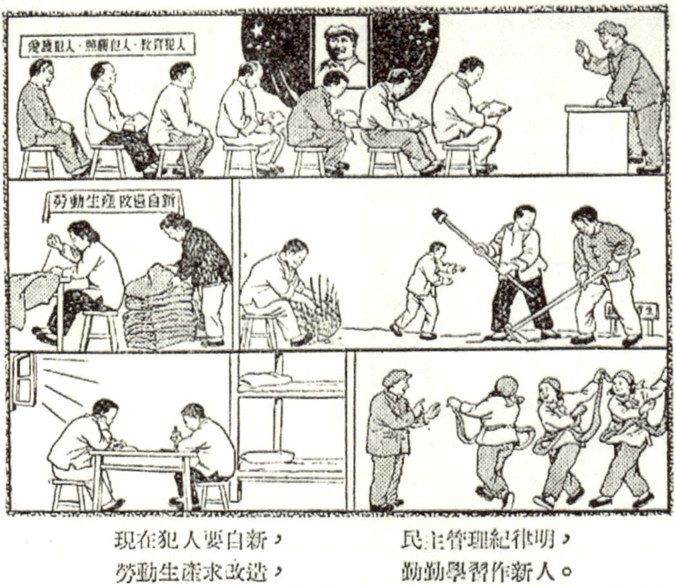

FIGURE 8.2. "Now criminals have to renovate themselves." A page from a larger work showing the superiority of PRC socialist law over what was deemed corrupt KMT law. *Jiefang qianhou dabutong*, materials compiled by Shen Tongheng, Huadong huabao chuban, 1950, available through Chicago Center for Research Libraries.

justice of the PRC's Supreme People's Court. He was a fascinating character—an old lawyer from a bygone era but one who saw the future in socialist glory. Shen spoke about transforming old judicial officers and creating an institution for establishing the study of new Chinese law. He said that China was in the midst of reemerging and creating a new people's law to cement the people's dictatorship and train more juridical talent. Shen saw the need to start work on three fronts: (1) raise the revolutionary authority of juridical people's workers, (2) retrain the old society's juridical officers, and (3) train new juridical workers. A new institution of legal learning could do just that. He urged students and everyone to embrace Marxism-Leninism-Maoism and Soviet legal knowledge to complete this process. Dong Biwu, one of the PRC's founding legal intellectuals, spoke in turn and announced that this changeover would be difficult and painful, especially for intellectuals. Transforming legal ideology would allow one to serve the people and be a juridical worker for the masses. At the same event, Deputy Attorney General Lan Gongwu said jurists from the old society needed to dispose of their legal ideals and baggage from the past, "overcome the sickness of individualism, overcome their denigration of labor, and such ideas as looking down on the masses, and only then can they be a juridical worker for the people."[14]

Shen Junru made clear the government's position on the judiciary and law at the National Committee of the Chinese People's Political Consultative Conference, on June 17, 1950: "The old courts of the judicial system for oppressing and fooling the people have been abolished. The judicial system which is dependent on the people, related to the people, and convenient to the people, has been set up."[15]

Not long after in the summer of 1950, China took possession of the approximately one thousand Japanese prisoners the Soviet Union had offered. These Japanese were labeled publicly in the Chinese press and in government documents as "war criminals" before any investigation or trial had opened. The carefully calibrated handover was completed at the border crossing of Suifenhe. Approaching the fifth anniversary of Japan's surrender, in 1950 Judge Mei Ruao wrote in the Chinese press that he saw potential in China's former enemy. However, he observed that the US occupation and US "fascist and selfish policies in Japan" over the last several years were ruining everything. Mei specifically mentioned that the occupation was crushing the JCP and that JCP leader Itō Ritsu had vocally pushed back. Itō, Mei wrote, proclaimed that "even if you topple one of us, ten will rise." This was an ironic declaration. Only three years later, communist leaders in Beijing would illegally sequester and then incarcerate Itō for more than twenty-five years with no charges and no trial. This was not known at the time to those outside of the core CCP leadership, so Mei obviously still held out hope for the future of Japan in the hands of Japanese communists. This belief is perhaps why Mei engaged as a consultant on the CCP war crimes investigation teams. To advance, he wrote, Japan had to oppose US imperialism and fight the occupation.[16]

Continuing his public role of talking about war crimes and China's relations with Japan, Mei authored an article in 1952, "All of the Asian People's Hopes for the Japanese People." He declared that "Japan has been strapped to the American tank and is one of the most seriously threatened by war amidst this extreme revitalization of militarism."[17] Mei referenced Japanese leftist Kōra Tomi's comments about Japan's remilitarization, as well as Hoashi Kei and others concerning Japan's wanting to turn away from its aggressive past. Mei quoted Japanese left-leaning politicians who pointed out that change in China's relations with Japan was possible. Using the words of Kōra and others, Mei wrote that he knew the Japanese wanted peace, not war, and that they "do not want to be dragged 'on the stupid path toward suicide.'"[18] Several years

FIGURE 8.3. Cover of the Chinese book *The True Situation of American Imperialism Propping up Japan*. Xinhua, ed., *Meidi furi zhenxiang* (Shijiazhuang: Huabei xinhua shudian, 1948).

later in a Chinese radio broadcast, Mei reiterated a similar message, saying that how the Chinese dealt with Japanese war criminals was "strictly just and benevolent" because "it shows the spirit of high levels of humanitarianism."[19]

The Start of CCP War Crimes Investigations

Wang Shilin was a young man studying law at Chaoyang University when the war with Japan started. He then headed south as the war worsened, kept studying, and ended up as part of the new legal team that was rebuilding the country. Soon after the announcement of liberation in autumn 1949 he was drafted into the CCP central government's efforts to study war crimes and put together an investigation team. At first the staff were not informed of what they would be doing—it was all top secret. After it was explained, team members were told their work was classified. Wang was not even permitted to tell his family about his new post. He said that he was initially sent from Taiyuan to be part of the investigation team in Beijing, which was trying to assist the legal staff to squeeze in all the necessary study of law so that they would be properly prepared to advance the prosecution team's investigations. The team received lectures from Judge Mei Ruao (the Chinese judge who had served on the Tokyo Trial) and a number of other high-profile legal practitioners with international experience. It was clear the CCP was pulling out all the stops to ensure proper procedures on the long road to the potential for having war crimes trials or at least creating a legal record of Japan's imperial misdeeds. Wang could not recall the specifics of Mei's lectures, but we can guess at some of their content based on the small array of Mei's media commentary. The PRC wanted to draw closer to Japan, and a new imperialist demon had been found in the United States, on which to heap vitriol. Legal clerk Li Fang recalled that real investigations of the Japanese prisoners only began after the Korean War concluded, when he was summoned to Beijing in December 1953 from the Hebei Provincial Public Security Bureau to the Beijing Procuratorate Office.[20]

Most of the PRC legal team members have died, but their reminiscences were recorded for posterity in two volumes, entitled *Recollections of Reforming the War Criminals*.[21] Wang recalled that he and the others did not know much about the Tokyo Trial when they started their jobs, but they knew that such a trial had taken place in Japan's capital. From the outset, most were not too keen on their new employment. Wang personally did not think the Japanese war criminals merited trials. It turns out that not only did the investigation teams have to study law and history, but the CCP leadership also had to spend time and effort to persuade investigators to complete their tasks. This was not a foregone conclusion, because initially many investigators did not want to comply with the directives. Wang explained that the decision not to summarily execute the Japanese POWs was made by Premier Zhou Enlai. Zhou explained to the investigation teams at one meeting that executing the Japanese was not an action that would gain justice for China, although he did not use those exact words, Wang said. It was obvious that China's communist central government paid careful attention to ensuring that the investigations ran smoothly. The goal was to orchestrate careful and deliberate probes while pressuring the Japanese war criminals to admit their crimes. The Communist Party wanted to be able to predict the outcome of the trial. The ultimate aim was an admission of guilt that would then be declared in open court. A few months after Wang finished preparatory study and training in Beijing, he was dispatched farther north to Fushun Prison (officially known as the Fushun War Criminals Management Center) in Liaoning Province for a time. He said he was not there very long, and he was quickly returned to Taiyuan.

Wang intimated the careful approach he took when investigating Japanese prisoners such as Tominaga Juntarō and Jōno Hiroshi. Jōno was a former military officer who teamed up with the KMT leaders in Shanxi Province immediately after Japan's surrender to organize Japan's imperial revival. Tominaga was in his fifties and also a former military officer. In his confession he admitted to working undercover as a railway police officer. Initially Tominaga was reluctant to talk. Wang voiced to me the frustration he felt when facing Tominaga's recalcitrance to advance the investigation, because if someone did not talk, then nothing happened. It took months of extra work and patience, something Wang admitted he struggled with at the outset. Wang added that the investigations took time to move forward because the team itself had to learn how to treat the Japanese prisoners. They could not just start out by calling these men "war criminals," because the Japanese officers did not conceive of themselves as such.[22] So, the investigators used proper titles and names with the prisoners and kept pushing. This took months and then years. This decision was a noticeable trend, because when I interviewed Wang, he never defaulted to the often-used term in China of "Japanese devils" when talking about the war criminals.

On the Road to PRC War Crimes Trials

One of the methods the PRC used to restore order was through a new application of law. Dong Biwu, future chief justice of the PRC's Supreme People's Court and legal scholar for China's new communist legal ideology, offered commentary on the nature of law and why the Chinese needed to learn more. In June 1954 at the Sixth National Public Security Meeting, in what must have been a long-winded report, Dong pointed out problems with training the masses to use and understand political and legal ideology. Carefully laying out his premise with several examples, Dong elucidated that the imperialists and counterrevolutionaries "want to break our inevitability, they want to destroy our institutions and our law. They know they cannot achieve this openly so they use secretive methods or loopholes in the law to their advantage. They use the fact that our law is not yet complete, exploit weak deficiencies in our work, most especially taking advantage when we let down our guard." Dong explained that the masses not only needed to understand the law but also needed to respect it, because "if the masses do not respect the law that will give our enemies a convenient opening. If the masses respect the law our enemies will not be able to find a way to gain an advantage."[23] A stable and legally cognizant new China was therefore a secure and robust People's Republic of China.

Unfortunately, much of PRC commentary on law is not case law but a system where higher courts release an opinion saying "correct" or "absolutely correct." There was very little legal reasoning involved.[24] Regardless, in the full throes of passion midway through his report, Dong Biwu then turned to the issue of training the next generation of socialist legal workers. This change would not be easy, he expounded, because there were many judicial clerks formed in the old style with outdated legal training. Legal knowledge during the Republican era was not a science, Dong stated, but "Lenin said that socialism is a science." The new legal workers would need to unlearn their previous habits and adapt to the idea that socialist law was formulaic. To throw away the old and learn the new took time, he instructed. And we need to construct new schools to teach this law as well, he added.[25]

Most Chinese leaders realized that molding new Chinese law with no reference points was untenable, and their greatest asset was to learn from the Soviets. And while technical advice abounded, doubt remains concerning what sort of legal specialists came to China and trained new specialists. China had to work hard to rebuild its legal environment, but it was not always clear whether it was trying to adopt Soviet law or merely struggling to gain international attention.[26] There were not that many Soviet legal specialists compared with the immense number of other technicians. There are numerous competing lists but no official and final tabulations. One scholar calculated that the USSR sent only twenty-four legal specialists to China, fifteen of whom were installed at People's University; others have slightly higher numbers. For a vast country of virtually half a billion people, only a small number of nonnative legal scholars trickled in and then stayed in China for only a short time, maybe a year or two at best.[27] From 1949 to 1960 approximately eighteen thousand Soviet specialists of all stripes worked in some capacity in China. Regardless of their actual numbers, these legal specialists were like a "drop in the ocean," according to another estimate.[28] And while the PRC prided itself on many of the advances in jurisprudence it borrowed from the USSR, including mandating a defense lawyer for defendants and a public trial, not all citizens would have necessarily known about any given law. After all, it was not until 1988 that the Chinese state decided that all laws must be published.[29]

Training also worked in the other direction, with Chinese visits to the Soviet Union. One of the first missions was led by Shi Liang, the minister of justice. Shi Liang was a key author of new laws for women in the PRC and also wrote about the further need to renovate Chinese law in the new era when socialism was supposed to shine brightly.[30] Shi was unique in many ways. One of the few female lawyers in China, she graduated from the Shanghai Law Academy in 1927, when there were only three female graduates.[31] Lucky to survive the anti-Rightist purge of 1958, Shi would be quietly excused from public life until her resurrection in the early 1980s.

Shi Liang made it abundantly clear that reforming the law also meant reforming people's attitudes toward it. In a report to the government on August 13, 1952, she put forward her thoughts. This report was also later published in the *People's Daily*.

> The thorough reform and reorganization of all the levels of the people's courts is an important step in consolidating the people's democratic dictatorship and guaranteeing the economic construction of the state. This concerns not only reassigning staff within the people's courts, but it is also a question of purging the remnant reactionary legal ideology and ways of doing business of the old Chinese Nationalist Party. For this reason, it is necessary to begin in a planned and step by step manner, by mobilizing the masses from top to bottom toward a campaign to oppose the old judicial viewpoints and to reform all the judicial organs.[32]

Shi Liang was indispensable in coordinating a mass of meetings and education programs to redo China's legal infrastructure and to train cadres.[33] It took from the first several years after Mao's announcement of a new China until about 1953 to establish courts in every region. The CCP leadership also tried to put women into as many new positions as possible. The size of the staff that served legal agencies expanded under her tutelage from 1950 to 1956.[34] Shi was also crucial to how Mao later prosecuted war crimes trials against the Japanese. Her team became a key conduit of information about how law operated in the Soviet Union, and these techniques seemed to have informed how investigations were managed. Shi led the three-month mission to the USSR with members of the Supreme People's Court, Supreme People's Procuratorate, the Ministry of Justice, and professors of legal studies.

The mission began on April 11, 1955, and the group returned on July 10, 1955. Those joining included twelve jurists and eight translators.[35] In her published mission reports, Shi Liang claimed she was surprised that even though the USSR was established thirty years prior, the people still had remnants of imperial or capitalist thinking. So, she believed, the law still needed to clamp down on them. The aim was not to punish crime that had already taken place; she also paid attention to issues that would lead to crime in the future. Educating the masses about the law, the courts, and what the party was doing was key, she instructed.[36] In another report, several members of the mission stated, "The court is an important weapon for the party and the state in guiding the people forward in socialism." They continued, "As such, trials are not divorced from political meaning nor do they advance in isolation." Of course, one had to scrupulously follow legal principles and rules of evidence, they agreed. In the end, the authors of the report tended toward exaggeration and claimed that Soviet investigations were so good and scientifically advanced that all crime immediately was uncovered. Regarding selecting and training members of the court, the report found that the members must reflect party and government policies and were key because "they are one tool of the fight to realize policy."[37] Shi later softened her stance on who could perform legal work, perhaps by 1957, owing to the torpid pace of educating competent staff. On a later trip to the USSR she remarked that she saw czarist-era lawyers at work and realized that in China, lawyers trained during the Republican era could still be employed to stem national shortages. They might not be able to be judges, but they could do real legal work, she opined.[38]

Wang Huai'an wrote a similarly laudatory article about the mission's findings, noting that "the cadre legal staff of the Soviet Ministry of Justice is extremely talented, and their work experience is very rich."[39] Wang Huai'an had attended National Sichuan University law school but dropped out shortly before graduating and left for Yenan, the Chinese communist stronghold, in 1940. He was falsely persecuted as a spy in 1943 and spent three years under arrest. Later, he would spend twenty years in labor camps after his subsequent PRC arrest in 1958.

Wang Ruqi, also part of this first mission to the USSR, was propaganda section chief in 1955 and instrumental to the major restructuring of the Chinese marriage law. She finished her legal studies at elite Fudan University in prewar Shanghai and wrote a draft of the important new law in postwar China concerning marriage. The marriage law was one of the many new ways of renovating China and had two purposes. The first order aimed to eradicate the vestiges of what was determined to be "feudal": multiple wives and related hierarchical family relations, which were believed to retard China's modernization. Second, "mass legal education was to contribute to linking state and society through knowledge, boost popular legitimacy for the young regime, and create the 'new' socialist masses that abided by policies, laws, and party doctrine."[40]

Minister of Justice Shi Liang wrote that the marriage law was not just a step forward for China but revolutionary in its scope because it broke the bonds of feudal relationships and guaranteed the establishment of a democratic household marriage. However, like most other legal staff participating in the creation of a new legal state, and connected to the prosecution of Japanese war crimes trials, Wang Ruqi's time in the limelight was short-lived. In the summer of 1957 many juridical staff suffered at the hands of another counter-revolutionary wave and she was sent to other posts, though never directly purged like so many others. Wang returned to the center stage of Beijing, where she served as a defense attorney for the Gang of Four trial in late 1980.[41]

As China embarked on research concerning how to construct a new legal system, on February 28, 1955, officials in the Supreme People's Procuratorate discussed releasing about five hundred Japanese prisoners the following month and they wanted to hear opinions on such a potential decision. China's Ministry of Foreign Affairs replied that it held no particular opinion, but taking such a big step before the Bandung Conference in April 1955 could have merit. (Bandung was the first postwar international conference of African and Asian states to discuss their roles in the decolonized world order.) However, the ministry suggested that China should be careful with making this publicly known because officials would not want to be misread as celebrating Japanese prime minister Hatoyama Ichirō's ascension to office. Or maybe the PRC should release a smaller number of prisoners before the Bandung Conference, officials queried, and then make a statement about those remaining afterward?[42]

The CCP also struggled with what to do about China's intellectuals, as it did concerning how to create a new legal structure out of whole cloth while lacking the staff. It could not summarily dismiss everyone, because talent, technicians, and able-minded cadres were in desperately short supply. In this vein in July 1955, Dong Biwu, Shen Junru, and Zhang Xiruo all delivered comments at the Second Session of the 1st National People's Congress. After Dong spoke, Shen followed up with a short discussion on intellectuals: "During the construction of a socialist society and the great struggle of using socialism to reform society intellectuals are for the near future important troops in that battle. However, on the other hand, we must recognize these intellectuals are born from the capitalist class or lower capitalist class and thus are inherently deeply flawed."[43]

Intellectuals who later became communist cadres, like Shen Junru, had to make sure they constantly affirmed their own personal journey of transformation regarding their background and attitudes. At the July 1955 meeting, Shen made a statement to the gathering:

> Have I or have I not intimately drawn myself into the Communist Party?
>
> Am I arrogant or emotionally full of myself?
>
> Am I not capable of serving the people with all my heart and spirit, and serving society?
>
> I believe we intellectuals must at this time investigate ourselves, sternly require ourselves to earnestly study Marxist Leninism, study Mao

> Zedong's works, train ourselves amidst this unfolding revolution, and advance education widely among the people, all before we can claim to have been reformed into a new individual in the new society. This all needs to be accomplished before we can contribute to socialism's great efforts.[44]

This moment of legal fermentation during "the 1954–1957 interlude represents the potential golden age of law in Communist China. The concern in that country with due process and normal, stable juridical relations impressed the Soviet legal clan favourably."[45] Unfortunately, it would not last.

On the Eve of the Trials of Japanese War Criminals

A consultancy group was formed and put to work to deal with the long and numerous individual investigations that teams in Fushun and Taiyuan had coordinated for years. According to instructions from Zhou Enlai, in January 1956 a group of legal minds including Tan Zhengwen, Jia Qian, Wang Ruqi, and Mei Ruao debated sentencing guidelines.[46] The members focused on the principle of being magnanimous but still advancing the notion of adjudicating and dealing with war crimes.[47] Contrary to contemporary accounts and the media in China, the CCP was not solely concerned with Japanese war crimes. At the time, the PRC widely defined what had caused the century of humiliation, and there was much responsibility to be shared.

Six years had passed since the Japanese prisoners had been delivered to the PRC's border rail station in 1950. Stalin had died in March 1953, and Soviet leader Nikita Khrushchev delivered his famous "On the Cult of Personality and Its Consequences," condemning Stalin in a secret session of the 20th Party Congress on February 25, 1956. Rumors of its content abounded, but it was hard to nail down. By June, the entire contents were published in the *New York Times*, and Stalin's crimes were exposed to the world.[48] Khrushchev's denunciation of Stalin surprised the Chinese, particularly Mao, who would soon be busy constructing his own cult of personality. But we should be careful in ascribing too much to the moment as the start of the souring of Sino-Soviet relations as "it artificially inflates the differences between the Soviets and the Chinese." In short, "Khrushchev appeared to downplay class struggle and sought peaceful coexistence with the United States. Mao criticized these policies as 'revisionist,' setting the stage for the ideological conflict that fully unfolded in the 1960s."[49]

At the end of March 1956, Soviet ambassador to China P. F. Yudin discussed with Mao the ramifications of Khrushchev's epoch-making speech. The two agreed that Stalin's mistakes should be avoided in the future, but Mao seemed less worried, Yudin wrote. Mao answered that, "evidently, there will be these types of mistakes again." This was because, in Mao's view, "there are still too many vestiges of the past."[50]

Importantly, while downplaying Stalin's mistakes, Chinese officials, like Zhou Enlai, did not wish to make any international gaffes in their dealings with Japanese war criminals. As detailed in a Chinese Ministry of Foreign Affairs report that was sent to the Central Committee, the government was worried that if the trials improperly employed international law, or that if a venue misquoted the law, especially while the PRC had not officially recognized international law, new China would not look good on the international stage.[51] The courts and the government needed to be prudent so as not to cause themselves national and international embarrassment.

By the spring of 1956, Chinese officials had formalized the manner in which they would use the six-year-long investigations they had opened against the Japanese war criminals. They noted how such a decision related to other groups the PRC deemed as war criminals. The official history of China's public security operations acknowledged that the KMT put Japanese war criminals on trial but asserted that the Chinese Nationalists "failed to reflect the true wishes and hopes of the Chinese people." The KMT did not bring to justice, in the vocabulary of the PRC, the three kinds of "domestic war criminals." These were the sixty-one high-ranking members of the Manchukuo administration (including ministers and Manchu royalty), about ten people who served in the Mongol United Autonomous Government, and KMT war criminals. All together they added up to just under one thousand individuals.[52] The Manchukuo war criminals, as the CCP deemed them, proved reluctant to reform in the initial years. Li Fang, who was head of the prosecutorial investigation team formed to interrogate and reform the prisoners, recalled that the Manchukuo prisoners "had knowledge related to previous laws and because they thought we should tell them that confessions to their crimes would be used against them later in court some stubbornly refused to acknowledge their crimes." Li went on to say that the CCP investigation teams did not just question the prisoners, they educated them. Wars were won or lost depending on who was just or unjust. For example, Li said, imperial Japan had invaded China and subsequently lost. In the War to Resist America and Aid Korea (how the Chinese refer to the Korean War), the imperial United States was defeated by the Chinese and the Korean people.[53]

Luo Ruiqing, chief of the Public Security Ministry, detailed how he categorized war responsibility in China. The first group, he explained in a March 1956 public speech "concerning problems with war crimes," were Chiang Kai-shek's nationalist soldiers taken prisoner during and after the civil war. Some were summarily executed, he noted. The second group were Japanese war criminals, and the investigations against them had been proceeding for some time, Luo remarked. The third group included the last emperor of Qing China, Pu Yi, and some sixty-one "fake Manchukuo" war criminals, including former ministers and others, Luo pronounced. In 1956, high-ranking CCP officials were still using the term "war criminals" for all these parties, which signified in some sense that Chinese Nationalist POWs were being consolidated with Japanese war criminals and former members of the Manchukuo leadership who were not Japanese. As part of their reeducation, Luo highlighted, KMT prisoners were toured around to factories, mines, water projects, and cultural sites. The report quoted an incarcerated KMT officer, General Liao Yaoxiang, who is said to have exclaimed: "Although I am a criminal bequeathed from an outdated society, I am still a Chinese. I cannot be but sincere in my fervent desire to support the great and holy projects that are now being undertaken to restore the motherland."[54]

Toward the end of his speech, Luo, almost as an aside, mentioned thirteen Americans held in China. He told the audience that all of them have "already been sentenced according to the law," which was more than one could say about the so-called trials of KMT prisoners who were usually summarily imprisoned with no trial. Luo offered further details on the incarcerated Americans, such as that some were taken around China to see the ways in which the country was rebuilding itself. Luo offered the example as a PRC mode of success when treating such foreign criminals.[55]

In April 1956, the CCP made public its announcement about how it would deal with Japanese war criminals. The Chinese Ministry of Foreign Affairs held internal top-secret discussions about coordinating its policy with the Soviets. In view of this issue, Liao Chengzhi expressed two points. Liao was the go-to man in postwar Sino-Japanese relations. He had grown up in Japan and was bilingual, serving elite bilateral relations and for a long time fronting PRC policy toward Japan. At this juncture the two policies were not unified, so, first, China should inform the Soviets, he ventured. Second, if China does inform the Soviets, Liao wrote, it might be a good idea to just hand them a copy of the Chinese decision and explain the Chinese policy on Japanese war criminals. Officials voiced concerns that the Japanese trials were going to take place more than ten years after the conclusion of World War II. Sino-Japan relations had changed, the report noted, so China should aim to implement a policy that was magnanimous. The Chinese explained these points to a high-ranking officer of the Soviet embassy.[56] At this time, the central core of the CCP was still talking about how to deal with the three groups of war criminals: the Japanese, the "fake" Manchukuo government officials, and other counterrevolutionaries, as they deemed KMT officials and officers.[57] As the final preparations for the trials of Japanese war criminals were under way, the central government sent out its opinion on how to punish these disparate groups and other counterrevolutionaries who were all now seemingly lumped together legally. They needed to be punished appropriately. "We need to prudently investigate," the directive said.

> Concerning the group of criminals including Pu Yi and other domestic and Manchurian traitors, along with Kang Ze, Du Yuming, Wang Yaowu and other civil war criminals, whether we should take the most egregious among them and merely execute them, or treat them magnanimously without using the death penalty but give them appropriate sentences according to their cases, is the question. Moreover, we also have to think whether we should continually acquit those who do not need to be sentenced for all charges or successively give amnesty to those who demonstrate repentance, to the biggest war criminals who make efforts to atone, and then use them as effective political capital? This problem is something worth prudently studying.[58]

The same directive discussed the fact that the war crimes trials of traitors, Japanese, and those from former Manchukuo could also be used to isolate the enemy and strengthen China's own position. But, the report noted, China needed to be careful because even though these men had already spent a long time in prison, there would still be those in Chinese society poised against this decision because the masses had suffered direct harm.[59] Communist officials labeled the KMT officials and soldiers captured as "war criminals," even though technically in a civil war these men had not committed crimes against humanity, or peace, and it was not a war in the legal sense. It is clear that CCP authorities struggled with layers of doubt in a legal haze, oftentimes mixing how to deal with counterrevolutionaries and the problems of Japanese war criminals in the same or related policy proceedings.

In the end, the CCP chose two locations for its public trials against Japanese war criminals—Taiyuan, Shanxi Province, and Shenyang, Liaoning Province. Both temporary courtrooms had theatrical lighting installed, and both events were recorded on film, though not released to the public until the twenty-first century. The stage was, literally and figuratively, set. In a sense, any trial is an event that creates a specially defined space. Trials are procedures that fulfill important social rituals to announce the pursuit of justice. An arena of justice needs to be "embedded in a social fabric" for it to have significant meaning for the society.[60] Law is the process within that space where justice is found or the process of justice is presumed to occur. A tribunal is a venue where different actors come together to find resolution or assign responsibility and mete out punishment. At the same time, trials define national territory. States seek to delineate the borders of what crimes will and will not be charged under the jurisdictions they control. But what drove the PRC to pour money and time into pursuing Japanese war criminals long after other courts had adjourned concerning these issues around the rest of the region?

The war crimes trials in communist China that took place in the two venues of Taiyuan and Shenyang stretched from June to July 1956, charging only forty-five of the highest-ranking Japanese with war crimes. All the other remaining Japanese prisoners, including the initial almost one thousand who were "gifted" from the USSR, had been repatriated in waves preceding these trials.[61] Many facts about the war crimes trials of the Japanese were unknown until recently. For example, why was a building in the north of the city of Shenyang, which required daily transportation of the prisoners and staff, used as the location for one set of the CCP tribunals? It turns out that officials had discussed holding the court in Fushun, where the prison was located, but no appropriate building or room was grand enough in scale. The building selected in Shenyang was the Beiling Cinema, which was a working movie theater both before and after the war crimes trials.[62] Shenyang was deemed a fitting location because it was precisely where Japanese war crimes began with the September 18, 1931, Manchurian Incident. Chinese lawyer Lian Xisheng, who worked on the trials, claimed "former Tokyo Trial Judge Mei Ruao, who had joined the training teams for the CCP trials, suggested the location of Shenyang. 'Shenyang was where the 9.18 Incident happened so we should hold judgement in Shenyang. There the crimes were committed, so the trial should be there. This is the way to provide the world education and a warning; it is a way to guard peace, and contain malevolent forces.'"[63]

In late June 1956, on the eve of the military tribunals of Japanese war criminals in Taiyuan, Shanxi Province, Supreme Court procurator Zhang Dingcheng spoke at the Third Session of the First National People's Congress. Zhang was pleased that 1955 had been a high point for the country in achieving its socialist goals, and he announced that China had won the struggle against counterrevolutionaries. The country was now arresting, investigating, and bringing criminals to court, while following the rule of law correctly. Toward the end of his remarks, Zhang got around to the "Japanese war criminal elements," as he categorized them. Being benevolent toward the Japanese war criminals was "in our longer-term interest," Zhang said. This policy demonstrated China's magnanimous spirit but "can also show the power of our nation's people and the great force of world peace." Such moves will also "gain the sympathy of the Japanese people and support of those around the world who cherish peace."[64]

Chief Judge Jia Qian presided over the 1956 Shenyang trials. Jia was a graduate of one of Republican China's top law schools before heading into the hinterland to join the CCP during the war of resistance against Japan. One of the people who helped arrange the defense teams was Wang Ruqi, a top Ministry of Justice official, a Republican law graduate, a participant in Shi Liang's 1955 tour to the USSR, and a key drafter of China's new marriage law. These former Republican-era lawyers had years of personal experience with the Chinese Nationalist judicial system, which probably had a much deeper impact on their understanding of the law and judicial process than abstract socialist theories they had recently read concerning a judicial system they barely knew. But to acknowledge a positive Chinese Nationalist legal debt was career suicide, so instead anything that looked like formal Republican-era legality had to be represented as Soviet.

FIGURE 8.4. Shenyang 1956 war crimes trial courtroom, now a museum.

The long effort in investigating Japanese war crimes and then consistently having the prisoners write and rewrite their confessions was designed to get them to admit their atrocities. One result of these sessions was that many Japanese prisoners promised to reform and then did so when they eventually repatriated to Japan. This was a fundamental element of the whole process. Feng Jingyu recalled such a moment. He had attended the entirety of the Shenyang trials and had assisted in the drafting of the language for the verdicts. Feng was the political section editor of the *Progressive Newspaper*, a local Shenyang newspaper. Feng witnessed Fujita Shigeru (former lieutenant general of the Japanese imperial army) pledging his life to antiwar efforts and promoting peace. Fujita did just that upon repatriation with his role in the formation of the Liaison Group of Returnees from China (*Chūgoku kikansha renrakukai*, hereafter referred to as the Liaison Group).[65]

But there were also problems with the communist trials, including those of special military tribunals for Japanese war criminals. CCP judges were often army judges, few had postsecondary education, and "legal training [was] not compulsory until 1983."[66] In addition, the euphoria over Beijing's announcements to stand as the most benevolent nation toward Japan was short-lived when PRC agencies started to analyze the actual situation. A report from June 28, 1956, concerning Japanese reactions to the Chinese announcement of prisoner releases and trials caused much consternation in elite PRC circles. In general, newspapers in Japan and public opinion were positive regarding China's moves, the report noted. However, challenges remained and attitudes were not wholly consistent, the report enunciated.[67]

Even before the ink was dry on the CCP trial verdicts, China was nonetheless congratulating itself on a job well done. The Political Division Enemy Military Operations Section of the People's Liberation Army kept tabs on Japanese reactions to the prisoners' repatriation. China highly estimated the impact of its war crimes trials education, release program, and overall process. Arima Torao, a prisoner and former head of the Railway Police School in Manchukuo, gave an interview to a Japanese newspaper.[68] Arima had been handed over from the Soviets to the Chinese in the big exchange in June 1950.[69] This Chinese report mentioned another news article, but I have been unable to find corroboration in any Japanese sources to verify this news event that the Chinese cite. They had supposedly interviewed former Japanese soldier Kawanishi Kinji, who upon returning home to Tokyo learned that his three brothers had died and only his mother survived the war. The article recorded that his mother, "tearfully embracing her son upon his return," said, "Regardless of what happens I will never again let him go." Kawanishi's mother "thanked China for its humane treatment of her son and for nursing him back to health when he was ill."[70]

Confessions

The CCP trials not only reformed prisoners and fashioned "Japanese devils" back into being men, but the courts also offered concrete forms of justice to the Chinese public for crimes that had never been recognized during either the last years of KMT rule on the mainland or the first years of the PRC. This plan was orchestrated in terms of the level of care investigators took in their prolonged and detailed interrogations of Japanese prisoners from 1952 to 1956, as Wang Shilin explained regarding his experiences.[71] These materials were then used to ensure a "correct" verdict but also to push the successful admission of Japanese guilt in court when the time came. These confessions of the CCP-convicted Japanese war criminals were published in a set of ten volumes in 2005, followed by a few reprints over the years.[72] The forty-five confessions were later truncated and translated in online versions around 2014. The final moment of revelation came in 2015 when the first tranche of 120 volumes of *all* the confessions of about eight hundred Japanese war criminals was produced. The vast majority of these men were granted early release and not put on trial, but the record of their actions in their own words remains, even though the Chinese public was denied access to it for the past sixty years.[73] Obviously, years of work remain to analyze more fully the contents of these confessions, as well as their meaning and significance. However, one key confession, that of Major General Uesaka Masaru, provides a key link to the tragedy narrated in this book's introduction. Uesaka was the military leader involved in the poison gas incident in Beituan Village, where I interviewed Li Qingxiang at the start of this book. In the preface to Uesaka's investigation, images of the atrocities for which he took responsibility are printed in the 2015 version of the confession. One of them shows a photograph of bones lined up before a memorial cenotaph in the village.

On December 7, 1954, Uesaka confirmed the photos and the incident in Japanese and then in translation that these were the bones of his victims. The Japanese confession is a bit over the top in terms of language and style and probably does not reflect his own words but rather employs a repeated set of phrases that are consistent throughout many of the confessions. Uesaka refers to his actions as "an atrociously inhuman massacre that defies language." And yet, he still confirmed the incident on May 27, 1942, in Beituan Village when the Japanese military used poison gas to kill Chinese civilians.[74] Uesaka

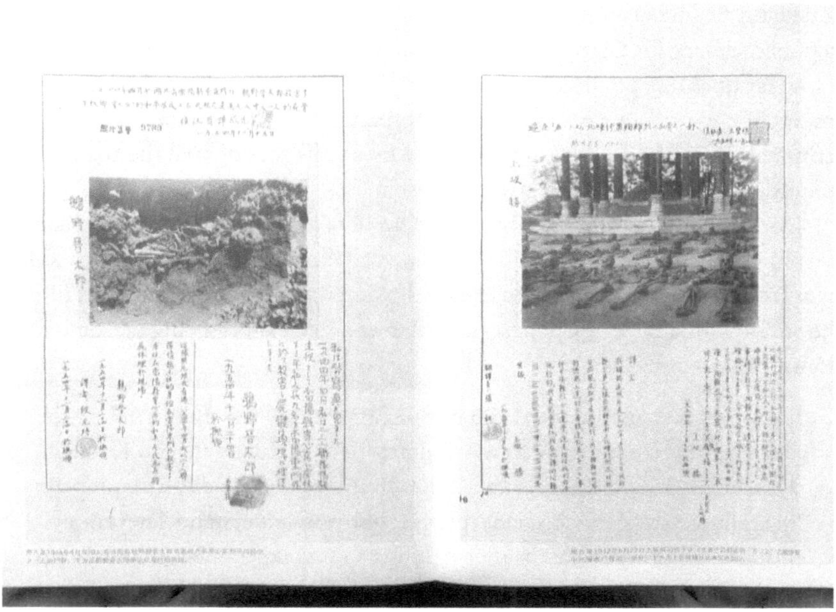

FIGURE 8.5. Published version of confessions from Uesaka Masaru and Uno Shintarō.

admitted to having used the green and red gas containers in Beituan. Soldiers threw this "poison" into tunnels, causing asphyxiation or enough pain for the rebels to try to escape from underground, where the Japanese would shoot them as they fled, he explained. Uesaka wrote that the orders to kill the suspected Eighth Route Army soldiers and civilians came from him.[75] In tightly handwritten Japanese, as with the Chinese translation, Uesaka personally recorded this admission.[76] His trial was held with Suzuki Hiraku and a group of eight in Shenyang from June 9–19, 1956.

CCP officials designated Wang Minqiu as Uesaka's defense lawyer. CCP defense teams existed, but, until recently, insight into their motivations, or even what they did, had remained thin on the ground. While memoirs abound from the guards and reeducation campaigns of the prisoners, scant records exist from the legal side. There are also very few declassified archives that detail their activities. Wang was the head of the Northeast China Branch School for Central Government Political Cadres, and he had been dispatched to Shenyang to lead the court's legal teams. One of the lawyers who worked on the team, Quan Deyuan, recalled a car ride he shared with Wang. During the ride Wang pulled some letters out of his leather satchel, turned to Quan, and said, "These are all letters sent to lawyers at the military tribunal from people in Guangdong,

Zhejiang, Shanghai and elsewhere. These letters all reproach us and ask 'You are a public servant for China but help defend the beastly Japanese imperial fascists. How far does this go to defend the position of the Chinese people?'" Wang lamented to Quan, "I can understand the people's hatred of the Japanese war criminals but they do not comprehend why at this sort of trial the regulations requiring that we must have lawyers present."[77]

Lian Xisheng, who was only twenty-three years old, harbored a similar internal conflict about being a defense lawyer for Japanese war criminals. He was from Tianjin and was five years old when the Japanese arrived. At fifteen he studied for a bit in a Japanese school in the city, experiencing life under colonial occupation. Lian said,

> If I am to be truly honest, I did not willingly think we should offer a defense for the Japanese. Afterward, many people cursed us and I can understand their emotional state. At that time a lawyer's work had not been formally established so many people did not understand lawyers and thought that lawyers just said nice things about bad people, or said things that helped the Japanese, these men who killed so many Chinese. However, we had to prudently complete the plan that we initiated and defense is one link in the trial. Without it, a civilized trial ceases to be just that.[78]

Lian added it that was hard to defend against the testimony revealed at court. "The prosecution side had already done a lot of work. Not only did they have material evidence but they also had many who would testify. The evidence was very specific and factual. For example, there would be someone who would come to court and testify, showing the back of their neck where there was a knife wound, a wound from being cut by a Japanese. How do you offer a defense in the face of that sort of evidence?"[79]

Testimony came from far and wide. One villager from Beituan managed to travel all the way to Shenyang to give testimony, although not everyone remembered this when I interviewed them in the village. Li Dexiang went into horrific detail in his testimony at Uesaka's trial on June 12, 1956. After detailing how the "devils" (his label for the Japanese military) closed up tunnel vents with futons and then threw poison gas down into the tunnel entrances or air vents to kill or force those hiding to come out, he explained his personal situation. He came up from the tunnel inside a neighbor's home. As soon as he stuck out his head, "the devils [the Japanese military] seized me. They said they wanted the guns and the hand grenades, the armaments of the 8th Route Army. I said I am just a kid and did not know about such things. The Japanese devils didn't believe me. They beat me with a wooden baton, pushed me down, then had me get up and forced me to take off my clothes. There were about

50–60 of us who had been captured by the Japanese. They also took off all the women's clothing just to humiliate them."[80] After describing the litany of Japanese crimes against civilians, including murder and rape, Li continued with his own story. The Japanese soldiers dragged him to his own house, where there were many people in the courtyard, including his mother, his younger brother, and elder sister. They pushed many people into the house and, using sorghum and surrounding materials, set fire to Li's home.

The testimony became overwhelming for Li, and the court record details that he cried at several intervals. At one point, Li turned to Uesaka, the accused, and said,

> I am the only one left from my family of six. You killed five members of my family, you completely burned down our house, the only asset we owned. All of my misfortune is entirely of your inhumane Japanese devil making. My being here saying a few words in no way dissolves my hatred for you. You not only created this painful calamity for me but you also did the same to all the families in my village, and equally caused the same to millions of civilians. How many children lost their mothers, how many mothers and fathers lost their children, how many young women lost their husbands? All of this horrible inhumanity was caused by you, you Japanese devils. Today I call on this court to sternly mete out punishment to these murderous culprits.[81]

Uesaka had been arrested in 1945, was ultimately sentenced to eighteen years in prison for his crimes, and was released in August 1963. His years incarcerated in the USSR and China before trial were counted as part of his sentence.

Confessions of a Kind

The story of how these war crimes were discussed in postwar Japan is equally important and played a large role in galvanizing feelings of injustice. In fact, the official postwar record of the Japanese imperial army's battles in Beituan Village does not mention the use of poison gas. The account acknowledges the number of Chinese dead at one thousand, which was similar to the accounts of Chinese witnesses. But the authorized Japanese military compilation only includes a description of the troop movements as they approached Beituan and that they had intelligence it was going to be riddled with tunnels. The official record blandly states, "We found the tunnel entrances and closed them off with a mass of enemy soldiers inside. We crushed the enemy and suffered 3 deaths and 5 wounded on our side. The security of this village and the surrounding areas greatly solidified after this."[82] The skirmish ended in success, according to the official postwar analysis, "due to the spiritual rigor of the Japanese military and the stern military command and control that gained the understanding of the Chinese people."[83]

This imperial record drew on Japanese regimental histories, including the personal recollections of Major Ōe Yoshiwaka, who was a battalion commander within the 163rd Regiment.[84] An intrepid Japanese journalist, Ishikiriyama Hideaki, who had studied at Beijing University, grew deeply interested in what really happened at Beituan Village.[85] He wondered how Chinese villagers could be telling one story while the Japanese imperial army recounted something different. He was fortunate enough to locate Ōe's report and realized a glaring error. Major Ōe had clearly written that his battalion had used poison gas to "annihilate" the Chinese enemy.[86] Somehow or other Ishikiriyama managed to track down Ōe, who was still alive and well in the early 1990s, and requested a personal interview. At first, Ōe insisted that what he had written in his personal report was that the Japanese troops had used gas but that it was "sneezing gas," a weapon that does not kill. It just incapacitates, he added. After a long argument Ōe admitted that he probably had used some form of gas in battle against the Chinese.[87] But if Ōe had admitted using poison gas, a war crime, why was that not showing up in Japan's official military record?

To get to the bottom of it, in 1998 Japanese photojournalist Arai Toshio and *Asahi Newspaper* reporter Honda Masakazu went to the publishing house that produced the official military history to complain and request an explanation from the lead editor of that volume, Morimatsu Toshio. After waffling, Morimatsu eventually revealed to the two Japanese journalists that because using poison gas was illegal in international law he had been instructed "from above" not to write those elements into the official Japanese military history.[88] For years Ōe's personal record was available for consultation in the reading room of Japan's Ministry of Defense archives. Suddenly, in 2003 it was no longer allowed to be seen.[89] What became obvious was that somewhere down the line there were a growing number of manifest inconsistencies in the military record compiled by Japanese officials.

From the end of the war until today, former military and official Japanese government efforts have tried to both hide and conserve what they deem as a true record of the war so they can write up their "correct" version of history. It is not dissimilar to what Nazi architect Albert Speer attempted with his secret diaries, trying to explain his side of the Holocaust genocide.[90] What is disconcerting within the history of Japan's poison gas war crimes in China is that these years of back and forth between Japanese researchers and ministry hesitation have delayed the wheels of justice.[91] But these impediments were not just of Japanese making. The United States and, in part, the Soviet Union were also complicit in their respective bids to keep the investigations into some war crimes far from glaring courtroom eyes so that the information could be monopolized for their own potential national military utilization.[92] Which Japanese war crimes were prosecuted was the result of an international game of cat and mouse, as were the stories of which trials were able to be researched long after the war was over, if the archives were deemed sufficiently declassifiable.

The Case against Sumioka Giichi

Taking a cursory look at the declassified and fully published confessions of former Japanese war criminals offers a new window into the CCP investigations and 1956 war crimes tribunals. The trials shake off their monolithic appearance when we can see behind the curtain concerning what aspects of Japanese military activity they concentrated on and perhaps why these forty-five men were chosen to stand trial while others were released. The confessions also provide insight into the sort of justice the CCP believed it was pursuing.

Sumioka Giichi was first charged in a Taiyuan court on June 12, 1956, along with Jōno Hiroshi, in a trial of eight defendants. The trial began early at 8:30 a.m. Perhaps this was scheduled to avoid the afternoon heat in what was then known as the Hall of Self-Reflection, built by General Yan Xishan, but what is now the Shanxi Hotel. Until 1949, even though Shanxi Province was theoretically part of China, the warlord General Yan Xishan managed the region as a personal fiefdom. In the 1940s the hall was a two-story building that stood at the end of a large courtyard, fronting a big lake in the center of Taiyuan city, the provincial capital. Taiyuan was one of the two communist war crimes tribunal sites in 1956 as it contained one of the, if not the largest and most spacious, halls in the region. Later, the Hall of Self-Reflection was torn down and on the same site a large resort hotel was erected. The park adjacent to the hotel houses another famous building that Yan Xishan built in honor of his father's birthday. In English, the building has several names but is usually called the Propitious Tower. It was here that, at the end of the war, Japanese lieutenant general Sumita Raishirō and KMT general Yan colluded to create collaborator battalions of Japanese soldiers. These were initially a division of around ten thousand Japanese soldiers who were coerced, or volunteered according to some sources, into continuing to wage war with the KMT against the CCP after Japan's surrender.

Among a long list of charges against Sumioka were (1) staying on in Shanxi after Japan surrendered and trying to resurrect Japan's defeated empire and

(2) rounding up prisoners and using them for "live target practice." To toughen up new Japanese recruits and accelerate their training to deal with a Chinese enemy that was showing deep reserves of resistance, the goal was not to waste bullets. Instead, young imperial soldiers were put into close contact with the enemy to get used to killing another human being without hesitating. Sumioka explained that the prisoners were a mix of Chinese Nationalist soldiers, Eighth Route Army soldiers from CCP anti-Japanese guerrilla forces, and others.

Sumioka's published confession reads almost the same as the court record. After going through all his crimes—some of which included battles with the Communist Eighth Route Army and a long list of killing civilians—he arrives at the part where he bayonetted Chinese prisoners. On July 26, 1942, he was serving as second lieutenant instructor for education of the First Year Soldier's Machine Gun Platoon stationed in Taiyuan City. Colonel Yasuo Masatsuna wanted his new soldiers "to receive real armed training in bayonetting the enemy in combat" and chose the horse track just outside of the Small Eastern Gate of the city as the site. Sumioka was Yasuo's aide-de-camp and participated in the roundups and "live target" training. Sumioka detailed in his confession, and then later to the court, that on that day in late July he brought out about 220 first-year soldiers, officers, and 220 prisoners, most of whom were anti-Japan CCP Eighth Route Army soldiers, but others were mixed in as well. He then lined up both groups to face each other. In the confession we can see Sumioka is not using his own language but perhaps has adopted the language of his captors when he explains "this mass slaughter," which is a very Chinese way of referring to the event.[93]

Sumioka observed that it was obvious the new Japanese soldiers were reluctant. In the court record he recalled, "At the time, the new recruits could only really injure the victims, they could not kill them. So, I took my own knife, faced the new soldiers to show them how it was done, and stabbed the [Chinese] prisoners in the chest killing them."[94] On that specific day, Major General Tsuda Moriya, who had commanded this sort of field training, arrived to observe the exercise. Sumioka said there was one prisoner who escaped on this day and later there was a report about him in a *Xinhua* newspaper.[95] In August, the same practice was repeated with about seventy prisoners, many of whom were women and students. They screamed "Long Live China!" when about to be stabbed, and many Japanese soldiers missed their mark. Sumioka had to show them, or when that proved insufficient shoot the prisoners himself. Sumioka signed off on his own graphic confession on March 16, 1955.[96]

In these CCP trials, judges and prosecutors posed questions to the defendants. After the presentation of Sumikoka's confession, the judge wanted to add a bit more context to exactly what happened on the racecourse with the killings. He recommended including the affidavit of Zhao Peixian. Zhao did not attend the trial, but his accusation was read into the court record. Zhao had been imprisoned in the Taiyuan Prisoner Camp. During the war it was surrounded by electric and barbed wire. Zhao testified: "On the dark and damp ground we slept, ate, crapped, pissed, and were treated like pigs. It stunk of sweat, piss and excrement, baked by the heat of the hot sun our flesh was slowly rotting. Those whose bodies were already weak fell ill after a few days and died! Those who were relatively strong, were gradually whittled down to being nothing more than skin and bones."[97] Zhao's testimony narrated his narrow escape:

> On July 26 it was our turn to be taken for live target practice. At 3.30pm eighty of us from the 'wu section' were divided into four groups, and from the Xiaodongmen [Small Eastern Gate] we were taken to a cemetery amidst the trees. Immediately a group of about 100 armed fascist bandits (the Japanese army) arrived, took the first group of 20 of my revolutionary brothers, stripped off their shirts, tied both hands behind their back, and lined them up [. . . .] [The testimony continued] [. . .] raising their bayonets the soldiers screamed as they rushed toward us. We are brave warriors of the revolution, continuing the glorious traditions of the 8th Route Army, pledged to die rather than give in! Facing down the bayonets we let loose streams of abuse. At the top of our lungs screaming: "Long live the Communist Party! Long live the victory in the war of resistance! Down with Japanese imperialism!" It was soon the third group's turn, the group I was in. [A Japanese soldier tied each prisoner up and kicked Zhao down, forcing him to kneel.] I thought: "I can't be slaughtered like a sheep, I must struggle against them as I face death." [. . .] Just before the enemy had removed his bayonet from the chest of my comrade before me, at this moment pregnant with tension, I escaped my ropes, jumped across a ditch and flew with my back to the enemy. I was lucky to have escaped.[98]

Having heard Zhao's testimony, Sumioka was asked if he had any response. He said, tearfully, "I have just heard the accusations from Zhao Peixian, and while I cannot take full responsibility, I still am a part of the Japanese militarism that killed those people. As such, I implore the judge to give me a stern sentence. This punishment itself expresses a minute fraction of apology toward the victims and the Chinese people. This expression of apology is extremely small, but in its absence I have no other way of seeking apology for my offense."[99]

Problems with This Format of Justice?

When these confessions were made to the Chinese investigators during the 1950s, the details were not released to the public in China or Japan. However, Japan's public was greatly aware of the atrocities Japanese imperial soldiers had committed, as these appeared in news reports of the various trials of Japanese war crimes and what the Liaison Group published. These were the war criminals formerly imprisoned in Shenyang and Taiyuan who were released by the CCP after being investigated and who admitted their crimes. After establishing their organization they immediately set out publishing exposés of their former crimes in books that quickly sold out. But one problem was when the soldiers were initially repatriated, the Japanese media were dubious as to how the PRC trials had taken place after ten years of incarceration. The *Asahi Newspaper* asked in its June 23, 1956, editorial, Were the trials not implemented a bit too hastily? What was obvious with such skepticism was that the Japanese public had not been primed to understand that the Chinese communists had already been investigating the Japanese war crimes for years and had made a decision based on a pragmatic foreign policy and domestic concerns to let the lesser war criminals go and put the major ones on trial. The CCP trials were, in part, predetermined because the defendants had already admitted their crimes. At the same time, the Japanese newspaper expressed concern, no doubt voicing an opinion that resonated throughout the archipelago, that it was clear to most Japanese that the defendants' postwar circumstances were random. Not only were Japanese suspicious of the nature of the "victor's justice" of such trials, but in general there was seemingly an arbitrary aspect to the laws and sentences handed down at the trials, the Japanese media reasoned. There was no uniformity, which in part mirrors Liu Tong's summary findings of the KMT trial history. "It causes one to have grave doubts about what exactly the justice of humanity is," the *Asahi* editorial complained.[100]

These confessions were employed to great effect in the 1956 PRC trials, but then they disappeared. They were first unearthed for the Japanese media in the late 1990s, and readers were astounded at the depravity of the former imperial army. War crimes trials, like those of Tokyo and elsewhere, had in many ways already depicted the horrors of war, but for many Japanese such stories were mainly only accessible in specialized history tomes and were not part of the mainstream media. Arai Toshio, an award-winning photojournalist, had secured the confessions directly from Fushun Prison.[101] This was big news on April 5, 1998, when it was scooped in the *Asahi Newspaper*.[102] The discovery split Japan's academic community mainly along political lines. Historian Fujiwara Akira, emeritus professor at the time, said that these confessions, when transposed against other materials, "showed the fairness of the Chinese trials." Yoshimi Yoshiaki, known in other circles for his work on wartime history and the comfort women issue, assessed that such confessions were valuable because they offered a rare, detailed record from officers at the army division commander level concerning war responsibility and the establishment of comfort women stations. The more conservative historian Hata Ikuhiko opined that while the materials were historically useful, how the prisoners had undergone conversion or "brain washing" remained a mystery.[103]

Not everyone took the Japanese confessions at face value. Tanabe Toshio is a long-standing Japanese revisionist who sometimes treads a dubious path of investigation. He sees these sorts of confessions as part of Japan's history problem. "I have concluded on the basis of personal investigations the fact that masochistic history ideas, anti-Japan historical views and such, or critical views of early modern history have been constructed on the basis of unfairness and a lack of common sense," he writes.[104] Tanabe believes that ideas about Japan's historical "wrongness" were built on the holy trinity of Honda Katsuichi's book *Journey to China*, reporting from China itself, and the confessions and diaries of those who were detained in China for war crimes after the war. This would include the work of the Liaison Group. Tanabe labels those who produced such material as "charlatans," but who have also become the "darlings of the media," which in his case refers to media that is supposedly liberal.[105] Tanabe is not completely full of hot air. He compared Suzuki Hiraku's personal diary, which ended up in Tokyo's Ministry of Defense archives, with his Chinese-produced confession, which was released in 1998 to much fanfare in the left-wing Japanese magazine *Sekai* (World).[106] In short, Tanabe does not believe the Chinese confessions. In the Chinese version, Suzuki provided a confession of using poison gas to kill Eighth Route Army prisoners instead of detaining them, though he says he had ordered his men to repatriate them to their respective provinces of origin. According to Tanabe, in the personal diary Suzuki kept (deposited in Japan's Ministry of Defense archives), he wrote that the army used smoke cannisters and tear gas to flush out those in the tunnels and finish them off. This same gap between personal diary and official military record appeared when investigating the official military record of actions in Beituan Village and personal memoirs. The official confession in China from Suzuki admitted crimes, whereas, according to Tanabe, Suzuki's personal diary stored in Japan does not refer to these actions. Tanabe proposes, as several others have, that the cannisters used were filled with sneezing or tear gas, not poison. Suzuki's personal diary is as detailed as his confession in China was but less damning, and Tanabe chooses to believe the less aggressive iteration. An additional issue is that Suzuki also wrote in his Chinese confession about his supposed experience of spreading plague in China, which even historian Fujiwara Akira admitted was probably an amalgamation of stories Suzuki had heard from other prisoners. Tanabe is not having it and challenges progressive historians for believing one part of the confession and not other parts. In the end, Tanabe manages to cast doubt in some places, but he is also selective in evidence that is less damning in all cases. Nonetheless, skepticism remains.

Regardless of the use of poison gas as a military terror tactic, what remains important to underline is that neither the KMT during its 1946–1949 trials nor the CCP in its 1950s investigations really dug into these issues on their own. In fact, the PRC never really investigated poison gas or biological war crimes. Chinese communist leaders grudgingly accepted the USSR-selected war criminals and then asked those Japanese to confess. But aside from this select few, no domestic Japanese war criminal cases were independently uncovered by Chinese investigations outside of the Soviet ones. Similar to the KMT, the PRC limited its pursuit of these poison gas war crimes in what appeared to be a bid to more quickly improve postwar Sino-Japanese ties.[107]

The End of Justice?

The Liaison Group, the repatriated Japanese former war criminals who coalesced into a major lobbying and educational force, has unfortunately been largely forgotten outside of Japan. Almost to a man, these former Japanese officials and military officers took on the new mantle of expressing war responsibility because they brought back their experiences and used them to ensure that Japan's peace education exposed the darker side of the historical narrative that was normally absent—Japan as perpetrator.[108]

The returnees started arriving back in Japan in the mid-1950s and quickly pressed for compensation from the state. In 1957, an initial group held its first big national meeting at the end of September and established itself formally in Tokyo with thirty members. Their goal was to assist war criminal repatriates in restoring some semblance of order to their postwar lives. They also aimed to help members financially since they were meeting with much hardship, discrimination, and police harassment. But the group's secondary goal was more overtly political and strove to oppose Japanese militarism. Their first book, of personal memoirs about the war crimes they committed, was published as *The Three Alls*, referencing the Japanese wartime imperial military policy of the enemy's total annihilation in China: "kill all, burn all, loot all." The publication met an explosive readership demand and within three weeks had sold fifty thousand copies.[109] At the same time, the Liaison Group wanted to promote better Sino-Japanese ties, so the group cooperated with the veneration and repatriation of the remains of Chinese forced laborers in Japan. Tsuji Masanobu pilloried the book for setting back Sino-Japanese relations when they were on the eve of improving, he said. Other rightists could not forgive former imperial soldiers for exposing Japan to international embarrassment.[110]

The Liaison Group continued activities in Japan through its books and journal, as well as numerous trips to China and the establishment of a committee to seek stronger Sino-Japanese ties and to recognize the violent nature of Japan's war. The museum exhibit now curated at the Fushun War Criminals Management Center began in 1987, and a lot of the materials were donated or collected from former Japanese inmates. The group's influence was not instantaneous but gestated slowly over time. In 1989, Japan's public broadcasting corporation, NHK, filmed a TV special, "War Criminals' Confessions from Fushun and Taiyuan War Criminal Management Centers," which detailed for the first time the experiences these men had undergone in China. The confessions episode was part of a larger show concerning the war in general, which was broadcast each night over four nights in August. The public broadcaster had recorded almost forty hours of interviews, many of them part of, or related to, the Liaison Group for what was ultimately edited to a forty-five-minute episode. The show gained an unprecedented 12 percent of the viewing market on those nights, an astounding twelve million Japanese viewers.[111]

While the Japanese public's reaction to the Liaison Group was earnest but slow to develop, Beijing's own analysis of the evolution of how it had "reeducated" those Japanese is worth considering. The CCP's internal assessment of the confession exercises was written up on the eve of the Cultural Revolution, on June 10, 1964. The Fushun Prison put together its analysis just after the last Japanese war criminals had been repatriated to Japan, and the investigation aimed to analyze the entirety of the project from the prisoners' arrival in 1950 and over their fourteen years of incarceration.[112] The 1960s report reflected what Wang Shilin had revealed in his interview with us. Prison executives divided the fourteen years into four stages. Stage one was the first year until the following summer, which saw the Japanese prisoners push back against the system and continue to show distaste for the Chinese staff. Stage two took place over the next two years, until about March 1953. During this period the prisoners were shocked by China's victory in the Korean War. Slowly they began to soften in the face of the benevolent and humanistic attitude the Chinese took toward them. They began to study and think about Japan's war of aggression. Stage three came around the autumn of 1954, as the investigations into the Japanese officials' confessions intensified. Even if they admitted that Japan's war was invasive and not one of liberation, it was still difficult for them to question the validity of their own behavior as anything criminal. Stage four was their final acceptance and acknowledgment of their guilt and social recognition around the summer of 1956 as the trials began.[113]

And then, after all that work, the trials were over, and once again Chinese public debate about counterrevolutionaries took up more media attention than worrying about Japanese war criminals. By the end of the 1950s, Mao's policies of destruction were evident in the legal sphere, but sadly little had been created to replace it. The Hundred Flowers Campaign had initially launched in the spring of 1956, just as trials of Japanese were taking place. From that spring through 1957, much domestic discussion about China's orientation and criticism of the CCP emerged. The campaign came to a shuddering halt and turned volte-face with the subsequent anti-Rightist campaign, beginning in June 1957, almost a year after the war crimes trials of Japanese finished and "justice" was then subverted to politics. This move was a defensive measure by Mao, pushback against the intellectual criticism that the party had requested and then duly received much more of than anticipated.[114] It was here that the beginning of the end started: three thousand lawyers in 1957 reduced to four for the ensuing decades (1958–1980). By 1959, the Ministry of Justice was completely abolished, and the rule of law would not reemerge on the mainland until the early 1980s.[115] However, even as courts were dismantled and the law was put to sleep, the legacy of injustice would percolate to the surface and continue to disturb Sino-Japanese relations on both sides of the East China Sea.

Chapter 9

The Pathology of Justice in Post-Occupation Japan

While the Chinese were investigating and processing their socialist formulations of justice, the Japanese government and society struggled over the same situation but in the opposite direction. How could a defeated nation "own" justice? This would center on redefining the meaning of the trials and critiquing the form of justice the Allies had pursued.

Preparations for how to compete with the vision of justice being meted out in China and elsewhere began even before Japan regained its sovereignty with the implementation of the 1952 San Francisco Peace Treaty. Behind the scenes, in preparation for the return of Japan's political sovereignty, Toyota Kumao and his team in the Ministry of Justice were putting together a new strategy for a change in the Japanese public's attitude toward war crimes and former war criminals.[1] Former naval captain Toyota Kumao headed an office within the Second Bureau of Demobilization (formerly the Ministry of the Navy), which was charged with keeping naval officers out of legal trouble, defending them if things went to trial, and collecting trial records and evidence as the means to offer a defense or apply for later clemency. This group was active from the end of 1945 until the 1970s, suggesting that some portions of the former Japanese military and leadership were keen to keep their names disconnected from the idea of war responsibility. Aiming to coordinate a policy for compiling a record of war crimes trials to be used as a reference for the larger plans, Toyota wrote about a consultation meeting and detailed how the historical summary should be organized like a plan of attack. This preparation concerned how to mobilize parliament and coordinate files, among other matters. The plan called for encouraging the Japanese government and recommending the restoration of privileges to war criminals. Toyota noted the need to get all of this systematized in advance of when Japan's peace treaties were to be enacted. He suggested using lawyers groups and family associations of the war bereaved in a media campaign to guide public opinion. His team discussed ways of gathering necessary materials to deal adequately with the legal issues concerning compensation problems of "third country nationals," referring obliquely to Taiwanese and Koreans who had been convicted in war crimes tribunals. One of the most interesting elements of Toyota's plan was the recognition that once sovereignty was restored, Japan needed to have the complex planning in place in order for it to be effective for the former soldiers who required it. The first step to attain this "was to create a solid foundation for the public to perceive that those connected to war criminals (including families) were victims of the war."[2]

Toyota's group wanted to incorporate bereaved family members' grievances into the general sacrifices made during the war in the cases of war criminals in a bid to secure government aid. This inclusion would serve as a further linkage between regular deaths in the war and those who were executed, the plan enunciated. The burial remains or bones of the war criminals who died abroad were to be returned in the same manner as those who were deemed "regular battlefield deaths." Also, the group outlined the need to further examine the issue of getting executed war criminals enshrined in Yasukuni and how to keep a focus on public opinion. Importantly, this move would take place on a national scale by going to each region and getting those locales to schedule "comfort the spirits" events in geographic coordination for those who died during the war.

The plan also detailed "operations for managing political public opinion." This media campaign was directed at raising awareness among the people about the true situation of war criminals, according to conservative Japanese officialdom. Public materials from international law specialists and their associations, talking about the related issues, needed to be produced and distributed. Letters from families that "have emotional appeal," materials from the last wills and testaments of executed war criminals, and materials from Japanese who were abused as POWs themselves would need to be collected, the plan observed. Toyota's blueprint recommended using such materials in different media campaigns to influence government policy. The group intended to use and release these resources in newspapers and magazines after the implementation of the peace treaty (around April, the plan noted). While one cannot prove that these plans were actually implemented as they were outlined, their goals seem fairly consistent with what happened in Japan after the San Francisco Treaty. The ultimate thrust, the plan noted, was to get those in positions of authority to empathize with the predicament of war criminals. An additional goal was to get the minority judgments of the Tokyo Trial publicly published. This was a reference to Judge Radhabinod Pal's dissent, which, like most of the other elements of the Tokyo Trial, took decades to be fully released. Finally, the plan referenced a need to organize and publicly produce background notes about Allied atrocities and illegal activities as a counterbalance to the charges against Japan.[3] Having plans at hand was crucial to coordinate the collection of war crimes materials from tribunals outside of Japan, the report assessed.[4]

Within the plan, a fascinating diagram from 1950 shows how the Ministry of Justice kept up with what was happening to Japanese war criminals domestically and those still incarcerated abroad. It is telling that the Japanese government was more anxious about its former soldiers after the war than it had been concerned about their well-being during the war. The handwritten spreadsheet displays Sugamo Prison, Australia's Manus Island prison, and detention centers in the Philippines, Burma, Singapore, Hong Kong, and other locations. Officials tabulated a general summary of prisoner daily activities, conditions of food, work, clothing, daily necessities, entertainment, medical and communication circumstances, and so forth.[5] All of these debates and decisions ultimately paved the way for the Japanese government to eventually claim the souls of those executed as war criminals and have them enshrined at Yasukuni Shrine.[6]

Intense negotiations and discussions had led up to the San Francisco Peace Treaty, enacted on April 28, 1952. Debates had revolved around whether Japan should enact a multilateral peace with all its previous enemies, including China and the USSR, or a more singular orientation toward US interests and excluding the communist nations. In the short term, US leverage won the day. But this did not mean such policy weighed in on all features of political life in newly sovereign Japan. One of the first policies the Japanese government declared days later was a pronouncement of how the nation should view its war criminals. At an April 30, 1952, press conference, Attorney General Kimura Tokutarō stated that he wanted to put forward processes to grant amnesty to BC class war criminals.[7] The next day, Kimura issued a more affirmative directive to other government offices that war criminals who had died while incarcerated would be considered as "deaths in public service" and that currently jailed war criminals would be legally treated as having been "detained" or "arrested." This meant previous welfare and military benefits that had been denied to those men and their families would now be permitted. Such a government pronouncement issued from the Ministry of Justice to relevant government agencies effectively meant that on the level of domestic Japanese law, those prisoners would no longer be defined as war criminals.[8] On June 21, 1952, the Japanese Federation of Lawyers handed Prime Minister Yoshida Shigeru and Attorney General Kimura a memo of the federation's opinion to have all the war criminals released because such a move undergirded the real principles for establishing a lasting peace.[9] Several months later, Kimura became minister of justice in the fourth Yoshida Shigeru cabinet, but he was perhaps better known as the backbone of postwar movements that fiercely opposed communism and harkened back to the heady prewar days of ultranationalism.[10]

Kimura's announcement, which amounted to a national volte-face concerning Japanese war criminal responsibility, was not a shock to most. The political tide had been building for months. In mid-November of the previous year, at the Japanese Diet Committee on Judicial Affairs, Attorney General Ōhashi Takeo had made statements in the Diet that once the occupation had ended, war criminals would no longer be deemed as such on the level of Japanese domestic law.[11] Because foreign governments conducted these trials, he claimed, they did not have legal validity in the eyes of Japanese domestic law. In a sense, what Ōhashi was saying was that Japanese prisoners would be treated in accordance with Japanese law as prisoners, but not as special "war criminals" as they had previously been defined. Such a change in terminology allowed Japan to treat the verdicts or review the trials as it deemed fit, according to its own legal standards and policies.[12] In fact, even before conservative political elements within Japan's former imperial superstructure began pushing a narrow interpretation of the Tokyo Trial, outspoken conservative opinion leaders were using Judge Pal's dissent to that end. In 1952, Tanaka Masaaki, who had been secretary to General Matsui Iwane (executed for Class A war crimes), published a book in which he argued that Judge Pal had pronounced Japan not guilty. The book, whose original title was *The Argument for Japan's Innocence: Judging the Truth*, has been republished and repackaged a bit over the years. In the same year, a second popular book emerged in the form of Yoshimatsu Masakatsu's partially translated and edited version of Pal's dissent, *Refuting the History of the War: Japan Was Innocent*.[13] Both tomes had excellent sales and championed Japan as "not guilty" in the Tokyo Trial, perverting to some extent what Pal had intended. Pal had noted that the trial was unlawful on the level of international law, but he did not claim that Japan had acted nobly in any measure, nor had he diminished the problems inherent in Japanese imperial rule.[14]

Not everyone in Japan agreed. The always-vocal-until-they-were-banned JCP and the budding Japanese Socialist Party (JSP), formed in the late autumn of 1945, both voiced strong opposition. These minority parties reasoned that unless Japan took measures of its own to both atone for and delve into the causes of the crimes of war, peace in Asia would be short-lived. And both parties' positions stemmed from how they saw the validity of the Tokyo Trial. The JCP "uncritically accepted the Tokyo Judgment. The JSP accepted the judgment but explicitly argued that the trial had serious flaws, including the failure to subject the Allied powers to the same standards of criminal justice."[15] It is important to note that conservative powers picked up the criticisms of the JSP but not its intent.

Early Postwar Interactions with China

Contrary to Chinese stories about Mao's unique form of benevolence toward postwar Japan, it appears that the decision to "reeducate" Japanese suspected war criminals did not solely emerge from Soviet pressure or from internal PRC plans. An additional avenue of pressure interestingly developed from increased contact with disparate Japanese groups and bilateral meetings from the early 1950s. This is a hitherto unexplored facet of the postwar Sino-Japanese relationship that influenced decisions concerning war criminals. Such efforts also reflect the nature of entangled pasts, in "that the past that is remembered—the object of memory—must itself be placed in a transnational context and be seen as a product of processes of exchange and influence."[16]

In the summer of 1950, the head of the Japanese Red Cross, Shimazu Tadatsugu, had traveled to Monaco to represent Japan at an International Red Cross meeting. At a party, he ran into PRC Red Cross representative Li Dequan. Shimazu asked Li if she could investigate the whereabouts of Japanese whose repatriation had not yet taken place from China, including more than three hundred Red Cross nurses.[17] Opportunities for communication between mainland China and Japan were few and far between but held immense importance for bilateral relations.[18]

In April 1952, concomitant to the implementation of the San Francisco Peace Treaty, the ROC (Taiwan) signed a special and separate peace treaty with Japan. The USSR was also trying to shore up its international support, and at the beginning of April the Soviets held an international economic conference in Moscow to sponsor trade between the Cold War blocs. Even with the knowledge that Japanese were still detained in China, but unclear on the actual numbers, the two countries were keen to organize new but unofficial economic agreements. The first of these was created through the personal visits of several Japanese Diet members, including Kōra Tomi, Hoashi Kei, and Miyakoshi Kisuke. Kōra Tomi was a Diet member of the upper house and the first Japanese woman to get a PhD from Johns Hopkins University, having also studied at Columbia University. Hoashi Kei was a former member of the upper house of parliament and representative of the Japan–China Trade Promotion Association. Miyakoshi Kisuke was a member of the lower house and director-general of the Federation of Japanese Parliamentarians to Promote Sino-Japanese Trade. Rebuilding the national economy and infrastructure was important to both Japan and China.[19]

The Japanese group was not officially permitted passports to travel to China because Japan did not legally recognize the PRC. The Yoshida government also used a clause within the Japanese passport law to deny anyone a travel pass if there were potential issues of national security. At this time, Yoshida Shigeru concurrently held the posts of both prime minister and foreign minister, so he had much bureaucratic power in hand. Regardless, the Japanese leftists pulled a ruse to travel, and the game was on. The members used their privilege as former and current members of the Diet to exit the country and then took roundabout travel itineraries to eventually find their way to the meeting in Moscow.[20] In the USSR, during their travels from Khabarovsk to Vladivostok, Kōra and the others were able to learn firsthand what was happening with the remaining Japanese detained as prisoners and war criminals. In Moscow, their invitations to Beijing had already been prepared, and they traveled from there to China as, unofficially, the first Japanese government representatives in the postwar era to enter Beijing. (JCP leaders had already snuck into Beijing previously.) On May 15, 1952, Sun Pinghua, who had studied in Japan during the war, met the group at Beijing's airport and welcomed them to new China. Sun had been placed in the group that would coordinate with the Japanese, specifically owing to his experience while working briefly for the Manchukuo government and his years of study in Japan. His interpretation, however, was not always praised.[21]

On June 1, 1952, the First Sino-Japanese Trade Agreement was announced by Hoashi, Miyakoshi, and Kōra. The main Chinese interlocutor was Nan Hanchen from the China Council for the Promotion of International Trade.[22] It was an unofficial trade agreement as the Japanese delegates were opposition party members and did not represent the government in power.[23] The Yoshida cabinet had put up all sorts of obstacles, but the group's efforts paid off. Getting home after their trip to China was another matter. Kōra recalled that all three were refused reentry to the USSR for their return journey on the pretext that news about them would harm Soviet relations with Japan. The other two eventually went home by way of Hong Kong, whereas Kōra was invited to Switzerland to present her account of how Japanese POWs were faring in the Soviet Union.[24]

Upon their return, Hoashi and Miyakoshi joined the speaking circuit around Japan, reporting on their findings in the USSR and China. They conducted a whistle-stop tour in Tokyo, Osaka, Kyoto, and finally Nagoya, where a riot ensued. On the evening of July 7, 1952, a collection of labor unionists, students, and North Korean–linked activists numbering five thousand, according to some reports, welcomed the two Diet members for an event celebrating their return. After the festivities, newspapers reported that the North Korean flag and a red flag were raised. Police tried to stop the demonstration and a clash ensued. Protesters threw Molotov cocktails, numbers grew, more police were called in, and a massive riot ensued. In the end, more than twenty people were injured and ninety arrested.[25] The newspapers noted what was happening to many of the Japanese prisoners in the USSR, some having been charged as war criminals and serving sentences after trials that were poorly understood.[26] Kōra said in a press conference in Hong Kong that the PRC had calculated about twenty-five thousand Japanese were still living in China.[27] She returned to Japan on July 27, 1952. The Japanese media highlighted criticism from some of the nurses and technicians who were able to repatriate in this initial stage. The nurses and technicians refuted reports of Hoashi and others, which had been produced in the Chinese press. The repatriating doctors and nurses said that with the exception of those Japanese who were believers in communism, everyone else wanted to repatriate and life was difficult in the PRC.[28]

In December 1952, two years after initially being asked, the Chinese finally officially responded to Japan's query about Japanese who stayed behind. Beijing radio announced to a very surprised Japanese public that approximately thirty thousand Japanese were still living in China. Things developed fairly quickly after this admission, and the Chinese invited Uchiyama Kanzō, head of the Japan-China Friendship Association, to lead a delegation to China composed of himself, the Japanese Red Cross chief, Shimazu Tadatsugu; head of the Peace Liaison Group, Hirano Yoshitarō; Upper House Representative Kōra Tomi; and seven others.[29] This was the start of "people's diplomacy," the heart of a new form of Chinese international relations in the absence of official diplomatic recognition. In part, this Chinese strategy built on the CCP's wartime policy of treating the Japanese people as innocent and blaming the Japanese military leadership for the war. This also meant further separating those who had been in positions of authority as having responsibility, whereas other public officials of lower ranks had merely made mistakes and did not have the same burden.[30]

Even with the ups and downs in Japan's relations with China, it was not until late January 1953 that Kōra Tomi finally received an official passport to travel to China. Japan had resumed its sovereignty, and although travelers were limited in the amount of money they could take out of the country, international travel was still procedurally tricky and permitted for only a select few. Once again, the Japanese government initially dragged its heels providing Kōra with travel documents, which delayed the group's departure for a few weeks. Early 1950s official Japanese government policy toward China was complex for a variety of immediate postwar political reasons. "In essence, the Yoshida cabinet employed a double-tongued policy and promoted Sino-Japanese economic relations, while denouncing China publicly in order to save its face with Washington."[31] Once the Japanese group got to the mainland, they met with Chinese officials to discuss the as-yet-unrepatriated thousands of Japanese as well as meetings to expand trade. Uchiyama's group met with a variety of Chinese delegates, including Red Cross head Li Dequan and Japan hand Liao Chengzhi.[32] The groups agreed on enough steps to get the ball rolling once again to advance in March 1953 Japanese repatriation of the more than thirty thousand Japanese still residing in China who wished to return to Japan.

However, 1953 was also a pivotal year for a confrontation with the conservative forces at work in Japan and their efforts to define the meaning of Japan's recent war. Parliamentarian Kita Reikichi, a member of the Liberal Party, queried the government about its goals for raising the morals of the country. Politicians on both sides of the spectrum were worried about the supposed decline of social values in the postwar period. In response, Minister of Education Okano Kiyohide explained, "Postwar the people have completely lost their confidence. For me this is most regrettable." He went on to detail that he did not wish to enter into a debate about whether the Greater East Asian War was bad. He wanted the Japanese people to find some historical fixtures on which they could restore their pride. Regardless of the outcome of the war, he said, "the fact that the Japanese are superior I think I can prove. At the very least, the fact that they were at war with many of the world's countries for four years points to Japanese superiority we can say. I will probably be told that I am exaggerating ethnic hubris, or rather that this is a feudalistic way of thinking. But I think because we have completely lost our confidence, I want Japanese who have lost confidence to such an extent to claim this feeling back so that is why I am saying things like this."[33]

PRC assessments noted the Japanese discomfort with its predicament, concerning how to analyze its recent past. An "internal eyes only" report within the Chinese government from March 28, 1953, stated that it was important to consider the mind-set of Japanese returnees from Shanghai and their attitudes toward repatriating. The internal investigation noted that many Japanese felt that this repatriation was very sudden and the majority did not wish to repatriate. Only about twenty-nine wanted to return to Japan. The internal report detailed that the Japanese said they liked their lives in new China and were afraid of unemployment in Japan. The report labeled some as communists or "progressives." These Japanese repatriates were afraid of being blacklisted in Japan by the Yoshida government, something that later experience proved accurate in many cases.[34] Some even cried and would not fill out the necessary forms, saying in the end, "If you order us to repatriate that will be the only way we will return." Others said that because China now had access to advanced USSR technology, Japan was no longer necessary.

According to the report, other Japanese said they would repatriate and carry on the revolutionary struggle. Some Chinese public security officers who were mobilizing the Japanese for repatriation spoke to them in rather stern language, saying, "We don't need you now that we have advanced Soviet technology." Or, "if you don't take up this opportunity to repatriate, it will be too difficult in the future." Such statements, the report cautioned, cause the overseas Japanese distress and should be stopped. One group of Japanese in Tianjin gathered to repatriate admitted upon return to Japan that they would study Mao Zedong thought. Many gave tearful goodbyes upon embarking on the ship, according to the PRC analysis.

But the same report noted several deficiencies in the repatriation process: there were many ill Japanese among the groups repatriating. Those from Hebei Province, with more than three hundred Japanese, had more than fifty who were ill. Other areas sent Japanese who had communicable diseases and mental issues, as well as pregnant women who were about to give birth. Additionally, there was no uniformity of monetary assistance given to those who were going to repatriate. Some groups were provided a bit of financial assistance, others a month's salary.[35]

The March 28, 1953, report also analyzed the mental states of those Japanese repatriating from Shanghai. The internal analysis concluded that the Japanese were of many minds regarding repatriation. Some factory workers and technicians believed that this was China's way of dealing with the Yoshida government's comments that China was detaining Japanese so Tokyo insisted the Japanese repatriate. Many women said that their lives were stable in China and they questioned why the Chinese government was forcing them to repatriate. Others felt that with US president Dwight Eisenhower's administration just beginning, the situation would become tense in the future. Others accepted returning to Japan if they could take their Chinese wives and children with them. If forced to separate, members of that group announced that they would jump into the ocean, presumably committing suicide. Others had already taken Chinese names, so it was obvious they were not keen on returning to Japan. This sort of internal report for Chinese high-level officials admitted that given all these problems related to repatriation, the issue demanded serious attention.

The "reactionary" Japanese government, the report pointed out, also wanted to use repatriating Japanese for intelligence purposes to learn whether Japanese war criminals were still being detained in China. Rumors around China maintained that tens of thousands more were detained in the north. Others said that the searching of Japanese baggage upon departure was too stringent and that this left a bad feeling because the Chinese officials were breaking personal items. Some felt Japanese women were singled out and embarrassed, the reported noted, so Chinese officials took steps to correct this and began using female inspectors.[36]

Man in the Iron Mask, Communist Style

While Japanese leftists of all stripes were traveling in competing groups to China and the Soviet Union to link with partners, gain advice, and direct the winds of political change back in Japan, the JCP was falling apart. The harbinger of what could have become the catalyst for domestic pressure within Japan to investigate its own war crimes was tragically lost to infighting and political backstabbing. Nowhere was this dissolution more evident than in the tragic story of Itō Ritsu.

Photographs of Itō Ritsu from 1948 show a confident man in the full splendor of his thirties with swept-back black hair, sporting a handsome face with pronounced cheekbones. Itō's experience was very different from those of his two main CCP postwar rivals—Tokuda Kyūichi and Nosaka Sanzō. Tokuda had spent almost two decades in harsh conditions imprisoned in Japan. Nosaka Sanzō had been abroad, helping the CCP in Yenan for much of that time, while keeping the political fires of international socialism burning bright far from the hearth of Japanese imperialism.

In the early 1950s the JCP faced an internal dilemma: which party line to follow? Nosaka pushed for a softer line but faced Cominform criticism, which wanted the Japanese to be violent in the promotion of the revolution. This friction produced further factionalism within the JCP regarding which party to follow and what revolutionary line to take. In late June 1950 the Korean War exploded, but the US occupation authorities had already stopped publication of the Japanese communist flagship newspaper *Red Flag*, which by this point had grown into a media force in Japan. Starting with only ten thousand

FIGURE 9.1. CCP criticism of "Imperious America pressing Yoshida, oppressing the democratic people, and shutting down the *Red Flag* newspaper." Image is from box 29, "17 Chinese communist propaganda postcards," Preliminary Inventory of the Zhongguo Gongchandang Issuances, HIA.

copies in October 1945, with its original publication calling for justice in Japan, *Red Flag* reached a distribution of three hundred thousand by the beginning of 1950. Its departure from Japan's public media arena was significant.[37] On June 6, 1950, SCAP ordered the "removal from public life" of twenty-four members of the JCP's central committee, which essentially shut down its functioning as a political party.

This era soon witnessed bickering about policy and adherence to ideology that caused fissures within the left-wing leadership. Trotskyites, petty bourgeois, deviationists, sectarians, and other epithets were thrown at each of the factions. These arguments sadly overwhelmed the original aims to topple the emperor and establish political rights for the disenfranchised.[38] In the interim, labeled as the "Molotov cocktail period" by some, many of the purged leaders went underground or voyaged in secret to China by boat, to wait things out.[39] Nosaka, Tokuda, and Itō found themselves in political exile on the mainland. Further political divisions soon appeared. In December 1952, at a JCP safe house in Beijing, surrounded by high walls and monitored by public security guards, Itō was questioned by his comrades. Itō recounted that he was told

Moscow had directed the JCP to hold this meeting. Tokuda was in China but not present. In part, this was because Tokuda's long years in detention had broken his health and he had already been in a Beijing hospital for three months. Nosaka and other party luminaries were present, including Nishizawa Takaji, and several CCP members, Li Chuli, and Zhao Anbo.[40] Zhao often served as translator between the Chinese and Japanese communist party elements because of his strong language skills gained from having studied in Japan. At this initial meeting, Nosaka pulled out a piece of paper and claimed that instructions from Moscow, meaning Stalin, intimated that Itō should immediately be removed from party duties. Although Itō had already been accused several times in the immediate postwar period, the party had found him not guilty in the Sorge affair. Nosaka told Itō that to clear everything up about the Sorge incident, party leaders required him to write yet another self-criticism.[41]

The group that was detaining Itō changed buildings, and from that time for about a year Itō was kept under house arrest in Beijing.[42] Ironically, he said that he felt something like this might happen when he secretly went to China. At that time, Japan was still under occupation rules and no official travel abroad was permitted, particularly to communist countries. It is obvious that Itō got swept up in intraparty politics as well as the conflict between the JCP and the CCP and their mutual reliance on Soviet leadership. His house arrest began on December 24, 1952. Along with extensive self-criticisms constantly being requested, during his initial sequestering he was treated well and had a servant boy in the house for food and errands, who also brought in water for cleaning. Doctors were called when Itō fell sick.

As Japanese political representatives traveled more frequently to China for improved relations, and tens of thousands were repatriating, former Japanese communist leader Itō Ritsu was being more carefully withdrawn from public view. Throughout the end of 1952 and into 1953 the JCP and CCP leadership kept pushing and asking Itō if he was a spy. Had he been the one who had given up Richard Sorge in Tokyo during World War II? In the midst of this, in March 1953 Stalin died and deeper fissures opened up between the JCP and the CCP.

By the end of 1954, Nosaka Sanzō, leader of the JCP, and other high-ranking members of the JCP had stricken Itō from party membership rolls for having been in contact with an officer of the special higher police during the war and for supposedly having given succor to the imperialist United States in the immediate postwar period. In China, Itō was moved several times under guard and eventually was put in prison. From this time until Itō returned to Japan in 1980, Nosaka Sanzō denied this entire story. Itō always felt that unless Nosaka had been complicit, the Chinese would never have thrown him in prison. Itō was never formally charged, only detained in various Chinese prisons for decades. He was literally thrown into a dungeon along the lines of dark fiction that Alexandre Dumas made famous in his nineteenth-century story, *The Man in the Iron Mask.*

Had Itō become a symbol of ideological conflict among the various East Asian communist parties, or was he being punished in China because the Japanese could never find sufficient evidence to pursue him in a Japanese court? Regardless, the JCP was intent on using extralegal measures to silence one of Nosaka's main competitors for party leadership. As Itō languished in a series of Chinese jails, efforts to augment Sino-Japanese relations continued unabated throughout the 1950s. In September 1953, a group of twenty-three Japanese politicians and industrial experts and businessmen formed a mission to China to further expand trade and received an enthusiastic welcome. Zhou Enlai's first postwar meeting with a Japanese was with Ōyama Ikuo, head of the Peace Protection Committee.[43] By the end of October 1954, Japan and China had already signed their second trade accord. Hatoyama Ichirō took the reigns as prime minister and exchanged letters with Beijing, on August 29 and October 20, 1954, saying that Japan needed to resolve issues related to Japanese stranded in China, including the problems concerning Japanese war criminals.[44]

This era continued to see a steady flow, mostly of Japanese to China, of interaction and attempts toward reconciliation and reconstructing a more formalized system for trade and political relations. At the same time, both sides were a bit wary of the other. On September 5, 1954, Beijing broadcast a shortwave radio roundtable program of seven Japanese former soldiers who had been granted amnesty by the PRC and who would soon be repatriated. The family of one soldier, Nishii Kenichi, had not received any word from him since his mobilization in September 1943 and had woken early to travel to a self-defense forces' site to hear the transmission. The broadcast was full of static and hard to decipher, but when Nishii's mother, wife, and eldest daughter heard his voice, for the first time in twelve years, they held their breath, the *Asahi Newspaper* reported.[45]

An "internal eyes only" Chinese report from September 28, 1954, examined the situation of meetings with formerly released Japanese military officers and Diet members of Japan's left-wing political parties. Socialist party members Tanaka Toshio and Kameda Tōgo, among others, including kabuki actor Nakamura Kan'emon, met with a group of former Japanese soldiers who were granted clemency and released. The Chinese government had invited Tanaka to visit China from July 30, 1954, and he returned to Japan on October 21.[46] Kameda was an old leftist and labor organizer who had written several books on China and related issues.[47] Nakamura was a thespian, a kabuki performer who had gotten wrapped up in a political scandal and sought refuge in China for a number of years.

As more Japanese visited China, some of them were able to observe or meet with former Japanese POWs and war criminals. Tanaka, Kameda, and Nakamura held a roundtable with about twenty former Japanese imperial soldiers to whom the CCP had given amnesty. Tanaka explained to them, according to the Chinese assessment of the event, that rural life in Japan was more prosperous than the urban areas, and that land reform had been fairly successful. The former soldiers asked Tanaka if their livelihoods would be protected once they returned home. Tanaka replied that if they had technical skills they would find work, but the subtext of his comments was that unemployment was the future for those who had no skill set. The Chinese report stated that during the meeting the former soldiers incessantly posed questions and Tanaka responded, sweating from being placed in a difficult position. The Japanese soldiers asked him if the Japanese government would pay for their repatriation, and Tanaka explained that because these men had chosen to stay and fight with KMT warlord General Yan Xishan, after Japan had already declared surrender, such funds would not be forthcoming. Some of the soldiers showed disappointment with Tanaka's comments. The men immediately responded that they had been forced to remain and join forces with KMT troops, which rendered Tanaka speechless. The former soldiers were more conciliatory toward Kameda and Nakamura, the report indicated.[48]

Many of the men who talked with Tanaka showed their displeasure. Others said, "What Tanaka is talking about seems more like propaganda from his party. . . . He's not really saying anything factual." Others retorted that Tanaka wanted them to go back to the rural areas so that they would not continue the struggle in the urban areas. Kameda's talks met with a better reception, and his remarks received great applause from the former soldiers, the report noted. The final paragraph of the internal Chinese report detailed that, after this meeting, many former Japanese soldiers came to realize that Japan's socialist party was a "faker" but that "the communist party was the people's party." It was only because they received education from the liberation army, the PLA, that they claimed to have realized the true aims of the socialist party and now understand the need to unite behind them, the report concluded.[49] After three years abroad, in November 1955, Nakamura proclaimed to the media that his return was a "Triumphant Repatriation."[50]

In late September 1954, an academic/political delegation traveled to China to celebrate the fifth anniversary of the People's Republic. The mission included LDP member Yamaguchi Kikuichirō, JSP member Suzuki Mosaburō, Sino-Japan Friendship Association head Matsumoto Jiichirō, and others.[51] On

October 11 they engaged in a broad set of talking points covering economics and diplomacy with Chinese premier Zhou Enlai and also touched on the war criminal issue. Zhou informed the mission that some Japanese soldiers who fought with KMT general Yan Xishan and committed atrocities had already returned home. There were still one thousand or so war criminals remaining in China, Zhou remarked. KMT leader Chiang Kai-shek dealt with those who took part in the invasion of China. The ones left in China belonged to one of two categories, Zhou explained: (1) those taken prisoner by the Soviets and returned to China and (2) the one hundred or so who committed crimes while with the post-1945 Chinese Nationalist forces. Zhou stated that all these individuals were permitted to communicate with their families through the Chinese Red Cross, a point that would be touched on by Red Cross head Li Dequan when she visited Japan. China wanted to resolve this problem quickly, Zhou added. The PRC followed its wartime practice of refraining from killing Japanese POWs. However, among these prisoners were those who committed serious war crimes, so the PRC could not treat them the same and explained that it was looking into how to deal with them, Zhou underscored to the Japanese visitors.[52]

On October 12, 1954, the PRC and the USSR released a joint statement concerning their new policy toward Japan. The gist of the statement was an acknowledgment of the fact that Japan had emerged from the occupation once again as an independent nation, and launched an appeal of sorts for the Japanese to break from the military dictates of the United States.[53] On the same day, the Soviet Union removed the military forces it had stationed at Port Arthur on China's Liaodong Peninsula. Both the PRC and the USSR were pressing Japan that the time was ripe to consider reestablishing diplomatic relations.[54] On his way home in late October 1954, which involved a stop in Hong Kong, Tanaka Toshio held a press conference where he remarked that he supported the recent Sino-Soviet statement on relations with Japan because it would help restore diplomatic relations with those two countries.[55] It is apparent that the CCP was greatly interested in keeping an eye on the pulse of public opinion in Japan in part because of the great information gap that had grown since 1949. So few were the conduits of news and knowledge over the short geographic distance that Chinese leaders leapt at anything they saw as potentially adverse to their stance.

On the last day of October 1954, the long-awaited visit of the Chinese Red Cross representative, Li Dequan, finally arrived. Japanese newspapers had been drumming up interest in her and the potential for change that a high-ranking Chinese official visit might bring. When she arrived, the *Asahi Newspaper* announced that a "grand reception team" awaited her at the Tokyo airport.[56] The

Japanese media was clear she had been invited in a private capacity by the Japanese Red Cross and was thus not "an official guest." Nonetheless, the public were elated. Li brought a list of the thousand or so Japanese on the rolls as war criminals to be tried. The papers asked that they not be used as political hostages but be dealt with in a civilized manner. Japanese newspapers noted that while many Japanese Diet members had visited China and traveled around unaccosted, some of the right wing in Japan threatened to make Li's trip difficult. This should not happen, and Li should be able to travel around Japan freely and without worry, Japan's media underscored.[57] Li embodied three elements of change and transformation that fascinated the Japanese public. In the political realm, "left-leaning social organizations, intellectuals, and activists saw the Li visit as a valuable step forward in the restoration of China-Japan friendship and East Asian peace." Japanese women saw in Li an example of the heights to which gender equality could be reached outside of Japan. At least in the minds of many at the time, this parity had been achieved in the PRC and demonstrated how far Japan still had to go to attain such a milestone. Finally, Li was a beacon of hope for bereaved families "who would learn from the Li delegation if their soldier sons, husbands, and fathers would finally be coming home." For them, "her visit was a blessing that offered relief from painful uncertainty."[58] Li brought over the first official Chinese enunciation of who was detained as a Japanese war criminal in China, and she handed over lists of names. It is important to recognize that she came under the auspices of the Red Cross, not as a CCP member, which she was not. With her deputy Liao Chengzhi, Li had undertaken the first large-scale Chinese mission for new China to visit Japan.

The Chinese Red Cross, Japanese Red Cross, and the Japan-China Friendship Association released a memo of understanding on November 3, 1954.[59] They publicly put forward the steps to be taken for how repatriation would proceed and included a proviso that children born from the union of Japanese and Chinese under the age of sixteen would be considered Chinese, but a child above sixteen would be allowed to choose his or her citizenship and thus repatriate if desired. Article 7 of the memorandum touched on the war criminal issue. Some would be released, as Premier Zhou had already told a Japanese delegation about a month prior, and the Red Cross would represent the governments in the absence of official diplomatic channels. But other war criminals, those who had committed serious crimes, would remain in China to fulfill their sentences. In these cases the Red Cross organizations of both countries would aid in exchanging letters and packages.[60] If the Japanese side wanted to know about the terms of incarceration, where they were being held, their sentences, and other related matters, the Chinese said they would consider publicly releasing this information and would consult with the relevant ministries.

On December 4, 1954, an "internal eyes only" Chinese report on Japanese journalists visiting the city of Tianjin assessed that Chinese cooperation with the Japanese journalists, in which they let them into their homes and allowed them to interview repatriates, surprised the visiting Japanese.[61] Such internal Chinese reports, like the Americans before and the Japanese authorities after 1952, were responsible for interviewing repatriates to analyze the mood of the nation and the direction in which national attitudes were leaning. A report from December 15, 1954, contained an interview with Fukuda Kumajirō on the situation in China after his return. Fukuda was Japanese and a former high-level technical consultant in Beijing. He became a POW in Dalian (Dairen in Japanese) at the end of the war and was detained by the CCP. He had been in charge of a chemical plant at that point. Fukuda said that in 1949 the CCP arrested many owing to the activities of counterrevolutionaries. Fukuda was very critical of Chinese courts that dealt with counterrevolutionaries. Others opposed these Chinese courts, which had no defense counsel, and there was no written law that could be utilized. Fukuda said, "China thinks it has already learned enough from Japanese technicians so it can send them home but I feel China is still thirty years behind Japan." The five-year plan would not be able to get China to where it aims to go, he believed. Fukuda wrote a piece in the Japanese magazine *Mainland Problems*, in which he revealed his impressions of new China. He penned that China participated in the Korean War so that citizens would shift their focus from domestic problems and displeasure toward the war.[62] The internal Chinese report detailed Fukuda's whole article, and investigators seemed vexed about it.[63]

In the April 1955 issue of the Japanese magazine *Sekai*, Murata Shōzō talked about his trip to China. Murata had been a prewar entrepreneur, minister in the wartime cabinets, and suspected postwar war criminal who was arrested but eventually released. He later became an adviser in the Foreign Ministry and assisted with the reestablishment of diplomatic relations. Murata claimed that Japan had preconceived notions of the Communist Party and the PRC, but they were wrong. The PRC is not narrow minded, he told readers. After all, he managed to get a face-to-face meeting with Zhou Enlai that lasted four and a half hours, Murata wrote. Murata said, "We ought to accept the notion that a new neighbor to this country has risen," meaning that new China should be treated afresh. Japanese used to think of old China as dirty, but now everything was clean. Murata also said that Zhou told him that the Chinese would like to forget the past, because "in the long-range view of history, the disputes in the past fifty or sixty years mean very little." The two discussed trade issues to a great extent because that was the focus of Murata's visit.[64]

While China had been officially closed off to the Japanese, former imperial lines of communication and negotiation remained open. These were not always the same avenues for reconciliation one would have imagined, but they demonstrate Japanese and Chinese efforts to remove the obstacles put in place by the burgeoning Cold War alliances and attempts to establish a new stage on which to build future political relations. Sadly, while the main role to bridge this divide was lost to the JCP, which slid into decline and theoretical squabbles, other Japanese groups stepped into the fray to push the dialogue forward.

Chapter 10

Behind the Curtain

Forces Shaping Sino-Japanese Postwar Attitudes toward Justice

Chinese Nationalists across the strait in Taiwan were paying close attention to communist Chinese visits to Japan as well as Japanese calls to the new China. KMT leaders were not pleased with such developments and commented about it in their discussions of Japanese attitudes toward the ROC in the mid-1950s. In an ROC Ministry of Foreign Affairs report from November 1955, the compilers made it clear that they were unhappy with Japan's acceptance of Li Dequan, Guo Moruo, and the visits of other "bandits," as they termed various CCP and other leaders. The report added that allowing the "fake Taiwan independence party" to visit did not enamor the ROC to Japan. Japan's attitude was "clearly unfriendly" toward us, the report enunciated.[1] ROC misgivings were not unfounded, but a core of stalwart Japanese support within the higher echelons of government still wanted to maintain strong ties to Taiwan.

Even though Japanese war criminals were being released by Beijing, Itō Ritsu did not come into contact with another "criminal" in his prison until the start of 1955. This prompts the question: given how busy everyone was with trying to reestablish relations and rebuild trade with Japan, why even waste time with Itō? Was he Mao's trump card, or Zhou's? The JCP had obviously abandoned him, so what was the motive for keeping him around?[2] At one point even Itō himself could not figure out his misfortune; he surmised that he really had no future and would soon be executed or die during imprisonment.[3]

We can learn a bit more about Itō's tragic fate by retracing the life and times of Zhao Anbo. Before the war, Zhao had traveled to Japan to study and then returned to China to join the CCP resistance movement. He later met JCP leader Nosaka Sanzō in Yenan, China, at the end of 1940. Zhao began serving as Nosaka's translator and wrote that the two were inseparable for five years. In 1951, Wang Jiaxiang, head of the International Liaison Department of the CCP, called Zhao to Beijing from Shenyang. Zhao was tasked with the responsibility of managing propaganda toward Japan and receiving Japanese guests. Few people knew much about Japan, so there was much work to do and he was kept busy. In addition, Zhao stated that he was doing all the interpreting for Mao Zedong, as well as CCP generals Zhu De and Liu Shioqi. Zhao revealed part of why he was called from Shenyang to Beijing by Wang was to assist with testy relations between the two JCP leaders, Tokuda and Nosaka, who were in self-exile in Beijing. They had arrived in late 1950 and early 1951. Tokuda told Zhao that the reason he traveled secretly to Beijing was to keep an eye on Nosaka because "who really knows what he's been saying."[4] There was little trust among competing factions in the JCP.

In a 1990s interview Zhao Anbo elaborated on the role he played between JCP leaders and Itō Ritsu. Zhao explained that JCP leaders had asked him to "get rid of" Itō Ritsu, which he refused to do.[5] Zhao's revelation set off a Japanese media firestorm, revealing the long trail of damage caused by the Itō scandal. The Japanese historian who interviewed Zhao wrote that the editorial staff at the magazine chose to "shelve the piece." She estimated that after a three-decade interim of frosty relations, the mood between the two communist parties was finally thawing, and perhaps the editors at the Japanese magazine thought Zhao's disclosure would inadvertently impede political resolution.[6]

News of the censored interview fed a further uproar in Japan and renewed interest in the whole Itō Ritsu drama, along with the explosive issue of Nosaka's supposed complicity. In the final analysis, according to Zhao's recollections, after the JCP moved its central bureau to Beijing, the leaders entreated the Chinese to remove Itō Ritsu. At the time, the JCP was split into two factions: the international clique and the emotional clique. Tokuda, Nosaka, and Itō were part of the emotional clique, hoping to create a more lovable communist party. Hakamada Satomi and Miyamoto Kenji were part of the international clique, hewing more closely to USSR guidance of violent revolution.

Zhao confirmed that the request to handle the Itō situation came from both Nosaka, head of the emotional clique, and Hakamada, leader of the international clique. Zhao remembered that Nosaka used the words "deal with" (*shori*), while Hakamada was much more explicit in 1955, saying to Zhao that he "wanted Itō killed" (*koroshite hoshii*).[7] After Tokuda's death and the dissolution of the international clique, the two sides eventually reunited. CCP leaders estimated the whole debacle was a problem internal to JCP leadership squabbles and did not wish to intervene. The Itō story also suggests a larger struggle within China concerning justice. The CCP leadership took a variety of stances in implementing what it deemed as justice, but there was little uniformity. There was one plan for notable Japanese war criminals, one for JCP brethren, and a third for domestic KMT "war criminals," as well as other formulations as one moved down the scale of publicity and political hierarchy.

At the same time as Itō was settling in for a long incarceration, moves were afoot that tried to push forward Sino-Japanese diplomatic rapprochement. As an outgrowth of the pro-communist World Peace Conference in 1954, Indian leaders opened the Asian Conference on the Relaxation of International Tension in New Delhi from April 6–10, 1955. Famed Japanese writer Hino Ashihei attended with the Japanese mission and then journeyed to China. During his trip he visited Fushun Prison and wrote about the detained Japanese war criminals.[8] Hino received a guided tour of the prison facilities and was introduced to those incarcerated. He recalled that it was a very different environment from what prisoners experienced in the previously Allied-managed Sugamo Prison in Tokyo. The prisoners in Fushun had undergone a "human renovation" through a ten-year process of "thought reformation," he wrote. However, Hino observed, when considering the plight of these men, they were still languishing in incarceration a decade after the war had finished.[9]

On April 18, 1955, the famous Bandung Conference opened, and Japanese envoy Takasaki Tatsunosuke met his Chinese counterpart, Liao Chengzhi. The two advanced talks for trade and bilateral political negotiations on the sidelines. The UK embassy in Beijing commented that even though progress had been made, there was still an imbalance in Sino-Japanese relations. A September 14, 1955, editorial in China's *People's Daily* made a contrast between the Japanese in China who were treated well and the Chinese in Japan who had been used for forced labor. The PRC criticized Japan for continued failures to investigate the crimes committed against these Chinese. Tens of thousands of Japanese who wanted to return to Japan from China were allowed and even encouraged to do so. However, Japan had done nothing for Chinese nationals in Japan. In some ways this story emerged because the Japanese government insisted that some forty thousand Japanese were still unaccounted for in China. China responded, stating that Tokyo had not accounted for the forty thousand Chinese it had taken during the war for forced labor.[10]

Just prior to the *People's Daily* article, in August 1955, the first meeting in Hiroshima of the World Conference against Hydrogen and Atomic Bombs convened. Representatives from China and the USSR attended. The moment was ripe for engagement, but it was also contentious. Antileft groups hired an airplane to drop anticommunist leaflets, while left- and right-wing political groups clashed outside the hall.[11] August 6, 1955, marked a decade since the end of World War II, but Japan and China had still not signed a peace accord. Chinese representative Liu Ningyi joined the World Conference in Hiroshima that day. He was the deputy head of the All China Federation of Trade Unions. Following the ceremonies and back in Tokyo, Katayama Tetsu, along with Kazami Akira, who was in part responsible for the establishment of the People's Federation to Protect the Constitution, met with Liu at his downtown hotel. The federation wanted to keep Japan's pacifist constitution, while the opposition assessed that the postwar constitution was foisted on Japan by the victorious Americans and was therefore unjust. Liu was in Tokyo to attend an informal discussion with federation members at the Prince Hotel in Shinagawa.[12] Endō Saburō made the decision to make an appearance as well.

Endō, a former imperial officer, had been at the center of the military intrigue during and after the war.[13] Worried that the country in the early postwar was sliding into panic mode, Endō pushed for a meeting with Prime Minister Higashikuni to offer ideas to which the people could cling to for hope. Endō, like many others, was later arrested and poised to be charged with war crimes, ultimately spending about a year in Sugamo Prison. He was released without charge in January 1948.[14] Endō was also an example of conversion, perhaps rare among high-ranking military circles, where he shifted from a hawkish stance, to being a pragmatist, to supporting peace initiatives with communist China. Endō had not started out as pro-Chinese, although he certainly developed in that capacity over the years.

Upon meeting Chinese representative Liu, Endō explained that Japan would not interfere in the PRC's relationship with Taiwan, because that situation was akin to a spat between a husband and wife. Endō said rather bluntly, which Liu enjoyed, "The Taiwan issue is a matter of domestic concern and we will not meddle." However, Endō added that "if this relation is resolved using military force we cannot just sit back and watch from the sidelines. If military force is used against Taiwan this could turn into WWIII and this might then entail the use of a hydrogen bomb," which of course everyone wished to avoid.[15]

Endō suggested that stopping the cycle of retaliation was the way to move forward. Endō said that Liu listened and that he would relay this message to his superiors. Endō thought Liu was just being polite, but not long after, Katayama Testu received a letter from Chinese representative Zhang Xiruo, formally inviting him to the PRC. Katayama, in turn, invited Endō.[16] Other sources offer a slightly different background to this story. Isogai Rensuke, who had been an imperial army "China expert," was supposedly in consideration. In the immediate postwar period, the KMT had put Isogai on trial. He was found guilty as a war criminal and sentenced to life in prison but was eventually repatriated from China to Japan. In October 1954, on his first postwar visit to Japan, Liao Chengzhi unofficially traveled to Isogai's villa on the coast of Chiba Prefecture.[17] Initially, the Chinese invited Isogai to head a mission from Japan composed of former military veterans to China. But when Isogai went to get a passport photo, there were some problems and Isogai was refused travel permission by the Japanese government. In his place, according to some accounts, the Chinese invited Endō Saburō to assist in the mission. Endō detailed in his diary his motivation to see for himself what was really happening in China: "First, I want to see whether the people under communist authority are living in fear. Second, I want to determine if there are harbingers of the regime's demise. Third, I want to ascertain if they have ambitions of revenge against Japan."[18]

In the meantime, Tsuji Masanobu, who was on his way home after a September 1955 visit to the USSR, stopped in Beijing and met with Zhou Enlai. According to some sources, Tsuji was also being courted to lead a group of former imperial veterans to China because he was seen to wield influence in Japan. It is interesting that China ultimately rejected Tsuji as a former veteran to head such a mission but accepted his visits while he was a Diet member a couple of years later in 1957.[19]

For his part, Endō knew that Kishi Nobusuke, as chief whip of the newly formed ruling party the Liberal Democratic Party (LDP), was not at all interested in letting a group of former imperial soldiers go to China. Kishi felt they would just be used for propaganda purposes and be wined and dined, to be shown only one side of new China.[20] Endō insisted that former military men understood the delicacy of the situation and surely would not be satisfied with "attending banquets."

There were excursions to China by different Japanese groups and individuals around this time, so it is possible Kishi suspected ulterior motives. JSP member Nomizo Masaru met with Zhou Enlai on October 3, 1955, and while he supported China's policies toward Taiwan as a "domestic matter," he still broached the topic of Japanese war criminals.[21] One of the first official group of Japanese parliamentarians, headed by Kanbayashiyama Eikichi, visited China in autumn 1955 and released a joint statement with CCP leader Peng Zhen on October 17. A few days prior, Kanbayashiyama and his group had met with CCP chairman Mao Zedong and Premier Zhou Enlai. After exchanging pleasantries, Kanbayashiyama broached the war criminals question concerning repatriation after their release. He told his Chinese counterparts, "I know this is a difficult question but please consider their families. So I just want to put this suggestion out there and hear your opinions on the matter." Mao responded: "You cannot talk about this problem in that way. This problem is an issue for the Chinese people; China and Japan, our two countries have still not concluded their state of war, have not restored diplomatic relations, so to talk about this problem is a bit premature. This is not the same matter as the repatriation of overseas Japanese. The war crimes problem is a result of the war but the overseas civilians is not the result of the war." Zhou Enlai then chimed in and said, "You visited the war criminals, what do you think? We have already dealt with a portion of this problem. If their war crime was light we already released some." Kanbayashiyama then backtracked a bit after this remonstration, adding that his concern was for the families in Japan. After hearing Zhou's explanation, he expressed his gratitude and said they would not bring it up again. Zhou pressed a bit, asking, "You visited the war criminals. If there is a specific problem, like some are sick, or if they are not being treated well, or cannot write letters to their families, please tell us."[22]

Even with political support from some quarters, the Japanese government's ambivalent stance toward a renovated relationship with China was due in part to bureaucratic continuity with the prewar period. The continued service of many wartime Japanese bureaucrats and politicians, who had taken up significant postwar political and economic leadership positions, advanced conservative wartime attitudes into the postwar period. Kishi Nobusuke was one such imperial figure who had worked in key wartime government agencies and in Japan's puppet kingdom of Manchukuo. He was arrested but never indicted as a war criminal. Kishi waxed poetic about Japan's imperial efforts. Revealing a brashness that reeked of nostalgia, he demonstrated a noted absence of reflection concerning the less than savory aspects of Japan's imperial era and why the Japanese administration was hesitant to allow military veterans to reorient interpretations of Japan's "glorious" wartime past.

> On the numerous occasions when I made state visits to the various countries of SE Asia, I recalled Manchukuo. At the time, Asia was in the throes of its economic resurgence and this reminded me of how we built the ideal and racially harmonious country of Manchukuo. So many young Japanese filled with idealism crossed the sea to prepare and take a stand against the West in the boundless and plentiful material treasure house of Manchukuo. Afterward, the facilities, infrastructure, technology and manpower they left behind lives on within the Chinese economy. Japan's destiny in the future is, of course, unchanged from before and remains united with Asia's economic regeneration. To accomplish this feat the experience and reflection on what was done prior in Manchukuo can serve as a most valuable reference guide.[23]

Ultimately, after completing all the travel preparations, a small group led by Katayama Tetsu departed on November 6, 1955, from Tokyo and returned a month later. Endō recalled his meeting with CCP general Peng Dehuai, where he learned that the delay in special tribunals to adjudicate Japanese war criminals was due to the CCP desire to wait until the emotions of the Chinese people had softened so that the Chinese judgments against the Japanese would be less harsh. Such a rationale, of course, was not exactly accurate since the Chinese were not of one mind regarding such a policy, but the reasoning probably sounded good to Japanese ears.[24]

Katayama's group met Mao and Zhou directly. Endō regaled Mao with a story of how he had been sent to Sugamo Prison as a war criminal.[25] While being processed, Endō received two right shoes, not a pair of left and right. The shoes were too big, Endō joked, and his toenails grew in, pushing his feet left. The upshot was that when he walked, he ended up ambulating toward the left, suggesting that politically he was also now leaning left.[26] Mao, according to several accounts, enjoyed the tale. After meeting Endō and being entranced with his fresh attitude toward new China, Mao explained that rather than meeting with more Japanese leftists, he hoped to meet more former military men like Endō. Endō returned from his mission to China on December 7, 1955, and spoke to the Japanese press and radio, explaining that Mao and Zhou wanted to meet with former imperial Japanese military officers.[27]

On March 3, 1956, Inoue Masutarō, director of foreign affairs for the Japan Red Cross Society, held a meeting in Beijing with his Chinese counterparts. The repatriation of Japanese who had remained in China had proceeded smoothly over the previous few years, and now the Japanese wondered about the remaining Japanese war criminals still detained in China, more than a decade after the war had come to a close. Katayama Tetsu had announced the release of war criminals in the Japanese media, so Japanese society was expecting them back, the Japanese visitors explained. Peng Yan, a representative from the China side, responded that he and his team had "no more information than you." Inoue said, "The question of war criminals should not be an object of political bargain. This question is fundamentally a judicial one. Therefore, the release of war criminals should be granted according to the Chinese Criminal Law. Therefore, even after the opening of diplomatic relations, you need not release them in case your criminal law requires so." Peng agreed that China would not make Japanese war criminals part of any political bargain. The Japanese contingent received over 1,224 letters from the war criminals to give to their families, and letters from the Japan side were handed to the Chinese to be forwarded to the Japanese war criminals.[28]

Esler Denning, British ambassador in Tokyo, informed London on April 13, 1956, about the growth of the recently established Japan-China Cultural Association. Denning wrote that it grew from the November 1955 visit of the People's Federation to Protect the Constitution to China, led by Katayama Tetsu, and the December 1955 Guo Moruo visit to Japan. Regardless of this progress, Chief Cabinet Secretary Nemoto Ryūtarō had already announced on March 27 to push forward measures to restrict what Nemoto called "useless visits of Japanese to China." The Japanese government had taken notice that not everyone who traveled to China, which they estimated at eight hundred, had the correct travel documents, so it was obvious that some passed through other countries. MOFA officials wanted to investigate whether there was a way to design an alternate passport that would make these visits more difficult. This British dispatch voiced that the Chinese had invited a group of thirty former Japanese officers, and such a move was of interest. According to the British assessment, Japan's MOFA seemed to think former soldiers would be level-headed and not easily duped by Chinese propaganda to provide an overly positive assessment. The analysis postulated that before the war, many of the young officers of the Japanese army were communist, so perhaps the CCP had this in mind.[29]

After Endō returned to Japan, the next step was to wait for the formal invite from Zhang Xiruo and then form a group of former military officers to visit China. Two hundred former imperial soldiers applied for the mission. Endō and his team chose eighty, then they pared that down to a list of thirty-four. But the Japanese government in 1956 was not so accommodating. Endō assessed that the leaders were worried about upsetting the United States. It is possible that Japanese politicians and Foreign Minister Shigemitsu Mamoru were also anxious about left-leaning former soldiers or those who had been incarcerated by the CCP or USSR and were pro-communist, or supposedly spies. Endō felt his biggest obstacle was Tsuji Masanobu, who by this point was a mainstay within the LDP and a politician with political might. As we now know, Tsuji had been pursuing his own path to lead a mission to China.

From the end of 1955 through 1956, Mao Zedong, but moreover Premier Zhou Enlai, made numerous overtures to the Japanese for improved relations, if not more frequent high-level meetings. In May 1956, when Zhou met a Japanese peace delegation, he told them that "last year we met with about 800–900 Japanese friends who visited China."[30] A May 11, 1956, Chinese internal report for high-ranking officials detailed the still-unresolved issue of Japanese war criminals incarcerated in Taiyuan, Shanxi Province. At stake was their psychological condition. The report stated that before the indictments had been opened, Japanese in Taiyuan under detention had some "premonition" about how trials might proceed in the near future. The staff had been talking a lot with Jōno Hiroshi and eleven others. Jōno and the other prisoners appeared to want to admit their crimes, the report suggested, but "mentally their tendency toward apprehension and to psychologically struggle remained deep." Some evenings, officials reported, the prisoners were so agitated they could not sleep. The Japanese detainees feared the outcome of the trial, according to the report, and never being able to return to Japan.[31]

On June 6, 1956, Endō met with Kishi to plead his case. Eventually a consensus was reached, and on August 12, 1956, Endō officially left for China with his team of Japanese veterans. They had provisioned to go as a group of thirty-five, but Japanese officials said that number was too high and so only fifteen former officers departed.[32] The group traveled to Changchun, Anshan, Shenyang, and eventually made it to Fushun Prison just after the war crimes trials had been concluded. Liao Chengzhi suggested that if Mao met with visiting former soldiers, the effort would have a lasting impact.[33] Mao did just that, by greeting each of the former Japanese officers and shaking their hands. Mao told them how the Chinese, in part thanks to the officers, have rallied together. Mao made sure to mention that China respected the Japanese emperor system, and at one point he asked Endō to pass on his respects to the emperor.[34]

The impact of Endō's former Japanese military officer mission was not lost on other foreign embassies keeping track of what was happening in China and on potential rapprochement between China and Japan. UK foreign office officials believed that China had invited former imperial Japanese officers in a bid for "impressing people who are not automatically sympathetic to the regime." The British assessment focused on how Zhou Enlai invited Endō as an explicit strategy to avoid having only left-wing ideologues observe new China.[35] After visiting the PRC and then returning in 1956, Endō subsequently pulled together many former vets and took them on several more missions to China in a bid to restore relations from 1956 to 1972.[36] The director of the Taiyuan War Criminals Management Center, Wang Zhendong, wrote about Endō's visits and the impact of discussions with his imprisoned former detainees. Initially, Endō only listened to them recount their war crimes, but upon subsequent visits he was moved to talk about his own participation in Japan's war of aggression.[37]

At the end of February 1957, Tsuji Masanobu was once again in a meeting with Zhou Enlai in Beijing. A few days prior on February 25, Prime Minister Katayama Tetsu had resigned due to a long-term illness, but Tsuji had already departed on a two-month, twelve-nation tour including Gamal Abdel Nasser's Egypt, Josip Tito's Yugoslavia, and elsewhere. The goal was to convince potential Allied nations that Japan was not merely a client state of the United States and that Japan wanted to create partnerships with African and Asian nations. In late April 1957, just after Kishi Nobusuke's cabinet took over, JSP member Asanuma Inejirō produced a joint communiqué with Zhang Xiruo, who by this point had become the chair of the Chinese People's Foreign Affairs Study Association. The announcement called for advancing the friendship of the two countries and pushing toward diplomatic relations. The communiqué also called for the abolishment of the production, use, and holding of nuclear weapons.[38]

A confidential British embassy dispatch from China on May 9, 1957, drew attention to the growing number of visiting Japanese delegations, which the embassy signaled as a portent that a normalization of political relations was in the air sooner than previously suspected. Movements of the Japanese delegations were widely reported in the Chinese press, the embassy noted, so much so that space devoted to noncommunist entities was unusual. A JSP visit with Asanuma Inejirō was underlined as important because the socialists openly said that they supported China, the dispatch explained.[39]

However, even after all these Chinese tactical moves, by 1957 the Japanese were reevaluating the Chinese war crimes trials and repatriating prisoners. They were not impressed and seemed to have arrived at the opposite conclusion that the CCP had been careful in its treatment of the incarcerated Japanese.[40]

Shifting Landscape of Memory in Japan

As the 1950s melted into the 1960s, Japan's attitudes at the higher altitudes of governance began to lean more conservative. We can see this already in the return to power of wartime elites and their retrograde attitudes. Prime Minister Kishi Nobusuke's comments in Japan's parliament concerning responsibility over forced Chinese labor in April 1958 are indicative of this conservative swing. This was around the time that Chinese laborer Liu Lianren was found in the mountains of Hokkaido, after hiding there for thirteen years following the end of World War II. In the Diet, JSP politician Tanaka Toshio asked the prime minister about the illegality of the cabinet decision to allow forced labor when Kishi had been in the wartime cabinet. Tanaka stated that "the fact is obvious that these people did not enter the country [Japan] of their own free will," and Tanaka wanted to know how the government assessed this history. Kishi responded bluntly, mostly skirting the issue. "The government does not have any materials that would shed light on the situation at the time. There is, in truth, no way for us to confirm what occurred." He added, "However, the real problem is we have not been able to ascertain if those people were brought by force, or if they were those who came on their own having accepted [a contract]. Whether the government has responsibility is something at this point in time, I believe, that has not yet been made clear."[41]

Throughout the 1960s and the era of the Vietnam War, Japan's postwar youth grew angrier toward their parents' generation. This division within Japanese society continued to widen, as seen through the anti-security-pact riots that led to months of unrest on the streets of most major Japanese cities. For more than a year, from the spring of 1959 to the summer of 1960, about thirty million Japanese took part in protests. The US occupation had attempted to remake Japan in its own vision, but after the 1952 resumption of Japan's sovereignty, the Japanese were keen to redo what many felt had merely been imposed from above.[42] Returning to the stage of power in 1957, Prime Minister Kishi Nobusuke would railroad through the Diet, during that fateful summer of 1960, a new security alliance with the United States. The terms of the agreement were actually an improvement over what Japan had previously ratified, but the manner in which Kishi manipulated the situation galvanized public anger because it stank of wartime government backhandedness and ignored democratic processes.

Many more traditionally minded Japanese politicians and bureaucrats began to devise a strategic move away from apology toward a more concrete affirmation of the imperial past. To do this required a reanalysis of the Tokyo Trial and the lesser BC class war crimes tribunals. Tucked away in the deep recesses of the national archives in Tokyo is evidence of such a plan. Toyota Kumao, who had previously assisted imperial naval officers to avoid war crimes prosecution in the immediate aftermath of the war, drafted a set of proposals on March 19, 1964, concerning the establishment of a study group to investigate the Tokyo Trial. It is clear that Toyota aimed to use the findings as part of what he deemed necessary for "future countermeasures" in international and domestic policies. The proposal had many iterations, and one draft from April 23 details how the study group would examine all the charges of the Tokyo Trial: Was it aggressive warfare or a form of defense? Was the trial the misapplication of ex post facto law? Where did the role of individual responsibility lie on the axis of international law? What about the emperor's responsibility? Toyota's proposal strove to reconsider the trial verdicts in light of these issues. More drafts were produced, and budgets were outlined. Much of this work seemed to be at the behest of the Ministry of Justice.[43] The plan, which eventually was implemented, involved both legal scholars and a variety of economic and media talent, including a few individuals from the Ministry of Justice. The matters the group would analyze were numerous, so a large budget of approximately 100 million yen (about US$1 million) was set aside to be used over what was envisioned as a two- to three-year schedule. The group set its sights on examining the Tokyo Trial, BC class war crimes trials, and the Nuremberg trials as well.

The study group's goal, in part, appeared to question the validity and findings of the war crimes trials, and the intention was less to serve as an open commission to examine the larger legal and political concerns. A memo in the files from April 25 detailed that the major goals of the group would be to investigate (1) jurisdictional rights, (2) ex post facto law, (3) the crime of conspiracy, (4) questioning if invasive war was a crime, and (5) the issue of individual responsibility in international legal trials.

Participants included, among others, professor of law Ichimata Masao, professor of politics Tsunoda Jun, and lawyer Sakano Junkichi, along with the administrative assistance of two individuals from the Ministry of Justice, Toyota Kumao and Inoue Tadao. Ichimata's section would lead the international law discussions, and diplomatic history would be covered under Tsunoda's group. The actual management of the war crimes trials would be scrutinized by Sakano's crew. Ichimata was a professor of law at Waseda University, and Tsunoda had graduated from Tokyo's First Higher School and had been part of the editorial team that put together the series *Japan's Road to the Pacific War*.[44] Sakano had been active as a defense lawyer at the Tokyo Trial for Class A war criminal Army General Itagaki Seishirō. Sakano had also served as a witness for the prosecution in the BC class trials of Lieutenant General Okada Tasuku, but his testimony served to support the defendant in a surprising discussion of the legal issues at stake.[45]

The study group formally began in June 1964, the year that Japan hosted the Olympics. Prime Minister Ikeda Hayato had died later that year, and following on Kishi Nobusuke, his predecessor, Ikeda had focused on increasing Japan's economic growth.[46] The study meeting took place with the assistance and guidance of the Ministry of Justice, in part and perhaps because Kaya Okinori was minister of justice from 1963 to 1964. Tellingly, when Kaya had been paroled from prison in 1955, a large "gathering to offer solace and encouragement" was held in his honor at the expensive Chinzansō Hotel in Mejiro, Tokyo. From 1962 to 1977, Kaya headed up the politically influential Japan Association of War Bereaved Families (*Izokukai*), and under his leadership the group added "'honoring the glorious war dead' (*eirei no kenshō*) to their traditional slogans of world peace, social welfare, and the prevention of war."[47] The schedule of all the meetings, from the preparatory meeting on June 15, 1964, to the mostly bimonthly meetings, extended to more than one hundred gatherings. The last meeting, the 107th, was held on March 24, 1969. Normally, four intellectuals would assemble for discussions, with Toyota and Inoue in attendance most frequently as observers. The initial meetings were held at Tokyo's Lawyer's Association Hall (Hōsō kaikan).

A handwritten memo on Ministry of Justice stationery offered insight into why so many found it necessary to form this study group. The pursuit of Japanese for war crimes was unprecedented in the history of civilization. And thus there might be many important issues the Japanese could glean from examining the trials on the level of criminal law and international law, the memo disclosed. The group claimed that it hoped to probe international law through the ideas about self-defense and how evidence was presented at the Tokyo Trial. And they planned to debate the idea of self-defense while looking at the issues from a lawyer's point of view. The processes of the trial as well as its torpid pace were key points for investigation. In addition, the study group conducted interviews with notables such as Japanese and American lawyers who were involved. Finally, they aimed to gauge the influence of Nuremberg on the Tokyo Trial.

Regardless of the important legal questions that the study group focused on, they assiduously avoided one major historical topic: Why did the Allies believe they had to implement special trials to pursue justice against Japanese war criminals? In short, without looking into the pervasive and excessive brutality of Japanese imperial military and political rule, such trials would not have been necessary. Starving POWs and rampant abuse of prisoners and Chinese were so commonplace that they were a standard feature of Japanese imperial expansion. Focusing exclusively on legal issues, to the exclusion of moral questions and issues of the rule of law within the empire, and avoiding how the Japanese managed the empire meant that the Tokyo Trial study group was looking at only half the puzzle. They concentrated on Allied legal responsibility toward those whom the study group assessed were "victims" of the war crimes trials, namely the Japanese.

As the study group moved into its third year, it added the examination of the Pal dissenting judgment in the Tokyo War Crimes Trial. A long memo from June 9, 1966, discussed the necessity for research into BC class trials as well. In the end, the study group published a book about this and other related projects.[48] Ichimata stated that the group would not make any profit from the book, but "it is vexing that this mistaken history is what is now so prevalent." He added, "I also want to put this into print for the young people who do not know history."[49] This project in the 1960s was a trend that has never lapsed.[50]

However, the conservative sway in Japan did not always run in a straight line through all of society. Social discontent continued to find release through the younger generations, percolating into a massive social volcano when students at Ritsumeikan University in Kyoto defaced the campus's archetypal war memorial statue. The *Listen to the Voices of the Sea* statue represented the suffering of wartime drafted students.[51] The statue had emerged from a social movement, which in turn had been galvanized by a 1949 book of the same title.[52] Nothing can surpass the intense emotional depths that this statue embodied for many concerning sacrifices made in the name of the war.[53] The book became a movie, which was a box-office hit in Japan the following year. However, postwar students witnessing the US-led war in Vietnam during the 1960s were different. They believed those who had previously erected the statue failed to do anything of merit to stop Japan's war and were thus blameworthy. In the eyes of the 1960s generation, the *Voices of the Sea* statue had become the false prophet for pushing peace and needed to be toppled. In the same manner that political debates about the role and meaning of statues in the United Kingdom and the United States during the later 2010s divided generations who ascribe significance to public art based on their own historical experience, Japan was no different. An editorial in the *Asahi Newspaper* from May 21, 1969, asked if the students understood the actual meaning of the statue as antiwar and that it had been funded by the proceeds of sales of books edited from collections of letters that student draftees had written during World War II. But the editorial then explained that blame should not be placed solely at the feet of the students for their lack of compassion. After all, the previous generation bore responsibility for not offering a full explanation of the war. The students accused the previous generation: "Why didn't you flee the battlefield, why didn't you drop your guns and leave? If you didn't do this then you were nothing more than a fascist." These deep-seated emotions fed the anti-US hegemony, anti–Vietnam War movement in Japan. The editorial concluded by saying that it was not just an imperial war of aggression that required examination—Japan needed to delve into the state and the terror of authority to explain its past. Obviously, Japanese have failed to teach these lessons to the next generation, the editorial wrote, which is why Japan found itself at this current impasse.[54]

"White Terror" in Taiwan

Japan was not the only country to experience conservative governments that were more interested in reestablishing order than they were in rooting out the origins of their own war crimes. Owing to a disparity in geopolitical circumstances, Japan's postwar evolution differs greatly from Germany's (West Germany until 1990). In Europe, Germany was confronted on the west by France, which had reintegrated its democratic government, and the United Kingdom.

There was pressure in the region for Germany to conform. Until the 1990s, to the east, West Germany faced its rival, East Germany, whose leaders took delight in propagating how little West Germany had acknowledged its Nazi past and how many former war criminals remained in government. Not only did Japan not face repeated pressure or inquiries after the initial postwar years, but its regional neighbors were constrained under their own punitive and tight political conditions. So, rectifying Japan's past was one of the last thing on their minds. In addition, because Japan had closely allied with the United States in the early stages of the Cold War, US pressure to discuss war crimes dissolved rather abruptly as well.

This quick turnaround can also be seen with the example of the ROC, more commonly known as Taiwan, or Formosa by many Westerners until the 1990s. Taiwan is currently more interested with righting the wrongs of a half century of domestic martial law and coming to terms with those excesses, rather than parsing over Japanese atrocities that took place either on Taiwan or on the mainland when the KMT was in power prior to 1945. That social pressure, combined with years of Chinese Nationalist efforts to curb public discussion of these issues, makes for a very different core public opinion toward the Japanese imperial era.

Taiwanese memory of Japanese imperial history cuts against any transnational veneer because of this complexity. Moreover, today's Taiwanese seem less concerned about Japan's excesses than they do about the much longer reign of difficulty they lived under with KMT rule from 1949 until the later 1980s. This era is known as the age of "white terror" (*baise kongbu* in Chinese), which should be thought of as the continual exertion of state violence. The KMT declared martial law on May 20, 1949, and this state of enforced security persisted until July 14, 1987. During this era of extrajudicial abuses, which were more extreme in the early 1950s, the KMT defined all who opposed any KMT political goals as "subversive" and thus a traitor to the ROC. Ironically, this was fairly similar to the sort of counterrevolutionary panic the CCP was trying to contain along the same lines at a similar moment.[55] There is no one definitive accounting of those killed, incarcerated, or abused during the long decades of the white terror in Taiwan. Estimates suggest there were "some 3,000 to 4,000 executions," of "roughly 140,000 political trials conducted by ROC martial-law courts (including some 30,000 retrospectively deemed 'improper')."[56] Not all of these trials took place in the early years, and many stretched to the very end of KMT military rule on the island.

One can get a feeling of the sort of suppression the Taiwanese public faced from an early postwar interview with KMT general Sun Li-jen. He was disappointed with the continued internecine political spats within the military elite in Taiwan, and in 1955 he was put under house arrest for thirty years under the false suspicion of having tried to foment a rebellion. Sun heaped scorn on the Chiang Kai-shek regime.[57] Things did not improve, even after a decade and growing US support of what the United States, with no irony, called "free China." In 1961, famed legal scholar of China Jerome Cohen recounted that one lawyer in Taiwan told him, "Judges were commonly believed to be so corrupt that lawyers joked that 'honest' judges only kept the bribe given by the winning party."[58]

By the 1960s many Taiwanese had grown interested in Formosan self-determination. This was due, in part, to the KMT political disenfranchisement of native Taiwanese. The enormous budgets the KMT spent on its military and youth leagues were to Peng Ming-min reminiscent of Hitler youth organizations. With the arrival of the KMT, Taiwan had ossified—labor unions were illegal, there was no opposition party, and representatives in the national legislature remained frozen in time from 1947 with no new elections. In fact, the national congress would not reflect reality until decades later. Peng and his supporters produced a manifesto that contested this standoff and drew attention to these issues. He was arrested in 1964 and court-martialed. Sentenced to eight years, he was then freed by Chiang Kai-shek's decree. The news media in Taiwan, controlled by the government, broadcast that Peng had confessed but was released due to the generalissimo's largesse. However, Peng was far from truly free and remained under constant surveillance. He decided to escape the rising pressure and violence. Without telling his family, he fled to Sweden, and in 1970 he traveled to the United States to seek asylum.

Regardless of the government pressure to tamp down popular discontent, along with control of the media and the courts, discussions of the February 28 Incident were never far from the surface, be it on the government or civilian side. It was still such a divisive political issue in the early 1980s that KMT authorities crafted a new policy in 1983, labeled as the "clearing away the dust plan" (*fuchen zhuanan*). The aim was to keep the incident from being further openly debated, and the government suggested that anyone who did bring it up was by nature a pro-independence Taiwanese political agent. To stifle such arguments, a group went around and collected an enormous number of documents related to the incident, compiled oral histories, and collated police reports in a move to establish the definitive account. The materials were published in a twenty-nine-volume series as part of the KMT plan to start to direct the discussion and no longer let it be directed by Taiwan independence supporters or other groups.[59] In 1986, an extension of the plan managed to publish a book in the United States, *Brushing Away Dust from the Mirror of History*. The book was a crusade by the KMT intelligence agencies to separate the Taiwan independence movement from "the truth" of what had happened in 1947 and to render it mute as a tool to criticize KMT abuses.[60] The book painted the Taiwanese as innocent dupes of the communists, described the KMT's handling of the situation as "benevolent and accommodating," and tried to underline incidents of Taiwanese assisting mainlanders as demonstrative of "brotherly love."[61] Interestingly, within a few years after this and only two years after martial law was lifted, Taiwanese society was rocked into a new discussion sparked by a feature film: Hou Hsiao-hsian's cinematic opus, *City of Sadness*. The film portrays the legacies of the colonial era, the aftermath of the February 28 Incident, and the ensuing era of the white terror. His efforts visually depict "what is ultimately beyond words—the experience of cultural suppression, dislocation and disconnection, and the weight of historical rupture, violence, and pain."[62] Because of the impact of this film, as well as a variety of other domestic and international elements, within a decade Taiwan was holding national elections and was on the path toward instituting full democracy.

Owing to such political changes over the last few years, Taiwan had invested national finances toward compensation for transitional justice. But its critics emphasize that the focus on money has denied any substantive investigation of the legal and political systems within which these abuses flourished. Two Taiwanese academic detractors summarize the situation as one where "without experiencing social processes like public hearings held by a truth commission or wide dissemination of the results of research, the public's knowledge of the dark past is simplified and fragmented. Furthermore, with respect to dealing with the perpetrators, no institution has ever been initiated. This illustrates Taiwan's situation as a case of transition without justice.'"[63]

CHAPTER 11

Evaporating Legal Memory and KMT War Criminals

The concept of how and why the push for "global justice" emerged from the aftermath of World War II was crucial to the political shaping of East Asia. However, public pushback and political criticism of the law and how it had been orchestrated in China began almost immediately after the 1956 trials of the key Japanese war criminals. The Shanghai legal world soon opened a struggle against Wang Zaoshi and Yang Zhaolong, notable lawyers who were pilloried for their supposed Republican-era views on law. In an official 1957 discussion touting China's new legal system, disparaging the West became a focal point. One member retorted:

> Look at America's fatuous democracy. [. . .] To concretely express true legal rule you have to look at the social order. Last year in America there were 2.5 million juvenile offenders and American prisons in a year see more than one hundred riots. The main reason is because they use torture to deal with criminals. What kind of rule of law is this? In Shanghai prisons we do not even have bedbugs and if the criminals get ill they can stay in the hospital. Our criminal rates are falling so what kind of rule of law is that?[1]

This was, of course, false. At the time the PRC was rapidly constructing a *laogai* (reform through labor) incarceration system, where forced labor was employed as a means to punish criminals and those who held opposing views regarding socialist law. Ministry of Justice legal scholar Yang Zhaolong did not see the evolution of law in China from the same rosy standpoint and was quoted as having said that China "had no law upon which it could depend." To him this meant that "bad elements could act without fear of consequences and good people did not feel protected."[2]

In mid-July 1957, Minister of Justice Shi Liang jumped on the bandwagon abandoning important tenets of the rule of law. Once Mao sounded the alarm against what he deemed as counterproductive law, the race to line up as his minion was on. Even though the legal edifice on which the PRC managed to prosecute Japanese war criminals in a bid to gain international legitimacy was still fragile, Shi disparaged Yang, Wang, and others for pushing "poisonous attacks" on the people's legal work under party direction. These men criticized the "purge of counter-revolutionaries" as "a shame" and a "mistake," something with which Shi Liang disagreed. She explained in a talk at the Fourth Session of the First National People's Congress that "everyone knows the elimination operations are entirely necessary and we could even ask if we had not conducted these would we have such peaceful days as we now have?" She did admit that the purges had their faults, but that did not mean China should suspend all such operations. Rather, the authorities needed to be more vigilant when finding cases of malfeasance and correcting them, Shi opined. Shi Liang went on to complain that such individuals, those rightists, wanted a US-style rule of law. And those same individuals say "suppressing counter-revolutionaries is 'unconstitutional' or 'contravenes the law.' Whose constitution, whose law?" she asked. She then admitted that, yes, this move goes against KMT law, but that was the aim from the beginning.[3]

For all the years of effort that CCP officials had spent on investigations, the war crimes trials honeymoon of the Japanese was short-lived. Internal party criticism of Judge Jia Qian, who presided over the first Shenyang military trial in the summer of 1956, began not long after the conclusion of the trials. Jia was worried about the deficit in legal knowledge of his fellow judges because China's courts would be observed by the world. According to his former secretary, "After forming the legal teams for the special military tribunal Jia Qian several times requested that everyone needed to earnestly study Chinese and international law and strictly implement those ideas."[4]

On February 15, 1958, the CCP voted to purge Jia Qian from its ranks. This was a seismic shift in legal power—subordinating the judicial branch to the political arm. Like other legal workers, Jia Qian was critical of merely eradicating all prior Chinese law. The decision was censorious of his comments concerning traditional law, and he was quoted as having said, "Old law has tens of years of experience and leaves a cultural legacy. I can accept criticism of it but we cannot wipe it away in one stroke." Jia Qian was also a fierce advocate of the independence of the court, and he perceived that party questions concerning legal cases was tantamount to meddling in justice. He believed defendants should have the benefit of the doubt in court, which the party found aggravating while trying to round up counterrevolutionaries. Party dissatisfaction had seemingly little to do directly with Jia's actions at the trials of the Japanese, but he was castigated for decreasing former Japanese Manchukuo administrator Furumi Tadayuki's sentence. Regardless, his suggestion was not carried out, because CCP leaders disagreed.[5]

In mid-February 1958, the party showed its displeasure with another judge, Zhu Yaotang, who had been deputy chief of the Shenyang military tribunal trials of the Japanese. Zhu was also expelled from the party rolls. His criticism of the CCP's quick methods of delivering death sentences in other tribunals drew ire. Zhu stated that trial committee members' problems were numerous and that records were too simple, often recording the proceedings with just one word: "kill" or "judgment." "Zhu has distorted the facts, saying the judicial committee deliberated death penalty cases for just three minutes each, one minute in one case, and authorized some ten or so in one morning." Internal party complaints noted that Zhu had the temerity to support Jia Qian's "antiquated" views on law. The party pointed out for particular scorn how Zhu emphasized the rights of the accused.[6]

Yang Xianzhi was expelled at the same time as Zhu, also after serving as a military tribunal judge in the Shenyang cases. Yang affirmed "judicial independence" and chafed at party interference in judicial matters. He also "savagely" criticized central cadre policies. He was accused of "ignoring the time and place of the conditions of the struggle" while "single-handedly trying to affirm legal science and publicly promote 'the presumption of innocence.'" Such ideas were seen as anathema to the revolutionary process and Mao's political goals after 1957.[7] The criticism of Judge Hao Shaoan, also part of the Shenyang war crimes tribunals, followed a pattern similar to the others. Protesting too much for independence of the judiciary and admitting that legal staff were essentially not good or incompetent were the charges leveled at him.[8] Yuan Guang, deputy chief judge at the Shenyang trials, appears to be one of the few highly ranked Shenyang war crimes tribunal judges who was never purged.[9]

In late April 1958, just shy of two years after the Taiyuan trials of Japanese war criminals in Shanxi Province, the party expelled Judge Zhang Xiangqian. He had served on the military tribunal for the June 9–19, 1956, Japanese war crimes trial of eight Japanese prisoners in Taiyuan, including Uesaka Masaru,

Suzuki Hiraku, and Fujita Shigeru, among others. Zhang graduated from law school in Beijing and was forty-six in 1958. The charges against him were that he had expressed in "word and deed" opinions as a rightist with a group that included Jia Qian, Zhu Yaotang, and others. Zhang believed in the independence of the judiciary, "and from the outset opposed the party's direction of judicial proceedings." The party saw Zhang "as a rightist element of the capitalist class and through the decision of the party court branch all party members are unanimous in the decision to purge him from the party register." Zhang proclaimed that judicial workers were "utterly hopeless" because they did not study and were not thorough. And he had the audacity to "oppose dogmatism." The last damning point of the internal party analysis of his supposed crimes was that "Zhang's mistakes are absolutely not random and have roots in their class element and historical origins." This referenced the fact that Zhang came from a "wealthy peasant household" and "received a capitalist legal education at university." However, even after entering the party he had supposedly not been able to reform himself, the analysis stated.[10]

On the one hand, the CCP made a clear attempt to implement justice and act magnanimously toward Japanese prisoners during the initial years of the nascent rise of the PRC. However, almost immediately after the military tribunals concluded, the records of those trials were buried, along with the notion that law could help adjudicate historical reconciliation. Sadly, by 1958 the memory of justice and benevolence found in some measure in those trials of Japanese war criminals had been pushed to the dark recesses of administrative drawers. Because the legal knowledge gained and talent experienced at trial were stifled shortly after the verdicts were delivered, the potential cultural legacy and dividend of the trials remained stunted.

KMT War Criminals

The PRC's public security ministry assessed that reeducating KMT soldiers was often harder and took longer than work on the Japanese war criminals. This was because the Chinese military men were disciples of Chiang Kai-shek and believed he was the legitimate ruler of the Chinese government.[11] Interviews with former CCP guards and those who worked with KMT war criminals, as well as memoirs from the KMT prisoners themselves, provide a window into the mind-set of the CCP and how the party configured its response to the incoming KMT high-ranking officers late in China's civil war and then after.[12] Early on, PRC officials labeled KMT prisoners as "war criminals," like the

Japanese, but also called them traitors and reactionaries. Moreover, the CCP considered its reform policies aimed at KMT prisoners as different from plans imposed on Japanese officers and officials.

Lei Hao worked on the reeducation campaigns of KMT war criminals. However, even though the CCP had for years categorized KMT prisoners with this legal classification, and incarcerated them, trials were rarely ever held. They were, in essence, mainly prisoners without a sentence, and their treatment was therefore very different from how justice for the Japanese war criminals was adjudicated. For the CCP, it was important to gain a public confession of guilt and malfeasance from the Japanese on the trial record and in public. To be frank, there was little justice for the KMT prisoners, just reeducation and incarceration. The KMT prisoners were less clear regarding the CCP's plans. At the beginning of 1949, Lei arrived in Beijing and went to work in the Gongdelin Prison. There he came into contact with KMT prisoners Kang Ze and Dong Yisan, who were kept in solitary cells.[13] Dong had been sent to the United States to study wireless communication technology toward the end of the war and was made part of the military defense staff until he was taken prisoner by the CCP during the civil war in 1948. Kang was a famous KMT officer whom Lei called a "walking dictionary." From the early 1930s, Kang had been a leader in the propaganda war against the KMT's enemies and later helped run the *China Daily* newspaper, which had the stated aim of propping up Chiang Kai-shek. Mao Zedong mentioned Kang by name in his seminal April 25, 1956, speech, "The Ten Major Relationships."[14]

In that speech, given on the eve of the CCP's announcement about its trial policy to release most of the minor Japanese war criminals and pursue only the top leadership, Mao outlined his policy for tracking down and punishing counterrevolutionaries. He distinguished between those within the general society and those within the government itself, for whom he had no pity. But with the general prisoners, and particularly toward incarcerated KMT officials, Mao's tone was more measured and very pragmatic.

> Even war criminal Emperor Pu Yi who was taken as a prisoner, and the sort of people like Kang Ze, we do not kill. We do not kill them not because they have not committed crimes worthy of execution but because killing them has no merit. If you kill someone like this you will have to compare them later with the others that follow and you will end up killing more people. This is the first issue. The second issue is you can incorrectly execute people. History proves that a head falling to the ground cannot connect back to a body again. It's not like with garlic chives, when you chop them off they grow back. Cut a head off incorrectly and even if you

> want to do it over to correct your mistake, there is no way. The third issue is elimination of evidence. Suppressing the counter-revolution requires evidence. The case of a counter-revolutionary can frequently serve as living testimony against other case of counter-revolution. We can prosecute them if we have the legal means. However, if we eliminate them we will no longer be able to find any evidence. Such a move would only benefit the counter-revolution and would not assist our revolution. The fourth issue is that if we kill them we first cannot increase production, second we cannot raise our levels of science, third they cannot help in our "eliminate the four pests campaign," fourth we cannot increase our national defense, and fifth they cannot help us regain Taiwan. If you kill prisoners, you will get a reputation of killing prisoners for yourselves. It is historically proven that this reputation is negative.[15]

By 1950, not long after the establishment of new China, there were about eighty KMT prisoners in Gongdelin Prison, and by the end of 1955 their reeducation had begun. This was just about the time when the investigations of most Japanese war criminals had ended and their trials were being prepared. There had been numerous small sites of KMT prisoner detention around China—in Chongqing, Xian, Wuhan, Nanjing, Shenyang, Zhangjiakou, and elsewhere—but by 1956 a move was under way to "consolidate" the KMT war criminals into a few major detention sites. Former high-ranking KMT officials got sent to Beijing and housed in Gongdelin, which was just outside the city borders.

Like the Japanese war criminals, the KMT prisoners did not easily accept their predicament and did not believe in the reeducation program. Some even tried to escape. One such prisoner who was initially detained at the Shanxi, Hebei and Chahar Provinces (Jin-Cha-Ji) Military Zone Detention Center was Lieutenant General Yang Guangyu.[16] Owing to lax guarding, he managed to escape but did not get far. It was the dead of winter, and both of his legs succumbed to heavy frostbite. He was brought back, but the wounds had already turned gangrenous. As a result, both of his legs were amputated. Afterward he was incarcerated at Gongdelin Prison.[17]

The CCP guards believed they were just as righteous as the KMT. But they did seem to evince compassion rather than cruelty, at least at that time. The Fushun War Criminals Management Center, the keystone of the PRC's renovation plan for Japanese war criminals, was reopened to prisoners in June 1950, just before the Japanese arrived from the USSR. Jin Yuan was there from the start. Jin was part of the Korean-Chinese minority in northeast China, had learned some of the Japanese language in his youth, and later joined the CCP's

Eighth Route Army during the war. He began as a section chief, became deputy warden, and then was prison warden in 1964, the year all the Japanese were released.[18] In September 1956, Jin said that with the exception of high-ranking KMT officers in Gongdelin Prison, the rest of the KMT prisoners were eventually moved to Fushun. They came in waves from detention sites dotted across China. In September 1963, the Chongqing War Criminals Management Center closed, and those prisoners were transported to Fushun. Over a period of years, from the autumn of 1956 to the spring of 1968, the transfer of KMT political prisoners was completed, Jin wrote, and all eventually made their way to Fushun in northeast China.

Jin Luxian was a Chinese Catholic priest incarcerated for using foreign languages and considered a spy. Deemed a dangerous counterrevolutionary, he was jailed in numerous prisons throughout China—similar to the forgotten Japanese communist Itō Ritsu. Jin recalled a similar system of transport that had been used with the Japanese soldiers, of not telling prisoners where they were going when being moved around the country.[19]

> The train started, picked up speed, didn't stop at any station along the way—it was a special train. The next morning, the train slowly decreased speed and then suddenly stopped. We got off to see that it was yet another small station, the platform covered with armed soldiers. Once again we boarded vans and after half an hour entered a compound full of single-storey buildings and stopped in front of a large assembly hall. We lined up in order to listen to the instructions of the prison authorities. Only then did we learn that this was the Fushun War Criminals Management Centre.[20]

KMT war criminals underwent reeducation campaigns similar to what the Japanese had endured, but there were stark differences. Unlike the Japanese program that emerged in 1952, the CCP push toward reforming KMT officers did not ramp up until later in 1956. When they arrived, some KMT prisoners whispered, "We started out as counter revolutionaries and were sentenced, and now we have become war criminals. It's like adding another criminal charge. That's a bit much isn't it?" Seeing the name on the prison as "War Criminals Management Center" and the items that former and current Japanese prisoners had pasted up on the walls caused many KMT soldiers to feel despondent that they would never be able to leave and return home. Another depressing factor the men learned about was the 1956 Hungarian uprising. After all, what was happening in China did not occur in a vacuum. The KMT prisoners were justifiably now more anxious that what was going on in Hungary could spill over into China. In turn, their anxiety pushed them to believe that China could learn the lesson that it needed to be more vigilant, and if the Republic of China (Taiwan) attacked, the prisoners might be expunged as a form of revenge.[21]

Duan Kewen was a skeptic and one of the few KMT prisoners who managed to get to the United States after incarceration. He claimed that Manchu prisoners were favored, and at the top of the list were the Japanese, who received all the perks. Duan was angry that the Japanese who "butchered Chinese" were released first.[22] Duan's peripatetic life story demonstrates the vagaries of PRC policy toward KMT war criminals and how long it took to arrive at a unified national policy. When the war ended in 1949, Duan was in Changchun. He then traveled down to Beijing, where he was a businessman for two years before being arrested by the CCP government in February 1951. He was taken back to Changchun and detained for two years by the Public Security Bureau for "reflection." At the end of January 1953 he was sent to the Changchun People's Court and sentenced to life imprisonment. He spent a bit more than two months in prison and was then sent to a Changchun labor reform camp, where he fired bricks in a kiln all day. In the autumn of 1955, he was suddenly returned to the Changchun Prison and then in January 1956 was transferred to the Jilin Provincial Public Security Bureau. After one more transfer in September 1956, Duan finally arrived at the Fushun Prison, where he was incarcerated for the next twenty years.[23] He wrote that during his various detentions he was forced to write his "confession" numerous times. Duan reflected on why the CCP left him alone for so long before arresting him, and the only rationale that he could come up with was that the pressure of the Korean War must have postponed his arrest and then the suppression of other important "counter-revolutionaries" followed.[24] Duan wrote that during his initial incarceration he was kept in leg irons for five years.[25]

Many of the KMT officers did not believe in the CCP, of course, and there were "class contradictions," Jin Yuan wrote. Everyone had their own stance toward the label of war criminal. Jin noted that KMT cases were different from Japanese cases, which he had also managed at Fushun. The KMT soldiers, he wrote, for certain had committed serious crimes, but among them were many individuals who had contributed in the war against the Japanese and sacrificed for the Chinese people. These soldiers were Chinese nationals, but not all supported the same KMT cliques and therefore they did not share the same interests and privileges as the KMT leadership. Owing to this rather complicated set of circumstances, Jin recalled, "our reformation work with the KMT war criminals, compared with how we treated the Japanese war criminals and fake Manchukuo war criminals, was more carefully calibrated and painstaking."[26]

At the start of 1957, reform education began to steer KMT prisoners toward acknowledging their crimes. This process, Jin explained, was a series of three steps: first, "benevolence for frank admission of crimes"; second, "stern punishment for refusal"; and third, "rewards for those who successfully completed the process."[27] Not everything went smoothly, however. Internally, not all the guards or the investigators agreed with the government's initial policy not to render a verdict in the KMT cases. Prison officials were concerned that such a move would not allow the prisoners to admit their crimes. The reformation program needed to first get the men to internalize what they had done and press them to "rectify their own errors." But, after scouring through their case files, many offices around the country had merely listed the KMT prisoners as "war criminals" or as "counterrevolutionaries," so the record of their crimes was not systematically organized. At first the KMT prisoners were puffed up with pride. Only once they learned more about the consequences of their actions did they come to suffer regret and then start on the path toward accepting reforming education, Jin explained. One should note, however, that former KMT prisoners never dedicated a memorial to their incarceration at Fushun and never began a lobbying group like the Japanese Liaison Group.

Two of the more famous war criminals within the CCP prison ranks were former KMT generals Du Yuming and Huang Wei. As with the pragmatic usage of Japanese war criminals to promote better Sino-Japanese relations in the immediate postwar period, Mao was pleased with the capture of Huang and did not allow his execution. Instead, Mao believed Huang could be put to good political use.[28] Huang was implicated in the KMT military defeat at Huaihai and charged by the communists for having supposedly used poison gas. US State Department records, however, suggested that the "poison gas charge is an old one, bandied back and forth by both sides but never substantiated by either."[29] The Battle of Huai-hai (also called Chiang Kai-shek's Waterloo), in which close to two million soldiers came into fierce combat on a plain hundreds of miles wide, was one of the largest military campaigns of the Chinese civil war. The campaign was costly for both sides, but the losses were devastating for the Chinese Nationalists. More than 550,000 KMT soldiers were killed, wounded, or captured during the campaign. Although the PLA lost 150,000 men, it ended the battle in a stronger position because the communists gained the captured and defecting Nationalist troops. In short, the Huai-hai battle marked the beginning of the end of the civil war.[30]

When he was first captured in December 1948, Huang recalled that he did not give up his real name and rank. Nonetheless, the communists soon figured it out.[31] At the end of January 1949 he was transferred to Gongdelin Prison. Ironically, the facility had earlier served as a place to torture and kill Chinese communists during the Republican era of oppression against those who opposed the KMT. Huang admitted he was determined to prove the CCP's policy of magnanimity toward POWs was a lie, so he remained stubbornly opposed to their interventions. He kept his composure as an old-school general, supposedly held his head high, and never admitted his crimes. To be fair, Huang's supposed war crimes were never actually made clear during the interrogations. Was he a counterrevolutionary or something else?[32] In 1952, Huang wrote that he fell severely ill with tuberculosis, and his body was ravaged to the point that he could not leave the bed even to get to the bathroom for the smallest of necessities. He noted that China had an old saying: "During a chronic illness even dutiful children will leave your bedside." He was a "war criminal" and an enemy of the communists, and yet they continued to provide him the best of care. How was that possible? he wondered. For several years they fed him meat, eggs, and milk to strengthen his health, even during the most difficult of economic times.[33]

Huang was also one of the more colorful prisoners and an amateur scientist in the most expansive sense of the word. He grew obsessed with disproving scientific principles in his bid to invent a perpetual motion machine while incarcerated. His fixation stemmed from his belief that it would be "an inestimable contribution to all of humanity."[34] It is possible that another factor behind this passion was linked to the fact that he was languishing in prison, so focusing on this project offered him a way of avoiding reform, at least according to some in the public security bureau.[35] Lei Hao wondered why Huang was preternaturally absorbed with this impossible machine and concluded it was just a way for the former military general to deal with his change in life circumstances. Regardless of the criticism, Huang was seemingly serious about what he called his "Eastern Red Engine."[36] Huang also remained loyal to Chiang Kai-shek. Even as Huang changed within the reformation education, he never wavered in his fealty to Chiang, although he eventually saw the light.[37] His incarcerators saw him as obstinate. Jin Yuan, in charge at the Fushun War Criminals Management Center, must have had the central government's authorization, because great financial largesse was granted to allow Huang to build a model of the contraption. The prison held a grand unveiling, but, of course, the machine failed to perform.[38]

In the late 1950s, with great fanfare the CCP launched its "special amnesty" campaign toward KMT prisoners. On September 18, 1959, the *People's Daily* celebrated China's achievements on the tenth anniversary of its founding. To promote that success and the solidification of the "people's dictatorship," the newspaper produced a glowing editorial, "Turning Away from Evil and toward Virtue, the Future Is Bright," to champion the moment.[39] The announcement was not met with complete social acceptance, and there was some pushback. Regardless, on December 4, 1959, prisons in Beijing, Fushun, Jinan, Xian,

Chongqing, and Hohhot held amnesty meetings for some KMT war criminals. The year 1959 was significant for the PRC, marking the ten-year anniversary of the establishment of the new government. Mao was inclined to bestow an amnesty of sorts toward prisoners, mirroring his belief that this was a practice enacted by Chinese emperors in ancient times.[40]

It is clear that the process was somewhat muddled at times. Huang Wei recalled, much to his amazement since he was still stubbornly against the CCP reeducation process, that Zhou Enlai had originally put him on the 1959 list to be granted special amnesty. The authorities had even notified Huang's daughter, who was teaching at Qinghua University, to be prepared to come and get him. But the prison authorities rejected the proposal, saying that Huang had not yet sufficiently reformed, and to release him would cause great problems among the remaining war criminal prisoners.[41]

Many former KMT officers wrote memoirs, but none was as prolific or as toadying as that of Shen Zui. Shen had been a KMT spy and had worked under the notorious KMT officer Dai Li. Quoting Shen's own observations, one historian likened Dai Li to the most subservient of subjects to Chiang Kai-shek, implementing Chiang's will like a "dagger" behind the scenes but serving as his "butcher" publicly as head of the KMT's spy network, which at one point employed about twenty thousand people.[42] Shen had expected to be executed upon capture and admitted that he did not find the process of CCP thought reform easy. He believed the communists never demeaned him but kept pushing and pushing him in interrogations and discussions, with "dogged persistence" as he put it.[43] He was also one of the former KMT officers whose will eventually bent to his captors, ultimately writing numerous books about their benevolence and benefiting from the glow of their adulation. His stories also relate a dark humor at times.[44]

KMT war criminals were also employed as political window dressing for the CCP in its gestures to gain international legitimacy. Du Yuming was one such individual—a failed military general but a willing pupil as a prisoner. He had engaged the CCP consistently from the start of the civil war but lost every single battle, an impressive record. He, too, was captured during the disastrous Huai-hai campaign. At first, Du seemed less willing to change, in comparison with some of the others, but upon release he was quickly trotted out for international propaganda events.[45] Felix Greene, a British journalist, was invited to a banquet hosted by Premier Zhou Enlai toward the end of May 1960, and Du was present. Greene was "the US-based cousin of Graham Greene who became one of the most effective advocates of the Chinese cause both in print and in television documentary films."[46] Also in attendance was Manchukuo last emperor Pu Yi. British field marshal Bernard Montgomery was the guest of honor that night and was enamored with Mao. Not only did the UK military commander find Mao "delightful," but he added, "Like all sons of the soil he is a genuine democrat."[47] When Premier Zhou introduced PLA general Chen Yi and former KMT general Du Yuming, Montgomery was told, "These two fought each other. This one lost," Zhou said, pointing to General Du. Montgomery asked Du how it was possible to lose the civil war when he had a million men under his command. "Du responded, 'They all ran over to his side,' nodding toward Chen Yi. Chou En-lai [Zhou Enlai] threw back his head and laughed."[48] Du and Pu Yi had been released from detention only about five months prior, but their presence was deemed necessary to showcase PRC military competence and magnanimity toward past enemies. The CCP could demonstrate its new approach to foreign policy, and the meetings entertained foreign guests. Montgomery returned to the UK convinced that rumors of starvation after China's Great Leap Forward were false.[49]

As Mao did with KMT war criminals, CCP leaders believed it was imperative to keep the last Manchu emperor alive and well. He was a useful tool for international and domestic propaganda.[50] We can gain a further understanding through the fate of Li Yuqin, Pu Yi's fourth wife. In 1955, after a decade of incarceration in various locales, Pu Yi managed to get in touch with Li, and she visited him a few times in Fushun. Chinese authorities were keen on getting her to bolster Pu Yi's flagging health. In arranging for her visits, prison officials opened up a larger room for two, stocked it with better furniture and a large double bed, and even repainted the room. At this time, Fushun officials were also allowing visits to the incarcerated Japanese. The prison authorities passed a rule that war criminals with more than five years to go on their sentences could have their spouses live with them. Of course, Pu Yi had no time on his sentence since he had never been charged. He was, for all intents and purposes, a prisoner at the leisure of Mao, Zhou Enlai, and Luo Ruiqing, the head of the Public Security Ministry. However, Li Yuqin wanted a divorce, which the authorities did not want to grant and they pressured her to stay married. Eventually, she went to the government offices in Fushun City to file directly for divorce. She remarried and went to work for the Changchun city library. Pu Yi was released from Fushun in 1959 and remarried in 1962.[51]

As they had done with the Japanese prisoners, starting in 1956 the PRC officials also escorted KMT prisoners on many tours around the country to introduce them to new China.[52] Generally speaking, Japanese and KMT prisoners still fared far better than the average Chinese citizen in confinement.[53] However, not everything was in accord with the law in prisons or camps that housed KMT prisoners. Sometimes the situation went very much awry. Liu Binyan, a famous Chinese reporter who documented legal and political corruption within China and eventually chose exile to the United States, wrote about these issues when they first started to surface. He described the murder of a former young KMT soldier at a camp called Nenjiang. The murder was committed by a camp guard in full view of more than one hundred prisoners, and no one did anything. The prisoner, who was shot, died a slow and painful death in the prison yard while everyone watched, helpless to intervene.[54]

Comparing the confessions of the KMT and other war criminals is difficult. CCP obsession with acknowledging one's crime was central to its personal renovation process, but it is an interesting method in the face of the lack of actual trials for KMT prisoners. "To insist on a confession, repeatedly revised and extended, while at the same time knowing it is often produced simply to conform and avoid trouble would seem to place too low a value on sincerity, even if this is regarded as a first stage only."[55] It is obvious the CCP did not see Fushun merely as a prison but as a site of reeducation.[56] It was clear that Mao did not believe in the rights of man but in the right of the majority to bestow or deprive rights based on the class or background of an individual. Within a society still transitioning from one form of rule to another, confessions were also employed to assert new authority. Confessions demonstrated that a defendant was attempting to redeem himself within the utopian society, and this, doubly, served as a public record of the new state's legitimacy.[57]

Taiwan and KMT War Criminals—So Much for Loyalty

The issue of war criminals remained potent in China and Taiwan owing to strained cross-strait relations. Even though the Chinese had long since repatriated those who they claimed were the worst of the worst Japanese war criminals, delays of KMT "war criminals" dragged on. Decades after World War II had concluded, the issue of Japanese war crimes and the meaning of justice had transformed into something truly greater than the sum of its original elements.

By the early 1970s, Taiwan had been dislodged from its UN seat representing China, and the mainland Chinese communist government under Mao was invited to replace it. Seemingly the world had shifted, and yet the issue of World War II war criminals was still a high priority. In the early 1970s, CCP leader Mao began to receive word from his premier, Zhou Enlai, concerning the state of POWs still being held at Fushun Prison in Liaoning Province. But the memos were perplexing because the Chinese communist government had already repatriated the Japanese defendants, and the four dozen or so who had been sentenced to lengthy jail terms had already been released back to Japan, the last three to great political fanfare in 1964.

On May 19, 1971, Zhou Enlai notified Mao that no one from the Public Security Ministry had been checking on the KMT prisoners in Fushun Prison, and many were now gravely ill. With the Cultural Revolution in full swing, Zhou was anxious that the government would end up being criticized. He feared that people would say that Japanese "great war criminals are granted amnesty while the smaller [Chinese] war criminals are jailed until they die; foreign war criminals are released, but we incarcerate our own war criminals." This, Zhou attempted to explain in the memo to Mao, did not fit the CCP's goals for the revolution. Mao instructed Zhou to change what the prisoners were being given to eat, alter their labor requirements, or figure out some way to help them survive.[58] What communist officials realized was that KMT war criminals had been forgotten in the dungeons up north. In the end, the communist government was never quite sure exactly how many were released, because records were lost. Agreement on who was detained on what charges was also absent because the prisons and the rule of law had essentially been ignored for more than a decade and a half since the end of the 1950s.

What happened to high-ranking KMT war criminals was not only of consequence to propping up the domestic legitimacy of the PRC. This delayed clemency had an impact on Taiwan. In Taiwan, the term for KMT generals and others who were captured but never sentenced was "fierce loyalists." At least this was the generous label employed when the prisoners were kept at a respectful distance. But when the potential for formerly "tainted" prisoners to repatriate arose, KMT leadership showed the same sort of reluctance CCP leaders had shown in their suspicion of returning POWs from the Korean War. In the spring of 1975, when a select number of remaining KMT prisoners were offered a chance to depart to Taiwan, the KMT showed its true colors and rejected their requests.[59]

This last group caused a massive political scandal because ten men requested to return to Taiwan and the CCP leadership granted the application. This was Mao's propaganda ploy and he had declared the men were free to go anywhere after their release. On April 13, 1975, the ten amnestied prisoners left Beijing by plane and flew south, then took a train to Shenzhen. They were each given 2,000 Hong Kong dollars, some new clothes, and an exit visa for half a year, meaning they could apply to return to the mainland if so desired.[60] They were then escorted to the border. Once the former war criminals crossed the bridge to Hong Kong, reporters swarmed. The Taiwan press was not as forgiving or interested (the KMT was firmly a dictatorship at this point, reliant on a media that was heavily censored), and the Chinese Nationalist news companies barely reported the event. The Taiwanese media saw this move as part of Mao's strategy to gain more political capital—to appear benevolent, to show the world that mainland China was stable, and maybe with a longer eye toward future relations. By contrast, the early 1970s international changes had rocked Taiwan's world. The ROC had recently been booted from its seat on the UN, US president Richard Nixon had dined with Mao in Beijing, and Taiwan was unsure of its future. Generalissimo Chiang Kai-shek had just passed away in April 1975, and his son, Chiang Ching-kuo, was settling in during this delicate time of a transfer of power. For decades, Chinese Nationalists had billed themselves as the anticommunist stronghold and "free China," but now that policy was no longer paying dividends.[61]

The KMT sent out a variety of messages, at first saying it was pleased these men were being released and wanted to return to the "motherland," a strange turn of phrase since none of the incarcerated prisoners had ever been to Taiwan. But a few days later at a media event, a KMT party spokesman said that while Taiwan welcomed all anticommunists, this did not include spies from the CCP. KMT leader and Chiang Kai-shek's son, Chiang Ching-kuo, felt "only the personnel captured in raids on the mainland since 1950 would be considered for settlement in Taiwan."[62] It is possible Taiwan rejected former KMT war criminals because it believed this acceptance would destabilize the KMT's long-standing "three no's policy": no contact, no negotiation, and no cooperation with the Chinese communists.[63] Initially, when the ten said they wanted to go to Taiwan, CCP leaders said they would pay the costs and Taiwan showed a welcoming attitude. Soon after, the KMT assessed that the men were "tools" for a CCP liberation plan of Taiwan and denied their repatriation.[64] One released prisoner, Zhang Tieshi, grew so despondent over the postponement that he committed suicide in a Hong Kong hotel.[65] The CCP was in a quandary over what to do and set up a commission to study the issue. The remaining nine men were told that if they wanted to return to China and work, that was fine. If they then later chose to try to go abroad, this was equally acceptable. Or they could even "stay in Hong Kong," CCP officials advised. In the end, almost half eventually returned to the mainland, and a few chose to stay in Hong Kong. Several made it to the United States.

A few years after Taiwan rejected the KMT former prisoner return, the island country welcomed a defecting high-ranking communist officer, PLA Air Force squadron commander Fan Yuanyan. It seems KMT officers who became prisoners were no longer believed loyal, but CCP officers who brought military hardware with them to Taiwan were seen in an entirely different light. Defecting with his Chinese fighter jet to Taiwan earned Fan the sizable reward of 150 kilograms of gold with no tax strings. "Massive rewards" and the presentation ceremonies were central to the ritual of celebrating these mainland military defectors as "anticommunist heroes."[66] Fan landed in what was still deemed "free China," and the *Washington Post* quoted him as noting the lack of justice in China as a reason for his departure. "Comrades, it's the Communists who forced me to do this. I just cannot take it anymore. I came here to seek freedom and human rights which are totally lacking on the China mainland."[67] The great irony, of course, was that Taiwan was far from such a land at that time.

It is interesting to consider just how different the CCP's multiple prisoner reeducation programs were: the Japanese war criminal process; the one eventually set up for people not actually tried, the KMT prisoners; and the draconian system that developed for what many Chinese peasants would end up facing in the prison labor system. In particular, we should pause for a moment and demonstrate the stark contrast between these two mainland China policies for those defeated in war, the CCP's former enemies. These more magnanimous plans were implemented during an era of revolution, but with an eye to the idea that former enemies could be reformed. Obviously, that reform came with many conditions and a long duration of incarceration, but it still kept an end goal in sight. Compare that policy with practices employed by the US military and intelligence services in the twenty-first century. US forces and the government found it difficult to practice full legal representation for all prisoners of war since there was little belief that those captured during the wars in Iraq and Afghanistan would reform.

When the United States suffered the 9/11 attack, an unnamed US intelligence official explained how the country should respond. "What's needed is a little bit of smacky-face. Some al-Qaeda just need some extra encouragement."[68] With no understanding of how US officials had behaved in the past, a new American machismo asserted that the United States would defeat terrorism only with superior military prowess. Somehow or other the United States had forgotten what it learned immediately after World War II. A US Strategic Bombing Survey report, published in 1946, emphasized that "while defeat is a military event, the recognition of defeat is a political act."[69] In the postwar period, militaries demobilize, but civilian societies do not follow in the same way, and that is why intelligence, propaganda, and a strategy for after the battle are exceedingly important. But what should really give us pause concerns the issue of what follows incarceration and interrogation. If governments, like China, were interested in war crimes trials to showcase their benevolence, then, in some fashion, that policy worked. By contrast, US efforts at Guantanamo and elsewhere appear to be ham-fisted. A critical FBI interrogator explained, "After getting intelligence from terrorists, at some point we have to prosecute them. We can't hold people indefinitely. Whether it is one year later or ten years later, eventually a trial becomes necessary; otherwise they'll have to be released."[70] Close to eight hundred men were processed through the detention center opened in January 2002 in the US base of Guantanamo, and thirty-five remain. As of 2022, only twelve were ever charged in a military tribunal.[71]

Chapter 12

Owning the War

Constructing the Contours of National History, 1970s–1980s

In the autumn of 1971, the political situation in East Asia began to change, though no one could have guessed its ultimate direction. On October 25, the PRC became the new official representative of China to the United Nations, and Chiang Kai-shek's representatives were declared to have "unlawfully" occupied the seat.[1] This was the international scene, but the US government did not switch its embassies until full diplomatic credentials had been negotiated and exchanged, something that did not occur until the start of 1979. Slowly over the decade, the PRC appropriated the mantle of international recognition from Taiwan and regional power dynamics began to shift. After being off the international radar screen, because of neglect but also the long interregnum of self-imposed exile and revolutionary fervor gone awry, PRC leadership emerged from the shadows. Toward the end of October 1971, Premier Zhou Enlai gave Japan's *Asahi Newspaper* a late-night interview, one of China's first after the announcement that the PRC would replace the ROC on the UN Permanent Security Council. The Japanese news item took the headlines of the first three pages of the newspaper.[2] But all was not quiet. The Lin Biao Incident had occurred just before China's international reemergence and threatened to undo everything. In September 1971, supposedly fearing for their lives, Marshal Lin Biao and family flew to the USSR, but their plane crashed over Mongolia. All the passengers died. Mao had previously deemed Lin as his grand successor, so many questions remain unanswered, even today. The impact of Lin's supposed failed coup allowed Mao and Zhou Enlai to purge the politburo of those who were labeled as or actually were Lin's allies. Liu Shaoqi had already been axed in the heat of the Cultural Revolution. The 1960s into the 1970s was an era that demonstrated the sort of postwar imbalance that had developed between China and Japan, even just looking at the most cursory figures. Japanese travel to China in 1969 saw 2,643 Japanese visit, but only seven Chinese journeyed to Japan. By 1971, the figures were 5,718 and 74, respectively.

Zhou Enlai was keen to show the world that the PRC was now in command of its future and that it would proceed cautiously. However, in the UN, China regarded talk of Taiwanese independence as out of bounds. In addition, perhaps in an attempt to snuff out rumors that the Chinese were unaware of what was happening in the rest of the world and therefore not ready for the international role newly thrust upon them, Zhou showed the *Asahi* journalists "internal eyes only" reports and foreign news sources to which only high-ranking CCP officials had access.[3] But that did not mean the handover was seamless. US national security advisor Henry Kissinger, during his November 1971 secret meeting with Ambassador Huang Hua, PRC permanent representative to the UN, believed that China was caught off guard by its sudden entry into the international vortex of the United Nations. Kissinger assessed the Chinese as rudderless concerning what to do, not enthusiastic and "feeling its way in an unfamiliar environment."[4] Not everyone took that stance. Some assessed the Chinese UN team as "first rate," suggesting that Huang was a long-standing diplomat with excellent language skills, as were his underlings.[5]

Several months after the epoch-making interview with one of Japan's leading newspapers, US president Richard Nixon practiced with chopsticks so that he would not embarrass his hosts at the enormous banquet held for him in Beijing in February 1972.[6] Notwithstanding that restoring official relations with the PRC was the goal for both the United States and Japan, actual negotiations hit a few obstacles, and it was not until the late 1970s that official treaties were signed. Change came, but it evolved slowly due to so many political and economic impediments. The 1960s into the 1970s was a volcanic period for China owing to the seismic political aftermath of the Cultural Revolution, which might be best symbolized by one item, the "Little Red Book" of Mao's quotations. Initially, it was an "ideological field manual for soldiers" to help them gain access to Mao's thought, which would be a "spiritual atom bomb of infinite power."[7] At one point, it was the most printed book in the world, and the overproduction was rumored to have been kept in massive air-conditioned storehouses once Maoism waned.[8]

During this same era, Japan had been advancing its own economy and trying to assure the world, after the somewhat more security-focused foreign policy of Prime Minister Kishi Nobusuke, that the country was more interested in trade and economics. "By 1969 50 percent of Japan's Overseas Development Aid (ODA) went to Southeast Asia. Japan thus began to follow a path that would later see it become the largest provider of ODA to the Third World."[9] Much of this aid shifted to China after 1972. As China emerged back into the world arena through the 1970s, the World Bank and Japan were largely responsible for the economic foundations on which China developed. "Japan provided more than three quarters of China's total bilateral loans totaling $10 billion (1.6 trillion yen) in the years 1979–1995. The massive capital infusion into China was a product of China's changed development priorities and economic performance."[10]

On July 27, 1972, Japan's Kōmeitō Party head, Takeiri Yoshikatsu, held a long meeting with Chinese premier Zhou Enlai. They exchanged diplomatic platitudes, but the Chinese wanted Japanese commitments to trade, aid, and access to the outside world. Zhou was semiconciliatory but firm: "The ties of trade and friendship are deep. It has been 27 years since the war, but relations between Japan and China span 2,000 years back to the Qin Dynasty. The previous 27 years is only but a moment."[11] While seemingly flexible in their attitudes toward the history of World War II, the legal issue of Taiwan remained a looming problem for Sino-Japanese negotiations. Zhou stated that China understood from its own experience during the Qing era, when indemnities were placed on it for the Boxer Rebellion, that reparations could be burdensome and obviously saw China's move not to request them as a great propaganda coup.[12] Zhou explained, "Chairman Mao has said that he will renounce the right to seek reparations. If we seek reparations, this would place a burden on the Japanese people. This is something that the Chinese people fully understand."[13] The next meeting played up how the Japan-China relationship was an improvement over that of the United States and China. Zhou told his Japanese interlocutors: "We have returned 30,000 Japanese, including war criminals. We have carried on friendly attitudes. Friendship, memoranda, and trade are paths that the former minister Matsumura [Kenzō] opened up. Japan knows this. The US does not have this. They have even less of cultural exchanges. Ping-Pong diplomacy lapsed last year, but it has been reestablished. Ping-Pong is the reason that Nixon conducted secret diplomacy to reestablish relations. That ball is very important."[14]

As Japan embarked on a new era with the PRC, Tokyo was forced to close formal relations with Taiwan. This proved difficult. The question for the

Japanese was: how could they create a legal word salad that allowed them to deny what had been a lawful treaty with the KMT and replace it with one that gave preference to Mao's communist leadership on the mainland? This move was all the more painful because many KMT leaders had long-standing ties to Japanese politicians and bureaucrats, having studied together before the war and sharing vague but potent positions covering Pan-Asianism and Japan's future role in East Asia. China long held that Taiwan was a "renegade province," and dealing with it without going through Beijing muddled in China's internal affairs, a protocol to which the PRC strictly adhered for its own practice and as a foreign policy. Some Japanese, like Shiina Etsusaburō, a long-standing bureaucrat and close confidante to former prime minister Kishi Nobusuke, hoped that Japan could maintain independent relations with both Chinas. Ultimately that proved impossible, at least according to the letter of the law.

The Japanese wasted no time in opening up new portals for relations with the Chinese. Prime Minister Tanaka Kakuei, who replaced Satō Eisaku after he managed to get Okinawa returned to Japanese sovereignty, jumped at the chance to go to China and sign a joint communiqué with Premier Zhou Enlai. This would be the "first sustained diplomatic relations between a sovereign Japan and the Chinese mainland since 1938."[15] This détente was epochal for several reasons. Japan and China had had no diplomatic relations for decades yet finalized arrangements on September 27, 1972, after only four days. Japan's diplomatic treaty with the USSR, a communist entity like China, took more than a year and a half. With South Korea the talks elongated to fourteen years until a treaty was concluded in 1965. The key was that for the Japanese it was politically necessary, and savvy, to *not* immediately pursue a peace treaty with China, a formal diplomatic move that was not signed until 1978. The 1972 document was symbolically a "joint communiqué" and thus did not need to be ratified by the Japanese Diet. In this manner, key Japanese politicians and diplomats used a unique strategy to begin relations on the right foot in a calculated way to avoid domestic roadblocks that had previously tripped them up.[16]

The CCP under the leadership of Premier Zhou Enlai also realized the necessity of preparing the groundwork for mainland Chinese public opinion to accept these new moves toward what appeared to be sudden rapprochement with the long-despised Japanese. According to Wu Jinan, who headed public opinion investigation campaigns in China, many Chinese did not understand why China had to suddenly reestablish relations with Japan. Many interviewed were against Japanese prime minister Tanaka's proposed visit to China, and emotional opposition ran high among the middle-aged and elderly. Wu and his colleagues assessed the situation and told their higher-ups that a public lack of support, if not active opposition, risked derailing the situation and creating an uncomfortable rift. CCP leaders and heads of the propaganda bureau came up with a solution, which was to publicize and paint the establishment of relations with Japan as a key policy decision that would aid the PRC's strength in countering Soviet revisionism and US imperialism in the region. Even more cleverly, the plan detailed, this move would quell future Japanese militarism because entering into formal relations with the PRC would pressure Japan to accept China's five principles of peaceful coexistence. In short, all the reasons to oppose the visit from Tanaka were logically dismembered through advance propaganda campaigns.[17]

Other events also held the potential to upset the delicate changes woven into place. Deaths of key CCP leaders in the mid-1970s confused the PRC's political situation, as did Mao's poor preparation for a successor. Premier Zhou Enlai, who had served loyally for so many years and been China's mouthpiece for foreign policy for decades, died on January 8, 1976.[18] Marshall Zhu De, the Communist Party's most venerated military general, died in July 1976. From early 1974 on, Mao was increasingly incapacitated. He had a cataract operation and could not read. Parkinson's disease rendered him virtually speechless. Mao finally succumbed to his panoply of maladies in September 1976. The CCP had no real plans for a transition after Mao's death, and the chaos of the previous decade during the Cultural Revolution had stunted national trust in every regard.

However, even with Chinese détente and renewed engagement with Japan and the world, by the late 1970s China was once again on the back foot. It had squandered its economy, the people were grossly unhappy in the domestic rule of law, and the leadership was in shambles. Hua Guofeng had been chosen as Mao's eventual successor, but he engendered little enthusiasm. US official Thomas Gates, head of the US liaison office in Beijing, met Hua in 1976 and called him colorless and found him full of caution.[19] Within a month of Mao's death, a "bloodless, but successful coup d'état" took place within the central corridors of Chinese power. In October 1976, the new first vice chairman of the CCP, Hua Guofeng, ordered the arrest of the Gang of Four.[20] Their trial would not take place until several years later, but the moment was pregnant with significance. At the same time, party stalwart Hu Yaobang made an initial move for some form of administrative reversal of the mountain of "miscarriages of justice" (*yuanjia cuoan* in Chinese) that had plagued China during the previous decades.[21] Millions of Chinese had been falsely accused and/or found guilty of arbitrary or specious charges of being a counterrevolutionary or undermining the state. Justice would be brought to China, but this required investigating history, because unraveling how these injustices had occurred would involve analyzing the political situation that had allowed these legal contraventions to happen. And behind the political situation lay the taboo of indicting Mao, Maoism, and potentially unlocking further and massive social discontent that had built up over the years. It is important to consider just how much the Cultural Revolution had cut China off from the rest of the world. Premier Hua Guofeng, who succeeded Mao as party leader, first journeyed abroad to Yugoslavia and Romania in 1978 as China's top leader. With the exception of participation at the UN by PRC representatives, the last trip abroad by a top Chinese leader had been almost twenty years prior, when Mao returned to Moscow in 1957.[22]

In 1979, when Deng Xiaoping took the political reins of China behind the scenes (he never took a formal title and Hua Guofeng remained chairman of the CCP from October 1976 to June 1981), the country was in political disarray and economic freefall. Grain production had fallen lower than it had been in 1957, and the per capita income stood at a dismal rate. Factories were still working with equipment received from the USSR in the 1950s.[23] Deng was not sprightly for a leader to start anew; he was already in his mid-seventies. He had survived three nonfatal purges: first during the rise of the CCP, in 1966 at the dawn of the Cultural Revolution, and in 1976 just after Zhou's death and five months before Mao's. If Deng and his Chinese counterparts had learned two things, they were (1) how deeply Chinese culture had depreciated under Mao's reign and (2) how desperate the PRC was to send students abroad to learn. Modernization could not happen without new talent and new technology.

Not long after Mao lay in state off Tiananmen Square, a few blocks away "Democracy Wall" began to take shape. From 1977 to 1978, all sorts of large poster campaigns cried out for justice against corrupt cadres and listed popular complaints about all the injustice that had occurred in Chinese society during the previous two decades under Mao's reign. These massive posters and diatribes were hung on city walls in a specific quarter. At the same time, thousands of others from the hinterlands flocked to Beijing to press the government to remedy the wrongs that had been done to them, hoping that their grievances would be heard.[24] But as with so many previous movements, this form of social venting soon turned into mass embarrassment for the party.

Wei Jingsheng, a former Red Guard and electrician, was one of the most prolific protesters. His writings were published in a samizdat journal at the time. After initially tolerating Wei's criticisms of the state, the authorities arrested and jailed him in 1979 for promoting democracy.[25] Wei was damning of his incarceration; he was held in the same prison from which Japanese communist Itō Ritsu was released at almost the same time. Wei wrote, "Torture at Qincheng has been even worse than that which used to be carried out by the Nationalists in the 1940s."[26] Mu Xin, former editor at the *Guangming Daily*, experienced Qincheng Prison. Years later he commented that the prison practiced cruel and unusual punishment.[27]

While imprisoning Chinese citizens who posted criticism of the PRC government, CCP leaders were by this time considering the release of Japanese communist Itō Ritsu. Enough of a thaw had occurred in China for the incarcerated former Japanese communist leader Itō to be rediscovered in his Chinese prison cell. After twenty-seven years in a series of Chinese prisons, with no charges placed against him, Itō was suddenly summoned one day in October 1979 and told by prison officials: "The Japanese Communist Party requested you to be sequestered and questioned, and you have been left for a long time in this jail. Moreover, considering your health, we believe it inadvisable for this to continue any longer. From the standpoint of 'revolutionary humanitarianism' the Central Committee of the Communist Party of China has decided to grant you release." Itō was told he could either stay in China or return to Japan.[28] Regardless of his ultimate decision, he was counseled to "please not reveal any of your political opinions while in China."[29]

It was only at this moment that Itō saw PRC national currency for the first time. His physical condition had deteriorated to the point that the PRC authorities hospitalized him several times to ensure that he could successfully repatriate to Japan. It was clear that the CCP did not want his death on their hands. Itō quickly started up correspondence with his long-suffering wife, who had not known his whereabouts or even whether he was alive. She quickly wrote back, and things moved along in preparation for his return to Japan.[30] When Japanese embassy staff in Beijing asked him some questions in preparation for his return, it was obvious they were not fully apprised of the situation. Defiant until the end and keen not to implicate the JCP or his Chinese hosts, Itō tersely replied, "I will not say a word." When asked "What were you doing in China and where were you meeting with high level communist cadres?" Itō answered, "I was studying but fell ill. For a long time I was convalescing. And more than that I will not talk about."[31]

It appears that initially Itō still regarded the Japanese government as the enemy even though it was his own party that had set him up. His return was discussed in the Japanese Diet, and some members of parliament, not clear about the background of the story, went so far as to claim that Itō was seeking asylum in China. This was, of course, a gross misrepresentation. In September 1980, Itō repatriated to Japan and was taken from his plane in a wheelchair. His speech was slow and slurred, but he appeared happy. His reappearance as if from a long lost time machine was a national shock, especially considering that he was assumed to be dead. The extent of his suffering was soon noted in Japan's parliament and was surely a commentary on the behavior of the JCP that put him into such circumstances as well as Chinese incarceration standards. Parliamentarian Tsukamoto Saburō pointed out: "According to reports, he cannot see very well and he has hearing loss. He speaks haltingly and at the Japanese Embassy he was only able to communicate by writing because he suffers so greatly from impairments. . . . From this sort of speculation imagining that he was illegally detained and that he submitted to an investigation in the form of a lynching was probably the judgement arrived at by most Japanese who harbored common sense."[32]

China's release of key Japanese prisoners was symbolic of the overall shift in managing a more open and transparent legal system. In February 1979, the *People's Daily* published an article on how to establish a healthy legal system in China. Marshall Ye Jianying told those assembled at the press conference that "our socialist legal system from the founding of the country has not had the most favorable healthy establishment. Lin Biao and the Gang of Four dug this hole for us and under the guise of 'strengthening the dictatorship of the proletariat' they merely grabbed who they wanted and opened up on the people and officials a fascist dictatorship. We now understand these lessons that a country must have law and a system."[33] Ye went on for much longer, detailing why a robust legal system was necessary and then linking it to Chinese socialism. Ye, along with Hu Yaobang, launched the first salvo that demonstrated the reign of the arbitrary would now be slowly dismantled.[34]

The flagship newspaper the *People's Daily* is the mouthpiece of the CCP. Its editorials are used as commentaries in weekly study sessions. All editorials and content arise from the party, and the paper transmits the message. Rarely is there independent analysis critical of the power structure as one finds in democratic media. Before commentary is produced, the article goes through a selection of ideas process, drafting of the wording, and finally revision or censorship. These strict procedures mean that what is published in the main media organs is essentially a government consensus policy to be broadcast from the top down.[35] So, an editorial appearance of Ye's comments indicated that the party approved of this direction.

Almost coincident with Wei's trial and Itō's repatriation, from November 1980 to January 1981, China held its most important tribunal to restore political stability and the CCP's reputation—the Gang of Four trial. The newly reintroduced "rule of law" through the courts put into play a Communist Party historical bid to completely disengage Mao from responsibility for the debacle of the Cultural Revolution and to place it at the feet of the Gang of Four. Deng himself put a lid on criticism of Mao because he believed that this form of soul-searching would not heal the nation.[36] The year 1980 was significant for China because it fundamentally restored a renewed attention toward the pursuit of justice. However, this resurrected interest also created two new problems. The first was the rectification of those who had been illegally or incorrectly charged during the previous two and a half decades of the Cultural Revolution, its aftermath, and the years preceding it since the 1957 anti-Rightist movement. The second was the rise of historical investigations into the war with Japan, memories and introspection that had essentially been dormant since the closure of the 1956 trials of the Japanese war criminals years before. The last few years of the 1970s had witnessed epochal changes in both how China was seen internationally and how it was being understood.[37]

Not only did the history of injustice greatly hamper China's evolution toward modernity, but the party had also carved up society into a new feudal sort of class structure in which the sins of the father were visited upon the whole family for subsequent generations. This family origin labeling system greatly retarded economic development. These class categories stuck around for a bit but were greatly reduced or removed after the Cultural Revolution.[38] Regardless of the massive number of cases over decades of malfeasance, by 1982 all the cases of injustice were supposedly examined and the whole process was surprisingly deemed complete. The total number of people whose cases were reexamined reached 2.3 million.[39] According to official statistics from August 1980, 23,921 people had been executed during the Cultural Revolution.[40]

Gang of Four Trial

As declarations about history were being crafted for public consumption, history was also being judged in China, once again in a courtroom. Post–Cultural Revolution China opened its most famous trial on television to demonstrate legal reform and a supposed return to a just society. From November 1980 to early 1981, four years after Mao's death, elements of the former state leadership were charged with crimes in a public setting, complete with the trappings of a courtroom. The Gang of Four, singled out as responsible for the nation's calamities, were Zhang Chunqiao, a vice prime minister of the State Council; Wang Hongwen, a vice chairman of the CCP; Yao Wenyuan, a secretary of the CCP in Shanghai; and Mao's wife, Jiang Qing. Besides the gang, others were implicated in the trial, including five military officers and Lin Biao, accused of having plotted to overthrow Mao. But the main focus was the gang, a radical clique that fell from grace after Mao's passing. The case was tried in a special court under China's Supreme People's Court, reinstated after a two-decade hiatus. Forty-nine witnesses were called to testify, and 651 pieces of evidence were submitted.[41] In January 1981, the court found all guilty, and sentences ranged from sixteen years in jail to death. An editorial in the *People's Daily* announced, "This is the people's verdict, history's verdict, a just verdict."[42] The death sentences were commuted, but Jiang Qing died by suicide years later.

The case was important legally for the supposed transition of the return to the normal socialist legal system, but also as a moment of post-Maoism. It was, in part, a legal spectacle in ways similar to the war crimes trials the Chinese had held of the Japanese about twenty-five years prior. Fei Xiaotong, a famous Chinese sociologist, was rehabilitated from obscurity to serve as a judge at the Gang of Four Trial. His career had been cut short by China's political waves of counterrevolutionary fervor. Fei wrote that twenty-three years of his life were wasted during that era, when he was pushed out of society and forced to clean toilets.[43] In his estimation, "the immense significance of this trial is that it announces China is on the road toward opening an important new door to establishing a healthy socialist rule of law."[44]

In the internationally published English record of the trial Fei was even more strident toward the defendants in the introduction, which was entitled "Reflections of a Judge." It is important to remember that Fei had no legal education; he was a sociologist who had been trained decades earlier in the United Kingdom. He proclaimed to the world that with this trial China had turned a corner with new legal procedures. He took pains to point out that the leaders on trial in this court had violated criminal law, unlike others who had merely made political errors. This was precisely the point that Deng and others were trying to make to save Mao and Maoism. Fei was careful to use the analogy of a ship advancing at high speed but headed by a navigator—in this case, Mao—who had made an error in navigating. In his extended analogy, the Gang of Four, in charge of the ship, formed cliques and started plotting. The navigator might have steered the ship incorrectly and needed to answer for this action. However, the other culprits tried to exploit that situation "for their own despicable ends," Fei proposed.[45] Fei was pleased with the trial and ranked it highly. "It must be remarked, however, that these perpetrators of crimes in the end were given a just trial and justly adjudged by history. Some writers abroad have likened the trial to those held in Nuremberg and Tokyo after the Second World War. This is rather appropriate in my view."[46] Most Western scholars probably did not view the trial on the same broad scale of justice that Fei did but perhaps more akin to the judicial process to bring calm to what had been a large-scale lawless society and to combine to the extent possible these stories of injustice into a single narrative of the past that would serve future PRC political stability.[47]

At its base, "the Gang of Four trial was an expression of justice inseparable from its transitional context, the transition from the Cultural Revolution to the post-Mao era. It was a political show trial to be sure, but the historian must take this fact as an impetus for further inquiry and not as the final judgment."[48] The dilemma for the struggling PRC was how to modernize and gain power and wealth while toeing the line on communist political theory and retaining supposed Chinese values. One could say this is still an issue for the current administration under president Xi Jinping. The Gang of Four trial created an official verdict on the past for public consumption.[49] In fact, one could argue, as I have, that war crimes trials are in a sense official verdicts of the past. The Gang of Four trial revealed the long absence of law and education in China. Perhaps because there were so few lawyers of talent from which to choose, or because she had a high profile, Jiang Qing initially had hoped to have former minister of justice from the 1950s, Shi Liang, serve as her defense counsel. Shi declined, but she did accept "Deng Xiaoping's personal request to review a draft of the Special Procuratorate's indictment in July 1980. She also continued to serve on the Standing Committee of the National People's Congress and as vice-chair of the multiparty Chinese People's Political Consultative Congress."[50]

One would think the Gang of Four trial would in no way be linked to the pursuit of justice against Japanese war criminals, but that was not the case. The global conversation about jurisprudence and the law had not been limited to the West.[51] But what had occurred in China meant that expertise in the law was in short supply. The nation would have to rely on the experiences of the small cadre of legal experts who had been politically quarantined since the days when war crimes were pursued against the Japanese. One example of these deeper and unexplored linkages can be seen in the career of Qiu Shaoheng (Henry Qiu), whom we already briefly encountered with the 1946 Shibuya Incident and subsequent trial of Taiwanese in occupied Japan. Qiu's professional advancement is a fascinating example of the importance of examining the "legal flows" of juridical ideas around Europe and East Asia.

Qiu had graduated from Soochow University, China's first university that taught Western law in English. In the immediate postwar period this rare set of skills, along with his proficiency in the English language, made Qiu valuable as an internationally trained lawyer in a country that suddenly required his unique talents so that it could join the international community and prosecute Japanese war crimes. Not only did Qiu serve at the Tokyo Trial, but he also took part as one of the few Chinese members of the Allied effort to deal with internal Japanese imperial hierarchies coming into conflict with the tragedy of postwar reality where former Japanese imperial subjects, the Koreans and Taiwanese, wallowed in legal purgatory. Finally, because of his participation in two Allied trials in the 1940s, Qiu was once again needed on the legal stage when China reinstated the rule of law after the disastrous decade of the Cultural Revolution.

In early 1980, Special Court Chief Justice Jiang Hua called on Qiu to be a key "consultant" to the Gang of Four trial. There were many judges on the case, but the sole consultant was Qiu. Until 1979, Qiu had been teaching English at the Shanghai Foreign Language Institute but then returned to Beijing.[52] He designed the Chinese courtroom for this momentous trial, which aimed to bring order back to the chaos as a "symbolic space for China's transition to legal modernity." Qiu based much of the setting, including curtains and color scheme, on his experience from the Tokyo Trial because he believed that this trial venue had created the definitive atmosphere of legality for the proper pursuit of justice.[53] This special tribunal in Beijing was not just for domestic consumption but served as a bid for China to represent its restored legal credentials to the international community. Nothing was left to chance, including figuring out how to deal with Jiang Qing's refusal to accept the court's jurisdiction and Zhang Chunqiao's refusal to speak in court. Qiu supposedly spent days scouring legal records for a precedent and succeeded in finding a 1977 case from Charlotte, North Carolina, where the defendant was so abusive of the court that it disturbed the trial proceedings. The court ordered the defendant out and proceeded with the prosecution. Qiu translated this US precedent, and even though it had no legal standing in a Chinese court, the authorities were happy to see that they had some legal footing if and when problems arose and defendants in the dock disrupted the court.[54] Equally important were Qiu's English-language skills, which were employed by the party to propagate a positive message of the trial proceedings to the world through the state's English-language press and other media.[55] Qiu gave an interview to the Xinhua News Agency on January 29, 1981, concerning the Gang of Four trial. He was very careful to state that the trial was fair. He added, "A defendant in a Chinese criminal court is presumed neither innocent nor guilty." The goal of China's criminal procedures, he remarked, was more to assess accurate findings about what happened and then apply the law.[56] So much for justice.

Years later, after serving as a consultant in the Gang of Four trial, Qiu was instrumental as a mainland lawyer in the drafting of the Basic Law of the Hong Kong Special Administrative Region.[57]

The CCP's Resolution on Mao and History

The Gang of Four trial attempted to bring some measure of closure to a chaotic era, but it also uprooted confusion about responsibility. The way forward appeared to be the creation of a second historical declaration. This pronouncement was designed as the means to redirect Chinese society—to urge it back on the track of a productive form of state socialism and to rectify the wrongs suffered by many. PRC leaders build consensus and thus ideological legitimacy of their rule. Because there are no firm guidelines for the handover of power from one leader to the next, formulating a document that is then issued as a directive serves as a mandate for the continuation of authority. "The only way leaders have to establish legitimacy, even such hegemonic leaders as Deng and Mao, remains the transfer of their own personal preferences into collective decisions, regardless of the methods they may use." In this way, "the process of formulating a document becomes a process of politically legitimizing personal preferences of leaders."[58] Since the information system is closed, and the mass media can sometimes but not always gain access to these documents, "obtaining documents thus helps officials to control the masses."[59]

Once again Deng Xiaoping was at the forefront, thinking about how to salvage a ruling party that had clearly demonstrated its inability to properly govern over the previous several decades. Deng copied what the communists had done in 1945—create a commission that would deliver a historical verdict to the people concerning what had happened. From 1980 to 1981, Deng and his team worked on their draft statement. Deng Liqun was instrumental, but it appears that even though he was leader on paper, Deng Xiaoping maintained the final gavel strike on what was written. The always-present Hu Qiaomu, longtime Mao theoretician and confidante, played a grand role as well. Political theorist Hu was a magician of party word craft and had formed part of the committee that put forward the first resolution on historical questions back in 1945. Thirty-five years later, the main sticking point was how to fly the banner of Maoist thought while at the same time criticize Mao. Moreover, how to avoid creating mistrust toward the party? The proclamation contained parts that reaffirmed the correctness of Mao's historical position and thought but also allowed the country to bypass political upheaval by noting that this ideology also had failures. During the Cultural Revolution, Mao made mistakes, they admitted. But when "looking at Mao and this era we need to seek out the truth from facts and analyze it. When looking at the last thirty years of our nation's history since the new China, we must do the same and assess what was successful and what was a mistake. The aim of all of this is to realign our unity and to come together."[60] But, as Deng also said, China should not conduct all this analysis in too much detail, which essentially meant that citizens should grin and bear it.

This Chinese historical resolution document parallels the war responsibility (*sensō sekinin*) investigations the Japanese completed. Certainly, the two commissions were different in that the Chinese murdered their own and Japan was imperialist in its aggression. Japanese also murdered their own if one thinks of forced group suicides in Okinawa toward the end of the war or the idea of a "dog's death" that Fujiwara Akira enunciated. But Sino-Japanese efforts are similar in the nature of trying to come to terms with governments that were fundamentally flawed and led their respective countries in disastrous directions. But Deng was clever and said that Chinese could not just criticize Mao and be done with it. China needed, in Deng's assessment, a systematic framework that could assist society to change and advance.

The *Resolution on certain questions in the history of our party since the founding of the People's Republic of China* passed at the sixth plenary session of the 11th Central Committee of the Communist Party of China, in June 1981. Serving as the new way forward, this historical declaration affirmed over numerous pages that the party was responsible for creating new China and its achievements were great. But somehow or other the party and the country had gotten derailed from the true policy of following Marxism-Leninism-Maoism. At one point the team that drafted the paper wrote, "History proves the line the party has put forward in this era of transition is completely correct." Such emphasis would make it hard to criticize the party or its decisions because it had now attached itself to national success and salvation. Additionally, Mao had erred, but the conclusion was that his success was greater than his errors in leading China on the new path. Additional articles in the lengthy document declared that "only socialism can save China," and "without the Chinese Communist Party there is no new China." Toward the end the resolution stated that the party "dares to squarely face and correct its mistakes and is resolved to and has the power to prevent a repeat of these sorts of grievous errors that were committed in the past. After all, our party's mistakes and frustrations were only transitory phenomenon." An important emphasis was that "the party will also proceed with righting the injustices suffered by the population."[61]

The goal was not to find truth or develop a new direction for the country. The aim was to save the system from itself. The motivation for a second historical declaration hinged on how to realign a political system that had gone badly wrong and save it from another revolution that would surely have upended things and pushed the country toward further friction. Everyone involved was essentially willing to avoid admitting that the emperor (Mao) had no clothes. How could one dispute the revolution as having been incorrect after already investing about a half century in its evolution? As a way around these conundrums, and in a move that helped deify Mao away from the man himself, the committee decided to divvy up the Maoist era. The first seven years after establishment of the new country were now seen as "good." That was an easy decision. The ten years of the Cultural Revolution were "bad" and should be negated. That left two other eras that were tough to delineate. The problem was that there was some sort of cataclysm almost every year: the anti-Rightist movement of 1957, the Great Leap Forward in 1958–62, and the famine of 1959–62, to name just a few. Many had lived through at least some of these transitory phases, had seen people become sick and die from famine, or knew others who had been unjustly accused and/or punished. But when leaders met and discussed this era, they all fell silent.[62]

There Can Be Only One History!

Mainland Chinese ideas about a unified interpretation of history continue to ossify and corral Chinese society. Starting in the 1980s, and then with renewed vigor in the 1990s, the CCP has upgraded patriotic education as a cornerstone of teaching Chinese youths to love their country in a certain way with a specific view of the past. This is undergirded by a litany of newer dictates to further solidify national opinion. An official CCP history website has a collection of President Xi's declarations on history and the party's anxiety concerning what it deems "historical nihilism" (*lishi xuwuzhuyi*).[63] Historical nihilism is a loaded term that means not only that the PRC and Chinese history in general are now clarified by the government but also that only legalized versions are permitted in public discourse owing to party decisions that improper history would harm the state. This is partly what is believed to have happened in the former USSR, which eventually denied the legacies of Lenin and Stalin leading to its downfall.[64] This conviction that negative historical opinions brought down the USSR pervades the higher circles of the PRC leadership. To investigate the issues, the party, in coordination with the Chinese Academy of Social Sciences, produced an eight-episode special television documentary, *Preparing for Danger in Times of Safety: The Historical Lesson of the Perishing Soviet Communist Party*, in 2006.[65] In July 2013, the Xinhua News Agency reported that three agencies of the PRC government—the General Office of the Communist Party of China, the General Office of the State Council, and the General Office of the Central Military Commission—had collectively produced a document: "Ideas on work to further strengthen martyrs' memorials." A move was afoot for the nation to entwine in solidarity concerning the historical sanctity of those who sacrificed themselves. The goal was that "their spirit would become the source of energy to galvanize all the peoples of the country to implement the People's Republic great flourishing and unremitting struggle."[66]

The PRC has enacted several new laws over the past few years under President Xi Jinping that further aim to congeal a unified public opinion toward not only generic history but specific historical examples as well. A special website devoted to coverage of China's seventieth anniversary of its founding posted an explanatory article: "Why does China need to establish a law to protect its heroes?" Chinese president Xi frequently quotes a famous aphorism in response: "To get rid of a people's country you first need to eradicate their history." Through history the CCP seeks to affirm that its rule and political choices are the sole future path for the nation's well-being. This idea then gets tied up with hero worship. Consequently, because Japan played a significant role in harming China during World War II, when many of these heroes emerged, a tenuous link between modern history and anti-Japanese emotion has been formed.

This public and official sentiment about "proper history" further escalated in a law adopted at the 2nd Session of the Standing Committee of the Thirteenth National People's Congress of the People's Republic of China, which came into force on May 1, 2018. Officially known as the "Law of the People's Republic of China on the Protection of Heroes and Martyrs," it is comprehensive at thirty articles long. In the law, citizens' historical views are now intimately linked with the promotion of state socialism, the power of the state, patriotism, and "strengthening the spirit of the flourishing China Dream." Article 3 is indicative of this feature: "The achievements and spirit of heroes and martyrs are the central embodiment of the Chinese People's collective historical memory and core values of socialism."[67] Article 5 created a new public holiday on September 30 to mark Martyrs' Day, where a commemorative ceremony was designated to be held at the Monument to the People's Heroes, a tower in the center of Tiananmen Square in Beijing.[68]

Xi Jinping has led the CCP to set down a legal opinion that China controls law outside of its borders as well.[69] These new ideas concerning how law should be used as a tool of the state for control of historical opinions, as opposed to serving as a lever to bolster the rights of citizens, emerged in part from the introduction of Nazi legal thinker Carl Schmitt's writings into China in the late 1990s.[70] Mainly pushed by legal scholars at the prestigious Peking University, adherents of this path believed that law needs to protect the state from outside enemies, which would of course put it into conflict with international norms. The evolution of this thought process suggests the growth of a belief that the introduction of new legal norms destabilizes Chinese society. Consequently, "China needs to free itself from Western legalism and promote the creation of a new model of governance."[71]

Japan's Ideas of Justice Are Still Enrobed in Discussions of the Tokyo Trial

The Japanese state does not dictate in the same way as the PRC how history should be viewed, but it has demonstrated similar tendencies toward official conservatism since the late 1980s. However, this was not always the case, and at one point change seemed imminent. For example, on June 20, 1984, in a lower house foreign affairs committee meeting, Takazawa Torao, a Socialist Party politician, asked if the foreign minister had seen recent Japanese news reports about the imperial army's use of poison gas on the Chinese mainland during World War II. A Japanese researcher had uncovered incontrovertible proof on a secret Japanese military map that detailed the numerous locations where the Japanese imperial army had used mustard gas and other poison gases in China.[72] Takazawa wanted the foreign minister's reaction. Minister of Foreign Affairs Abe Shintarō affirmed the government's supportive position and was adamant that the situation required further investigation.[73]

Within almost a decade, the tone of the domestic discussions changed. In an upper house Diet debate on November 30, 1995, delegate Tachiki Hiroshi, a member of the JCP, asked about the Japanese imperial military's use of poison gas during the war. In response, Director General of the Defense Agency Akiyama Masahiro said the imperial military had used nonlethal weapons like "sneezing gas" and such, but if they used munitions like "mustard gas" or fatality-inducing agents, the record was not clear enough with archival evidence to declare with certainty.[74] Even though personal military records, like Ōe Yoshiwaka's, and news reports about other archival evidence were known, to say nothing of the evidence and the testimony of the Chinese peasants from the 1956 trials in communist China, some quarters of Japanese officialdom had grown more skeptical because that information was supposedly not contained in their own repositories.

From the mid-1990s onward, Japan's discussions about the US-imposed postwar constitution centered on a set of questions pertaining to history. In 1997, former prime ministers Nakasone Yasuhiro and Miyazawa Kiichi, both elder statesmen by this point, held a series of debates in the *Asahi Newspaper*. The exchange was revealing in that it showed how the conversation had evolved in Japan concerning justice. In their first installment, the two started off with Nakasone saying that the postwar constitution was fifty years old and the Meiji era had lasted sixty years. The time was ripe to have an inspection and check the status of Japan's current constitution in ten years to see if it fit historical developments. (Why constitutions were so frail they need to be "oil checked" every six decades Nakasone did not elaborate on.) The less hawkish Miyazawa responded that the postwar constitution was something that, while good, came from the United States, and this meant that it did not really emerge from the will of the Japanese people. Miyazawa opined that the peace constitution was a good document, and the cost of energy and time to the people would not be worth the effort to redraft. He added that Japan should not wish to alienate its neighboring countries and invite misunderstandings. But the central point for Nakasone in the discussion was that Japan's peace constitution had fundamentally cost Japan its autonomy. Nakasone freely admitted that the constitution had brought peace and prosperity to Japan, but that it was the outcome of the alliance with the United States, among other contexts. Nakasone told the newspaper that surely Japan had grown rich and that high-level growth was nonmilitary, which was admirable. But, he added, "our country has an empty soul."[75] Nakasone was, of course, harking back to the idea that the Tokyo Trial and other war crimes trials left a national stain on Japanese history, which was hard to expunge. Nakasone assessed that Japan's war against the West should be differentiated from its war in Asia. The former was a war of self-defense, the latter a war of aggression. This, in turn, also colored his perception of the Tokyo Trial as improper because it did not distinguish between these events.[76] After the war, this mind-set created a masochistic sense of self in Japan on which the conservative wing wanted to locate the origin of contemporary Japanese malaise. This Tokyo Trial–centered view of history does not permit Japanese to maintain a sense of pride, goes the reasoning.

Miyazawa disagreed and retorted that after fifty years Japan had turned into a good country, so the result was something to evaluate highly. Japan had advanced to this age, Miyazawa noted, precisely without using military force. The country must strongly guard against the use of force to avoid making the same mistakes of the past. Nakasone did not dismiss this opinion, but he parried that Japanese needed to talk more about the nation and not make those discussions a taboo.[77]

Over the next several installments the two continued to chat about the nature of the constitution and efforts to alter it throughout the 1960s, which never resulted in any successful change. In their fifth round of conversation, published on April 26, 1997, Nakasone brought up his decision to be the first prime minister to publicly visit the Yasukuni Shrine in 1985. He made the visit because the war dead were there, he said, and to not go in an official capacity would deny their memory, which the country had pledged to uphold. But, Nakasone rejoined, he did not know that war criminals were enshrined there. He was also surprised that his visit was used in political squabbles in China, which probably in part forced out Chinese president Hu Yaobang. Miyazawa concurred and said that he saw Yasukuni as a place for symbolizing the spirits of those who gave their life for the nation. Neighboring countries can say what they like, but we are not bound by their comments, he expressed.

The *Asahi Newspaper* then posed a vexing question to both statesmen, asking why it was the case that many who wanted to change the constitution were also supporters of the view of history that labeled the war as one of "liberation," as the Greater East Asian War. Nakasone ventured first and said clearly that he was against those who pushed a positive interpretation of Japan's imperial history. But he also denounced General MacArthur's Tokyo Trial view of history, where Japan was guilty of a conspiracy to dominate East Asia. The war with the West was a regular war, Nakasone intoned, while war in China and Southeast Asia was an "aggressive war," and the two needed to be considered separately. Japan had apologized, but passing a resolution of apology through the parliament would be rash, Nakasone believed. Nakasone assessed that Japan's current constitutional provisions for peace and the respect of human rights were strong, but "the concept of justice has grown very weak."

Miyazawa offered that such arguments about the war always seem to lead to this point. He, too, believed that at times blood had to be shed for justice and freedom. And that idea resonated with him. However, Japanese must talk about this very prudently as a topic of political discourse. When a Japanese police officer was killed in Cambodia during a 1993 UN peacekeeping mission, the whole country quickly responded that all Japanese participants should immediately be pulled out. Miyazawa was in charge of UN work then and criticized this as a weak social response. Nakasone complimented Miyazawa for his efforts but added that if Japan tried to solve the problem of terrorism with money, this demonstrated that the country harbored no actual concept of justice.[78]

The debate might not have arrived at any conclusion, but the discussion revealed that even well into the 1990s, the issue of the Tokyo Trial and the form of justice it delivered still deeply shaped the Japanese political landscape.

Chapter 13

Afterlives of the Damned

The Commemoration of Justice and Injustice, 1990s to the Present

To get to Li Qingxiang's village of Beituan, the one I wrote about in the introduction, required several forms of transportation. High-speed rail, which the Chinese have been laying down at an unprecedented pace all around the country, gets you fairly close. This meant that the last leg of the journey was still two hours by car, or in our case, by a rented small bus—a Toyota. The Japanese brands are very reliable, I was told by the driver. Beituan Village presents a crucial locus of interest in determining, perhaps finding justice for, Japan's wartime actions and what people wish to remember about the war.

In addition to trying to ascertain the lived experience of those who had seemingly found some justice through the CCP courts, such as at least one of the residents from Beituan Village who had testified at the 1956 Shenyang Trial, it was important to talk with others who had direct experience. In the city of Fushun, the actual location of the Japanese War Criminals Management Center, I interviewed a former nurse, Zhao Yuying. Sporting an ingratiating smile, the elderly Zhao lived in a two-room apartment with a large kitchen and comfortable furniture. According to her published oral history, on July 16, 1950, she arrived at the city of Suifenhe to wait for the Japanese prisoners in the small town. The train arrived on July 18, she remembered.[1] Later, after ushering the Japanese war criminals back to Fushun, Zhao and a small group of doctors returned to Suifenhe to receive a second trainload of the Manchu war criminals from the USSR. On August 1, these men finally arrived by train, and the young Zhao saw the last Manchu emperor, Pu Yi, for the first time. He sported dark glasses and wore a Western suit, standing about 170 centimeters tall. He appeared to be in his forties, she recalled. Former Manchukuo prime minister Zhang Jinghui, who was in his seventies, was also present. He was short and looked "old and decrepit," Zhao said.[2]

In our interview Zhao did not offer much more than what she had already expressed two decades prior in her oral history.[3] She did talk about all the diseases that the Japanese prisoners had when they arrived and the fact that, like Wang Shilin, she was not informed of the nature of her work before it started. She met the POWs at the rail station and then realized what her job was going to entail. Much of our interview repeated what Zhao had said elsewhere, but I seemed to have been the first person to ask her about the KMT war criminals at the same prison where she worked. She responded that she never saw them and that they only came in later. This latter part was, of course, not true since we know the KMT prisoners trickled in by 1955, but it is possible the staff were separated. However, Zhao's reply implied that the various groups of prisoners were kept apart—"puppet" Manchukuo officials were separated on one wing, and Japanese war criminals were kept in a different area. KMT officers were impounded elsewhere. Interestingly, the museum (which was formerly the prison) does not detail these aspects of the history and mainly focuses on the Japanese war criminals along with detailing the life of the last emperor, Pu Yi.

In Zhang's apartment I continued with the next interview of former director of the Fushun War Criminals Management Center Hou Jiahua. Hou had worked at the prison since 1986, when it was turned into a museum, and she was instrumental in the establishment of the first exhibit and reconstruction. This would have been around the same time that the Unit 731 museum just outside of Harbin was built, along with the Nanjing Massacre Memorial Museum and similar memorial sites throughout China, signaling a national return to remembering World War II history. But, as happened in Beituan Village and with the Taiyuan POW site as Liu Linsheng told me, part of the impetus to build these memorials was spurred by former Japanese war criminals and others coming back to China, giving money, donating items, and pushing for such commemoration of both the war and China's postwar magnanimity. As I previously detailed, this wartime history was buried from just after the conclusion of the trials in 1956 until the 1980s. Importantly, in the interviews I conducted, everyone clammed up when I asked them about their lives after 1956, as if their lives never altered course and everything had stopped. I questioned Zhao what she did after Fushun, but she responded she had worked there for nine years, which would have taken her up to 1959, when KMT prisoners were there and many of the Japanese had already been released. She deferred from going into detail concerning how life changed after most of the Japanese POWs had departed. It was as if there was only one tale to tell, and that was the story of the Chinese benevolence toward the Japanese. That narrative was decoupled from any other elements of domestic or international history. It was unlinked to anything else, floating out there in an endless cycle in which a single story repeats its own greatness.

Former director Hou was an interesting interview and not reticent to offer her sharp opinions. She told me that she hated the Japanese, but it was not from personal experience or really any conviction. She explained that partly this was perhaps the result of having grown up watching so many anti-Japanese movies, including *Tunnel Warfare* and others.[4] She despised the Japanese but also realized she had to do her job. She did not appreciate my question whether the Japanese prisoners had been brainwashed in their reformation, she intimated. If they had been forced, she bristled, why would these men come back year after year to Fushun to thank their former jailers? Hou Jiahua was the person who received these visiting teams from Japan and then worked with the Liaison Group. These men were able to showcase their personal journeys of psychological transformation when they brought their families with them, or returned to China as old men to say thank you and to remark that the prison was their "place of rebirth."[5]

But what about the deeper legal issue of the eleven years these men had spent in incarceration before they were put on trial? Was that not a form of extended pressure—you cannot go home until you change, if ever? Was there not severe, and thus extralegal, inducement to change? Sadly, this conversation was a nonstarter and connected back to the impossibility of digging in further concerning the question of justice that lurks under the surface of Chinese trials of Japanese war criminals. Questioning even a fraction of the process gets mistaken for historical revisionism or denial of the truth—now punishable by law.

Another aspect I grew to understand from talking to former guards and legal staff involved with the extensive CCP trials, like Wang and Zhao, was the idealism of youth of those who were involved. Many were in their twenties or early thirties, idealist communists or at least prepped for a national shift from what they believed was a corrupt former KMT administration. They saw an avenue for change and talked about that era with smiles and in fond terms with me. The fact that most of them never discussed it in any interviews or wrote much about it until the 1990s also tells us volumes about the meaning of those trials, for so long kept silenced while waves of political violence internal to China continued to rumble.

FIGURE 13.1. Japanese former war criminals' apology stele at Fushun War Criminals Management Center ("To the anti-Japan martyred heroes, we apologize for our crimes")

Taiwan (The Republic of China)

At the outset of its rule in 1949, the KMT government was practical about how to gain legitimacy for its cause. And on the island of Taiwan, where in the immediate aftermath of Japan's surrender pro-KMT memorials were in short supply, Chinese Nationalist leaders did what many authorities have done in the past. They remade the former enemy's commemorative sites into their own. Several of the major Japanese Shinto shrines on Taiwan were quickly repurposed as Chinese Nationalist "martyr's shrines" to economize.[6] This happened at approximately fifteen sites around Taiwan and not just at the periphery.

The main Japanese imperial Protect the Nation Shrine (*Gokoku jinja*) in the center of Taipei in the immediate postwar period was transformed into the Taiwan provincial martyr's shrine. Later, when Taiwan became its own country, this shrine was nationalized and served as the one at which foreign guests would pay their formal respects on official visits to the Republic of China. Afterward, it was renamed the People's Revolutionary Martyrs' Shrine.[7] Such memorials helped "to engender and consolidate social *practices* of visitation."[8] Political change began to slowly percolate in Taiwan beginning in the 1990s. Elections of the permanent government representatives did not actually happen until the early 1990s, with full elections in 1996, when Lee Teng-hui became Taiwan's first democratically chosen president.

This fascinating evolution should cause us to reflect on the same "anchors of history" that we dealt with toward the beginning of the book. While noting that "heritage is not history," we can still understand how the two categories are deeply intertwined, particularly during periods of political handover. "While history is the study of the past, the use of the past in heritage-making is dictated by present-day concerns."[9] Memorials to fallen soldiers or national sacrifice communicate "intangible values like honor, sacrifice, and spirit" to the population.[10] Did the Taiwanese find it ironic that locales that had only months prior touted alignment with the Japanese emperor were suddenly switched over to fealty to Chiang Kai-shek? It is hard to tell. But at the edge of Japan's former empire, that was precisely the problem with defeat. How militaries memorialize defeat while not being defeatist partly emerged in the Tokyo Trial. The Allies crafted a story of the war and this "masochistic" view of history pushed Japan's conservative side to oppose this attitude and to prop up alternative meanings of the war in response.

The connective tissue of this narrative between war and postwar, or war and political legitimacy at the far fringes of Japan's former empire, did not end with defeat or the refashioning of Japanese imperial shrines into Chinese Nationalist military commemorative sites. In March 2009, a brand new repatriation ceremony was designed to celebrate the repatriation of bones of former KMT soldiers who had died in Papua New Guinea as POWs. Many of these men were the Chinese POWs detailed in earlier chapters. Here was an interesting moment of historical significance. These men had been soldiers for the ROC, and thus represented China. But that government was no longer in control of mainland China and had shifted to Taiwan. It is not clear whether the PRC launched a formal protest, but eventually the former KMT soldiers were repatriated to Taiwan in a grand ceremony.[11] Taiwan was now incorporating a new history for itself in some measure. These spirits/bones were placed into Taiwan's National Revolutionary Martyrs' Shrine even though by the standards set by the United Nations Taiwan was no longer an internationally recognized state.[12] This event was not without impact, because memorials shape the "contours of a historical event. They affirm what should be regarded as crucial to it, and what is understood as extraneous or 'outside.'"[13] It is possible this was all just part of Taiwan's push to regain diplomatic relations with Papua New Guinea, having lost and retrieved it several times since that country's independence from Australia in 1975. But the ceremony and money spent demonstrate something deeper, an attempt to ensure that Taiwan's new history remains linked to the ROC's longer story of postwar legitimacy as well.

The PRC also wedged in on the proceedings, claiming that several Chinese communist soldiers had given their lives in Rabaul. Competition between the mainland and Taiwan to maintain grave sites abroad and memorialize those fallen in the name of China remains a potent symbol even in the twenty-first century. In fact, in the words of one historian, these graves of "past wars have become bones of contention. The forgotten war graves have become the sites of contestation. The spirits of these soldiers and civilians have become sources of sovereign power, allowing both the PRC and the ROC to re-envision their common history prior to their Civil War."[14]

But history is not just about remembering; it is also about forgetting or excising. Nowhere is this more physically felt than in a park a short drive from Taiwan's international Taoyuan Airport. Almost forty-five minutes from central Taipei, many of the old or no longer necessary statues of Chiang Kai-shek are stored in an open field. The park was created by the mayor of Daxi and is called the Cihu Memorial Sculpture Park. The intent was to maintain the Chiang legacy but deal with a surfeit of statues that were no longer required to embellish the front of every school and public building.[15] However, the actual impact, according to some foreign assessments, is more like a "memorial dump."[16]

At the same time, over the past several decades since the birth of democracy in Taiwan, an assessment of the past still lags and people continue to press for justice. In Taiwan's case, while pressure on Japan is low but persistent, it remains in sharper relief concerning domestic issues. Taiwan president Tsai Ing-wen created the Truth and Reconciliation Committee, which promised a report on an investigation into transitional justice concerning the February 28 Incident. This is indeed a laudable goal. For her government, greater focus is not on the era of Japanese colonialism but the much more recent KMT egregious actions of the February 28 Incident and the era of "white terror."[17] The Memorial Foundation of 2.28, headed by Professor Hsueh Hua-yuan, now hosts a new museum dedicated to the February 28 Incident and a foundation.

FIGURE 13.2. "Lost Chiangs" Cihu Memorial Sculpture Park in Taiwan.

Repurposing Victory

The CCP copied on mainland China what the KMT did in Taiwan, repurposing a former enemy's monuments. In the PRC's case, the CCP took the KMT World War II victory monument in the center of Chongqing, the wartime Chinese capital, and remade it into a monument commemorating the 1949 communist victory. There is a large public square in the center of the downtown, now known as Liberation Monument Square. Originally, the Chinese Nationalists celebrated the defeat of Japan and their role with the erection of a seven-story octagonal tower with a slogan running down the side of it, reading "Anti-Japan War Victory Monument." On October 1, 1950 (as China perched on the precipice of joining the Korean War), the CCP refaced the tower and changed the commemorative appellation from a "victory monument" to a "Liberation Monument."[18] The Chinese central government, however, did not always share the provincial city governments' opinions about the protection of national heritage. For the village of Pingfang and the city of Harbin nearby, pushing for a war crimes museum concerning Japanese Imperial Army Unit 731 was not necessarily in their interest. In fact, "during the 1950s and 1960s the provincial authorities in Harbin endeavoured to demolish the entire Pingfang

FIGURE 13.3. New Unit 731 Museum on outskirts of Harbin.

site, in order to erase memory of the war there."[19] A confidential US embassy report from Harbin corroborates this view. The report details information about Chinese attitudes toward war crimes memorials during Senator Henry Jackson's August 20–26, 1983, visit to northeast China. At that time, the ruined factory, as it was termed, was "not prominently identified from the road and the visit was only arranged at Senator Jackson's specific request." The report notes that "the ruined main building" was "unmarked except for a small sign in Chinese."[20] When I first visited in 1996, the site was still fairly unremarkable and scant educative facilities existed. Twenty years later, this location now pulsates with historical meaning in the new architectural monument of an expanded museum and its very archivally detailed exhibits. This pales in comparison with what the building and museum have become today. China is pouring money into museums and cultural sites of memory, paradoxically more numerous the further the history recedes into the past.

This reformatting of monuments and heroes can also be seen in popular culture expressions of history. The valiant KMT soldiers who tried to fight off the Japanese at the 1937 Sihang Warehouse Battle in Shanghai were celebrated by Chinese media as "the eight hundred heroes," even though they numbered only 423.[21] In 1975, a Taiwanese film championed this history. In 2005, mainland Chinese news grew excited over a rekindled interest in the Sihang Battle and the KMT's role in attempting to push back the Japanese, even though it signaled the ultimate demise of KMT power in Shanghai. In 2014, President Xi Jinping publicly praised the eight hundred heroes.[22] In 2018, mainland Chinese movie producers wrapped up a new film about the famous warehouse battle with epic special effects and backed by a colossal budget. But for reasons that were never clear, the release was suddenly canceled, days after it was pulled from a Shanghai film festival.[23] However, a year later, the movie was released with international fanfare and very briefly shown in IMAX theaters in London as well.[24]

Japanese Commemorations of the "Damned"

The shift from victim to hero demonstrates the shifting landscape of the cultural heritage bolstering the varied historical interpretations of Japan's war crimes trials, particularly the Tokyo Trial. The "Martyr's Graves of the Seven Great Men" is a commemorative stone outdoor mausoleum in Aichi Prefecture dedicated to the seven Class A war criminals executed on the final judgment of the Tokyo Tribunal.[25] But the seven war crimes "martyrs" did not just find themselves in Buddhist commemorative site by accident. These executed Japanese war criminals ended up in three sites in Japan.

After these seven war criminals were hanged by American executioners in December 1948, their bodies were driven to the Kuboyama Crematorium in Yokohoma. Two Japanese lawyers, Sanmonji Shōhei, who had worked on Koiso Kuniaki's case at the Tokyo Trial, and Hayashi Itsurō supposedly conspired to steal some of their ashes. The two lawyers did not want to allow Japanese leaders to be anonymously disposed of by the Allies. They did not manage to get the bulk of the bones after incineration, but some of the leftover ashes were apparently swept up and preserved.[26] Exceedingly detailed US records point to the contrary, in that the occupation authorities went to extraordinary lengths to ensure that they could "refute any possible claim that one or more of these war criminals are still alive or that anyone has all or any part of their ashes."[27] Regardless, a group of Japanese bent on what they believed would maintain the dignity of the accused formed, and head temple priest Ichikawa Iyū etched that story in stone. It can be found on a stele located to the side of the Kōzen Temple near the Yokohama funeral home.[28] Some Chinese writers have painted the incident in a more devious and conspiratorial tone.[29]

A decision was then made to move the remains, dust essentially if it ever existed, to the Rising Asia Kannon Temple in Atami, Shizuoka Prefecture. This temple had an important backstory, having been created at the behest of Japanese general Matsui Iwane as a way to commemorate imperial soldiers who died in the war for China. Matsui requested that a shrine to the China Incident be erected in 1940. It became, ironically, the same site at which he would be memorialized years later. The temple grounds are a location that promote the idea that Japan's war in China was righteous and sought to liberate Asia. Tanaka Masaaki wrote that Matsui "loved China more than anyone," although one would have to admit Matsui had a funny way of showing it.[30] On the sixtieth anniversary of the establishment of the Rising Asia Temple, Tanaka Masaaki was by this point the head of the Association to Protect the Rising Asia Temple.[31]

In the inaugural temple newsletter, Tokutomi Tasaburō, son of liberal Meiji turned wartime strident nationalist journalist Tokutomi Sohō, instructively wrote what the temple stood for. Tokutomi was a classmate of Tanaka Masaaki's from the army's 58th class. This was the officer class of slightly more than one thousand second lieutenants who had graduated from the Imperial Japanese Army Academy just before the war finished, in June, and most were purged during the occupation. Tokutomi laid out the three main canonical elements of the temple:

> First: To offer solace to the spirits of the war dead (including those executed)
> Second: To exonerate those for the so-called Nanjing Massacre
> Third: To correct the Tokyo Trial historical view[32]

Several years later, Sejima Ryūzō made some favorable comments about the Rising Asia Kannon Temple in the newsletter. For Sejima the temple embodied the Japanese spirit because it allowed for the celebration of the fallen spirits of both Japan and its previous enemies.[33] Sejima was a high-ranking imperial military officer who was caught by the Soviets at the end of the war, brought forward to testify at the Tokyo Trial, and then detained for more than a decade in the USSR. He managed to have a second life after release and became head of a large and financially successful Japanese conglomerate. In 1959, with calligraphy from a former prime minister, a memorial stone with the words "7 Martyrs Memorial" was erected.[34] Finally, in 1978, a portion of the remains were removed from the Rising Asia Kannon Temple to Mount Sangane in Aichi Prefecture.[35]

The 1970s saw a resurgence of interest in the Tokyo Trial and the BC class war crimes trials within Japan because some intellectuals felt it was precisely this era of war crimes tribunals where postwar Japan had rebooted. At the same time, this was the moment that generated numerous problems for postwar Japanese society because the people never came to terms with their colonial and imperial military responsibility. The Japanese "miracle" of economic rebirth by the 1970s had undercut its successes. As the famous Japanese playwright Kinoshita Junji wrote, "The war and defeat had bequeathed to Japanese society historical 'caverns' and 'distortions,' in other words unresolved issues, or a 'syndrome.'" Kinoshita was alluding to the problem of how to match Japan's postwar economic success with how it conceived of the justice and injustice found within the trials. To be sure, Japanese committed war crimes, but many of the trials, particularly at the BC class level, were of a variety where the verdict almost seemed random and justice was not always served.[36] Kinoshita had penned the drama *Between God and Man* as a stage play in the early 1970s. His message in the play was not to generate a discussion about the guilt of the twenty-eight defendants at the Tokyo Trial, but rather to push the idea that responsibility lay within the audience. "The guilty are among us; the guilty are none other than us; we have no place to take this burden, and lay it bare except within ourselves."[37]

As Japan moved through the 1970s, commemoration of the war developed into a larger international issue concerning what to do with the former historical sites such as the Sugamo Prison site, where Japanese war criminals had long been held. The complaints of JCP representative Ueda Kōichirō in the upper house of the Japanese parliament in 1980 mirror the background I presented toward the beginning of this book. He was incensed that a former war criminal became minister of justice and that Kaya Okinori was able to gain cabinet approval to protect sites related to former war criminals' imprisonment. In parliament Ueda remarked that "the idea to protect these various sites is rather unthinkable isn't it?"[38]

An example of how public monuments can impact their surroundings and private understanding of the past can be observed in the monument to the seven Class A war criminals. From 1965 onward, the site subsequently developed into a commemoration compound, housing 128 graves of other war criminals. There is also the "Memorial Tower to Sixty Patriots," erected in 1968, which memorializes sixty war criminals (of all classes) who were executed at Sugamo Prison. This is located on the grounds of the Kōmyō Temple in Yokohama, just down the road from the Kōzen Temple. This site emphasizes the Tokyo Trial as a form of "victors' justice." The back of the stone lists the names of those convicted and an epitaph: "The recorded names are those who unselfishly offered their service to the nation in the Greater East Asia War. Regardless, they suffered extreme sentences at Sugamo in trials unilaterally imposed by former enemies. We mourn them and enshrine their spirits here to offer solace, imploring future generations to ensure their legacy."[39] Not everyone agreed with the commemorative stele to war criminals, and there have been instances of vandalism against the sites.

In 1996, former Takushoku University president Odamura Shirō announced that "we should try to correct what we call the war." To reclaim the war and its meaning for the Japanese, he wrote, the people cannot let the war be called by other labels. It must be called "The Greater East Asian War," he publicly stated. Odamura heaped disdain on the Tokyo Trial for having distorted the meaning of the war. "This trial was full of prejudice and falsehoods, and the fact that it was nothing more than a tragedy of revenge borrowing the term of a trial is already something well established with proof among numerous intellectuals. Moreover, this scar still cuts deep in our national psyche."[40]

History Never Ends

In its bid to quickly discard the tools of empire, Japan's imperial forces in China buried, left behind, or abandoned chemical weapons at "more than 90 locations across 18 Chinese provinces or municipalities." The Chinese estimate this at approximately two million chemical weapons; the Japanese count puts that number at slightly half with seven hundred thousand. Either number means mountains of harmful weaponry leaking into the environment.[41] In late summer 2003, workers in Heilongjiang Province unearthed several drums of formerly buried Japanese chemical weapons at a construction site. Dozens of people suffered injuries and one man died.[42] Over the years such incidents have continued to surface all over China, but the Japanese government's responses have been slow. Even eight decades after Japan's aggression in China, the long arm of war crimes reaches into the current era and dampens international relations.[43]

As key Japanese intellectual pundits highlight, Japan has continually lacked strong political guidance concerning how to resolve crises in both the short and long term. The fact that the imperial Japanese military had to resort to barely trained pilots on kamikaze missions to try to eke out a victory in World War II has eerie echoes with what occurred during the March 2011 Fukushima nuclear accident when TEPCO management crafted the story of the "Fukushima fifty"—literally workers consigned to risk their lives to try to control the reactor meltdown. In both instances, the war and the nuclear disaster, the number of staff was fundamentally insufficient to complete the job; no one was prepared for a potential disaster, and there was no plan in place. According to Funabashi Yōichi, this idea continues to plague Japan in the conviction that the "people's spirit" can overcome material deficiencies and a lack of crisis management.[44] Unfortunately, the reality of both situations conclusively demonstrates this error in Japanese thinking.

In August 2014, Japan's *Asahi Newspaper* revealed letters of support Japanese prime minister Abe Shinzō had sent to the Okunoin Temple at Mount Kōya in Wakayama Prefecture that memorialized Class A and other war criminals. Abe hailed those executed by the Allied powers as "forming the foundation of this nation."[45] The wording of the commemoration made clear the tendentious Japanese reasoning: the Allied war crimes trials of the Japanese were based on hatred and revenge. Abe had been consistent in this message, arguing previously in the National Diet that on the level of domestic law, Japan has no war criminals. The owner of a popular hotel chain in Japan, APA, produced a revisionist book that denies the Nanjing Massacre and emphasizes the message that only Japan has been historically accused of wrongdoing.[46] The APA group donates generously to the main conservative lobbying arm of the LDP, the Japan Conference (Nippon Kaigi).

Nowhere, perhaps, are the ambiguous lines of law, war, and empire more blurred than with the historical issues concerning "comfort women." Over the past twenty years a range of endeavors by various pressure groups in East Asia and North America have pushed different political agendas in a bid to prove that the comfort women were only prostitutes, were all forced by the Japanese military into prostitution against their will, were a mix of both efforts, were all young girls violated by the state, and so forth. The truth of this tragic episode of history lies somewhere in between all these examples with no one single definition satisfying any one party. Historical inquiry posturing as political opinion has created a situation that has devolved to the point that questioning the prevailing politically correct wisdom in some settings has resulted in one scholar in South Korea being charged in criminal and civil court for her research. In the meantime, bilateral relations between Korea and Japan have come to a standstill.[47] In search of a way out of this deadlock that has already endured several years, Japanese leaders announced a sudden and decisive political decision in December 2015 with the agreement between Japanese prime minister Abe Shinzō and South Korean president Park Geun-hye concerning the issue of comfort women. This accord acknowledged "involvement of the Japanese military authorities at that time" and stated that the "Government of Japan is painfully aware of responsibilities from this perspective." Japan committed to contributing a large financial sum to be distributed to the victims by the South Korean government. But the agreement also included a fascinating clause that "the Government of Japan confirms that this issue is resolved finally and irreversibly with this announcement."[48]

However, history has no end and is always evolving, as are our interpretations of the past. To declare that history is finished, that a complete and total consensus had been reached, is destined to end in failure.[49] This is regrettably what occurred. Declaring that history had reached its final destination invited even more scrutiny of the ultimate historical interpretation that had supposedly been achieved. In true reconciliation, parties need to constantly engage; justice and reconciliation are two different processes. Justice is finite and has a declaration attached. Reconciliation is without end and is based on future behavior as well as the present. History never stops; we cannot put an end to discussions or debate. While we may applaud the Japanese and Korean governments for at least trying to depoliticize colonial and imperial history, this format could not attain its goals. Within moments of its announcement, loud complaints from both sides quickly emerged. A few outspoken South Korean educators have suggested that this form of "anti-Japan tribalism," where nothing is acceptable, is hurting South Korea internationally.[50]

One of the main functions behind war crimes tribunals is to manage society after a calamitous event. It is a venue where individuals present proof and make reasoned arguments to arrive at a judgment.[51] That verdict is then used as the basis for domestic legal order and employed in foreign relations with other countries. The battle in East Asia is now defined as a Sino-Japanese struggle but also, in part, one between Korea and Japan. And the battleground is the no-man's-land between memory and history. The fundamental problem centers on the issue that "to speak of a duty of memory is fine, but 'memory' may not be something that can be authoritatively fixed by a legal process."[52] Court testimony, archives, and records are evidence but not memory. And once the verdict is rendered, the legal aspects of justice are complete. Following the conclusion of a trial, the historians take over. They organize and interpret the materials bequeathed by a trial to put together a narrative for the people to digest for the future. This involves selection, deletion, and oftentimes trying to summarize a much more complex historical situation into simpler terms for the larger public to understand. The limitations of these processes and the gaps that arise within them confuse and irritate many.

Conclusion

The Poverty of Political Ambition in East Asia

Years ago, while sitting in the front row of a press conference concerning a Chinese lawsuit against the Japanese government for wartime compensation, I was spat on. It was not so much that the salivatory bomblet was directed at me but more that I was in its orbit of trajectory. The emitting Japanese lawyer was incensed that, yet again, his just cause of legal pursuit against Japan for a war crime of forced wartime labor had been tossed out of a higher court in Tokyo. He was, in fact, yelling in front of those of us assembled in a small side room where we gathered to hear about the continued legal frustration that his group consistently encountered. That moment stays with me because while much of this book has been about justice denied, or feelings of injustice created, there is still much to observe in the gap behind how mainstream Japanese society reacts and hopes to find reconciliation but is often stymied by its leaders and the conservative branch. Which brings me to a crucial point in this conflict between the memory of injustice and the search for justice: How much do we remember about other recent-history war crimes trials?

War crimes trials do not always work. In Serbia this pursuit of justice actually managed to assist the former pariah state in ignoring its past as a perpetrator.[1] This is not just the sense of "inverted justice" mentioned in the introduction. Rather, this is hijacked justice because domestic actors parrot the words of transitional justice but do not adhere to international norms. Many will recall accounts of what occurred in Rwanda: a slaughter of untold magnitude during only a few months between the Tutsis and Hutus.[2] War crimes trials continue to abound, but what do they achieve? In the early twenty-first century, perhaps even more confusing for many would be the Khmer Rouge trials. These trials gained more attention internationally than among the Cambodians, who arguably suffered the most. When placed in an international context, Japan's war crimes do not pale in comparison, nor are they more understandable. What does come into relief is the sense that such atrocities are not unique to Japan and that war crimes trials do not always seamlessly lead to postwar reconciliation.

At the same time, as much as I have argued in this book to not overextend the comparison between Germany and Japan, we can distinguish between the rhetorical aims of their politicians. The patriotic but sympathetic words of German federal president Frank-Walter Steinmeier are a case in point. In his moving May 8, 2020, speech from Berlin commemorating the end of World War II, Steinmeier called on his compatriots to bear in mind that Germany was responsible for the murder and suffering of millions. He also reminded his fellow citizens to not draw a line under their past, because that would lead to "denying the catastrophe that was the war and the Nazi dictatorship." Germany, he proclaimed, "can only be loved with a broken heart." Such a position is necessary so that no one devalues "all the good that has since been achieved."[3] Powerful words that sadly no Japanese politician seems capable of enunciating in public. Steinmeier's central point is that apology is a never-ending cycle of reflection. One can only be chagrined when comparing Steinmeier's elegant comments with those of Japan's longest-serving prime minister, Abe Shinzō. His tempered take on the situation in his August 2015 speech concerning the end of World War II marks a stark contrast: "In Japan, the postwar generations now exceed eighty per cent of its population. We must not let our children, grandchildren, and even further generations to come, who have nothing to do with that war, be predestined to apologize."[4] Here was a missed opportunity to move beyond putting Japan's own suffering front and center and press the government to consider how its past affected others. Abe's focus on apology fatigue instead of reconciliation is telling. Japanese conservatives delude themselves into parallel thinking as well. They constantly enjoy testing the argument: the Americans had no right to judge Japan because the United States dropped atomic bombs on Japanese cities. However, to me what this really smacks of is what the young American poet laureate spoke of at President Joe Biden's inauguration on January 20, 2021. Amanda Gorman, the poet, was decrying the damage done to the United States by the megalomaniac Trump and how the nation needed a period of self-reflection to heal from its hypocrisy. How strikingly similar, I thought, to what happened in some ways to Japan in its soul-searching in the postwar era. In her longer poem, Gorman reflected:

> It's because being American is more than a pride we inherit,
> it's the past we step into
> and how we repair it[5]

The past is not merely something to laud. Oftentimes it is a burden, Gorman explained. A nation's past cannot simply be something to be extolled; it carries a responsibility and it is a legacy that needs to be "repaired" to move forward. How fitting an ideology for nations other than just the United States.

The Chinese want to treasure the Nuremberg Trial and retain that master narrative to fit the same parameters for the Tokyo Trial. However, mainland scholarship on the topic has not kept pace with the international turn from hagiography of the trials to a more critical stance. And this is the core issue—one cannot accept a golden rule about these war crimes trials and then ignore how international attitudes have changed toward that history since 1945.

Even though wartime Japanese history has often, and not exactly fruitfully, been compared with Nazi Germany because of their Axis Alliance, a more fitting analysis would place Japan alongside France.[6] For Japan, Korea was seen as a vital frontier for international security, as was Algeria for France. Both Japan and France felt their imperialism helped civilize their colonial holdings. More importantly, in terms of historical memory, both Japan and France experienced an imperial blackout in the decades after their losses concerning both Algeria and Korea. Unlike Germany, which in fits and starts was coming to terms with its legacy of barbarism, France, like Japan, ignored this past and focused merely on aspects of retaining and restoring postwar power. If we think about war crimes, then the two cases are even more alike. Japan's failure to domestically pursue its war criminals stands out as unique, but the massive French massacres in Algeria and elsewhere that were never pursued remain an open wound for French society as well.[7]

Chinese Ideas about History

About fifteen years ago, a popular weekly supplement to the *China Youth Daily*, "Freezing Point" (*Bingdian*), published an article by Yuan Weishi that gained the venom of CCP leaders. Yuan had dared to write that China needed to investigate its own history, and it had a duty to educate the younger generation about that truth. This opinion displeased Chinese officials, who quickly shut the supplement down. Yuan drew a line between Japanese and Chinese textbook treatments of modern history. He also revealed an open secret, that patriotic education on the mainland has created problems.[8] This nationalist ideology propels both countries into a state of conflict, but blame cannot fall only on Japanese shoulders, he recognized.[9] Liu Jie, an eminent Chinese historian who works in Japan, proposes that herein lies a deeper problem. In facing the decades of unequal treaties and imposition from the Great Powers during the prewar era, Chinese leaders placed faith in a system above and outside of the law, namely revolution. This idea established the notion of "justice" as a value that superseded law and exceeded treaties, since neither had been helpful to the Chinese in the early modern era. The result, by the middle of the twentieth century, was the development of a specific mind-set. The Chinese suffered from what others did to them. Consequently, whatever the Chinese did in response was correct and patriotic.[10] Liu asked: did China want to be the country that championed justice and emphasized the results of its revolution and the concordant historical views such a narrative brings with it? Or did the PRC wish to become a country founded on the rule of law, which therefore cannot hold up the ideals of the revolution as the sole foundation for authority? These two historical views work in opposition, and only one can be ascribed to at a time. The current Beijing government would like the international community to believe that China has always supported multilateralism and the rule of law. China's minister of foreign affairs Wang Yi said as much in February 2020: "As the first founding member of the UN to sign its Charter, China has stayed true to the UN's founding aspirations and firmly defended the purposes of the Charter and international law."[11] But this assertion dulls the edges of truth because in reality it was the Chinese Nationalist government that signed this charter in 1945, not the communists.[12]

Did the Trials Bring about Peace?

The paradox of war crimes trials based on international law is that even with more than seven decades of accumulative experience, few would disagree with the idea that international law—as the UN Charter states, to "be centre for harmonizing the actions of nations in the attainment of . . . common ends"—has not fulfilled all the goals originally attached to its birth. The goals of peace, security, and justice are admirable, but they mean different things for different parties and vary widely in relation to those common ends.[13] Everyone calls for peace, but what it means for each party is so unique that discussions are not actually about international law but rather the meaning of the ideas of peace or justice. To say that international law is for peace and justice is only significant within a system where the meanings are "agreed and understood between the members of the system."[14] By contrast, even recent books, including the prolific output of the Center for the Tokyo Trial Studies of Shanghai Jiaotong University, frequently mention peace and the fact that the trials aimed at establishing it. But such books in mainland China do not detail how the trial managed to implement these important ideas.[15] In his long book on the fury with which the Allies investigated the atrocities visited on the European continent in the immediate postwar, A. T. Williams arrives at a different conclusion: "For all Nuremberg's value in confronting the overarching systems of Nazi inhumanity, the victims were only numbers. That's what law and trial invariably promises; an impersonal and imperfect reaction to human cruelty and human suffering."[16] The Europeans and Americans realized they needed to bring some measured response to the destruction caused by Nazi injustice or future generations would suffer. But Williams also realized that this form of trial would also end with a certain measure of inadequacy.

Ironically, even given the at-times frosty bilateral relations in the region, since 1979 East Asia has been more peaceful than ever before. However, that important transformation seems to have been overlooked because to do so would require admission that Japan no longer threatens the region. Strangely, little consensus exists concerning what this peace represents.

Monumental History Misses Much of the Story

The structures of a national history create zones of conflict and sites of commemoration that are not immune from influence on how this history is shaped. The first comes in the form of "monumental history," which is used to build domestic notions of nationalism. This formation is often pitted against "critical history," which is historical inquiry that aims to investigate the past regardless of how it lauds or denigrates the state.[17] The gap between these different genres of history is made clear in recent Chinese government maneuvers to more blatantly emphasize its version of history throughout the world, through the internet and propaganda platforms. Mainland Chinese historical scholarship is frequently forced to reflect what the state wants its citizens to believe. This is not history but rather mimicry.[18]

It is not just China, however, that leans on the glory of monumentality in history. In 1997, the Group of Young Parliamentarians Thinking of the Future of Japan and Historical Education formed. This group consists of one hundred Japanese parliament members from the ruling LDP. It was founded in part to push against what was felt to be the negative historical vision the supposedly liberal media in Japan publicized.[19] Furuya Keiji, a lower house member of parliament who headed the group at one point, blogged about Japan's need to avoid cultivating a masochistic national history.[20] The group produced two books of dubious quality that questioned Japanese war guilt and an "Investigation Report" on the Nanjing Massacre "problem" as they labeled it.[21] What is at stake here is that the issue of reconciliation encapsulates a debate in Japan concerning one's political stance toward empire *and* the war. The "Tokyo Trial view" of history (that Japan's empire was aggressive and wrong) is posited against the conservative view that empire was about the liberation of Asia and that the war was fought to protect Japan's security because it was forced into a corner.

Nations cannot be left to resolve historical issues on their own. Japan and China need to investigate their own histories, not just rely on national sophistry and feel-good commissions to get them through times of crises. James Baldwin, the noted and polemical American writer, said as much at the end of his address to the National Press Club in Washington, DC, on December 10, 1986. "And as long as you pretend you don't know your history you're going to be the prisoner of it."[22] Baldwin did not repeat the tired idea of being condemned to repeat history. Rather, he articulated that reconciliation could only occur when a full grasp of a nation's history, however distasteful and horrible, was undertaken. He was explicitly talking about the United States' problems with race and injustice. But he was also soberly acknowledging that staring history in the face regardless of one's identity or color was perhaps the most difficult task in which a society could engage because it required shelving one's assumptions and exploring uncomfortable and unfamiliar intellectual frontiers. Baldwin never lived to see this dream achieved; he died soon after his address. War crimes trials in Asia did not lead to reconciliation in East Asia, but they offered a first step forward. The choice for leaders and the various national populations in this age is to decide in which direction they will advance the ideas behind those verdicts. Or will citizens merely continue to repudiate these legal processes in a bid to bolster the shorter-term satisfaction of emotional victimization? The choice is theirs and ours. Nothing is inevitable.

Glossary of Japanese and Chinese Names and Terms

Abe Shintarō (安倍晋太郎)
Abe Shinzō (安倍晋三)
Adachi Hatazō (安達二十三)
Akiyama Masahiro (秋山昌廣)
Amō Eiji (天羽英二)
Anami Korechika (阿南惟幾)
Aoki Tokuzō (青木徳蔵)
Arai Toshio (新井利男)
Arima Torao (有馬虎雄)
Asanuma Inejirō (浅沼稲次郎)
Ashida Hitoshi ((芦田均)
Baba Tsunego (馬場恒吾)
Bai Buzhou (白步洲)
Bai Chongxi (白崇禧)
Beituan Village (北疃村)
Chen Cheng (陳誠)
Chen Shuliang (陳叔亮)
Chūkiren (中帰連, Liaison Group of Returnees from China [Chūgoku kikansha renrakukai, usually abbreviated to Chūkiren])
Cihu Memorial Sculpture Park (慈湖紀念雕塑公園)
Deng Liqun (鄧力群)
Ding Ruchang (丁汝昌)
Dingyuan (定遠)
Doihara Kenji (土肥原賢二)
Dong Biwu (董必武)
Dong Yisan (董益三)
Du Yuming (杜聿明)
Duan Kewen (段克文)
Endō Saburō (遠藤三郎)
Fan Yuanyan (范園焱)
Fei Xiaotong (費孝通)

Feng Jingyu (馮荊育)
Fujita Shigeru (藤田茂)
Fujiwara Akira (藤原彰)
Fukuda Kumajirō (福田熊次郎)
Furuya Keiji (古屋圭司)
Fuse Tatsuji (布施辰治)
Gao Wenbin (高文杉)
Gongdelin Prison (功德林監獄)
Green Wind Group (緑風会)
Guo Moruo (郭沫若)
Hakamada Satomi (袴田里見)
Hanayama Shinshō (花山信勝)
Hao Shaoan (郝紹安)
Hata Ikuhiko (秦郁彦)
Hatoyama Ichirō (鳩山一郎)
Hayashi Itsurō (林逸郎)
Hayashi Miki (林水木)
He Ming (賀明)
He Yingqin (何應欽)
Higashikuni Naruhiko (東久邇稔彦)
Higuchi Jinichi (樋口仁一)
Hino Ashihei (火野葦平)
Hirano Ryūji (平野龍二)
Hirano Yoshitarō (平野義太郎)
historical nihilism (歴史虚無主義)
Hoashi Kei (帆足計)
Honda Katsuichi (本多勝一)
Honda Masakazu (本田雅和)
Honma Masaharu (本間雅晴)
Hou Jiahua (侯佳花)
Hsia Ch'in (Xia Qin, 夏勤)
Hsueh Hua-yuan (薛化元)
Hu Qiaomu (胡喬木)
Hu Yaobang (胡耀邦)
Hua Guofeng (華國鋒)
Huang Hua (黃華)
Huang Wei (黃維)
Ichikawa Iyū (市川伊雄)
Ichimata Masao (一又正雄)

ichioku sō zange (一億総懺悔)
Ikeda Hayato (池田勇人)
Imamura Hitoshi (今村均)
Inada Tomomi (稲田朋美)
Inami Ninrei (伊丹忍礼)
Inoue Tadao (井上忠男)
Ishikiriyama Hideaki (石切山英彰)
Ishiwara Kanji (石原莞爾)
Isogai Rensuke (磯谷廉介)
Itagaki Seishirō (板垣征四郎)
Itō Ritsu (伊藤律)
Itō Toshiharu (伊藤利春)
Iwata Chūzō (岩田宙造)
Jia Qian (賈潛)
Jiang Hua (江華)
Jiang Qing (江青)
Jin Yuan (金源)
Jing Zhuguo (井助國)
Jōno Hiroshi (城野宏)
Ju Zheng (居正)
Kameda Tōgo (亀田東伍)
Kamisago Shōshichi (上砂勝七)
Kanbayashiyama Eikichi (上林山栄吉)
Kaneko Fumiko (金子文子)
Kang Ze (康澤)
Katayama Tetsu (片山哲)
Katō Rinpei (加藤鑰平)
Kawanishi Kinji (川西錦二)
Kaya Okinori (賀屋興宣)
Kazami Akira (風見章)
Ke Jingxing (柯景星)
Kiangwan (江湾, Jiangwan in contemporary Chinese)
Kido Kōichi (木戸幸一)
Kim Ch'on-hae (金天海, real name 金鶴儀)
Kimura Tokutarō (木村篤太郎)
Kinkaseki (金瓜石, Jinguashi in Chinese)
Kinoshita Junji (木下順二)
Kishi Nobusuke (岸信介)
Kita Reikichi (北昤吉)
Kiyose Ichirō (清瀬一郎)

Koiso Kuniaki (小磯國昭)
Komatsu Shinichi (小松真一)
Kōmyō Temple (光明寺)
Konoe Fumimaro (近衛文麿)
Kōra Tomi (高良富)
Kōzen Temple (興禅寺)
Kuching (古晉, written as 久鎮 during Japan's occupation)
Kuroki Shigenori (黒木重徳)
Kuzuu Yoshihisa (葛生能久)
Lan Gongwu (藍公武)
Lei Hao (雷皓)
Li An (李安)
Li Chuli (李初梨)
Li Dequan (李德全)
Li Fang (李放)
Li Fushan (李甫山)
Li Jiajing (李家璟)
Li Kenong (李克農)
Li Liang (李良)
Li Qingxiang (李慶祥)
Li Weixun (李維恂)
Li Yechu (李業初)
Li Yuqin (李玉琴)
Li Zhiqun (李志群)
Lian Xisheng (廉希聖)
Liao Chengzhi (廖承志)
Liao Yaoxiang (廖耀湘)
Lijixiang comfort women museum (利济巷慰安所旧址陈列馆)
Lin Biao (林彪)
Lin Jiangshan (林江山)
Lin Jinlong (林金隆)
Lin Taizeng (林泰曾)
Liu Jie (劉傑)
Liu Jisheng (劉繼盛)
Liu Lianren (劉連仁)
Liu Linsheng (劉林生)
Liu Ningyi (劉寧一)
Liu Shaoqi (劉少奇)
Liu Tong (劉統)
Liu Zijian (劉子健)

Lu Xinfang (盧新芳)
Luku Incident (鹿窟事件)
Ma Zhendu (馬振犢)
Matsui Iwane (松井石根)
Matsumoto Jiichirō (松本治一郎)
Matsumura Giichi (松村義一)
Mei Ruao (梅汝璈)
"miscarriages of justice" (*yuanjia cuoan* 冤假錯案)
Miyakoshi Kisuke (宮腰喜助)
Miyamoto Kenji (宮本顕治)
Miyazawa Kiichi (宮澤喜一)
Morimatsu Toshio (森松俟夫)
Mu Xin (穆欣)
Nabeyama Sadachika (鍋山貞親)
Nakamura Kan'emon (中村翫右衛門)
Nakamura Toyoichi (中村豊一)
Nakasone Yasuhiro (中曽根康弘)
Nan Hanchen (南漢宸)
Nemoto Ryūtarō (根本竜太郎)
Ni Zhengyu (倪征燠)
Nishii Kenichi (西井健一)
Nishizawa Takaji (西沢隆二)
Nomizo Masaru (野溝勝)
Norimura Kaneko (法村香音子)
Oda Makoto (小田実)
Odamura Shirō (小田村四郎)
Ōe Yoshiwaka (大江芳若)
Ōhashi Takeo (大橋武夫)
Okamoto Masano (岡本正野)
Okamura Yasuji (岡村寧次)
Okano Kiyohide (岡野清豪)
Okazaki Katsuo (岡崎 勝男)
Okino Matao (沖野亦男)
Ōyama Ikuo (大山郁夫)
Ozaki Hotsumi (尾崎秀実)
P. A. Shibaev (史白夫)
Pan Zhenya (潘震亚)
Park Chung-hee (朴正熙)
Park Geun-hye (朴槿惠)
Park Yeol (朴烈)

Peng Dehuai (彭德怀)
Peng Ming-min (彭明敏)
Peng Zhen (彭真)
People's Newspaper (民衆新聞)
Progressive Newspaper (前進報)
Pu Yi (溥儀)
Qin Dechun (秦德純)
Qincheng Prison (秦城監獄)
Qiu, Henry (Qiu Shaoheng, 裘劭恒)
Quan Deyuan (權德源)
Quan Weicai (權維才)
Saitō Takao (斉藤隆夫)
Sakano Junkichi (阪埜淳吉, also recorded at the Tokyo Trial as Banno Kunkichi)
Sanmonji Shōhei (三文字正平)
Sejima Ryūzō (瀬島龍三)
Shen, Yorkson (Shen Jinding, 沈覲鼎)
Shen Junru (沈鈞儒)
Shen Zui (沈醉)
Shi Liang (史良)
Shidehara Kijūrō (幣原喜重郎)
Shiga Yoshio (志賀義雄)
Shigemitsu Mamoru (重光葵)
Shimazu Tadatsugu (島津忠承)
Shimoda Takesō (下田武三)
Shimomura Kainan (下村海南, also known as Shimomura Hiroshi)
Shimomura Sadamu (下村定)
Shirakawa training grounds (白河訓練所)
Suifenhe (绥芬河)
Sumioka Giichi (住岡義一)
Sumita Raishirō (澄田睞四郎)
Sun Li-jen (孫立人)
Sunama Ichirō (砂間一良)
Suzuki Hiraku (鈴木啓久)
Suzuki Mosaburō (鈴木茂三郎)
Tachiki Hiroshi (立木洋)
Takasaki Tatsunosuke (高碕達之助)
Takayanagi Kenzō (高柳賢三)
Takazawa Torao (高沢寅男)
Takeiri Yoshikatsu (竹入義勝)

Takenaka Katsuo (竹中勝男)
Tamura Hiroshi (田村浩)
Tan Zhengwen (譚政文)
Tanabe Toshio (田辺敏雄)
Tanaka Hisakazu (田中久一)
Tanaka Masaaki (田中正明)
Tanaka Toshio (田中稔男)
Tanizaki Jun'ichirō (谷崎潤一郎)
Tiantaigang (天台崗)
Tilanqiao Prison (提籃橋監獄, Basket Bridge Prison)
Tōgō Minoru (東郷實)
Tōgō Shigenori (東郷茂徳)
Tokuda Kyūichi (徳田球一)
Tokutomi Sohō (徳富蘇峰)
Tokutomi Tasaburō (徳富太三郎)
Tominaga Juntarō (富永順太郎)
Toyoda Soemu (豊田副武)
Toyota Kumao (豊田隈雄)
Tsuda Moriya (津田守彌)
Tsugita Daizaburō (次田大三郎)
Tsuji Masanobu (辻政信)
Tsukamoto Saburō (塚本三郎)
Tsunoda Jun (角田順)
Ueda Kōichirō (上田耕一郎)
Uesaka Masaru (上坂勝)
Umezu Yoshijirō (梅津美治郎)
Uno Shintarō (鵜野晋太郎)
Wang Hongwen (王洪文)
Wang Huai'an (王懷安)
Wang Jiaxiang (王稼祥)
Wang Lin (汪霖)
Wang Minqiu (王敏求)
Wang Ruqi (王汝琪)
Wang Shilin (王石麟)
Wang Xiaoxian (王效賢)
Wang Yaowu (王耀武)
Wang Yi (王毅)
Wang Zaoshi (王造時)
Wanping (宛平)
Wei Jingsheng (魏京生)

Weihaiwei (威海衛)
Woo Yian (吳棪)
Wu Jinan (吳寄南)
Wu Xuewen (吳學文)
Xiang Zhejun (向哲浚)
Xiao Xiangqian (肖向前)
Yabe Teiji (矢部貞治)
Yamada Fūtarō (山田風太郎)
Yamaguchi Kikuichirō (山口喜久一郎)
Yamaguchi Mitsufumi (山口盈文)
Yan Haijian (嚴海建)
Yan Xishan (閻錫山)
Yang Guangyu (楊光鈺)
Yang Xianzhi (楊顯之)
Yang Zhaolong (楊兆龍)
Yang Zhenya (楊振亜)
Yao Wenyuan (姚文元)
Yasuda Muneharu (安田宗治)
Yasuo Masatsuna (安尾正綱)
Ye Jianying (葉劍英)
Yokota Kisaburō (横田喜三郎)
Yonai Mitsumasa (米内光政)
Yoshida Shigeru (吉田茂)
Yoshimatsu Masakatsu (吉松正勝)
Yoshimi Yoshiaki (吉見義明)
Yuan Guang (袁光)
Yuan Weishi (袁偉時)
Yuhuatai (雨花台)
Zainihon chōsenjin renmei (在日本朝鮮人連盟)
Zainihon chōsenjin sōren gōkai (在日本朝鮮人総連合会)
Zainihon daikanminkoku kyoryū mindan (在日本大韓民国居留民団)
Zhang Chunqiao (張春橋)
Zhang Dingcheng (張鼎丞)
Zhang Jinghui (張景惠)
Zhang Tieshi (張鐵石)
Zhang Xiangqian (張向前)
Zhang Xiruo (張奚若)
Zhang Zhirang (張志讓)
Zhao Anbo (趙安博)
Zhao Peixian (趙培憲)

Zhao Yuying (趙毓英)
Zheng Fulai (鄭福來)
Zheng Luda (鄭魯達)
Zhenyuan (鎮遠)
Zhiyuan (致遠)
Zhong Hanbo (鍾漢波)
Zhong Hanhua (鐘漢華)
Zhonghua Ribao (中華日報)
Zhou Enlai (周恩來)
Zhou Gengsheng (周鯁生)
Zhou Yangqing (周錫卿)
Zhu De (朱德)
Zhu Yaotang (朱耀堂)

Notes

Archives frequently cited have been identified by the following abbreviations:

AH	Academia Historica, Taiwan
AWM	Australia War Memorial
CARMD	China's anti-rightist movement database
CMOFA	Chinese Ministry of Foreign Affairs Archives
CMPD	China's mid-1950s political movement database
FRUS	Foreign Relations of the United States
HIA	Hoover Institute Archives, Stanford, California
IRCA	International Red Cross Archives, Geneva
IRRC	Chinese Communist Party Internal Reference Reports Collection, University Services Center, Chinese University Hong Kong
JPR	Japan's Parliamentary Record
KGNA	Kew Garden, National Archives
MJPHMR	Modern Japanese Political History Materials Room in the National Diet Library, Tokyo
MODA	Ministry of Defense Archives, Ichigaya, Tokyo
MOFAAJ	Ministry of Foreign Affairs Archives, Japan
MOFAT	Ministry of Foreign Affairs Archives housed in Academia Sinica
NAA	National Archives of Australia
NAJ	National Archives of Japan
NARA	National Archives, College Park, Maryland
RPP	Rosco Pound Papers at Harvard University Law Library
SLRA	Sir Leon Radzinowicz Archive, Florida State University
TBA	Tōyō Bunko Archives
YSA	Yasukuni Shrine Archives

Introduction

1. The documentary was broadcast in China in September 2020, but it is also available on DVD: *Yatai zhanzheng shenpan* (*Asia Pacific War Crimes Trials*), an eight-episode series, Shanghai jiaotong daxue dianzi yinxiang chubanshe, 2021. A book was later produced: Shanghai guangbo dianshitai jilupian zhongxin Chen Yinan gongzuoshi, ed., *Yatai zhanzheng shenpan* (Shanghai: Shanghai jiaotong daxuechubanshe, 2021).

2. The Beituan massacre is detailed in Itō Toshiharu's interview for NHK, NHK sensō ākaibuzu, sensō shōgen, produced November 4, 2011, https://www2.nhk.or.jp/archives/shogenarchives/shogen/movie.cgi?das_id=D0001100729_00000.

3. Li Qingxiang, interview, May 30, 2019, in *Yatai zhanzheng shenpan*, 180–181, 190–192.

4. Flora Sapio, Susan Trevaskes, Sarah Biddulph, and Elisa Nesossi, eds., *Justice: The China Experience* (Cambridge: Cambridge University Press, 2017); Barrie Sander, *Doing Justice to History: Confronting the Past in International Criminal Courts* (Oxford: Oxford University Press, 2021), 1–25.

5. Haiyan Lee, *A Certain Justice: Toward an Ecology of the Chinese Legal Imagination* (Chicago: University of Chicago Press, 2023).

6. Evelyn Goh, *The Struggle for Order: Hegemony, Hierarchy, and Transition in Post-Cold War East Asia* (Oxford: Oxford University Press, 2013), 159–201. For more on processes of reconciliation, see the series: Asano Toyomi, ed., *Wakaigaku no kokoromi: kioku, kanjō, kachi*, vol. 1 (Akashi shoten, 2021). (Unless otherwise noted, all Japanese books are published in Tokyo).

1. The Kaleidoscope of Defeat in East Asia

1. Fujiwara Akira, *Shōwa no rekishi*, vol. 5, *Nicchū zenmen sensō* (Shōgakukan shuppansha, 1994 edition), 68–73.

2. Zheng Fulai, interview, May 29, 2019, in Shanghai guangbo dianshitai jilupian zhongxin Chen Yinan gongzuoshi, ed., *Yatai zhanzheng shenpan* (Shanghai: Shanghai jiaotong daxuechubanshe, 2021), 150–151.

3. Masha Gessen, "What HBO's 'Chernobyl' Got Right, and What It Got Terribly Wrong," *New Yorker*, June 4, 2019, https://www.newyorker.com/news/our-columnists/what-hbos-chernobyl-got-right-and-what-it-got-terribly-wrong; Na Li, "History, Memory, and Identity: Oral History in China," *Oral History Review* 47, no. 1 (2020): 26–51.

4. "China's Best Ship Lost," *New York Times*, November 23, 1894; Hans van de Ven, *Breaking with the Past: The Maritime Customs Service and the Global Origins of Modernity in China* (New York: Columbia University Press, 2014), 111.

5. Yasuoka Akio, "Meiji 19nen nagasaki shinkoku suihei sōtō jiken," *Hōsei daigaku bungaku kiyō*, dai 36gō, (1990): 50–51.

6. Asai Sachiko, "Shinkoku hokuyō kantai raikō to sono eikyō," *Aichi shukutoku daigaku gendai shakai kenkyū hōkoku* 4 (2009): 58.

7. Weipin Tsai, "The First Casualty: Truth, Lies and Commercial Opportunism in Chinese Newspapers during the First Sino-Japanese War," in *Print, Profit, and Perception: Ideas, Information and Knowledge in Chinese Societies, 1895–1949*, ed. Pei-yin Lin and Weipin Tsai (Leiden: Brill, 2014), 227–234.

8. "China's Best Ship Lost," *The North-China Herald and Supreme Court & Consular Gazette* (Shanghai), November 23, 1894; S. C. M. Paine, *The Sino-Japanese War of 1894–1895: Perceptions, Power, and Primacy* (Cambridge: Cambridge University Press, 2003), 229–230.

9. "Ueno kōen de kaisai suru daiichi shukushō taikai no junjo," *Yomiuri shimbun*, December 8, 1894, morning edition.

10. Tsuchida Seijirō, *Tōkyōshi shukushō taikai* (Shūeisha, 1895).

11. Kinoshita Naoyuki, *Sensō to iu misemono: nisshin sensō shukushō taikai sennyūki* (Kyoto: Mineruva shobō, 2013), 1–18.

12. Tsuchida, *Tōkyōshi shukushō taikai*, 139.

13. *The North—China Herald and Supreme Court & Consular Gazette* (Shanghai), November 23, 1894.

14. "Shinkoku gunkan chinen ga nagasaki ni tōchaku," *Yomiuri shimbun*, July 12, 1895, morning edition; *The North—China Herald and Supreme Court & Consular Gazette* (Shanghai), August 16, 1895.

15. Zhong Hanbo, *Zhuwai wuguan de shiming—yiwei haijun junguan de huiyi* (Taipei: Maitian chubanshe, 1998), 53–54.

16. "Panoramakan," *Fūzoku gahō*, 123gō, (September 25, 1896): 26–28.

17. *Asahi shimbun*, February 10, 1895, Tokyo morning edition.

18. "Chinen no ikari kenpishiki," *Asahi shimbun*, May 28, 1942, Tokyo evening edition.

19. Kari Shepherdson-Scott, "Entertaining War: Spectacle and the Great 'Capture of Wuhan' Battle Panorama of 1939," *Art Bulletin* 100, no. 4 (2018): 81–105.

20. Zhong, *Zhuwai wuguan de shiming*, 3.

21. Letter from Major General of the Chinese Army Lee Li-Bai to SCAP, June 26, 1946, in "Yaoqiu riben guihuan guqiwu," Waijiaobu, Guoshiguan, 020—1-119-0013, AH. I thank Professor Chang Li for sharing his archives on this historical episode with me.

22. Letter from Lee Li-Bai to SCAP, July 15, 1946, in "Yaoqiu riben guihuan guqiwu," Waijiaobu, Guoshiguan, 020—1-119-0013, AH.

23. In February 1948, the Chinese Mission in Tokyo considered whether gifts that Wang Jingwei had sent to Emperor Hirohito could be returned to General Chiang Kai-shek and put on display at his residence in Nanjing as commemorative war victory items. See "Wang niri tianhuang yuwan kefou yunjing," No. 002000000456A, in Jiangzhongzheng zongton wenwu, diancanghao: 002-020400-00052-124, AH.

24. Chang-tai Hung, *Mao's New World: Political Culture in the Early People's Republic* (Ithaca, NY: Cornell University Press, 2011), 112.

25. Barak Kushner, "Anchors of History: The Long Shadow of Imperial Japanese Propaganda," in *Fanning the Flames: Propaganda in Modern Japan*, ed. Kaoru Ueda (Stanford, CA: Hoover Institution Press, 2021), 29–41.

26. Florian Schneider, *China's Digital Nationalism* (New York: Oxford University Press, 2018), 141.

27. Tor Krever, "International Criminal Law: An Ideology Critique," *Leiden Journal of International Law* 26, no. 3 (September 2013): 708.

28. Kerstin Bree Carlson, *Model(ing) Justice: Perfecting the Promise of International Criminal Law* (Cambridge: Cambridge University Press, 2018), 127.

29. Dan Gretton, *I You We Them: Journeys beyond Evil: The Desk Killer in History and Today* (London: Penguin Random House, 2019), 30–31.

30. Urs Matthias Zachmann, "Yokota Kisaburō—Defending International Criminal Justice in Interwar and Early Post-war Japan," in *The Dawn of a Discipline: International Criminal Justice and Its Early Exponents*, ed. Frédéric Mégret and Immi Tallgren (Cambridge: Cambridge University Press, 2020), 335–357; Matthias Zachman, "Loser's Justice: The Tokyo Trial from the Perspective of the Japanese Defense Counsels

and the Legal Community," in *Transcultural Justice at the Tokyo Tribunal: The Allied Struggle for Justice, 1946–48*, ed. Kerstin von Lingen (Leiden: Brill, 2018), 284–306.

31. Kim Christian Priemel, *The Betrayal: The Nuremberg Trials and German Divergence* (Oxford: Oxford University Press, 2016), 6.

32. Yuma Totani, "International Military Tribunals at Tokyo, 1946–1949: Individual Responsibility for War Crimes," in *Historical Origins of International Criminal Law: Volume 2*, ed. Morten Bergsmo, Cheah Wui Ling, and Yi Ping (Brussels: Torkel Opsahl Academic EPublisher, 2014), 31–65.

33. Higurashi Yoshinobu, *Tokyo saiban* (Kōdansha, 2008), 27–28; Yuma Totani, *The Tokyo War Crimes Trial: The Pursuit of Justice in the Wake of World War II* (Cambridge, MA: Harvard University Press, 2008), 20–23.

34. Hayashi Hirofumi, *Sensō hanzai no kenkyū: senpan saiban seikaku no keisei kara tokyo saiban bishikyū saiban made* (Bensei shuppan, 2010); Sandra Wilson, Robert Cribb, Beatrice Trefalt, and Dean Aszkielowicz, *Japanese War Criminals: The Politics of Justice after the Second World War* (New York: Columbia University Press, 2017), 77–78, provides the most recent reliable figures and demonstrates where discrepancies originate.

35. Wang Guodong, *Riben xijunzhan zhanfan boli shenpan shilu* (Changsha: Hunan renmin chubanshe, 2005); Grégory Dufaud, "Khabarovsk, 1949 L'autre procès des criminels de guerre japonais," *20&21 Revue d'histoire*, no. 148 (April 2020): 51–64; Valentina Polunina, "The Khabarovsk Trial: The Soviet Riposte to the Tokyo Tribunal," in *Trials for International Crimes in Asia*, ed. Kirsten Sellars (Cambridge: Cambridge University Press, 2016), 121–144.

36. Yun Xia, *Down with Traitors: Justice and Nationalism in Wartime China* (Seattle: University of Washington Press, 2017).

37. Aiyaz Husain, *Mapping the End of Empire: American and British Strategic Visions in the Postwar World* (Cambridge, MA: Harvard University Press, 2014), 2.

38. Robert Gildea, *Empires of the Mind: The Colonial Past and the Politics of the Present* (Cambridge: Cambridge University Press, 2019), 64.

39. Robert Cribb, "The Burma Trials of Japanese War Criminals, 1946–1947," in *War Crimes Trials in the Wake of Decolonization and Cold War in Asia, 1945–1956: Justice in Time of Turmoil*, ed. Kerstin von Lingen (London: Palgrave Macmillan, 2017), 121. Cribb elucidates these goals specifically in reference to Burma, but I believe they hold true in general for the European colonial powers and other Allied aims.

40. Beatrice Trefalt, "The French Prosecution at the IMTFE: Robert Oneto, Indochina and the Rehabilitation of French Prestige," in von Lingen, *Wake of Decolonization*, 51–67; Ann-Sophie Schoepfel, "Justice and Decolonization: War Crimes on Trial in Saigon, 1946–1950," in von Lingen, *Wake of Decolonization*, 168.

41. See Rana Mitter, *China's Good War: How World War II Is Shaping a New Nationalism* (Cambridge, MA: Harvard University Press), 2020.

42. Kamila Szczepanska, *The Politics of War Memory in Japan: Progressive Civil Society Groups and Contestation over Memory of the Asia-Pacific War* (London: Routledge, 2014).

43. Martti Koskenniemi, "Between Impunity and Show Trials," in *Max Planck Yearbook of United Nations Law*, vol. 6, ed. J. A. Frowein and R. Wolfrum (Leiden: Brill, 2002), 11; Neil Boister, "The Tokyo Military Tribunal: A Show Trial?," in *Historical Origins of International Criminal Law: Volume 2*, ed. Morten Bergsmo, Cheah Wui Ling, and YI Ping, (Brussels: Torkel Opsahl Academic EPublisher, 2014), 3–29. See also Otto

Kirchheimer, *Political Justice: The Use of Legal Procedure for Political Ends* (Princeton, NJ: Princeton University Press, 1962).

44. Koskenniemi, "Show Trials," 18.

45. Seumas Milne, "Hague Is Not the Place to Try Milosevic," *The Guardian*, August 2, 2001, https://www.theguardian.com/politics/2001/aug/02/warcrimes.serbia.

46. Koskenniemi, "Show Trials," 30; Jacques Vergès, *De La Stratégie Judiciaire* (Paris: Les edition de minuit, 1968), 104; Filip Strandberg Hassellind, "The International Criminal Trial as a Site for Contesting Historical and Political Narratives: The Case of Dominic Ongwen," *Social & Legal Studies* 20, no. 10 (2020): 1–20.

47. Koskenniemi, "Show Trials," 33.

48. Viet Thanh Nguyen, *Nothing Ever Dies: Vietnam and the Memory of War* (Cambridge, MA: Harvard University Press, 2016), 17; Woo Kyung Im, "Jiyizhizhan: quanqiuhua shidai minzu jiyi de liebian, fenghe ji qi xingbie," *Taiwan shehui yanjiu jikan* 70 (June 2008): 245–271.

49. Masi Noor, Nurit Shnabel, Samer Halabi, and Arie Nadler, "When Suffering Begets Suffering: The Psychology of Competitive Victimhood between Adversarial Groups in Violent Conflicts," *Personality and Social Psychology Review* 16, no. 4 (2012): 362.

50. Mariska Kappmeier and Aurélie Mercy, "The Long Road from Cold War to Warm Peace: Building Shared Collective Memory through Trust," *Journal of Social and Political Psychology* 7, no. 1 (2019): 538.

51. Lord Sumption, "The Limits of the Law" (27th Sultan Azlan Shah Lecture, Kuala Lumpur, November 20, 2013), online publication of the speech. Listen to his lecture "Law's Expanding Empire," *The Reith Lectures*, BBC, https://www.bbc.co.uk/programmes/m00057m8; Jonathan Sumption, *Trials of the State: Law and the Decline of Politics* (London: Profile Books, 2019).

52. Yukiko Koga, "Between the Law: The Unmaking of Empire and Law's Imperial Amnesia," *Law and Social Inquiry* 41, no. 2 (Spring 2016): 404.

53. Madoka Futamura, *War Crimes Tribunals and Transitional Justice: The Tokyo Trial and the Nuremberg Legacy* (Abingdon: Routledge, 2008), 65.

54. See Suping Lu's book review in *China Review International* 21, no. 2 (2014): 149–179. While Lu's criticism is in some ways valid, he misses the larger point that justice was not so easily pursued and became a pawn of larger forces.

55. Suzuki Chieko, "Maboroshi de wa nakatta hyakuningiri kyōsō," *Chūkiren*, no. 27 (Winter 2003): 3–12.

56. Karl Gustafsson, "Memory Politics and Ontological Security in Sino-Japanese Relations," *Asian Studies Review* 38, no. 1 (2014): 71–86; Shogo Suzuki, "Japanese Revisionists and the 'Korea Threat': Insights from Ontological Security," *Cambridge Review of International Affairs* 32, no. 3 (2019): 303–321.

57. Inada Tomomi, *Hyakuningiri saiban kara nankin e* (Bungei shunjū, 2007).

58. The Nippon Kaigi states its position toward the Tokyo Trial, borrowing heavily from Satō Kazuo, ed., *Sekai ga sabaku tokyo saiban* (Meiseisha, 2005). See: https://www.nipponkaigi.org/opinion/archives/865 (originally posted December 11, 2008, Nippon kaigi website, *Opinion*). Sugano Tamotsu, *Nihon kaigi no kenkyū* (Fusōsha, 2016); Daiki Shibuichi, "The Japan Conference (Nippon Kaigi): An Elusive Conglomerate," *East Asia* 34 (2017): 179–196; Sachie Mizohata, "Nippon Kaigi: Empire, Contradiction, and Japan's Future," *Asia-Pacific Journal* 14, issue 21, no. 4 (November 1, 2016): 9.

59. Mary Fulbrook, *Reckonings: Legacies of Nazi Persecution and the Quest for Justice* (Oxford: Oxford University Press, 2018), 353. See also Tony Judt, "The Past Is Another Country: Myth and Memory in Postwar Europe," in *The Politics of Retribution in Europe: World War II and Its Aftermath*, ed. István Deák, Jan T. Gross, and Tony Judt (Princeton, NJ: Princeton University Press, 2000), 305.

60. David Cohen and Yuma Totani, *The Tokyo War Crimes Tribunal: Law, History, and Jurisprudence* (Cambridge: Cambridge University Press, 2019), 256.

2. The Shape of Justice

1. "Yuandong guoji fatingshang de guaiju," *Jiefang ribao*, July 30, 1946.

2. Ju-Ao Mei, "China and the Rule of Law," *Pacific Affairs* 5, no. 10 (October 1932): 863–872.

3. Xiaoqun Xu, *Trial of Modernity: Judicial Reform in Early Twentieth-Century China, 1901–1937* (Palo Alto, CA: Stanford University Press, 2008), 91.

4. Fan Zhongxin, You Chenjun, and Gong Xianzhai, ed., *Wei shenme yao chongjian zhongguo faxi: Ju Zheng fazheng wenxuan* (Beijing: Zhongguo zhengfa daxue chubanshe, 2009), 24–26; Terada Hiroaki, "The Crowded Train Model: The Concept of Society and the Maintenance of Order in Ming and Qing Dynasty China," in *Law in a Changing World: Asian Alternatives*, ed. Morigawa Yasumoto (Stuttgart: Franz Steiner Verlag, 1998), 100–109.

5. Fan et al., *Wei shenme*, 26.

6. Fan et al., *Wei shenme*, 27–29.

7. Fan et al., *Wei shenme*, 47.

8. Yang Zhaolong, "Zhongguo falu jiaoyu zhi ruodian ji qi bujiu zhi fanglue," in *Yang Zhaolong faxue wenji*, ed. Yang Zhaolong, Ai Yongming, and Lu Jinbi (Beijing: Falu chubanshe, 2005), 229–243.

9. Glenn Douglas Tiffert, "Judging Revolution: Beijing and the Birth of the PRC Judicial System (1906–1958)" (PhD diss., University of California, Berkeley, 2015).

10. Tahirih Lee, "Orienting Lawyers in China's Tribunals before 1949," *Maryland Journal of International Law* 27, no. 129 (2012): 182. See also Pasha L. Hsieh, "The Discipline of International Law in Republican China and Contemporary Taiwan," *Washington University Global Studies Law Review* 14, no. 1 (2015): 87–129. Dongwu University was referred to in English as Soochow University, or Suzhou University in modern pinyin.

11. Li Xiuqing, "John C. H. Wu at the University of Michigan School of Law," *Journal of Legal Education* 58, no. 4 (December 2008): 549; John C. H. Wu, *Beyond East and West* (New York: Sheed and Ward, 1951), 66–67; Sei Jeong Chin, "Autonomy through Social Networks: Law, Politics, and the News Media in Modern China, 1931–1957" (PhD diss., Harvard University, 2008), 52.

12. I am grateful to Isaac Gagné for suggesting this idea. The language of thinking of justice as a commodity and a transaction is his.

13. Renmin fayuanbaoshe, ed., *Zhengyi de shenpan: jinian zhongguo renmin kangri zhanzheng shengli qishi zhounian* (Beijing: Renmin fayuanchubanshe, 2016), 422. See *Review of the Records of Trials before United States of American Military Commissions, Shanghai, China*, a review of its own record of trials that lists ten trials of Japanese and one trial of German nationals. Found at the ICC Legal Tools Database: https://www.legal

-tools.org/doc/282e93/pdf/. Chaen Yoshio, ed., *Bishikyū senpan beigun shanhai nado saiban shiryō* (Fuji shuppansha, 1989), 132–135; Timothy Brook, "The Shanghai Trials, 1946: Conjuring Postwar Justice," in *Zhanhou bianju yu zhanzheng jiyi*, ed. Lyu Fang-shang (Taipei: Academia Historica, 2015), 127–155.

14. "Tilanqiao jianyu—jingnei shouci qiaoxiang shenpan riben zhanfan fachui," September 3, 2015, in series *Zhengyi de shenpan zhi meiguo shenpan shanghai*, in the Renmin fayuanbao, tekan, from 2015 (available for download or online reading at the *People's Court Daily* [Renmin fayuanbao] website, http://rmfyb.chinacourt.org/).

15. RG 153, Records of the Office of the Judge Advocate General (Army), War Crimes Branch, China War Crimes File, 1945–1948, XIV-A thru XIV-F, box 12, War Crimes Files, Nanking, China, Master Index XIV-A Folder "War Crimes Summary," NARA.

16. Jonathan Mayhew Wainwright, *General Wainwright's Story: The Account of Four Years of Humiliating Defeat, Surrender, and Captivity* (Westport, CT: Greenwood Press, 1970; originally published in 1945), 245–246; *Prisoner of the Rising Sun: The Lost Diary of Brig. Gen. Lewis Beebe*, ed. John M. Beebe (College Station: Texas A&M University Press, 2006).

17. RG 153, Records of the Office of Judge Advocate General (Army), War Crimes Branch, Historian Background Files, box 2, Legal Section—SCAP, Shanghai, NARA.

18. Katō Tetsurō, *Hōshoku shita akuma no sengo—731 butai to Futaki Hideo seikai jīpu* (Kadensha, 2017), 23.

19. William S. Hamilton, *Notes from Old Nanking, 1947–1949: The Great Transition* (Canberra: Pandanus Books, 2004), 30.

20. WO 32/15509, Confidential Memo, subj: War Crimes against British Subjects in the Far East, June 14, 1946, KGNA.

21. Guillaume Mouralis, "The Invention of 'Transitional Justice,' in the 1990s," in *Dealing with Wars and Dictatorships*, ed. Liora Israël and Guillaume Mouralis (The Hague: Asser Press, 2014), 83–100.

22. Tanaka Hiromi, *Bishikyū senpan* (Chikuma shobō, 2002), 21.

23. Jeanne Guillemin, *Hidden Atrocities: Japanese Germ Warfare and American Obstruction of Justice at the Tokyo Trial* (New York: Columbia University Press, 2017), 116.

24. See Amanda Weiss, "'A Continuous Retrial': Trans/national Memory in Chinese and Japanese Tribunal Films," *Arts* 9, no. 1:2 (2020): 1–16.

25. Kaya Okinori, *Senzen/sengo hachijūnen* (Keizai ōraisha, 1976), 191.

26. Kaya, *Senzen/sengo hachijūnen*, 174.

27. Udagawa Kōta, "Senpan no sengo—senpan no sensō sekinin sensōkan sengo shakaikan," *Kikan sensō sekinin kenkyū* 78 (2012): 22–23.

28. Harold R. Isaacs, *No Peace for Asia*, 2nd ed. (Cambridge, MA: MIT Press, 1967; originally published in 1947), 195.

29. Isaacs, *No Peace for Asia*, 197.

30. "Japanese Appeal to U.S.," *Manchester Guardian*, September 15, 1945. See also Barak Kushner, "Imperial Loss and Japan's Search for Postwar Legitimacy," in *The Dismantling of Japan's Empire in East Asia: De-imperialization, Postwar Legitimation and Imperial Afterlife*, ed. Barak Kushner and Sherzod Muminov (London: Routledge, 2017), 48–65.

31. *Shōwa tennō jitsuroku*, December 10, 1945, volume 34, Iwanami shoten, 176 (digital version). I thank Katō Yōko for sharing this resource.

32. John D. Pierson, *Tokutomi Soho, 1863–1957: A Journalist for Modern Japan* (Princeton, NJ: Princeton University Press, 1980), 381–397; Tokutomi Sohō, *Tokutomi Sohō 'ganso yume monogatari'* (Kōdansha, 2015). Tokutomi also published a book in 1948, *The School of Defeat* (Haisen no gakkō), which examines the nature of the defeat for the Japanese public.

33. Nakasone Yasuhiro, *Jiseiroku: rekishi hōtei no hikoku to shite* (Shinchōsha, 2004), 33–34.

34. Nakasone, *Jiseiroku*, 32.

35. Hosaka Masayasu, *Tennō ga jūkunin ita* (Kadokawa bunko, 2001), 15.

36. John Dower, *Embracing Defeat: Japan in the Wake of World War II* (New York: W. W. Norton, 2000), 243–244.

37. Ariyama Teruo, "Sengo nihon ni okeru rekishi kioku media," *Mediashi kenkyū* 14 (April 2003): 7–9.

38. Narelle Morris, "Obscuring the Historical Origins of International Criminal Law in Australia: The Australian War Crimes Investigations and Prosecutions of Japanese, 1942–1951," in *Historical Origins of International Criminal Law: Volume 2*, ed. Morten Bergsmo, Wui Ling Cheah, and Ping Yi (Brussels: Torkel Opsahl Academic EPublisher, 2014), 388.

39. Andrew Levidis, "Politics in a Fallen Empire: Kishi Nobusuke and the Making of the Conservative Hegemony in Japan," in *In the Ruins of the Japanese Empire: Imperial Violence, State Destruction, and the Reordering of Modern East Asia*, ed. Barak Kushner and Andrew Levidis (Hong Kong: Hong Kong University Press, 2020), 161–184.

40. Ian Buruma, *Year Zero: A History of 1945* (London: Atlantic Books, 2013), 239.

41. Akira Iriye, "Historicizing the Cold War," in *The Oxford Handbook of the Cold War*, ed. Richard Immerman and Petra Goedde (Oxford: Oxford University Press, 2013), 16–17.

42. Tanaka Akihiko, *Ajia no naka no nihon* (NTT shuppan, 2007), 3–4.

43. Kent Calder and Min Ye, *The Making of Northeast Asia* (Palo Alto, CA: Stanford University Press, 2010), 227.

44. See Araragi Shinzō, Kawakita Atsuko, and Matsuura Yūsuke, *Hikiage tsuihō zanryū: sengo kokusai minzoku idō no hikaku kenkyū* (Nagoya: Nagoya daigaku shuppan, 2019); Araragi Shinzō, ed., *Teikoku hōkai to hito no saiidō* (Bensei shuppan, 2011).

45. Kawashima Shin, "'De-imperialization' in Early Postwar Japan: Adjusting and Transforming Institutions of Empire," in *Dismantling*, 30–47.

3. When the Hero of Your Story Is the Villain of Another

1. Lyu Fangshang, "Cong riji ji danganzhong guancha Jiang Jieshi duiri waijiao celue 1930–1940s," in *2003 niandu caituan faren jiaoliu xiehui ritai jiaoliu sentā lishi yanjiuzhe jiaoliu shiye baogaoshu*, Zhongyang yanjiuyuan jindaishi yanjiusuo, March 2004.

2. Anja Bihler, "Late Republican China and the Development of International Criminal Law: China's Role in the United Nations War Crimes Commission in London and Chungking," in *Historical Origins of International Criminal Law*, vol. 1, ed. Morten Bergsmo, Wui Ling Cheah, and Ping Yi (Brussels: Torkel Opsahl Academic Publisher, 2014), 507–540.

3. Odd Arne Westad, *Decisive Encounters: The Chinese Civil War: 1946–1950* (Stanford, CA: Stanford University Press, 2003), 69–70.

4. Shimomura Kainan, *Shūsen hishi* (Kōdansha, 1985), 301–304.

5. Diane Lary, *China's Civil War: A Social History, 1945–1949* (Cambridge: Cambridge University Press, 2015), 45.

6. For a critique of Pound, see Jedidiah J. Kroncke, "Roscoe Pound in China: A Lost Precedent for the Liabilities of American Legal Exceptionalism," *Brooklyn Journal of International Law* 38, no. 1 (2012): 2–67; Wen-Wei Lai, "Forgiven and Forgotten: The Republic of China in the United Nations War Crimes Commission," *Columbia Journal of Asian Law* 25, no. 2 (Summer 2012): 306–339.

7. *The Roscoe Pound Papers*, Part I: Correspondence, 1907–1964, reel 68 of 127, RPP.

8. *The Roscoe Pound Papers*, Part I: Correspondence, 1907–1964, reel 68 of 127, RPP.

9. Letter from November 7, 1946, *The Roscoe Pound Papers*, Part I: Correspondence, 1907–1964, reel 68 of 127, RPP.

10. Barak Kushner, *Men to Devils, Devils to Men: Japanese War Crimes and Chinese Justice* (Cambridge, MA: Harvard University Press, 2016), 80–82.

11. Xiang Longwan and Marquise Lee Houle, "In Search of Justice for China: The Contributions of Judge Hsiang Che-chun to the Prosecution of Japanese War Criminals at the Tokyo Trial," in *Historical Origins of International Criminal Law*, vol. 2, ed. Morten Bergsmo, Wui Ling Cheah, and Ping Yi (Brussels: Torkel Opsahl Academic Publisher, 2014), 143–175. See also Qing Dechun, *Qin Dechun huiyilu* (Taipei: Zhuanji wenxue chubanshe, 1967).

12. Li Lingling, *Fajie jubo, Ni Zhengyu zhuan* (Nanjing: Jiangsu renmin chubanshe, 2008), 42–43.

13. Li, *Fajie jubo, Ni Zhengyu zhuan*, 44.

14. David Cohen and Yuma Totani, *The Tokyo War Crimes Tribunal: Law, History, and Jurisprudence* (Cambridge: Cambridge University Press, 2019), 213; Son Ansoku, "Shanghai no 'ashū seiki'ga mita sengo nihon no seiji," in *Sengo nihon to chūgoku chōsen: Purange bunko o hitotsu no tegakari toshite*, ed. Ōsaki Hiroaki (Kenbun shuppan, 2013), 218–220.

15. Li, *Fajie jubo, Ni Zhengyu zhuan*, 44; Kayoko Takeda, *Interpreting the Tokyo War Crimes Trial: A Sociopolitical Analysis* (Ottawa: University of Ottawa Press, 2010); Kayoko Takeda, "The Visibility of Collaborators: Snapshots of Wartime and Post-war Interpreters," in *Framing the Interpreter: Towards a Visual Perspective*, ed. A. Fernández-Ocampo and M. Wolf (London: Routledge, 2014), 150–159.

16. Li, *Fajie jubo, Ni Zhengyu zhuan*, 45. These included Xiang's brother-in-law, Zhou Yangqing, along with Gao Wenbin, Zheng Luda, Liu Jisheng, and interpreter Liu Zijian.

17. Huang Zijin, "Kangzhan jieshu qianhou Jiang Jieshi de duiri taidu: yide baoyuan zhenxiang de tantao," *Jindaishi yanjiusuo jikan*, di 45qi, (2014): 143–194. For a fuller overview of Chinese Nationalist POW camps which housed Japanese solders see: Kishi Toshihiko, *Ajia taiheiyō sensō to shūyōjo—jūkei seikenka no hishūyōsha no shōgen to kokusai kyūsai kikan no kiroku kara* (Kokusai shoin, 2021).

18. Matsumoto Masao and Furusawa Toshio, *Geishunka: Chō Ikushō no chūgoku kakumei kaikoroku* (Meitoku shuppansha, 1978), 220–221.

19. Herbert P. Bix, *Hirohito and the Making of Modern Japan* (New York: Harper Collins, 2000, 360.

20. Tanaka Hiroshi and Matsuzawa Tetsunari, eds., *Chūgokujin kyōsei renkō shiryō: gaimushō hōkokusho zen gobunsatsu hoka* (Gendai shokan, 1995); and NHK, *Maboroshi no gaimushō hōkokusho: chūgokujin kyōsei renkō no kiroku* (NHK Publishers, 1994); Yukiko Koga, "Inverted Compensation: Wartime Forced Labor and Post-imperial Reckoning," in *Overcoming Empire in Post-imperial East Asia: Repatriation, Redress and Rebuilding*, ed. Barak Kushner and Sherzod Muminov (London: Bloomsbury Publishers, 2020), 183–197.

21. Barbara R. Ambros, *Bones of Contention: Animals and Religion in Contemporary Japan* (Honolulu: University of Hawaii Press, 2012), 208; Yuki Tanaka, *Hidden Horrors: Japanese War Crimes in World War Two*, updated ed. (New York: Routledge, 2018).

22. Japan's National Diet Library has digital copies of the main prewar and wartime cabinet decisions online (https://rnavi.ndl.go.jp/politics/entry/bib00428.php).

23. Hosaka Masayasu, "Sensō ni makeru to, ānaru Yamada Fūtarō to chūgokuhei horyo," *Sandei mainichi*, July 25, 2010, 52–55; Yamada Fūtarō, *Senchūha fusen nikki* (Kōdansha, 2002), 306–309.

24. Gavan McCormack, *The Emptiness of Japanese Influence*, rev. ed. (New York: Routledge, 2015), 253–255; Higaki Takashi, *Matsushiro daihon'ei no shinjitsu* (Kōdansha gendaishinsho, 1994).

25. Yukiko Koga, "Accounting for Silence: Inheritance, Debt, and the Moral Economy of Legal Redress in China and Japan," *American Ethnologist* 40, no. 3 (2013): 494–507; Yukiko Koga, "Between the Law: The Unmaking of Empire and Law's Imperial Amnesia," *Law & Social Inquiry* 41, no. 2 (Spring 2016): 402–434.

26. Tanaka and Matsuzawa, eds., *Chūgokujin kyōsei renkō shiryō*, 14–15.

27. Tanaka and Matsuzawa, *Chūgokujin kyōsei renkō shiryō*, 785.

28. NHK shuzaihan, *NHK supesharu maboroshi no gaimushō hōkokusho chūgokujin kyōsei renkō no kiroku* (Nihon hōsō shuppan kyōkai, 1994); William Brand Simpson, *Special Agent in the Pacific, WWII: Counter-intelligence; Military, Political and Economic* (New York: Rivercross Publishing, 1995).

29. Li Enmin, "Nicchūkan no rekishi wakai wa kanōka: chūgokujin kyōsei renkō no rekishi wakai o jirei ni," *Kyōkai kenkyū*, no. 1 (October 2010): 97–112; Richard Minear and Franziska Seraphim, "Hanaoka Monogatari: The Massacre of Chinese Forced Laborers, Summer 1945," *Asia-Pacific Journal: Japan Focus* 13, issue 26, no. 1 (2015): 1–46.

30. William Underwood, "NHK's Finest Hour: Japan's Official Record of Chinese Forced Labor," *Asia-Pacific Journal: Japan Focus* 4, no. 8 (2006): 6.

31. Tanaka Hiroshi, "Kaisetsu," in *Chūgokujin kyōsei renkō shiryō: gaimushō hōkokusho*, ed. Tanaka Hiroshi and Matsuzawa Tetsunari (Gendai shokan, 1995), 802.

32. Koga, "Between the Law," 407.

33. Ishitobi Jin, *Hanaoka jiken kajima kōshō no kiseki* (Sairyūsha, 2010), 38–39. "Shōwa sanjūgonen shigatsu nijūshichinichi teishutsu, shitsumon daigogō, chūgokujin kyōsei renkō junnansha ni kansuru shitsumon shuisho," April 27, 1958, available online at the House of Representatives, Japan website: http://www.shugiin.go.jp/internet/itdb_shitsumona.nsf/html/shitsumon/a034005.htm.

34. Ishitobi, *Hanaoka jiken kajima kōshō no kiseki*. The author's actual name is Higuchi Jinichi.

35. Nozoe Kenji, ed., *Hanaoka jiken o mita nijūnin no shōgen* (Ochanomizu shobō, 1993), 140–141.

36. Nozoe, *Hanaoka jiken o mita nijūnin no shōgen*, 25–27.

37. Lu Junsheng and Zeng Xiaowen, eds., *Nanyang yinglie: erzhan qijian babuyaniu-jineiya jingnei guojun jiangshi jilu* (Taibei: Guofangbu shizheng bianyishi, 2009), 25.

38. G. J. Douds, "The Men Who Never Were: Indian POWs in the Second World War, South Asia," *Journal of South Asian Studies* 27, no. 2 (2004): 183–216; Shanghai guangbo dianshitai jilupian zhongxin Chen Yinan gongzuoshi, ed., *Yatai zhanzheng shen-pan* (Shanghai: Shanghai jiaotong daxuechubanshe, 2021), 92–96.

39. Lu and Zeng, *Nanyang yinglie*, 36.

40. Lu and Zeng, *Nanyang yinglie*, 43. David Sissons incorrectly states that these Chinese brought to Rabaul were all from puppet Chinese militaries. D. C. S. Sissons, "The Australian War Crimes Trials and Investigations (1942–51)," p. 38, accessed July 15, 2020, https://www.ocf.berkeley.edu/~changmin/documents/Sissons%20Final%20War%20Crimes%20Text%2018-3-06.pdf. According to postwar Chinese oral history interviews, the Chinese dragooned into labor were from a variety of military and other backgrounds. See Tian Jitian, "Babai zhuangshi xingcunzhe de xuelei huiyi," in *Erzhan luri zhongguo laogong koushushi*, vol. 5, *Gangwan dangnianma*, ed. He Tianyi (Jinan: Qilushushe, 2005), 387–392.

41. Lu and Zeng, *Nanyang yinglie*, 183.

42. Lu and Zeng, *Nanyang yinglie*, 154–157. See also Lan Shichi, "Beizhiminzhe de zaoyu, diguo bufu de zeren: erzhanhou zaihaiwai beijuliu qianfan de taiwanren," in *Zhanzheng de lishi yu jiyi*, ed. Lyu Fangshang (Taipei: Guoshiguan, 2015), 348–388.

43. Yuma Totani, "Crimes against Asians in Command Responsibility Trials," in *Australia's War Crimes Trials 1945–51*, ed. Georgina Fitzpatrick, Tim McCormack, and Narrelle Morris (Leiden, The Netherlands: Brill Nijhoff, 2016), 266–290. Woo's name in English is spelled in a variety of ways: Woo Yin, Woo Yian, Woo Yien. See also "Treatment of Chinese Prisoners of War," Series Number AWM54, 1010/4/153, AWM.

44. See Peter Cahill, "Chinese in Rabaul—1921 to 1942: Normal Practices, or Containing the Yellow Peril?," *Journal of Pacific History* 31, no. 1 (June 1996): 72–91.

45. "War Crimes—Military Tribunal—MATSUSHIMA Tozaburo (Sergeant)," NAA: A471, 80915, 60 of the digital archived trial record, NAA. The island of Taiwan was more commonly referred to as Formosa in earlier times.

46. "War Crimes—Military Tribunal—MATSUSHIMA Tozaburo (Sergeant)," 21–34 of the digital archived trial record, NAA.

47. "War Crimes—Military Tribunal—HIROTA Akira (Major-General)," NAA: A471, 81653 PART B, 4 of the digital archived trial record, NAA; Yuma Totani, *Justice in Asia and the Pacific Region, 1945–1952: Allied War Crimes Prosecutions* (New York: Cambridge University Press, 2015), 106–111.

48. "War Crimes—Military Tribunal—HIROTA Akira (Major-General)," 7 of the digital archived trial record, NAA.

49. "War Crimes—Military Tribunal—IMAMURA Hitoshi (General)," NAA: A471, 81635 PART A, 109 of the digital archived record of the trial, NAA. There seems to be agreement with this from the Australian side as well. Emmi Okada, "The Australian Trials of Class B and C Japanese War Crime Suspects, 1945–51," *Australian International Law Journal* 16 (2009): 65. On the issue of legal status of Chinese POWs, see pages 67–68.

50. Georgina Fitzpatrick, "War Crimes Trials, 'Victor's Justice' and Australian Military Justice in the Aftermath of the Second World War," in *The Hidden Histories of War*

Crimes Trials, ed. Kevin Jon Heller and Gerry Simpson (Oxford: Oxford University Press, 2013), 337. At the end of the war, Imamura was initially tried and found guilty in Rabaul in 1947, under Australian jurisdiction. He was then transferred to the Dutch East Indies (Indonesia) in 1949 and put on trial a second time for war crimes of command responsibility. See Fred L. Borch, *Military Trials of War Criminals in the Netherlands East Indies, 1946–1949* (Oxford: Oxford University Press, 2017), 188–194.

51. Banzuiin Chōbei was a Tokugawa-era character who "allegedly fought against injustice, helped the weak, and defeated the strong." He supposedly opposed the shogun's henchmen who "tormented and bullied the townspeople of Edo." Eiko Maruko Siniawer, *Ruffians, Yakuza, Nationalists: The Violent Politics of Modern Japan, 1860–1960* (Ithaca, NY: Cornell University Press, 2008), 114.

52. Giorgio Fabio Colombo, "Sakura Sōgōro: Law and Justice in Tokugawa Japan through the Mirror of a Ghost Story," *Law & Literature* 29, no. 2 (2017): 334–336. Sakura contravened proper Tokugawa legal procedure and went over the heads of local lords to petition the shogun directly. He was executed by crucifixion.

53. Aso guni no eiyakubun (0295). The official call number and title are "Tōnan—soromon bizumaruku—163, Imamura Hitoshi taishō shūsen hiroku," MODA. I thank Aiko Otsuka for typing this out from the handwritten documents. It is unclear if this letter was ever dispatched to the troops.

54. Georgina Fitzpatrick, "The Trials in Rabaul," in *Australia's War Crimes Trials 1945–51*, ed. Georgina Fitzpatrick, Tim McCormack, and Narrelle Morris (Leiden, The Netherlands: Brill Nijhoff, 2016), 556.

55. Timothy Snyder, *Bloodlands: Europe between Hitler and Stalin* (London: Bodley Head, 2010).

56. Dipesh Chakrabarty, *Provincializing Europe: Postcolonial Thought and Historical Difference* (Princeton, NJ: Princeton University Press, 2000), 28.

57. "Mamoranakereba naranu heiwa, jūgonenkan de shakaishugi shiage," *Asahi shimbun*, December 7, 1955, Tokyo morning edition.

58. Uchiyama Kanzō, *Kakōroku: nicchū yūkō no kakehashi* (Heibonsha, 2011), 514–516.

59. Minji Jeong and Youseop Shin, "Post-war Korean Conservatism, Japanese Statism, and the Legacy of President Park Chung-hee in South Korea," *Korean Journal of International Studies* 16, no. 1 (April 2018): 68.

60. Carter Eckert, *Park Chung Hee and Modern Korea: The Roots of Militarism, 1866–1945* (Cambridge, MA: Belknap Press of Harvard University Press, 2016), 4; Miura Hideki, *Goshiki no niji: manshū kenkoku daigaku sotsugyōseitachi no sengo* (Shūeisha, 2015); Barak Kushner, "Introduction: The Search for Meaning in Defeat and Victory," in *In the Ruins of the Japanese Empire: Imperial Violence, State Destruction, and the Reordering of Modern East Asia*, ed. Barak Kushner and Andrew Levidis (Hong Kong: Hong Kong University Press, 2020), 1–24; Hamaguchi Yūko, *Manshūkoku ryūnichi gakusei no nicchū kankeishi: manshū jihen nicchūsensō kara sengo minkan gaikō e* (Keisei shobō, 2015).

61. Barak Kushner, "Ghosts of the Japanese Imperial Army: The 'White Group' (Baituan) and Early Post-war Sino-Japanese Relations," in "Transnationalism and Contemporary Global History," supplement, *Past and Present* 218, no. S8 (2013): 117–150.

62. Jiang Jieshi, "Junguan xunliantuan biye xueyuan de renwu," June 27, 1950, speech in *Zongtong Jianggong sixiang yanlun zongji*, vol. 23, 312–313, http://www.ccfd.org.tw

/ccef001/index.php. I would like to thank Professor Huang Zijin for allowing me to paraphrase from two of his at that time unpublished papers.

63. Jiang Zhongzheng, "Shijiu shiji yilai yazhou de xingshi he women fuguo jianguo de yaodao, (shang)," *Zongtong Jianggong sixiang yanlun zongji*, vol. 29, 96–99, http://www.ccfd.org.tw/ccef001/index.php. I would like to thank Professor Huang Zijin for allowing me to paraphrase from his then unpublished papers.

4. Laying Blame for Japan's War Responsibility

1. "Teki no hijindō, danko hōfuku shingata bakudan ni taisaku o kakuritsu," *Asahi shimbun*, August 9, 1945, morning edition.

2. Shimokawa Masaharu, "Shūsenji no rikushō Anami Korechika: izoku ga kataru jiketsu nanjūnenme no shinjitsu," *Seiron*, (November 2015): 312–325.

3. Georgina Fitzpatrick, "The Trials in Rabaul," in *Australia's War Crimes Trials, 1945–51*, ed. Georgina Fitzpatrick, Tim McCormack, and Narrelle Morris (Leiden, The Netherlands: Brill Nijhoff, 2016), 556–557; Fujiwara Akira, "'Tennō no guntai' no rekishi to honshitsu," *Kikan sensō sekinin kenkyu* 11 (Spring 1996): 62.

4. Norimura Kaneko, *Chiisa na chōsei—kodomo ga mita chūgoku no naisen* (Shakai shisōsen, 1989), 14.

5. Shirōchi Asunobu and Fujigawa Hiroki, *Chōsen hantō de mukaeta haisen: zairyū hōjin ga tadotta kunan no kiseki* (Ōtsuki shoten, 2015), 41–42.

6. Marc Gallicchio, *The Scramble for Asia: US Military Power in the Aftermath of the Pacific War* (Lanham, MD: Rowman and Littlefield, 2008), 29.

7. Christopher Bayly and Tim Harper, *Forgotten Wars: Freedom and Revolution in Southeast Asia* (Cambridge, MA: Belknap Press of Harvard University Press, 2007), 12.

8. "Shengli shoujiang (1)," 002000002120A, in Jiangzhongzheng zongtong wenwu, diancanghao, 002-090105-00012-272, AH.

9. Stephen B. Connor, *Mountbatten's Samurai: Imperial Japanese Forces under British Control, 1945–1948* (Warrington: Seventh Citadel, 2015), 77–93.

10. Bayly and Harper, *Forgotten Wars*, 49.

11. Hayes report to UK Ambassador and Lt. General Sir Adrian Carton de Wiart, September 13, 1945, from Rupert Wingfield-Hayes, "Witnessing Japan's surrender in China," *BBC News Magazine*, September 2, 2015, http://www.bbc.co.uk/news/magazine-34126445.

12. Akiko Hashimoto, *The Long Defeat: Cultural Trauma, Memory, and Identity in Japan* (New York: Oxford University Press, 2015), 8.

13. Komatsu Shinichi, *Ryojin nikki* (Chikuma shobō, 1975), 213.

14. Asahi Shimbun Company, *Media, Propaganda and Politics in 20th-Century Japan*, trans. Barak Kushner (London: Bloomsbury Academic, 2015), 62–69, 71–81.

15. Carol Gluck, "Sekinin/Responsibility in Modern Japan," in *Words in Motion: Toward a Global Lexicon*, ed. Carol Gluck and Anna Lowenhaupt Tsing (Durham, NC: Duke University Press, 2009), 94–97.

16. *Intermittent Diplomat: The Japan and Batavia Diaries of W. Macmahon Ball*, edited and with an introduction by Alan Rix (Melbourne: Melbourne University Press, 1988), 67, diary entry from June 6, 1946.

17. David Cohen and Yuma Totani, *The Tokyo War Crimes Tribunal: Law, History, and Jurisprudence* (Cambridge: Cambridge University Press, 2019), 144.

18. John Dower, *Japan in War and Peace: Selected Essays* (New York: New Press, 1993), 12.

19. Ishizaka Kimishige, "Shūsen zengo no tōdai to wareware ga uketa kyōiku," in *Nanbara Shigeru no kotoba: 8-gatsu 15-nichi, kenpō, gakumon no jiyū*, ed. Tachibana Takashi (Tokyo daigaku shuppankai, 2007), 31–32.

20. Nagai Hitoshi, *Firipin to tainichi senpan saiban: 1945–1953 nen* (Iwanami shoten, 2010), 62. See also Kerstin von Lingen, "Setting the Path for the UNWCC: The Representation of European Exile Governments on the London International Assembly and the Commission for Penal Reconstruction and Development, 1941–1944," *Criminal Law Forum* 25, no. 1 (2014): 45–76; Dan Plesch and Shanti Sattler, "Before Nuremberg: Considering the Work of the United Nations War Crimes Commission of 1943–1948," in *Historical Origins of International Criminal Law: Volume 1*, ed. Morten Bergsmo, Wui Ling Cheah, and Ping Yi. (Brussels: Torkel Opsahl Academic EPublisher, 2014), 437–473.

21. Dai 88kai teikokukaigi, shūgiin, honkaigi, dai2gō, September 5, 1945, JPR. See also Shindō Eiichi, ed., *Ashida Hitoshi nikki*, vol. 1 (Iwanami shoten, 1986), 213.

22. Dai 88kai teikokukaigi, shūgiin, honkaigi, dai2gō, September 5, 1945, JPR.

23. Dai 88kai teikokukaigi, shūgiin, honkaigi, dai2gō, September 5, 1945, JPR.

24. Higashikuni Naruhiko, *Higashikuni nikki* (Tokuma shoten, 1968), 204.

25. Tanaka Hiromi, ed., *Bishikyū senpan kankei shiryōshū*, vol. 3 (Ryokuin shobō, 2012), 33–35.

26. Nagai, *Firipin to tainichi*, 68.

27. "Senpan yōgisha no toriatsukai ni kansuru nihon seifu tōsho no sochi," within Senpan jimu shiryō (shōwa 16–20 nen) sono 1, Honkan 4B-023-00, Hei 11 hōmu 06335100, NAJ.

28. "Senpan yōgisha no toriatsukai ni kansuru nihon seifu tōsho no sochi," within Senpan jimu shiryō (shōwa 16–20 nen) sono 1, Honkan 4B-023-00, Hei 11 hōmu 06335100, NAJ. See also "Senpan mondai ni kansuru moto rikusō Shimomura Sadamushi no kōjutsu, Shōwa 42 nen 1 gatsu," part of the Inoue Tadao archives in Yasukuni kaikō bunko, YSA, 393.4e; Nagai Hitoshi, "Sensō hanzainin ni kansuru seifu seimeian—Higashikuninomiya naikaku ni yoru kakugi kettei no myakuraku," in "Teikoku" to shokuminchi—"dainipponteikoku" hōkai rokujūnen, ed. Nenpō nihon gendaishi henshū iinkai, *Nenpō nihon gendaishi*, vol. 10 (Gendaishiryō shuppan, 2005), 277–321; and Shibata Shin'ichi, "Nihongawa senpan jishu saiban kōsō no tenmatsu" (in *Dainiji sekai taisen—3, shūsen: fukuin to senryō*), *Gunjishigaku* 31, no. 1–2 (September 1995): 338–349.

29. "Senpan mondai ni kansuru moto rikusō Shimomura Sadamushi no kōjutsu."

30. Higashikuni, *Higashikuni nikki*, 239–240.

31. Tanaka Hiromi, ed., *Bishikyū senpan kankei shiryōshū*, vol. 1 (Ryokuin shobō, 2011), 331.

32. Suzuki Tadakatsu kanshū, *Shūsen kara kōwa made*, in series *Nihon gaikōshi*, vol. 26, ed. Kajima kenkyūjo shuppankai (Kajima kenkyūjo shuppankai, 1973), 37. Suzuki Tadakatsu in Amakawa Akira, ed., *Gendaishi o kataru*, vol. 6, *Suzuki Tadakatsu* (Gendai shiryō shuppan, 2008), 187–213. Toyota Kumao says this cabinet decision was never officially released. Toyoda Kumao, *Sensō saiban yoroku* (Taiseisha, 1986), 51.

33. Tanaka, *Bishikyū senpan kankei shiryōshū*, vol. 1, 330.

34. "Senpan yōgisha no toriatsukai ni kansuru nihon seifu tōsho no sochi." The Americans executed Homma in the Philippines in 1945.

35. Sugita Ichiji, "Sensō shūketsu ni tomonau kongo no taikan to teikoku ni tsuite," September 15, 1945, Chūō—sengo shori—80, MODA.

36. Okino Matao, *Ikeru shikabane no ki* (Tōhō shobō, 1999; originally published in 1946), 204; Todaka Kazushige, *Nihon kaigunshi* (PHP kenkyūjo, 2009), 220–221.

37. Nakata Seiichi, *Torēshii nihonhei horyo himitsu jinmonsho* (Kōdansha, 2010), 182–205. It was more unusual for a Japanese POW to be interrogated at Fort Hunt compared with the other secret Camp Tracy.

38. Yamada Akira, "Nihon no haisen to daihonei meirei," *Sundai shigaku*, 94 (March 1995): 147–148.

39. "Shinnihon kensetsu no michi," *Mainichi shimbun*, August 28, 1945, Tokyo morning edition; C. Clinton Godart, "Nichirenism, Utopianism, and Modernity: Rethinking Ishiwara Kanji's East Asia League," *Japanese Journal of Religious Studies* 42, no. 2 (2015): 235–274.

40. Mark Gayn, *Japan Diary* (Rutland, VT: Tuttle Publishers, 1984; second printing), 68.

41. "Senpan jimu shiryō (shōwa 16–20 nen) sono 1," Honkan 4B-023-00, Hei 11 hōmu 06335100, NAJ.

42. Dower, *Embracing Defeat*, 477.

43. Dower, *Embracing Defeat*, 480.

44. Inoue Tadao shiryō, "Sensō saiban ni taisuru nihon seifu no kihon taido narabi ni hōshin," 61023, 393.4. This is written on "Daini fukuinkyoku zanmu shoribu" stationery, no pagination, YSA. See also Toyoda, *Sensō saiban yoroku*, 48–62; Higurashi Yoshinobu, *Tōkyō saiban* (Kōdansha, 2008), 147–150. Udagawa Kōta digs further into preparations and inside Japanese maneuvering concerning the trial in *Tōkyō saiban kenkyū* (Iwanami shoten, 2022).

45. "Haisen no genin oyobi jissō chōsa no ken," October 30, 1945, Kakugiketsu (Cabinet Decision). Japan's national library has a website that details all key cabinet decisions (https://rnavi.ndl.go.jp/politics/entry/bib00678.php).

46. Tomita Kei'ichirō, "Haisen chokugo no sensō chōsakai ni tsuite—seisaku o kenshō suru kokoromi to sono zasetsu," *Refarensu* 63, no. 1 (January 2013): 92–93.

47. Yoshida Yutaka, *Nihonjin no sensōkan: sengoshi no naka no henyō*, rev. ed (Iwanami shoten, 2005), 31. Aoki remembers it as 24th in Shidehara's memoirs. See Shidehara heiwa zaidanhen, ed., *Shidehara Kijūrō* (Shidehara heiwa zaidan, 1955), 590.

48. Shidehara heiwa zaidanhen, *Shidehara Kijūrō*, 589.

49. Shidehara heiwa zaidanhen, *Shidehara Kijūrō*, 592.

50. "Shōwa 20nen 12gatsu 2nichizuke kizokuin [. . .] Matsumura Giichikun no shitsumon," in volume 1 of the collection Sensō chōsakai kankei shiryō, shū1244, MJPHMR. Matsumura was later purged from public office.

51. Tomita, "Haisen chokugo no sensō chōsakai ni tsuite," 85–108.

52. "Tensei jingo" column, *Asahi shimbun*, January 9, 1946, Tokyo morning edition. The translation is from GHQ/SCAP RG 331, box 3462, folder 576 (8), Nov 1945–Sept 1948, MJPHMR.

53. "Sensō chōsakai dai2kai sōkaigi, shōwa 21.4.4," in volume 1 of the collection Sensō chōsakai kankei shiryō, shū1244, MJPHMR.

54. "Sensō chōsakai dai2kai sōkaigi, shōwa 21.4.4," MJPHMR.

55. Inoue Toshikazu, *Sensō chōsakai: maboroshi no seifu bunsho o yomitoku* (Kōdansha, 2017). See also Hirose Yoshihiro, ed., *Sensō chōsakai jimukyoku shorui*, vol. 1 (Yumani shobō, 2015).

56. As quoted in Jongsoo James Lee, *The Partition of Korea after World War II: A Global History* (New York: Palgrave, 2006), 51.

57. Nisso shinzen kyōkaihen, ed., *Soren wa nihon ni nani o nozomuka: tainichi rijikai ni okeru soren daihyō no hatsugen/ Terebuyanko Kisurenko kyōjutsu* (Ōdosha, 1949), 45–46.

58. Nisso shinzen kyōkaihen, *Soren wa nihon ni nani o nozomuka*, 50.

59. Higurashi, *Tokyo saiban*, 149.

60. Higurashi, *Tokyo saiban*, 151–152.

61. Higurashi, *Tokyo saiban*, 153.

62. Higurashi, *Tokyo saiban*, 154–155; Barak Kushner, "Imperial Loss and Japan's Search for Postwar Legitimacy," in *The Dismantling of Japan's Empire in East Asia: Deimperialization, Postwar Legitimation and Imperial Afterlife*, ed. Barak Kushner and Sherzod Muminov (London: Routledge, 2017), 48–65; Urs Matthias Zachmann, "Sublimating the Empire: How Japanese Experts of International Law Translated Greater East Asia into the Postwar Period," in *Dismantling*, 167–181.

63. Komatsu, *Ryojin nikki*, 260–261.

64. Komatsu, *Ryojin nikki*, 262.

65. Yuki Tanaka, "Last Words of the Tiger of Malaya, General Yamashita Tomoyuki," *Asia-Pacific Journal* 3, no. 9 (September 2005): 7. The original Japanese text can be found in Satō Yoshinori and Morita Shōgaku, *Rosubaniosu keijō no ryūseigun: Yamashita Tomoyuki, Honma Masaharu no saigo* (Fuyō shobō, 1981), 34–44, for the whole personal reflection, and 39 for the above specific quote. Morita was the Buddhist cleric who took down these thoughts forty minutes before Yamashita's execution.

66. Duan Ruicong, "Zhanhou riben dui rizhan qijian waijiao junshi de fanxing shuping," *Kangri zhanzheng yanjiu*, dierqi, (2020): 67.

5. The Tyranny of Tiny Decisions

1. Daizaburo Yui, "Democracy from the Ruins: The First Seven Weeks of the Occupation in Japan," *Hitotsubashi Journal of Social Studies* 19, no. 1 (April 1987): 37–38.

2. "Sayoku no dōkō," Naimushō keihokyoku hoanka, no date but estimated at late August, in Awaya Kentaro, ed., *Shiryō nihon gendaishi 2, Haisen chokugo no seiji to shakai*, vol 2. (Ōtsuki shoten, 1981), 170–171. (This is document 70 in the archival collection.)

3. "Sayoku no dōkō," Naimushō keihokyoku hoanka, 171–172. (This is document 71 in the archival collection.)

4. Guillain recounts the whole episode and I have selected a few moments to quote from the larger Japanese language article in Robēru Giran, "Tokkyū o shakuhō saseta no wa, watashi da," *Bungei shunjū* 33, no. 19 (October 1955): 110–116. See also Yoshida Kenji, "'Shōgen,' shūsen no wahei kōsaku to seijihan shakuhō no koro: Yamasaki Sōichishi ni kiku (1)," *Ōhara shakai mondai kenkyūjo zasshi*, no. 626 (December 2010): 51–64.

5. "Japan Wants to Swap Silk, Rayon for Food: Will Ask for Barter to Avert," *Chicago Daily Tribune*, October 4, 1945.

6. Tokuda Kyūichi and Shiga Yoshio, *Gokuchū jūhachinen* (Kōdansha, 2017), 15–17. (The book was originally published in 1947.)

7. Rodger Swearingen and Paul Langer, *Red Flag in Japan: International Communism in Action, 1919–1951* (Cambridge, MA: Harvard University Press, 1952), 107.

8. Swearingen and Langer, *Red Flag in Japan*, 108.

9. Tokuda Kyūichi, *Tokuda Kyūichi zenshū*, vol. 5 (Gogatsu shobō, 1986), 386.

10. Tokuda and Shiga, *Gokuchū jūhachinen*, 74. See also Hyōmoto Tatsukichi, *Nihon kyōsantō no sengo hishi* (Shinchōsha, 2005), 26–30.

11. Tokuda and Shiga, *Gokuchū jūhachinen*, 74.

12. Mark Gayn, *Japan Diary* (Rutland, VT: Tuttle Publishers, 1984; second printing), 10.

13. John K. Emmerson, *The Japanese Thread: A Life in the U.S. Foreign Service* (New York: Holt, Rinehart, and Winston, 1978), 257; *J.K. Emāsonshi danwa sokkiroku* (Naiseishi kenkyū shiryō dai170shū) (Naiseishi kenkyūkai, 1973).

14. Swearingen and Langer, *Red Flag in Japan*, 111.

15. Emmerson, *Japanese Thread*, 258; Takemae Eiji, *Inside GHQ: The Allied Occupation of Japan and Its Legacy*, trans. Sebastian Swann and Robert Ricketts (New York: Continuum, 2001), 239–240.

16. Emmerson, *Japanese Thread*, 259.

17. Yui, "Democracy from the Ruins," 41.

18. Inoue Manabu, "1945nen 10gatsu tōka, 'seijihan shakuhō,'" *Mita gakkai zasshi* 105, no. 4 (January 2013): 761–776.

19. Robert Scalapino, *The Japanese Communist Movement, 1920–1966* (Berkeley: University of California Press, 1967), 45, 72; Central Committee Japanese Communist Party, ed., *Sixty-Year History of Japanese Communist Party, 1922–1982* (Tokyo: Japan Press Service, 1984), 120–145; Kurokawa Iori, *Sensō kakumei no higashi ajia to nihon no komyunisuto, 1920–1970* (Yūshisha, 2020).

20. "Shutsugokusha kangeikai, kyōsanha no kisei," *Asahi shimbun*, October 11, 1945, Tokyo morning edition.

21. Fuse Tatsuji, *Tennōsei no hihan: datō? shiji? kenpōkaisei (shian)* (Shinseikatsu undōsha, 1946).

22. Kamo Michiko, *Woa giruto puroguramu: GHQ jōhō kyōiku seisaku no jitsuzō* (Hōsei daigaku shuppan, 2018), 126.

23. "Tennōsei shiji wa kokumin no ippan kanjō," *Yomiuri shimbun*, December 9, 1945, morning edition.

24. Young-hwan Chong, "The Tokyo Trial and the Question of Colonial Responsibility: Zainichi Korean Reactions to Allied Justice in Occupied Japan," *International Journal of Korean History* 22, no. 1 (February 2017): 77–105.

25. T'ae-gi Kim, *Sengo nihon seiji to zainichi chōsenjin mondai: SCAP no tai zainichi chōsenjin seisaku, 1945–1952nen* (Keisō shobō, 1997), 164.

26. Apichai W. Shipper, "Nationalisms of and against *Zainichi* Koreans in Japan," *Asian Politics & Policy* 2, no. 1 (January 2010): 55–75; Deokhyo Choi, "The Empire Strikes Back from Within: Colonial Liberation and the Korean Minority Question at the Birth of Postwar Japan, 1945–47," *American Historical Review*, (June 2021): 1–30.

27. Kim Chanjun, *Chōsen sōren* (Shinchō shinsho, 2004), 27–28.

28. Deokhyo Choi, "Defining Colonial 'War Crimes': Korean Debates on Collaboration, War Reparations, and the International Military Tribunal for the Far East," in

Debating Collaboration and Complicity in War Crimes Trials in Asia, 1945–1956, ed. Kerstin von Lingen (Cham: Palgrave Macmillan, 2017), 46.

29. John Lie, *Zainichi (Koreans in Japan): Diasporic Nationalism and Postcolonial Identity* (Berkeley: University of California Press, 2008), 39–41.

30. Mark E. Caprio and Yu Jia, "Occupations of Korea and Japan and the Origins of the Korean Diaspora in Japan," in *Diaspora without Homeland: Being Korean in Japan*, ed. Sonia Ryang and John Lie (Berkeley: University of California Press, 2009), 31–32.

31. "Dokuritsu teishin chikau Boku Retsushi no kangeikai," *Yomiuri shimbun*, December 8, 1945, morning edition; T'ae-gi, *Sengo nihon seiji to zainichi chōsenjin mondai*, 209; "Chōsen dokuritsu no ippeisotsu ni shakuhō sareta Boku Retsu [. . .]" *Mainichi shimbun*, December 8, 1945, Tokyo morning edition.

32. "Dokuritu teishin chikau Boku Retsushi no kangeikai," *Yomiuri shimbun*, December 8, 1945, morning edition; T'ae-gi, *Sengo nihon seiji to zainichi chōsenjin mondai*, 210–211.

33. Lie, *Zainichi (Koreans in Japan)*, 42.

34. "Sensō sekinin ni kansuru kettei, Shidehara naikaku giketsutei," November 5, 1945, in Awaya Kentarō, ed., *Shiryō to nihon gendaishi 2—haisen chokugo no seiji to shakai (1)* (Ōtsuki shoten, 1980), 341–343; Akazawa Shirō, "Sengo nihon no sensō sekininron no dōkō," *Ritsumeikan hōgaku*, June 2000, 2607–2633.

35. Yoshida Kenji, "'Minshū shinbun' no shuhitsu toshite (jō): Sunama Ichirōshi ni kiku," *Hōsei daigaku Ōhara shakai mondai kenkyūjo zasshi*, December 2008, 59.

36. Yoshida, "'Minshū shinbun' no shuhitsu toshite (ge): Sunama Ichirōshi ni kiku," *Hōsei daigaku Ōhara shakai mondai kenkyūjo zasshi*, January 2009, 48–60.

37. The event was called the "Kaihō undō shutsugoku dōshi kangei taikai." Yoshida, "'Minshū shinbun' no shuhitsu toshite (ge)," 50.

38. "Sensō sekinin tsuikyū jinmin taikai," *Asahi shimbun*, December 7, 1945.

39. Gayn, *Japan Diary*, 9.

40. Gayn, *Japan Diary*, 11.

41. Gayn, *Japan Diary*, 12.

42. *Nihon rōdō nenkan*, sengo tokushū, vol. 22, which is reproduced online for the Ōhara Institute for Social Research at Hōsei University (https://oisr-org.ws.hosei.ac.jp/images/research/dglb/rn/rn_list/rn1949-387.pdf).

43. "Kyōsantō senpan meibo shukō," *Asahi shimbun*, December 12, 1945, Tokyo morning edition. According to some sources, the JCP's list included the names of some pro-Japanese Korean traitors.

44. "Sanshū no taishū yaku sanman—Nosaka Sanzōshi kikoku," *Asahi shimbun*, January 27, 1946, Tokyo morning edition.

45. Nihon kyōsantō shuppanbu, ed., *Jinmin no te de sensō hanzainin o* (Jinminsha, 1946), 3. The first postwar issue of the JCP's *Red Flag* newspaper (*Akahata*), produced on October 20, 1945, had also called for toppling the imperial system and establishing democracy, digital archive version on Japan's National Diet Library portal, https://www.ndl.go.jp/modern/img_r/100/100-001r.html.

46. Nihon kyōsantō shuppanbu, *Jinmin no te de sensō hanzainin o*, 23.

47. Nihon kyōsantō shuppanbu, *Jinmin no te de sensō hanzainin o*, 24.

48. "Sekai ni kasu rekishi meidai," *Asahi shimbun*, May 2, 1946, Tokyo morning edition.

49. David Wolff, "Japan and Stalin's Policy toward Northeast Asia after World War II," *Journal of Cold War Studies* 15, no. 2 (Spring 2013): 4–29.

50. J. P. Napier, *A Survey of the Japanese Communist Party* (Tokyo: Nippon Times, 1952), 12.

51. Rodger Swearingen, "Japanese Communism and the Moscow-Peking Axis," *Annals of the American Academy of Political and Social Science* 308 (November 1956): 64.

52. Napier, *Survey of the Japanese Communist Party*, 40–41.

53. Napier, *Survey of the Japanese Communist Party*, 45.

54. Charles Willoughby, *Shanghai Conspiracy: The Sorge Spy Ring* (New York: EP Dutton, 1952), preface, p. 5.

55. Chelsea Szendi Schieder, "The Only Woman in the Room: Beate Sirota Gordon, 1923–2012," *Dissent*, January 15, 2013, https://www.dissentmagazine.org/blog/the-only-woman-in-the-room-beate-sirota-gordon-1923-2012.

56. Chalmers Johnson, *An Instance of Treason: Ozaki Hotsumi and the Sorge Spy Ring*, expanded ed. (Stanford, CA: Stanford University Press, 1990), 200–201.

57. Johnson, *Instance of Treason*, 208.

58. JCP chairman Miyamoto Kenji was quoted as saying as much. "Jidai sakugo no hitotsu," *Asahi shimbun*, December 31, 1980, Tokyo morning edition.

59. Erik Esselstrom, "From Wartime Friend to Cold War Fiend: The Abduction of Kaji Wataru and U.S.-Japan Relations at Occupation's End," *Journal of Cold War Studies* 17, no. 3 (Summer 2015): 177.

60. Willoughby, *Shanghai Conspiracy*, 274 (italics are mine).

61. Willoughby, *Shanghai Conspiracy*, 314–315.

62. Institute of Pacific Relations, *Hearings before the Subcommittee to Investigate the Administration of the Internal Security Act and Other Internal Security Laws of the Committee on the Judiciary*, United States Senate, Eighty-second Congress, first[-second] session by United States. Congress. Senate. Committee on the Judiciary, 1951–1952, 748, https://archive.org/stream/instituteofpacif03unit#page/748/mode/2up.

63. Reto Hoffman, "What's Left of the Right: Nabeyama Sadachika and Anticommunism in Transwar Japan, 1930–1960," *Journal of Asian Studies* 79, no. 2 (2020): 3.

64. Brian Tsui, *China's Conservative Revolution: The Quest for a New Order, 1927–1949* (Cambridge: Cambridge University Press, 2018); Hao Chen, "Resisting Bandung? Taiwan's Struggle for 'Representational Legitimacy' in the Rise of the Asian Peoples' Anti-Communist League, 1954–57," *International History Review*, (May 2020): 1–21.

65. Chen Guting, *Zhanhou riben gongchandang de toushi* (Taipei: Zhongri wenhua jingji xiehui yanjiusuo, 1954), 69.

66. See "Schemes for Survival of the Imperial," in Hata Ikuhiko, *Hirohito: The Showa Emperor in War and Peace*, ed. Marius B. Jansen (Leiden: Brill, 2007), 88–159.

67. See Fujiwara Akira, Yoshida Yutaka, and Awaya Kentarō, eds., *Tettei kenshō shōwa tennō "dokuhakuroku"* (Ōtsuki shoten, 1991).

68. *Chokurei dai 511 gō*, in Ōkurashō insatsukyoku, ed., *Kanpō*, gōgai, November 3, 1946, the National Diet Library Digital Collections, http://dl.ndl.go.jp/info:ndljp/pid/2962456?tocOpened=1.

69. *Chokurei dai 511 gō*.

70. "Sanjūsanmannin ni onsharei taishatō nana shurui no kōhan'i ni wataru," *Yomiuri shimbun*, November 3, 1946, morning edition.

71. Katō Kyōko, *Shōwa tennō shazai shōchoku sōkō no hakken* (Bungei shunjū, 2003); Peter Mauch, "Emperor Hirohito's Post-surrender Reflections," *Journal of American-East Asian Relations* 29, no. 2 (2022): 221–228.

72. Ōe Hiroyo and Kaneda Toshimasa, "Kokuritsu kōbunshokan shozō 'sensō hanzai saiban kankei shiryō' no keisei katei to bishikyū sensō saiban kenkyū no kanōsei," *Rekishigaku kenkyū*, no. 930 (April 2015): 22.

73. Chūō—shūsen shori—546, "Dai 23 gunshireikan rikugun chūjō (rikushi nijūni-ki) Tanaka Hisakazu-shi ni kansuru chūgoku saiban kiroku, sono 4," MODA.

74. Alessio Patalano, *Post-war Japan as a Sea Power: Imperial Legacy, Wartime Experience and the Making of a Navy* (London: Bloomsbury Academic, 2015).

75. Fujiwara Akira, "'Tenno no guntai' no rekishi to honshitsu," *Kikan sensō sekinin kenkyū* 11 (Spring 1996): 61; Fujiwara Akira, "'Eirei' wa nan no tame ni shinda no ka—inujini o megutte," *Chūkiren*, 11gō, (December 1999): 2–15; Tanaka Hiromi, *Kesareta Makkāsā no tatakai—nihonjin ni surikomareta taiheiyō sensōshi* (Yoshikawa kōbunkan, 2014), 38–39.

76. "Sensō sekinin o toinaosu natsu," *Nihon keizai shimbun*, August 1, 1994, evening edition; Fujiwara, "'Tennō no guntai' no rekishi to honshitsu," 67.

77. Fujiwara, "Eirei wa nan no tame ni shinda no ka," 2–15.

78. Oda Makoto, *Nanshi no shisō* (Iwanami shoten, 2008), 5–6; Yoshida Yutaka, *Heishitachi no sengoshi: sengo nihon shakai o sasaeta hitobito* (Iwanami shoten, 2020).

79. Hirai Kazuomi, "Saikō Oda Makoto to beheiren: beheiren e no sanka to nanshi no shisō kagai no ronri," *Kokuritsu rekishi minzoku hakubutsukan kenkyū hōkoku*, dai 216shū, (March 2019): 19.

6. The Violence of Imperial Dissolution at the Periphery

1. Wang Lin, "Wo zai shangbai yu riben zhanfu yixitan," *Deqing wenshi ziliao*, di erji, November 1988, 92–94.

2. Marc Gallichio, *The Scramble for Asia: US Military Power in the Aftermath of the Pacific War* (Lanham, MD: Rowman and Littlefield, 2008), 75.

3. Shen Zhihua, *Saigo no tenchō: Mō Takuto Kimu Iruson jidai no chūgoku to kitachōsen*, vol. 1 (Iwanami shoten, 2016), 75–103. This was also the case of Chinese violence against the Japanese in a mass event known as the Tonghua Incident in February 1946. See "'Tsūka jiken' o happyō fukuinkyoku Yoshida rusu gyōmu buchō [. . .]," *Asahi shimbun*, December 4, 1952, Tokyo morning edition; "Shūsengo no higeki wasurenai, kyūmanshū tsūka jiken kara nanjūnen, shimin gisei, shinsō motomeru," *Nihon keizai shimbun*, February 3, 2016; Lu Minghui, *Tonghua "er san" shijian* (Beijing: Shijie zhishi chubanshe, 2006).

4. Adam Cathcart, "Nationalism and Ethnic Identity in the Sino-Korean Border Region of Yanbian, 1945–1950," *Korean Studies* 34 (2010): 25–26.

5. Cathcart, "Nationalism and Ethnic Identity," 32.

6. Hirata Koji, "From the Ashes of Empire: The Reconstruction of Manchukuo's Enterprises and the Making of China's Northeastern Industrial Base, 1948–1952," in *Overcoming Empire in Post-imperial East Asia: Repatriation, Redress and Rebuilding*, ed. Barak Kushner and Sherzod Muminov (London: Bloomsbury Publishers, 2020), 147–162.

7. Amy King, *China-Japan Relations after World War II: Empire, Industry and War, 1949–1971* (Cambridge: Cambridge University Press, 2016), 51.

8. Yamaguchi Mitsufumi, *Boku wa hachirogun no shōnenhei datta*, new edition (Sōshisha, 2006), 70–71.

9. Yamaguchi, *Boku wa hachirogun no shōnenhei datta*, 72–74.

10. Satō Takumi and Son An-Sok, eds., *Higashi ajia no shūsen kinenbi: haiboku to shōri no aida* (Chikuma shobō, 2007).

11. Lori Watt, "Embracing Defeat in Seoul: Rethinking Decolonization in Korea, 1945," *Journal of Asian Studies* 74 (2015): 153–174; Mark Caprio, "The Politics of Collaboration in Post-liberation Southern Korea," in *In the Ruins of the Japanese Empire: Imperial Violence, State Destruction, and the Reordering of Modern East Asia*, ed. Barak Kushner and Andrew Levidis (Hong Kong: Hong Kong University Press, 2020), 27–49.

12. Liu Ximing, *Weijun: qiangquan jingzhuxia de zuzi (1937–1949)* (Taipei: Daoxiang chubanshe, 2002).

13. Liu, *Weijun*, 374.

14. Wang Qisheng, "China's Response to Ichigo," in *Battle for China: Essays on the Military History of the Sino-Japanese War of 1937–1945*, ed. Mark Peattie, Edward Drea, and Hans van de Ven (Stanford, CA: Stanford University Press, 2011), 416–417.

15. Liu, *Weijun*, 385–386.

16. Sebastian Conrad, "The Dialectics of Remembrance: Memories of Empire in Cold War Japan," *Comparative Studies in Society and History* 56, no. 1 (2014): 6.

17. Hans van de Ven discusses this in *China at War: Triumph and Tragedy in the Emergence of the New China, 1937–1952* (Cambridge, MA: Profile Books, 2018).

18. Yoshimi Shunya, "1940 nendai haisen to sengo no aida de," in *Hitobito no seishinshi*, vol. 1, *Haisen to senryō—1940nendai*, ed. Yoshimi Shunya and Kurihara Akira (Iwanami shoten, 2015), 1-15; Barak Kushner, "Introduction: The Search for Meaning in Defeat and Victory," in Kushner and Levidis, *Ruins*, 1–24.

19. Awaya Kentarō, ed., *Shiryō nihon gendaishi, 2: haisenchokugo no seiji to shakai 1* (Ōtsuki shoten, 1980), 42.

20. "Taiwan no genkyō," Gaimushō kanrikyoku sōmubu nanpōka, Shōwa 21.2.10, bugaihi, Microfilm, K'0006, MOFAAJ.

21. Kan Lee, "The 'China Lobby' in Tokyo: The Struggle of China's Mission in Japan for General Douglas MacArthur's Military Assistance in the Chinese Civil War, 1946–1949," *Journal of Chinese Military History* 8 (2019): 29–51.

22. Adam Cathcart, "Bullets of a Defeated Nation: The 1946 Shibuya Incident," in Kushner and Levidis, *Ruins*, 111.

23. Cathcart, "Bullets of a Defeated Nation," 99; Barak Kushner, *Men to Devils, Devils to Men: Japanese War Crimes and Chinese Justice* (Cambridge, MA: Harvard University Press, 2016), 130–136.

24. Yang Zizhen, "Teikoku nihon no hōkai to kokumin seifu no taiwan sesshū: sengo shoki nittai kankei ni okeru datsu shokuminchika no daikō" (PhD diss. at Tsukuba daigaku [Kokusai seiji keizaigaku], 2012), 124–133.

25. Cathcart, "Bullets of a Defeated Nation," 112–113; Yoshimi Yoshiaki, "Senryōka nihonjin no chūgokukan, 1945–1949," in *Nicchū kankeishi no shomondai*, ed. Saito Michihiko (Hachiōji-shi: Chūō daigaku shuppanbu, 2009), 191–221.

26. Chen Tsui-lian, *Chonggou ererba* (Taipei: Weicheng chuban, 2017), 48.

27. Chen, *Chonggou ererba*, 54–56; Steve Tsang, "From Japanese Colony to Sacred Chinese Territory: Taiwan's Geostrategic Significance to China," *Twentieth-Century China* 45, no. 3 (October 2020): 351–368.

28. Victor Louzon, "From Japanese Soldiers to Chinese Rebels: Colonial Hegemony, War Experience, and Spontaneous Remobilization during the 1947 Taiwanese Rebellion," *Journal of Asian Studies* 77, no. 1 (February 2018): 170.

29. Kamisago Shōshichi, *Kenpei sanjūichinen* (Tōkyō sensho, 1955), 18–19.

30. Kamisago, *Kenpei sanjūichinen*, 20.

31. Victor Louzon, "L'Incident du 28 février 1947, dernière bataille de la guerre sino-japonaise? Legs colonial, sortie de guerre et violence politique à Taiwan" (Programme doctoral histoire Centre d'histoire de Sciences Po, Doctorat en histoire, Institut d'études politiques de Paris, Ecole Doctorale De Sciences Po, France, December 2016).

32. "Taiwan kara no hōkoku, taiwan gunkanku sanbōchō, October 18–23, 1945," in *Shiryō nihon gendaishi, 3: haisen chokugo no seiji to shakai 2*, ed. Awaya Kentarō (Ōtsuki, 1981), 281–282.

33. Peng Ming-min, *A Taste of Freedom: Memoirs of a Formosan Independence Leader* (New York: Holt, Rinehart and Winston, 1972), 48.

34. Peng, *Taste of Freedom*, 63–73.

35. Peng, *Taste of Freedom*, 161.

36. Wakabayashi Masahiro, *Taiwan no seiji: chūkaminkoku taiwanka no sengoshi* (Tokyo daigaku shuppankai, 2008), 43–44.

37. Chen, *Chonggou ererba*, 162; Jin Yilin, *Guomindang gaoceng de paixi zhengzhi*, rev. ed. (Beijing: Shehui kexue wenxian chubanshe, 2016).

38. Chen, *Chonggou ererba*, 76.

39. Ka Gilin, *Taiwan gendaishi:ni ni hachi jiken o meguru rekishi no saikioku* (Heibonsha, 2014), 85–86.

40. The US government recorded the incident in *United States Relations with China: With Special Reference to the Period 1944-1949* (Washington, DC: Government Printing Office, 1949), 926.

41. *United States Relations with China*, 927.

42. *United States Relations with China*, 931.

43. Chen, *Chonggou ererba*, 333–335.

44. *United States Relations with China*, 936.

45. George Kerr, *Formosa Betrayed* (Boston: Houghton Mifflin, 1965), 97.

46. Victor Louzon, "From Japanese Soldiers to Chinese Rebels: Colonial Hegemony, War Experience, and Spontaneous Remobilization during the 1947 Taiwanese Rebellion," *Journal of Asian Studies*. 77, no. 1 (February 2018): 173.

47. Takashi Fujitani, *Race for Empire: Koreans as Japanese and Japanese as Americans during World War II* (Berkeley: University of California Press, 2011).

48. Louzon, "From Japanese Soldiers to Chinese Rebels," 175.

49. Jan Kiely, *The Compelling Ideal: Thought Reform and the Prison in China, 1901–1956* (New Haven, CT: Yale University Press, 2014), 257.

50. Chen, *Chonggou ererba*, 454–455.

51. Hsu Hsueh-chi, "Manzhouguo zhengfuzhong de taiji gongwu renyuan (1932–1945)," in *Taiwan lishi de duoyuan chuancheng yu xiangqian*, ed. Hsu Hsueh-chi (Taipei: Zhongyang yanjiuyuan taiwanshi yanjiusuo, 2014), 19.

52. R. Ashton, Gill Bennett, and Keith Hamilton, eds., *Documents on British Policy Overseas*, series 1, vol. 8, *Britain and China, 1945–1950*, Great Britain, Foreign and Commonwealth Office (London: Routledge, 2002), 94–95 ("Note by A.L. Scott on Formosa," [F 6408/2443/10] 7 May 1947).

53. Julia Strauss, *State Formation in China and Taiwan: Bureaucracy, Campaign, and Performance* (Cambridge: Cambridge University Press, 2020), 127–129; Stephan Feuchtwang, *After the Event: The Transmission of Grievous Loss in Germany, China and Taiwan* (Oxford: Berghahn Books, 2011), 113–135; Fang-Long Shih, "Memory, Partial Truth and Reconciliation without Justice: The White Terror Luku Incident in Taiwan," *Taiwan in Comparative Perspective* 3 (March 2011): 140–151.

54. Fang-Long, "Memory, Partial Truth and Reconciliation without Justice," 143.

55. As quoted by L. K. Little in his interview of Sun in 1951, in Chihyun Chang, ed., *The Chinese Journals of L. K. Little, 1943–1954: An Eyewitness Account of War and Revolution*, vol. 3, *The Financial Advisor, 1950–1954* (London Routledge, 2018), 235.

56. Sayaka Chatani, *Nation-Empire: Ideology and Rural Youth Mobilization in Japan and Its Colonies on Taiwan* (Ithaca, NY: Cornell University Press, 2018), 257–263 for Taiwan; 264–270 concerning Korean youths.

57. Hayashi Miki, *Senpan ni torawareta shokuminchihei no sakebi* (Miyazaki: Ono kōsoku insatsu kaisha, 1988), 45. See also Shi-chi Mike Lan, "'Crime' of Interpreting Taiwanese Interpreters as War Criminals of World War II," in *New Insights in the History of Interpreting*, ed. Kayoko Takeda and Jesús Baigorri-Jalón (Amsterdam: John Benjamins, 2016), 193–223.

58. Barak Kushner, "Treacherous Allies: The Cold War in East Asia and American Postwar Anxiety," *Journal of Contemporary History* 45, no. 4 (October 2010), 1–34.

59. Michael Hoare, "Taiwan's Darker Past: Emerging Histories of the World-War II Prisoner of War Camps," European Association for Taiwan Studies, Paris, March 31, 2006 (a conference paper). See the film about former POW Ben Wheeler made by his daughter in 1981, https://www.nfb.ca/film/war_story/.

60. "Soldiering on to Seek War Crimes Justice," *South China Sunday Morning Post*, February 19, 1989; Daniel Schumacher, "Strategies of World War II Commemoration in Hong Kong and Singapore" (Dissertation zur Erlangung des akademischen, Grades eines Doktors der Philosophie vorgelegt von Konstanz University, 2013), 261.

61. Suzannah Linton, "Rediscovering the War Crimes Trials in Hong Kong, 1946–48," *Melbourne Journal of International Law* 13, no. 1 (2012): 284–348; Renmin fayuanbaoshe, ed., *Zhengyi de shenpan: jinian zhongguo renmin kangri zhanzheng shengli qishi zhounian* (Beijing: Renmin fayuan chubanshe, 2016), 264.

62. Jack Edwards, *Banzai You Bastards* (Hong Kong: Souvenir Press, 1990), 259–261. See UK national archives (WO 235/1028, KGNA) for the full trial record where Edwards details the abuse, maltreatment, and deaths in Kinkaseki.

63. Sarah Kovner, *Prisoners of the Empire: Inside Japanese POW Camps* (Cambridge, MA: Harvard University Press, 2020), 132–133; Utsumi Aiko, *Nihongun no horyo seisaku* (Aoki shoten, 2005).

64. See John Pritchard's critique on a POW website and critique of this view: https://www.fepow-community.org.uk/monthly_revue/html/atrocities.htm (accessed June 15, 2020).

65. Li Zhanping, "Chushi shangzhanchang—beipoluozhou zhanfu Lian Amu," *Lishi yuekan*, (246) (2008): 49–56.

66. Ts'ai Hui-yu and Wu Ling-ching, *Zuoguo liangge shidai de ren—taiji ribenbing* (Taipei: Institute of Taiwan History, Academia Sinica, 2008), 287–304, https://www.fepow-community.org.uk/monthly_revue/html/atrocities.htm.

67. Linda Holmes, *Unjust Enrichment: How Japan's Companies Built Postwar Fortunes Using American POWs* (Mechanicsburg, PA: Stackpole Books, 2001) and David Bergamini, *Japan's Imperial Conspiracy* (New York: William Morrow and Company, 1971) are problematic in this regard. Charles D. Sheldon, "Japanese Aggression and the Emperor, 1931–1941, from Contemporary Diaries," *Modern Asian Studies* 10, no. 1 (1976): 1–40.

68. "Jiaqiang duiriben xuanchuan," 0200000014875A, Ministry of Foreign Affairs memo, AH.

69. Hei11-hōmu 4A-18-1831, "Daisan kokujin (kankoku, taiwan) senpansha shakuhōmondai, senpansha engo mondai kankei shorui," written July 1953, NAJ.

70. Sugamo isho hensankaihen, *Seiki no isho* (Kōdansha, 1984), 587.

71. Sugamo isho hensankaihen, *Seiki no isho*, 32.

72. Sugamo isho hensankaihen, *Seiki no isho*, 545.

73. Sugamo isho hensankaihen, *Seiki no isho*, 437.

74. Barak Kushner, "Gōhōsei to teikoku—taiwan o jirei to shita nicchū kankei ni okeru 'seigi' o meguru tatakai," *Chūgoku 21* 45 (February 2017): 81–105.

75. Kimu Shijon, *Chōsen to nihon ni ikiru: chejutō kara ikaino e* (Iwanami shoten, 2015).

76. Ja-hyun Chun, "Delayed Reconciliation and Transitional Justice in Korea: Three Levels of Conditions for National Reconciliation," *Asian Journal of Social Science* 45 (2017): 295.

77. John Merrill, "The Cheju-do Rebellion," *Journal of Korean Studies* 2 (1980): 139–197; Su-Kyoung Hwang, *Korea's Grievous War* (Philadelphia: University of Pennsylvania Press, 2016).

78. Hun Joon Kim, *The Massacres at Mt. Halla: Sixty Years of Truth Seeking in South Korea* (Ithaca, NY: Cornell University Press, 2014), 14–15.

79. Hun, *Massacres at Mt. Halla*, 24.

80. Hun, *Massacres at Mt. Halla*, 29–36.

81. Hun, *Massacres at Mt. Halla*, 44.

82. Carter J. Eckert, *Park Chung Hee and Modern Korea: The Roots of Militarism, 1866–1945* (Cambridge, MA: Harvard University Press, 2016), 87. Koreans who fought for empire and remained in Japan became postwar social outcasts. See Maureen Cheryn Turim, *The Films of Oshima Nagisa: Images of a Japanese Iconoclast* (Berkeley: University of California Press, 1998), 219–222. Film director Ōshima Nagisa edited a documentary about their plight, *Wasurerareta kōgun*, which aired on Japanese television on August 16, 1963. Ōshima Nagisa, "People of the Forgotten Army," in *Cinema, Censorship, and the State: The Writings of Nagisa Oshima, 1956–1978*, ed. and with an introduction by Annette Michelson, trans. Dawn Lawson (Cambridge, MA: MIT Press, 1992), 71; "Wareware no hoshō darega, kokuseki naiga kōgun datta—zainichi kankokujin no sengo hoshō soshō," *Mainichi shimbun*, July 16, 1994, Tokyo morning edition; "Ōshima Nagisa kantoku, maboroshi no 30ppun sakuhin *wasurerareta kōgun*, konya hanseiki buri hōsō," *Asahi shimbun*, January 12, 2014, Tokyo morning edition.

83. See Su-kyoung Hwang, *Korea's Grievous War* (Philadelphia: University of Pennsylvania Press, 2016).

84. Wada Haruki, *The Korean War—an International History*, trans. Frank Baldwin, (Lanham, MD: Rowman & Littlefield, 2014), xv; Wada Haruki, "Chōsen mondai to wareware no sekinin," *Gekkan shakaitō*, (January 1985): 46–55.

85. Hirano Ryūji, "Chōsen sensō ni okeru tairitsu kōzō no kigen," in *Senryakushi toshite no ajia reisen*, eds. Akagi Kanji and Konno Shigemitsu (Keiō gijuku daigaku shuppan, 2013), 108.

86. Wada, *Korean War*, xxvii.

87. Tessa Morris-Suzuki, "Prisoner Number 600,001: Rethinking Japan, China, and the Korean War 1950–1953," *Journal of Asian Studies* 74, no. 2 (May 2015): 413.

88. David Cheng Chang, *The Hijacked War: The Story of Chinese POWs in the Korean War* (Palo Alto, CA: Stanford University Press, 2020), 60.

89. Chou Hsiu-huan, ed., *Zhanhou waijiao shiliao huibian: hanzhan yu fangong yishibian*, vol. 1 (Taipei: Guoshiguan, 2005), 14.

90. David Chang, *Hijacked War*, 14.

91. Huang Tiancai, *Wo zai 38duxian de huiyi* (Taipei: INK yinke wenxue chuban, 2010), 72–80; Shen Xingyi, *Yiwansiqian ge zhengren: hanzhan shiqi 'fangong yishi' zhi yanjiu* (Taipei: Guoshiguan, 2013), 212.

92. Chou Hsiu-huan, ed., *Zhanhou waijiao shiliao huibian: hanzhan yu fangong yishipian*, vol. 2 (Taipei: Guoshiguan, 2006), 303–304; Chou Hsiu-huan, "Jieyun hanzhan fangong yishi laitai zhi yanjiu, (1950–1954)," *Guoshiguan guankan*, 28qi, (June 2011): 124; Lan Shi-chi, "Cong 'womende' zhanzheng dao 'beiyiwangde' zhanzheng: Taiwan dui 'hanzhan' de lishi jiyi," *Dongyaguannianshi jikan*, di7qi, (December 2014): 224.

93. "Meiguo de xinlizhan chedi shibai le," *Renmin ribao*, January 25, 1954.

94. David Chang, *Hijacked War*, 6.

95. Pingchao Zhu, "'Disgraced Soldiers': The Ordeal of the Repatriated POWs of the Chinese Volunteer Army from the Korean War," *Journal of Chinese Military History* 4 (2015): 163; Jin Daying, "Accounts of the Chinese People's Volunteers Prisoners of War: A Translation" (master's thesis, University of Montana, 1993).

96. Zhu, "'Disgraced Soldiers,'" 192.

97. Bao Mingrong, "Zhongguo renmin zhiyuanjun zai kangmei yuanchao zhanzhengzhong de zhanfu zhengce," *Junshi lishi*, di 6qi, 2001, 11.

98. Zhu, "'Disgraced Soldiers,'" 168.

99. Zhu, "'Disgraced Soldiers,'" 174.

100. He Ming, *zhongcheng: zhiyuanjun zhanfu guilai renyuan de kanke jingli* (Beijing: Zhongguo wenshi chubanshe, 1998), 128; Zhang Zeshi, *Wo de chaoxian zhanzheng: yi ge zhiyuanjun zhanfu de liushinian huiyi* (Beijing: Jincheng chubanshe, 2010), 207–215.

7. The Geography of Power

1. In its first two years of incarcerating counterrevolutionaries in the former Ward Road Gaol, the CCP executed more prisoners than had been executed by previous administrations since 1900. Frank Dikotter, *Crime, Punishment and the Prison in Modern China* (New York: Columbia University Press, 2002), 366

2. *West Australian*, June 19, 1947.

3. As quoted in Kirsten Sellars, "Introduction," in *Trials for International Crimes in Asia*, ed. Kirsten Sellars (Cambridge: Cambridge University Press, 2016), 9.

4. William Sebald, *With MacArthur in Japan: A Personal History of the Occupation* (London: Cresset Press, 1967), 165.

5. Sebald, *With MacArthur in Japan*, 173.

6. Hanayama Shinshō, *Heiwa no hakken: sugamo no sei to shi no kiroku* (Asahi shimbunsha, 1949), 309–310.

7. Sebald, *With MacArthur in Japan*, 174.

8. Hanayama, *Heiwa no hakken*, 311.

9. Sebald, *With MacArthur in Japan*, 174.

10. "Riben zhongyao zhanfan shijiuming mengzongjing quanbu shifang bing xuanbu zhanfan qingsuan gao jieshu," *Shenbao*, December 25, 1948. The CCP's main organ, *Renmin ribao*, criticized MacArthur's decision more bluntly, "Riben zhongyao zhanfanren duo meidi jing weifa shifang," on December 31, 1948.

11. Kiyose Ichirō, *Hiroku tōkyō saiban* (Chūō kōron shinsha, 2002), 177–178.

12. *Senkō sanzenri* (Mainichi wanzu, 2008; originally published in 1950); translated by Nigel Brailey, ed., *Masanobu Tsuji's 'Underground Escape' from Siam after the Japanese Surrender* (Global Oriental, 2009).

13. Advertisement in *Yomiuri shimbun*, June 2, 1950.

14. "Reports on the Rearmament Activities of Tsuji Masanobu and Hattori Takushiro," declassified CIA memo, May 3, 1951, https://www.cia.gov/readingroom/docs/TSUJI%2C%20MASANOBU%20%20%20VOL.%201_0016.pdf.

15. RG 263, Records of the Central Intelligence Agency, Second Release of Name Files, Tschoudnowsky, Leonid to Tymewycz, Roman, vol. 2, box 130, Tsuji Masanobu folder, vol. 1, NARA.

16. RG 263, Records of the Central Intelligence Agency, Second release of name files under the Nazi War crimes and Japanese imperial government disclosure acts, 1936–2002 (reference set), Tschoudnowsky, Leonid to Tymewycz, Roman, box 130, Tsuji Masanobu folder, vol. 1, confidential Department of State memo, February 24, 1956, NARA.

17. Mark Mazower, *No Enchanted Palace: The End of Empire and the Ideological Origins of the United Nations* (Princeton, NJ: Princeton University Press, 2009), 122–127; Donna-Lee Frieze, *Totally Unofficial: The Autobiography of Raphael Lemkin* (New Haven, CT: Yale University Press, 2013), 89–97; Philippe Sands, *East West Street* (London: W&N Publishers, 2016).

18. Kerstin von Lingen, "Setting the Path for the UNWCC: The Representation of European Exile Governments of the London International Assembly and the Commission for Penal Reconstruction and Development, 1941–1944," *Criminal Law Forum* 25 (2014): 48; Valentyna Polunina, "The Human Face of Soviet Justice? Aron Trainin and the Origins of the Soviet Doctrine of International Criminal Law," in *Stalin's Soviet Justice: "Show" Trials, War Crimes Trials, and Nuremberg*, ed. David M. Crowe (London: Bloomsbury Academic, 2019), 127–144.

19. Rebecca West, *A Train of Powder* (New York: Viking Press, 1955; originally published in 1946), 3.

20. "Aoyama saijō no kaikōshiki," *Yomiuri shimbun*, December 24, 1948.

21. Hei11 hōmu 4A-021-00, "Shichi senpan kaikōshiki no omoide, Nagai Watarushidan kōbunsho," NAJ. The interviewee, Naigai, was interviewed by Inoue Tadao about his experiences on December 22, 1962.

22. Professor Yan Haijian, interview by the author in Nanjing, May 27, 2019.

23. "Zhanzheng zuifan chuli weiyuanhui duiri zhanfan chuli zhengce huiyi jilu," 020-010117-0039-0017a-0029a, part of the Zhanfan chuli zhengce (2) series, AH.

24. Bob Wakabayashi, "The Nanking 100-Man Killing Contest Debate: War Guilt amid Fabricated Illusions, 1971–75," *Journal of Japanese Studies* 26, no. 2 (Summer 2000): 307–340.

25. Benjamin Uchiyama, *Japan's Carnival War: Mass Culture on the Home Front, 1937–1945* (Cambridge: Cambridge University Press, 2019), 47.

26. Li Donglang, "Guomindang zhengfu dui riben zhanfan de shenpan," *Bainianchao*, di 6 qi, 2005, 27–35; Luo Junsheng, "Shi Meiyu yu zhanhou nanjing dui rijun zhanfan de shenpan," *Dangshi zonglan*, di 1qi, 2006, 20–26.

27. Honda Katsuichi, *Chūgoku no tabi* (Asahi shimbunsha, 1972); Honda Katsuichi, *The Nanjing Massacre, a Journalist Confronts Japan's National Shame*, trans. Karen Sandness (London: M.E. Sharpe, 1991), 125–135. See also Mukai Chieko, "'Mujitsu da!' Chichi no sakebi ga kikoeru," *Seiron*, (March 2000): 60–71.

28. Kasahara Tokushi, *Hyakuningiri kyōsō to nankin jiken: Shijitsu no kaimei kara rekishi taiwa e* (Ōtsuki shoten, 2008), 201.

29. Wang Junyan, *Riben zhanfan shenpan miwen* (Beijing: Zhongguo huaqiao chubanshe, 1995), 298.

30. Shanghai hongkouqu danganbian, *Dongjing shenpan* (Shanghai: Shanghai shudian chubanshe, 2007), foreword by Gao Wenbin, 3–4.

31. Zhang Linfeng, "Bu neng wanque de lishi—fang dongjing shenpan qinlizhe Gai Wenbin," *Lianhe shibao*, February 28, 2014; "Koushu: Gao Wenbin, wo suo jingli de dongjing dashenpan," *Sanlian shenghuo zhoukan*, August 15, 2014.

32. "Mengjun zaihua youguan zhanzui sheshi," 020-010117-005-146a-147a, AH.

33. Greg Leck, *Captives of Empire: The Japanese Internment of Allied Civilians in China, 1941–1945* (Bangor, PA: Shandy Press, 2006); Henry Pringle, *Bridge House Survivor: Experiences of a Civilian Prisoner-of-War in Shanghai & Beijing, 1942–1945* (Hong Kong: Earnshaw Books, 2011).

34. "Mengjun zaihua youguan zhanzui sheshi," 020-010117-005-149a-151a, AH.

35. Li Zhiqun, interview by the author, Shanghai, June 5, 2019.

36. "'Jiangyin zhihu,' 'changshu zhilang' zuori zhixing shizhong qiangjue," *Zhonghua ribao*, June 18, 1947.

37. Li Yechu, "Sharen mowang shanghai fufa jishi," *Shanghaitan*, no. 224 (2005): 16–20.

38. Li Yechu, "'Changshulang' yu 'jiangyinhu' de mori," *Shanghaitan*, (February 1989): 27.

39. Li Liang, *Guonanji* (self-pub., 2012), 19. I thank Dai Chengxian for helping me procure a copy of this self-published memoir.

40. Dai Chengxian, interview for the documentary series. Shanghai guangbo dianshitai jilupian zhongxin Chen Yinan gongzuoshi, ed., *Yatai zhanzheng shenpan* (Shanghai: Shanghai jiaotong daxuechubanshe, 2021), 153–156.

41. May 30, 2019, interview with Liu Linsheng, Taiyuan, Shanxi Province. The book is Liu Linsheng, *Zhongguo de aosiweixin: rijun 'taiyuan jizhongying' jishi* (Taiyuan: Shanxi renmin chubanshe, 2012).

42. The other one is the Shenyang WWII Allied Prisoners Camp Site Museum.

43. Tom Phillips, "China Rebuilds Its Forgotten 'Auschwitz' to Remember Japan's Brutality," *The Guardian*, September 1, 2015.

44. Li, "'Changshulang' yu 'jiangyanghu' de mori," 29.

45. Zhongguo dier lishi danganguan, Shanghai jiaotong daxue dongjing shenpan yanjiu zhongxin, ed., *Zhongguo duiri zhanfan shenpan dangan jicheng*, vol. 1 (Shanghai: Shanghai jiaotong daxue chubanshe, 2019), 4. (There are 102 volumes in the entire series.)

46. The center changed its name to the Research Institute of War Trial and World Peace at Shanghai Jiaotong University.

47. Liu Tong, *Dashenpan: guomindang zhenfu chuzhi riben zhanfan shilu* (Shanghai: Shanghai renmin chubanshe, 2021), see table on 876.

48. Liu, *Dashenpan*, 875–887; Yan Haijian, "Fanzui shudi yuanze yu zhengju zhongxin zhuyi: zhanhou beiping duiri shenpan de shitai yu tezhi," *Minguo dangan*, (January 2018): 135. See also Yan Haijian, *Guomin zhengfu shenpan riben zhanfan yanjiu*, Nanjing: Jiangsu renmin chubanshe, 2022.

49. Yan Haijian, "Kuanda yihuo kuanzong: zhanhou guomin zhengfu duiri zhanfan chuzhi lunxi," *Nanjing shehui kexue*, di 7qi, (2014): 146.

50. Yan Haijian, "Tongxiang zhanhou shenpan zhilu: mengguo dui erzhan zhanzui chengchu niyi shulun," *Nanjing shehui kexue*, di 2qi, (2016): 154.

8. Creating a Theater of Law in Mao's China

1. Alexander Pantsov and Steven Levine, *Mao: The Real Story* (London: Simon and Schuster, 2012), 368.

2. "First Conversation between N.S. Khrushchev and Mao Zedong, Hall of Huaizhentan [Beijing]," July 31, 1958, History and Public Policy Program Digital Archive, Archive of the President of the Russian Federation, APRF, fond 52, opis 1, delo 498, ll. 44–477; copy in Dmitry Volkogonov Collection, Manuscript Division, Library of Congress, Washington, DC, translated by Vladislav M. Zubok, http://digitalarchive.wilsoncenter.org/document/112080.

3. Sandra Wilson, "The Sentence Is Only Half the Story: From Stern Justice to Clemency for Japanese War Criminals, 1945–1958," *Journal of International Criminal Justice* 13, no. 4 (September 2015): 749.

4. "Faxue zhuanjia Mei Ruao fabiao tanhua [. . .]," *Renmin ribao*, March 14, 1950.

5. Sherzod Muminov, *Eleven Winters of Discontent: The Siberian Internment and the Making of a New Japan* (Cambridge, MA: Harvard University Press, 2022); Amy King and Sherzod Muminov, "'Japan Still Has Cadres Remaining': Japanese in the USSR and Mainland China, 1945–1956," *Journal of Cold War Studies* 24, no. 3 (2022): 200–230.

6. "Conversation between A. Vyshinsky and Mao Zedong, Moscow," January 6, 1950, History and Public Policy Program Digital Archive, AVP RF, f. 0100, op. 43, d. 43, papka 302, ll. 1–5; provided by O. A. Westad; translation for CWIHP by Daniel Rozas, http://digitalarchive.wilsoncenter.org/document/112676. Xu Jingli, "Sulian

zhaohui zhongguo zhengfu tiyi zu tebie guoji fating shenpan rihuang deng xijun zhanfan," *Guoji wenti yanjiu*, di 6qi, (2005): 63–67.

7. Mao Zedong, "Lun renmin minzhu zhuanzheng," *Renmin ribao*, July 1, 1949. See also Wen-Shun Chi, ed., *Readings in Chinese Communist Documents: A Manual for Students of the Chinese Language* (Berkeley: University of California Press, 1966), 8.

8. Alison Adcock Kaufman, "In Pursuit of Equality and Respect: China's Diplomacy and the League of Nations," *Modern China* 40, no. 6 (2014): 605–638.

9. Shao-chuan Leng, *Justice in Communist China: A Survey of the Judicial System of the Chinese People's Republic* (New York: Oceana Publications, 1967), xi.

10. Fukushima Masao, Ubugata Naokichi, and Hasegawa Ryōichi., *Chūgoku no saiban* (Tokyo keizai shinpōsha, 1957), 63.

11. Shao-chuan, *Justice in Communist China*, xii.

12. Andrei Y. Vyshinsky, *Law of the Soviet State* (New York: Macmillan, 1948), 5.

13. "Lectures in the General Principals of Criminal Law in the People's Republic of China," series 1, box 75, folder 3, p. 18, SLRA. This is a US Department of Commerce translation in March 1962 of a 1957 Chinese textbook on law for Chinese political judicial cadres.

14. "Xinfaxue yanjiuyuan chengli, Shen Junru yuanzhang zhici [. . .]," *Renmin ribao*, January 5, 1950. Dong's longer speech, "Jiu sifa gongzuo renyuan de gaizao wenti," January 4, 1950, is in *Dong Biwu faxue wenji*, ed. Dong Biwu faxue wenji (Beijing: Falu chubanshe, 2001), 26–37.

15. Henry Wei, *Courts and Police in Communist China to 1952*, series 1, no. 1, 1952, "Studies in Chinese Communism," research done for Maxwell Air Force Base, Alabama, published by Air Force Personnel and Training Research Center, Lackland Air Force Base Texas, December 1955, 8.

16. Mei Ruao, "Nihon no zento—nihon no kōfuku goshūnen o kinen shite kisu," in *Nicchū no hyakunijūnen no bungei hyōron sakuhinsen 4*, ed. Chō Kyō and Murata Yūjirō (Iwanami shoten, 2016), 115–123. (The original article was in Chinese: Mei Ruao, "Riben de qiantu—wei jinian riben touxiang wuzhounian erzuo," *Shijie zhishi* [May 16, 1950].)

17. Mei Ruao, "Quan yazhou remin duiyu riben renmin de qidai," *Shijie zhishi*, di 39qi, (1952): 5.

18. Mei, "Quan yazhou remin duiyu riben renmin de qidai," 7.

19. Mei Ruao's commentary, "Bai Jokō-shi no nihon senpan shorihyō," in *RP shiryō kaisetsuban*, Radio puresu tsūshinsha, (June 23, 1956).

20. Jin Weihua, "Li Fang: chuting gongsu riben zhanfan," *Jiancha fengyun*, no. 19 (2009): 64–68. The top-secret training was coordinated by the Supreme People's deputy procurator Tan Zhengwen. Tan worked with Li Fushan, Quan Weicai, Bai Buzhou, and Jing Zhuguo, among others. See also Edgar H. Schein, "Some Observations on Chinese Methods of Handling Prisoners of War," *Public Opinion Quarterly* 20, no. 1 (Spring 1956): 321–327.

21. The originals were first published under a different title in 2006, then repackaged and sold as part of the *Wenshi ziliao baibu jingdian wenku*, a series of the Top 100 most important historical collections. See *Huiyi gaizao zhanfan* (vols. 1 and 2), ed. Quanguo zhengxie wenshi he xuexi weiyuanhuibian (Beijing: Zhongguo wenshi chubanshe, 2013); in Japanese see Arai Toshio shiryō hozonkai, ed., *Chūgoku bujun senpan*

kanrijo shokuin no shōgen: shashinka Arai Toshio no nokoshita shigoto (Nashi no kasha, 2003).

22. Wang Shilin, interview in Taiyuan, Shanxi Province, May 30, 2019. See also Shanghai guangbo dianshitai jilupian zhongxin Chen Yinan gongzuoshi, ed., *Yatai zhanzheng shenpan* (Shanghai: Shanghai jiaotong daxuechubanshe, 2021), 207–208.

23. "Dong Biwu zai diliuci quanguo gongan huiyi shang guanyu zhengzhi falu sixiang gongzuo fangmian jige wenti de baogao," June 2, 1954, CMPD.

24. Jeffrey Kinkley, *Chinese Justice, the Fiction: Law and Literature in Modern China* (Stanford, CA: Stanford University Press, 2000), 18.

25. "Dong Biwu zai diliuci quanguo gongan huiyi shang guanyu zhengzhi falu sixiang gongzuo fangmian jige wenti de baogao," June 2, 1954, CMPD.

26. Percy R. Luney Jr., "Traditions and Foreign Influences: Systems of Law in China and Japan," *Law and Contemporary Problems* 52, no. 2 (1989): 135–136.

27. Tang Shichun, "Jianguo chuqi laihua sulian faxue zhuanjia de qunti kaochao," *Huanqiu falu pinglun*, di5qi, (2010): 135.

28. Tang, "Jianguo chuqi laihua sulian faxue zhuanjia de qunti kaochao," 140. The author here is quoting the work of Shen Zhihua. He Qinhua, "Guanyu xinzhongguo yizhi sulian sifa zhidu de fansi," *Zhongwai faxue*, di3qi, August 2002, http://h286851.w276.mc-test.com/Item/Show.asp?m=1&d=544; Yu Min-ling, "Xuexi sulian: zhonggong xuanchuan yu minjian huiying," *Zhongyang yanjiuyuan jindaishi yanjiusuo jikan*, di 40qi, (June 2003): 99–139.

29. Kinkley, *Chinese Justice, the Fiction*, 14.

30. Shi Liang, "Guanyu chedi gaizao he zhengdun geji renmin fayuan de baogao," *Renmin zhoubao*, di 35qi, 1952, 22–23.

31. Sun Huei-min, "Minguo shiqi shanghai de nulushi, (1927–1949)," *Jindai zhongguo funushi yanjiu*, (14) (2006): 51–88.

32. Shi Liang, "Report on Reform and Reorganization of the People's Courts (extract), August 13, 1952," from http://www.commonprogram.science/documents/Report%20on%20Reform%20and%20Reorganization%20of%20the%20People's%20Courts.pdf; Shi Liang, "Guanyu chedi gaizao he zhengdun geji renmin fayuan de baogao," *Renmin ribao*, August 23, 1952.

33. Liu Fengjing, "Sifa linian de chujiu yu buxin," *Zhongwai fashi yanjiu*, di 1qi, (2009): 96–105.

34. Zhou Tiandu and Sun Caixia, *Shi Liang: minmeng lishi renwu* (Beijing: Qinyan Press, 2011), 301–302.

35. Tang Shichun, "1955nian zhongguo sifa gongzuo fangsu daibiaotuan yu sulian fazhi xingxiang de suzao," *Zhongguo shehui kexueyuan jindaishisuo qingnian xueshu luntan* (2008): 475–490.

36. Shi Liang, "Dui sulian sifa gongzuo de jidian tihui," *Faxue yanjiu* (June 1955) : 13–15.

37. Ceng Hanzhou, He Lanjie, and Lin Hengyuan, "Fangwen suweiai fayuan de jidian tihui," *Faxue yanjiu*, (June 1955): 16–19.

38. Zhou and Sun, *Shi Liang*, 309.

39. Wang Huai'an, "Sulian sifa ganbu shi youxiu de, ganbu gongzuo de jingyan shi fengfu de," *Faxue yanjiu*, (June 1955): 22–24.

40. Jennifer Altehenger, "Simplified Legal Knowledge in the Early PRC: Explaining and Publishing the Marriage Law," in *Chinese Law: Knowledge, Practice, and Transformation, 1530s to 1950s*, ed. Madeleine Zelin and Li Chen (Leiden: Brill, 2015), 343.

41. Wang Ruqi, "Xinzhongguo lushi zhidu dianji," *Falu shuoshi lunpin* (JM Review), di1qi, zongdi14qi, (2014): 6–7; He Bihui, "Wang Ruqi: Xinzhongguo diyibu 'huninfa' zhibiren," *Shiji*, 1qi, (2012): 55–57. Wang Ruqi is also mentioned by Ōsawa Takeshi, "The People's Republic of China's 'Lenient Treatment' Policy towards Japanese War Criminals," in *Trials for International Crimes in Asia*, ed. Kirsten Sellars (Cambridge: Cambridge University Press, 2016), 160.

42. "Guanyu shifang riben zhanfan wenti de qingshijian, baogao, minglingdeng," Danghao 105-00220-06(1), CMOFA.

43. "Dong Biwu, Shen Junru, Zhang Xiruo zai diyijie quanguo renmin daibiao dahui dierci huiyishang de fayan, July 23, 1955," CMPD.

44. "Dong Biwu, Shen Junru, Zhang Xiruo zai diyijie quanguo renmin daibiao dahui dierci huiyishang de fayan, July 23, 1955," CMPD.

45. George Ginsburgs, "Soviet Sources on the Law of the Chinese People's Republic," *University of Toronto Law Journal* 18, no. 2 (Spring 1968): 182.

46. The team was assisted by Shi Liang, Zhong Hanhua, Chen Shuliang, Li Fushan, Zhang Zhirang, Pan Zhenya, and Zhou Gengsheng.

47. Sui Shuying, "20shiji wushiniandai zhongguo dui riben zhanfan de shenpan yu shifang," *Yantai daxue xuebao* (zhexue shehui kexueban), 19, no. 4 (October 2006): 461.

48. "The Secret Speech That Changed World History," *The Observer*, February 26, 2006, https://www.theguardian.com/world/2006/feb/26/russia.theobserver.

49. Sergey Radchenko, "The Sino–Russian Relationship in the Mirror of the Cold War," *China International Strategy Review* 1 (2019): 273–274.

50. "From the Journal of Ambassador P. F. Yudin, Record of Conversation with Mao Zedong, 31 March 1956," April 5, 1956, History and Public Policy Program Digital Archive, AVPRF, fond 0100, opis 49, papka 410, delo 9, listy 87–98; also Center for Storage of Contemporary Documentation (TsKhSD), fond 5, opis 30, delo 163, listy 88–99; see also Problemi Dalnego Vostok 5 (1994), 101–110. Translated by Mark Doctoroff, http://digitalarchive.wilsoncenter.org/document/116977.

51. "Guanyu zhencha riben zhanfan de zhuyao qingkuang he chuli yijian de baogaodeng," Danghao 105-00501-07(1), CMOFA.

52. Dangdai zhongguo congshu bianji weiyuanhui, ed., *Dangdai zhongguo de gongan gongzuo* (Beijing: Dangdai zhongguo chubanshe, 1992), 98–99. Zhang Xudong and Zhang Kun calculate 817 KMT war criminals imprisoned, though their sources are difficult to trace. Zhang Xudong and Zhang Kun, "Guomindang zhanfan gaizao shimo," *Bainianchao*, di6qi, (2016): 53.

53. Arai Toshio shiryō hozonkai, ed., *Chūgoku bujun senpan kanrijo shokuin no shōgen: shashinka Arai Toshio no nokoshita shigoto* (Nashi no kasha, 2003), 407; Jin Weihua, "Li Fang: chuting gongsu riben zhanfan," *Jiancha fengyun*, no. 19 (2009): 64–68.

54. Luo Ruiqing, "Guanyu zhanzheng zuifan wenti de fayan, March 1956," CPMD.

55. Luo, "Guanyu zhanzheng zuifan wenti de fayan, March 1956," CPMD. File FO 371/110212, "Arrests, Trials and Executions of Counter-revolutionaries in CPG: Conviction of Captured US airmen (Folder 4), 1954," KGNA. Nicholas Dujmovic, "Two

CIA Prisoners in China, 1952–73 Extraordinary Fidelity," *Studies in Intelligence* 50, no. 4 (2006): 21–36. See also John Delury, *Agents of Subversion: The Fate of John T. Downey and the CIA's Covert War in China* (Ithaca: Cornell University Press, 2022); John T. Downey, Thomas J. Christensen, and Jack Lee Downey *Lost in the Cold War: The Story of Jack Downey, America's Longest-Held POW* (New York: Columbia University Press, 2022).

56. "Chen Jiakang 28/4, Chen buzhang zhuli shenpi Chen Shuliang, March 27, baogao" (Top secret), Danghao 105-00502-04, CMOFA.

57. "Zhonggong zhongyang guanyu zhengqiu duijiang, ri, wei zhanfan he qita fangeming zuifan de chuli yijian de tongzhi," Zonghao (56) 049, April 11, 1956, CMPD.

58. "Zhonggong zhongyang guanyu zhengqiu duijiang, ri, wei zhanfan he qita fangeming zuifan de chuli yijian de tongzhi," Zonghao (56) 049, April 11, 1956, CMPD. Wang Yaowu was the translator for KMT general He Yingqin and Japanese general Okumura Yasuji at the surrender ceremony in September 1945 Nanjing.

59. "Zhonggong zhongyang guanyu zhengqiu duijiang, ri, wei zhanfan he qita fangeming zuifan de chuli yijian de tongzhi," Zonghao (56) 049, April 11, 1956, CMPD.

60. Leif Dahlberg, *Spacing Law and Politics: The Constitution and Representation of the Juridical* (Oxon: Routledge, 2016), 2–5 explains the visual aspect of being at court.

61. I explore the details of the trials in chapter 7, "Socialist Magnanimity: The CCP Trials," in *Men to Devils*.

62. "Riben zhanfan cengzai zheli tongche huiguo," September 3, 2015, Zhengyi de shenpan zhi xinzhongguo shenpan shenyang, *Renmin fayuanbao*, special edition.

63. "Riben zhanfan cengzai zheli tongche huiguo," September 3, 2015.

64. "Guanyu zhenya fangeming douzheng wenti he chuli juya zai woguode riben zhanzhengfanzuifenzi wenti: zuigao renmin jianchayuan Zhang Dingcheng jianchazhang zai diyijie quanguo renmin daibiao dahui disanci huiyishang de fayan, June 22, 1956," CARMD.

65. "Rang fachui qiaoxiang lishi de jingzhong," *Renmin fayuanbao*, September 3, 2014. The Liaison Group is normally referred to as *Chūkiren* in Japanese. For more insight into the group's postwar activities, see Ishida Ryūji and Chan Honbo (Zhang Hongbo in Chinese), *Shinchūgoku no senpan saiban to kikokugo no heiwa jissen* (Shakai hyōronsha, 2022).

66. Kinkley, *Chinese Justice, the Fiction*, 24.

67. "Riben zhanfan huiguo yihou de fanying, riben duiwo panchu shifang rizhanfan fanying, youguan shenpan zhanfan de cankao qingkuang gangyao," Danghao: 105-00503-11(1), CMOFA.

68. "Riben zhanfan huiguo yihou de fanying, riben duiwo panchu shifang rizhanfan fanying, youguan shenpan zhanfan de cankao qingkuang gangyao," Danghao: 105-00503-11(1), CMOFA.

69. "Shōkan yokuryū kakokusa ukabu kyūsoren tōroku kādo 252ninbun kaiji = tokushū," *Yomiuri shimbun*, August 10, 2019, Osaka morning edition.

70. "Beishifang de riben zhanzheng fanzui fenzi huiguohou—zaibiaoshi fandui zhanzheng he ganxie zhongguo de kuanda," *Renmin ribao*, September 11, 1956.

71. Wang Shilin, interview. See also Wang Shilin, "Canyu zhenxun riben zhanfan gongzuo de huigu," in *Huiyi gaizao zhanfan*, shangce, ed. Quanguo zhengxie wenshi he xuexi weiyuanhui (Beijing: Zhongguo wenshi chubanshe, 2013), 170–178.

72. Liu Meiling, ed., *Riben qinhua zhanfan bigong*, 10 vols. (Beijing: Zhongguo dangan chubanshe, 2005).

73. Xiaoyang Hao, "What Is Criminal and What Is Not: Prosecuting Wartime Japanese Sex Crimes in the People's Republic of China," *China Quarterly* 242 (June 2020): 529–549.

74. Uesaka Masaru's confession in Zhongyang danganguan, ed., *Zhongyang danganguancang riben qinhua zhanfan bigong xuanbian*, diyiji, vol. 1 (Beijing: Zhonghua shuju, 2015), preface.

75. Uesaka Masaru's confession in Zhongyang danganguan, *Zhongyang danganguancang riben qinhua zhanfan bigong xuanbian*, diyiji, vol. 1, 299.

76. Uesaka Masaru's confession in Zhongyang danganguan, *Zhongyang danganguancang riben qinhua zhanfan bigong xuanbian*, diyiji, vol. 1, 385.

77. "Lushi: wenming shenpan bukehuoque de yihuan," in *Zhengyi de shenpan zhi xinzhongguo shenpan shenyang*, series, special issue of *Renmin fayuanbao tekan*, September 3, 2015, online magazine, http://rmfyb.chinacourt.org/.

78. "Lushi: wenming shenpan bukehuoque de yihuan."

79. "Lushi: wenming shenpan bukehuoque de yihuan."

80. Wang Zhanping, ed., *Zhengyi de shenpan: zuigao renmin fayuan tebie junshi fating, shenpan riben zhanfan jishi* (Beijing: Renmin fayuan chubanshe, 1990), 441.

81. Wang, *Zhengyi de shenpan*, 441.

82. Bōeichō bōeikenshūsho, senshishitsu, ed., *Hokushi chiansen 2*, vol. 50 of the Senshi sōsho series, Asagumo shimbunsha, 1971, 169.

83. Bōeichō bōeikenshūsho, senshishitsu, *Hokushi chiansen 2*, vol. 50, 170.

84. Ishikiriyama Hideaki, *Nihongun dokugasu sakusen no mura* (Kōbunken, 2003), 35; Aiko Otsuka, "Narratives of a Fallen Army: Japanese Veterans' Concepts of Defeat and War Crimes Responsibility in World War Two" (PhD diss., University of Cambridge, 2019).

85. Ishikiriyama Hideaki, "Nihongun dokugasu sakusen no mura," *Shūkan kinyōbi*, (June 23, 1995): 48–50.

86. Ishikiriyama, *Nihongun dokugasu sakusen no mura*, 44–45.

87. Ishikiriyama, *Nihongun dokugasu sakusen no mura*, 50–53.

88. Ishikiriyama, *Nihongun dokugasu sakusen no mura*, 58; Arai Toshio, "Kyōjutusho wa, kō shite kakareta," *Sekai*, (May 1998): 68–136. This included the confessions of Suzuki Hiraku, Fujita Shigeru, Uesaka Masaru, Nagashima Tsutomu, and Sassa Shinnosuke.

89. See one unnamed Japanese researcher's blog where he notes problems when trying to access these records, "Kōhyō o habakaru naiyō nanode kōhyō dekimasen," on the blog *Hachirogun kenkyū memo*, November 17, 2010, https://smtz8.hatenadiary.org/entry/20101117/1290269562.

90. Marcus K. Billson, "Inside Albert Speer: Secrets of Moral Evasion," *Antioch Review* 37, no. 4 (Autumn 1979): 460–474; Gitta Sereny, *Albert Speer: His Battle with Truth* (New York: Knopf, 1995).

91. Matsuno Seiya, *Nihongun no dokugasu heiki* (Gaifūsha, 2005), 302–310.

92. David Cohen and Yuma Totani, *The Tokyo War Crimes Tribunal: Law, History, and Jurisprudence* (Cambridge: Cambridge University Press, 2019), 201–202; Jeanne Guillemin, *Hidden Atrocities: Japanese Germ Warfare and American Obstruction of Justice at the Tokyo Trial* (New York: Columbia University Press, 2017), 201–204; Boris Yudin,

"Research on Humans at the Khabarovsk War Crimes Trial: A Historical and Ethical Examination," in *Japan's Wartime Medical Atrocities: Comparative Inquiries in Science, History, and Ethics*, ed. Jing Bao Nie, Nanyan Guo, Mark Selden, and Arthur Kleinman (London: Routledge, 2010), 61.

93. Zhongyang danganguan, ed., *Zhongyang danganguancang riben qinhua zhanfan bigong xuanbian*, diyiji, vol. 5, 469; Onishi Yasumitsu, "Tamura Taijirō kenkyū (2) sanseishō senpan no shuki kara," *Mita daigaku nihongogaku bungaku*, (18), (June 2007): 75–85.

94. Shanxisheng renmin jianchayuan, ed., *Zhenxun riben zhanfan jishi (taiyuan), 1952–1956* (Beijing: Xinhua chubanshe, 1995), 300.

95. Zhongyang danganguan, *Zhongyang danganguancang riben qinhua zhanfan bigong xuanbian*, diyiji, vol. 5, 470.

96. Zhongyang danganguan, *Zhongyang danganguancang riben qinhua zhanfan bigong xuanbian*, diyiji, vol. 5, 471.

97. Shanxisheng renmin jianchayuan, *Zhenxun riben zhanfan jishi (taiyuan), 1952–1956*, 301; Zhang Yaojie, "Huorenba Zhao Peixian—rikou jizhongying zhenshi gushi," *Yanhuang chunqiu*, 7qi, (2005): 55–56. The original story of the use of POWs as human targets was published as "Jindi canhai fulu, rending 'huoruo bazi' gong qi cisha," *Jiefang ribao*, August 31, 1942.

98. Shanxisheng renmin jianchayuan, *Zhenxun riben zhanfan jishi (taiyuan), 1952–1956*, 302.

99. Shanxisheng renmin jianchayuan, *Zhenxun riben zhanfan jishi (taiyuan), 1952–1956*, 303. See also Wang *Zhengyi de shenpan*, 625–627.

100. "Chūkyō yokuryū senpan zenbu no shakuhō o," *Asahi shimbun*, June 23, 1956, Tokyo morning edition. A few months later the *Asahi* would suggest that the several hundred released war criminals from China repatriating to Japan had been "brainwashed" because they all criticized Japan in the same way. "Tensei jingo," *Asahi shimbun*, August 1, 1956, Tokyo, morning edition; However, a letter to the editor on the same day, August 1, in the *Asahi* newspaper, "Jishuteki ni sennō shimashō," suggested many Japanese leaned toward the type of personal reflection the former war criminals from China exhibited, in contrast to the released Class A war criminals who only criticized their incarceration and learned nothing from it. Petra Buchholz, "Confessions of Japanese POWs after Re-education in China," in *Broken Narratives Post-Cold War History and Identity in Europe and East Asia*, ed. Susanne Weigelin-Schwiedrzik (Leiden: Brill, 2014), 229.

101. Released in several issues of *Sekai* magazine starting in May 1998, 88–101. Arai Toshio and Fujiwara Akira, eds., *Shinryaku no shōgen: chūgoku ni okeru nihonjin senpan jihitsu kyōjutusho* (Iwanami shoten, 1999); Okabe Makio, Ogino Fujio, and Yoshida Yutaka, eds., *Chūgoku shinryaku no shōgenshatachi: "ninzai" no kiroku o yomu* (Iwanami shoten, 2010).

102. "Yūzai 45nin no kyōjutsusho, hōdō shashinka ga nyūshu 56nen chūgoku de no senpan saiban," *Asahi shimbun*, April 5, 1998, morning edition.

103. "Sensō no sugata, tantan to saibanmaeni 'kandai na shobun' chūgoku no nihonjin senpan kyōjutsusho," *Asahi shimbun*, April 5, 1998, Tokyo, morning edition.

104. Tanabe Toshio, "Chūgoku senpan Suzuki Hiraku chūjō no yūryo—Suzuki chūjō ga kakinokoshita chōbun no 'shuki' nihen wa kōkinka no 'kyōjutsusho' no shinraisei o hitei suru," *Seiron*, (October 1999): 274.

105. Tanabe, "Chūgoku senpan Suzuki Hiraku chūjō no yūryo," 274–287. His whole article tries to assert that point.

106. Suzuki Hiraku confession in Arai and Fujiwara, *Shinryaku no shōgen*, 18–19. See the original confession mention of poison gas in Zhongyang danganguan, ed., *Zhongyang danganguancang riben qinhua zhanfan bigong xuanbian*, diyiji, vol. 1, 57.

107. Yoshimi Yoshiaki, *Dokugasusen to nihongun* (Iwanami shoten, 2004), 272.

108. Ishida Ryūji, "Kandaisa e no ōtō kara sensō sekinin e: aru moto heishi no owarinaki ninzai o megutte," *PRIME*, 31gō, (March 2010): 59–72.

109. Chūgoku kikansha renrakukai, ed., *Kaette kita senpantachi no kōhansei* (Osaka: Shinpū shobō, 1996), 31–34.

110. Chūgoku kikansha renrakukai, *Kaette kita senpantachi no kōhansei*, 36–37.

111. Chūgoku kikansha renrakukai, *Kaette kita senpantachi no kōhansei*, 589–590. The show was *Senpantachi no kokuhaku bujun, taigen senpan kanrijo 1062nin no shuki*.

112. Ishida Ryūji, "Chūgoku no senpan shogū hōshin ni miru 'kandaisa' to 'genkakusa': shoki no senpan kyōiku o chūshin ni," *PRIME*, (32) (October 2010): 68.

113. Ishida, "Chūgoku no senpan shogū hōshin ni miru 'kandaisa' to 'genkakusa,'" 69.

114. Frederick C. Teiwes, *Politics and Purges in China* (New York: M.E. Sharpe, 1979), 275–329.

115. Kinkley, *Chinese Justice, the Fiction*, 24. For an exegesis on the anti-Rightist movement and legal excesses, see Sebastian Veg, "Testimony, History and Ethics: From the Memory of Jiabiangou Prison Camp to a Reappraisal of the Anti-Rightist Movement in Present-Day China," *China Quarterly* 218 (June 2014): 514–539.

9. The Pathology of Justice in Post-Occupation Japan

1. Toyota's plan related, in part, to BC class war crimes trials in Yokohama. See Kiyonaga Satoshi, *Senpan o sukue: bishikyū yokohama saiban hiroku* (Shinchōsha, 2015), 125–137. For global consideration of problems connected to the treaty, see Kawashima Shin and Hosoya Yūichi, eds., *San furanshisuko kōwa to higashi ajia* (Tōkyō daigaku shuppankai, 2022).

2. Hei 11nen hōmu 4B, 23, 6290, "Sensō saiban kiroku shiryō (sensō saiban no kiroku mokuji (an) shōwa 27nendo gyōmushi, nijūnana. ni. Nijūnana sensō saiban no kiroku henshū no hōshin (an), shōwa nijūhachi nendo gyōmu uchiawase hoka), by Toyota Kumao," January 1952, NAJ.

3. Hei 11nen hōmu 4B, 23, 6290, "Sensō saiban kiroku shiryō (sensō saiban no kiroku mokuji (an) shōwa 27nendo gyōmushi, nijūnana. ni. Nijūnana sensō saiban no kiroku henshū no hōshin (an), shōwa nijūhachi nendo gyōmu uchiawase hoka), by Toyota Kumao," January 1952, NAJ.

4. Hei 11nen hōmu 4B, 23, 6290, "Sensō saiban kiroku shiryō (sensō saiban no kiroku mokuji (an) shōwa 27nendo gyōmushi, nijūnana. ni. Nijūnana sensō saiban no kiroku henshū no hōshin (an), shōwa nijūhachi nendo gyōmu uchiawase hoka), by Toyota Kumao," January 1952, NAJ.

5. Heisei 11nen 4A-21-6340, "Sensō saiban kankei jimu shiryō bassui," shōwa 16–20, NAJ.

6. Nariaki Nakazato, *Neonationalist Mythology in Postwar Japan: Pal's Dissenting Judgment at the Tokyo War Crimes Tribunal* (Lanham, MD: Lexington Books, 2016), 144–145.

7. "Bishikyū senpan no shamen, Kimura hōmu sōsai genmei saiban kakoku ni shinsei, sensōhanzai," *Asahi shimbun*, April 30, 1952, Tokyo evening edition.

8. "'Senpan' ni taisuru ninshiki to naikaku sōri daijin no yasukuni jinja sanpai ni kansuru shitsumon shuisho," (teishutsusha Noda Yoshihiko, shitsumon dainijūichigō, heisei17nen 10gatsu 17nichi teishutsu), The House of Representatives, Japan, (*shūgiin*), 163rd Parliamentary Session, November 17, 2005, 21st question session, JPR; Utsumi Aiko and Udagawa Kōta, "Sensō to sabaki: ōsutoraria saiban to hikokunin," *Ōsaka keizai hōka daigaku ajia taiheiyō kenkyū sentā nenpō* (2016): 2–8, claim it was Attorney General Ōhashi Takeo who issued the directive. Sheila A. Smith, *Intimate Rivals: Japanese Domestic Politics and a Rising China* (New York: Columbia University Press, 2015), 99, 295.

9. "Senpan shakuhō ikensho nihon bengoshiren ga shukō," *Yomirui shimbun*, June 22, 1952, morning edition; Sandra Wilson, Dean Aszkielowicz, Beatrice Trefalt, and Robert Cribb., *Japanese War Criminals: The Politics of Justice after the Second World War* (New York: Columbia University Press, 2017), 164–195.

10. Eiko Maruko Siniawer, *Ruffians, Yakuza, Nationalists: The Violent Politics of Modern Japan, 1860–1960* (Ithaca, NY: Cornell University Press, 2008), 159.

11. "Ōhaba na onsha kōryo kōwa no hakkōshi ni Ōhashi sōsai tōben kakuiinkai," *Asahi shimbun*, November 13, 1951, Tokyo evening edition.

12. 12shū-hōmu iinkai, 12gō, November 14, 1951, JPR.

13. Tanaka Masaaki, *Pāru hanji no nihon muzairon* (Shōgakukan, 2001); Yoshimatsu Masakatsu, ed., *Senshi o yaburu: nihon wa muzai nari* (Nihon shoseki insatsu tōkyō shisha, 1952); Suzuki Chieko, "Maboroshi de wa nakatta 'hyakuningiri kyōsō,'" *Chūkiren*, no. 27 (Winter 2003): 6.

14. Kei Ushimura, "Pal's 'Dissentient Judgment' Reconsidered: Some Notes on Postwar Japan's Responses to the Opinion," *Japan Review*, no. 19 (2007): 218.

15. Hiro Saito, *The History Problem: The Politics of War Commemoration in East Asia* (Honolulu: University of Hawaii Press, 2017), 27.

16. Sebastian Conrad, *The Quest for the Lost Nation: Writing History in Germany and Japan in the American Century* (Berkeley: University of California Press, 2010), 245.

17. Wang Weibin, "Zai chūgoku nihonjin no hikiage ni kansuru ichikōsatsu," *Shūdō hōgaku*, 27kan, 2gō, (2005): 159.

18. Casper Wits, "Foreign Correspondents in the East Asian Cold War: The Sino-Japanese Journalist Exchange of 1964," *Modern Asian Studies* 54, no. 5 (2020): 1–37.

19. Li Feng, "1950nendai no nicchū bōeki kankei—nicchū bōeki sokushin dantai no katsudō o chūshin ni" (PhD diss., Kobe University, 2014).

20. Besshi Yukio, "Sengo nicchū kankei to hiseishiki sesshokusha," *Kokusai seiji*, dai75gō, (October 1983): 99.

21. Sun Pinghua (Son Heika in Japanese), *Chūgoku to nihon ni hashi o kaketa otoko* (Nihon kezai shinbunsha, 1998), 77.

22. Ishikawa Tadao, Nakajima Mineo, and Ikei Masaru, eds., *Sengo shiryō nicchū kankei* (Nihon hyōronsha, 1970), 23–24; Mayumi Itoh, *The Making of China's Peace with Japan: What Xi Jinping Should Learn from Zhou Enlai* (New York: Palgrave MacMillan, 2017), 14–21.

23. Okazaki Yūji, "Ikeda Masanosuke to sengo shoki nicchū bōeki (ge)—minkan bōeki kyōtei ni honsō—shōnai shusshin seijika no sokuseki," *Tōhoku kōeki bunka daigaku*

sōgō kenkyū ronshū, forum 21 4, (2002): 117–138; Amy King, *China-Japan Relations after World War II: Empire, Industry and War, 1949–1971* (Cambridge: Cambridge University Press, 2016), 83–86.

24. Kōra Tomi, *Hisen o ikiru—Kōra Tomi jiden* (Domesu, 1983), 171; "Kokkō kaifuku seba sōkan, soren no senpan e no taido," *Asahi shimbun*, June 30, 1952, Tokyo morning edition.

25. "Demotai ni keikan happō nagoyade 20yomei fushō 90mei kenkyo [. . .]," *Yomiuri shimbun*, July 8, 1952, morning edition.

26. "'Shinu mae ni kaeritai,' soren de senpan wa uttau," *Asahi shimbun*, July 16, 1952, Tokyo morning edition.

27. "Zanryūsha niman gosen?," *Asahi shimbun*, June 29, 1952, Tokyo morning edition.

28. "Kurushikatta chūkyō no seikatsu kikoku kangofura kataru, 'Hoashira no hōkoku wa ayamari,'" *Yomiuri shimbun*, August 19, 1952, Tokyo evening edition.

29. Besshi Yukio, "Sengo nicchū kankei to chūgoku gaikōkan (sono 1)," *Hokutō ajia kenkyū*, dai2gō, (October 2001): 180. See also Besshi Yukio, "Sengo nicchū kankei to hiseishiki sesshokusha—nihon gaikō no hiseishiki channeru," *Kokusai seiji*, (dai75gō), (October 1983): 98–113. Rachel Leow calls this "conference hopping" in "A Missing Peace: The Asia-Pacific Peace Conference in Beijing, 1952 and the Emotional Making of Third World Internationalism," *Journal of World History* 30, nos. 1–2 (June 2019): 33.

30. Zhao Xinli (Chō Shinri in Japanese), "Nicchū sensōki ni okeru chūgoku kyōsantō no tainichi puropaganda senjutsu senryaku" (PhD diss., Waseda University, published by Waseda daigaku shuppanbu in 2011); Mōri Kazuko, *Nicchū kankei: sengo kara shinjidai e* (Iwanami shinsho, 2006), 22.

31. Itoh, *Making of China's Peace with Japan*, 18; Kōra, *Hisen o ikiru*, 175–176.

32. Besshi, "Sengo nicchū kankei to chūgoku gaikōkan (sono 1)," 180. Meetings included those with Zhao Anbo, Xiao Xiangqian, Yang Zhenya, Wu Xuewen, and Wang Xiaoxian, among others.

33. Saburō Ienaga, *Japan's Last War: World War II and the Japanese, 1931–1945* (Oxford: Basil Blackwell, 1979), 252; Dai15kai kokkai, shūgiin, yosan iinkai, dai 19gō, February 9, 1953, JPR. The quote from the translation is not quite the same as Okano's original comments in the Diet. Sebastian Conrad, *The Quest for the Lost Nation: Writing History in Germany and Japan in the American Century* (Berkeley: University of California Press, 2010), 112–119.

34. Lori Watt, *When Empire Comes Home: Repatriation and Reintegration in Postwar Japan* (Cambridge, MA: Harvard University East Asia Center, 2009), 9–10.

35. "Cong shanghai huiguo riqiao de zhuyao sixiang qingkuang," March 28, 1953, IRRC.

36. "Cong shanghai huiguo riqiao de zhuyao sixiang qingkuang," March 28, 1953, IRRC.

37. Rodger Swearingen and Paul Langer, *Red Flag in Japan: International Communism in Action, 1919–1951* (Cambridge, MA: Harvard University Press, 1952), 104.

38. Swearingen and Langer, *Red Flag in Japan*, 94–95.

39. *The Japanese Communist Party, 1955–1963*, declassified CIA report, March 1964, 10.

40. Zhao Xinli, "Nicchū sensōki ni okeru chūgoku kyōsantōnai no 'chinichiha' to tekigun kōsaku," *Wasedaseiji kōhō kenkyū*, 95gō, (2010): 1–15.

41. Wada Haruki, *Rekishi to shite no Nosaka Sanzō* (Heibonsha, 1996), 251–255.

42. Itō Ritsu, *Itō Ritsu kaisōroku—pekin yūhei nijūshichinen* (Bungei shunjū, 1993), 15–18.

43. Yang Mingwei and Chen Yangyong, *Zhou Enlai waijiao fengyun* (Beijing: Jiefangjun wenyi chubanshe, 1995), 237. A memo of the meeting can be found at: *The World and Japan* website, managed by Professor Tanaka Akihiko, National Graduate Institute for Policy Studies (GRIPS), (https://worldjpn.net/indexPC-ENG.html), "Nicchū kankei ni kansuru Zhou Enlai chūgoku shushō no Ōyama Ikuo kyōju ni taisuru danwa," September 28, 1953.

44. Besshi, "Sengo nicchū kankei to hiseishiki sesshokusha—nihon gaikō no hiseishiki chyanneru," 102; Suga Eiichi et al., eds., *Nicchū mondai—gendai chūgoku to kōryū no shikaku* (Sanseidō, 1971), 15–16.

45. "Shamen motogunjin no kansō, pekin hōsō no zadankai kara chūkyō hikiage," *Asahi shimbun*, September 5, 1954, Tokyo evening edition.

46. "Riben guohui yiyuan Tianzhong Rennan huiguo," *Renmin ribao*, October 23, 1954.

47. These included Kameda Tōgo, *Bōkyō—pekin ni arite: nihonjin no omoeru* (Kōbunsha, 1956).

48. "Huode kuanshe qian riben junren yu riben zuopai shehuidang yiyuandeng jianmian de qingkuang," September 28, 1954, IRRC.

49. "Huode kuanshe qian riben junren yu riben zuopai shehuidang yiyuandeng jianmian de qingkuang," September 28, 1954, IRRC.

50. "'Zenjinza jiken (hokkaidō akabira jiken)' o kangeru," interview at the home of Minotsu Tatsumi, Shiga Village in Shiga Prefecture, produced on December 7, 2002, http://www.miike-coalmine.org/data/koe/zenshinza.html; Samuel L. Leiter, *Kabuki at the Crossroads: Years of Crisis, 1952–1965*, (Leiden, Netherlands: Global Oriental, 2013), 140–141.

51. "Shū Onrai no nihon kokkai giin hōchū daihyōdan gakujutsu shisatsudan to no kaiken ni okeru hatsugen 'nihon yūkō no kiso ni tsuite,'" in *Sengo shiryō nicchū kankei*, ed. Ishikawa Tadao, Nakajima Mineo, and Ikei Masaru (Nihon hyōronsha, 1970), 27–32.

52. "Shū Onrai no nihon kokkai giin hōchū daihyōdan gakujutsu shisatsudan to no kaiken ni okeru hatsugen 'nihon yūkō no kiso ni tsuite,'" 32; "Record of Conversation from Premier Zhou's Reception of the Japanese Parliamentary Delegation in China and the Japanese Academic and Cultural Delegation in China," October 20, 1955, History and Public Policy Program Digital Archive, PRC FMA 105-00158-02, 6–27; obtained by Amy King and translated by Stephen Mercado, http://digitalarchive.wilsoncenter.org/document/165370.

53. "Chūso tainichi kyōdō sengen (chūka jinmin kyōwakoku seifu oyobi souieto shakaishugi kyōwakoku renpō seifu no nihon ni taisuru kankei ni tsuite no kyōdō sengen)," collated on The World and Japan website, managed by Professor Tanaka Akihiko, National Graduate Institute for Policy Studies (GRIPS), (https://worldjpn.net/indexPC-ENG.html); Park Jung Jin, "North Korean Nation Building and Japanese Imperialism," in *The Dismantling of Japan's Empire in East Asia: De-imperialization, Postwar Legitimation and Imperial Afterlife*, ed. Barak Kushner and Sherzod Muminov (London: Routledge, 2017), 208.

54. Lian Shu, "1950nendai ni okeru chūso kankei to chūgoku no tainichi seisaku," *Ronsō gendaigo gendaibunka*, 20kan, (February 2019): 14.

55. "Riben zhongyiyuan yiyuan Tianzhong Rennan fabiao tanhua huanying zhongsu liangguo [. . .]," *Renmin ribao*, October 24, 1954.

56. "Ri Tokuzen joshira sakuyū nyūkyo," *Asahi shimbun*, October 31, 1954, Tokyo morning edition.

57. "Tensei jingo," *Asahi shimbun*, October 31, 1954, Tokyo, morning edition; Cheng Ma and Lin Zhenjiang, *Riben nanwang Li Dequan* (Beijing: Zhongguo shehui kexue chubanshe, 2017), 47.

58. Erik Esselstrom, *That Distant Country Next Door: Popular Japanese Perceptions of Mao's China* (Honolulu: University of Hawaii Press, 2019), 22.

59. "Shū Onrai no nihon kokkai giin hōchū daihyōdan gakujutsu shisatsudan to no kaiken ni okeru hatsugen 'nihon yūkō no kiso ni tsuite,'" 33.

60. "Shū Onrai no nihon kokkai giin hōchū daihyōdan gakujutsu shisatsudan to no kaiken ni okeru hatsugen 'nihon yūkō no kiso ni tsuite,'" 34.

61. "Riben jizhe laijin tanfang huiguo riqiao qingkuang," December 4, 1954, IRRC.

62. Fukuda Kumajirō, "Watashi no mita mama no chūkyō," *Tairiku mondai* 3, no. 11 (November 1954): 28–45.

63. "Riqiao Futian Xiongcilang huiguohou dui woguo qingkuang jinxing waiqu xuanchuan," December 15, 1954, IRRC.

64. "Interview with Chou En-lai, Shozo Murata Talks about His Trip," translated in "Political Relations between China and Japan (1955)," FO 371-115005, published, KGNA.

10. Behind the Curtain

1. "Riben duiwo taidu," Waijiaobu zhongri xuanan, anjuan diyice, zhonghua minguo 44nian 11yueqi, (11-EAP-02382), MOFAT.

2. Itō Ritsu, *Itō Ritsu kaisōroku—pekin yūhei nijūshichinen* (Bungei shunjū, 1993), 84.

3. Itō, *Itō Ritsu kaisōroku*, 93–94.

4. Mizutani Naoko, *Hannichi izen: chūgoku tainichi kōsakushatachi no kaisō* (Bungei shunjū, 2006), 101.

5. "Chō Anpaku hatsugen to rekishi no shinjitsu," *Zenei*, (April 1998): 98–108; Mizutani, *Hannichi izen*, 68. The truncated article was published as Chō Anpaku, Himeda Mitsuyoshi, and Mizutani Naoko, "Chō Anpaku kaisōroku—nicchū kankeishi no ichi danmen," *Sekai*, (October 1998): 280–294.

6. Mizutani, *Hannichi izen*, 98.

7. Mizutani, *Hannichi izen*, 99–100.

8. Masuda Chikako, "Hino Ashihei 'Akai kuni no tabibito' no seiritsu to shin chūgoku ninshiki: 'chūgokutabi nikki' tono hikaku oyobi shoshutsu zasshi sakujo mondai o chūshin to shite," *Kansai daigaku tōzai gakujutsu kenkyū kiyō*, 44kan, (April 2011): 29–47.

9. Hino Ashihei, "Bujun purizon no senpantachi," in *Akai kuni no tabibito* (Asahi shimbunsha, 1955), 300–308.

10. Memo from Peking to Foreign Office, September 15, 1955, "Sino-Japanese Relations," in "Political relations between China and Japan (1955)," FO 371-115005, published, KGNA. The article "Zhongri liangguojian qiaomin wenti de zhenxiang" was from September 14, 1955, in the *People's Daily*.

11. Ran Zwigenberg, *Hiroshima: The Origins of Global Memory Culture* (Cambridge: Cambridge University Press, 2014), 103.

12. "Shū Onrai sōri: nihon shimbun hōsō kankei chūgoku hōmon daihyōdan to kaiken," in *Sengo shiryō nicchū kankei*, ed. Ishikawa Tadao, Nakajima Mineo, and Ikei Masaru (Nihon hyōronsha, 1970), 52–54.

13. Endō Saburō, *Nicchū jūgonen sensō to watakushi: kokuzoku aka no shōgun to hito wa iu* (Nicchū shorin, 1974), 328.

14. Endō, *Nicchū jūgonen sensō to watakushi*, 343.

15. Endō Saburō et al., eds., *Moto gunjin no mita chūkyō: shinchūgoku no seiji keizai bunka shisō no jittai* (Bunri shoin, 1956), 22–23.

16. Endō et al., *Moto gunjin no mita chūkyō*, 24.

17. Kobayashi Kazuhiro, *Shinatsū ichi gunjin no hikari to kage: Isogai Rensuke chūjōden* (Kashiwa shobō, 2000), 238; Yang Daqing, "1950nendai ni okeru sensō kioku to asai wakai—moto nihon gunjin hōchūdan o chūshin ni," in *Tairitsu to kyōzon no rekishi ninshiki, nicchū kankei 150nen*, ed. Liu Jie and Kawashima Shin (Tokyo daigaku shuppankai, 2013), 191–222.

18. Miyatake Gō, *Shōgun no igon: Endō Saburō nikki* (Mainichi shimbunsha, 1986), 216.

19. Kobayashi, *Shinatsū ichi gunjin no hikari to kage*, 239.

20. Endō et al., *Moto gunjin no mita chūkyō*, 17.

21. "1955.10.03, Zhou Enlai zongli jiejian riben zuopai shehuidang Ye Gousheng tanhua jiyao," Danghao: 105-00210-07, CMOFA.

22. Ishikawa Tadao, Nakajima Mineo, and Ikei Masaru, eds., *Sengo shiryō nicchū kankei* (Nihon hyōronsha, 1970), 56–57. Mao and Zhou Enlai met with Kanbayashiyama's group on October 15, 1955. "Mao Zedong zhuxi jiejian riben yiyuan fanghuatuan tanhua jilu," Danghao: 105-00210-01, CMOFA.

23. Manshūkokushi hensan kankōkai, *Manshūkokushi* (Sōron manmō dōhō engokai, 1970), unpaginated section.

24. Endō et al., *Moto gunjin no mita chūkyō*, 48.

25. According to one Chinese Ministry of Foreign Affairs source, for which the date of October 28, 1955, must be a mistake, Endō compared his time in Sugamo Prison in Tokyo with the experiences of Japanese war criminals in Fushun, where they were treated with "great benevolence." "Mao Zedong zhuxi jiejian riben yonghu xianfa lianghehui fanghuatuan tanhua jiyao," Danghao: 105-00210-02 (1), CMOFA.

26. Shiroyama Hidemi, "'Moto gunjin hōchūdan' to Mō Takutō gaikō no senryakusei—chūgoku gaikō tōan kara miru gunkokushugi no seisan," *Soshio saiensu* 19 (March 2013): 78; Endō, *Nicchū jūgonen sensō to watakushi*, 482. Sun Pinghua (Son Heika in Japanese), *Chūgoku to nihon ni hashi o kaketa otoko* (Nihon kezai shinbunsha, 1998), 92–95.

27. In December 1955, Zhou Enlai met with a Japanese civilian group, led by Takenaka Katsuo, who were repatriating the remains of Chinese "heroes." "Zhou Enlai zongli jiejian zhongguo kangri lieshi yigu husongtuan tanhua jilu," Danghao: 105-00210-10 (1), CMOFA. See also Wang Hongyan, "Chūgokujin ikotsu sōkan undō to sengo chūnichi kankei," *Hitotsubashi ronsō* 119, no. 2 (February 1998): 267–283.

28. (Confidential) "Minutes of the Talk between Japanese and Chinese Red Cross Societies," Peking, March 3, 1956, "Criminel de guerre japonais en Chine. Rapatriement, 08/10/1954-11/07/1958, B AG 219 048-001, IRCA.

29. Confidential British dispatch from the embassy in Tokyo on April 13, 1956, from Esler Denning, in "Political relations between China and Japan (1956)," FO 371-120888, published, KGNA.

30. "Zhou Enlai zongli jijian riben heping daibiaotuan Gongqi Longjie dengren tanhua jilu," Danghao: 105-00500-02, CMOFA.

31. "Taiyuan zaiya riben zhanfan de sixiang dongtai " May 11, 1956, IRRC.

32. Shiroyama, "'Moto gunjin hōchūdan' to Mō Takutō gaikō no senryakusei," 79.

33. On September 4, 1956, Liao Chengzhi wrote Mao a letter lauding the efforts of the Fushun Prison reform of Japanese war criminals and how that re-education, and the trips to key sites around China, had a positive influence on the visit of former Japanese military officers. Liao advised Mao that meeting with such groups would be "immense" in helping to further solidify their changing opinions of new China. See Liao Chengzhi wenji bianji bangongshi, ed., *Liao Chengzhi wenji* (xia) (Hong Kong: Sanlian shudian, 1990), 808–809.

34. Shiroyama, "'Moto gunjin hōchūdan' to Mō Takutō gaikō no senryakusei," 80; Miyatake, *Shōgun no igon*, 218; Shiroyama Hidemi, *Chūgoku kyōsantō 'tennō kōsaku' hiroku* (Bungei shunjū, 2009), 12–13.

35. "August 27, 1956, British embassy Tokyo dispatch, from RW Selby," in "Political relations between China and Japan (1956)," FO 371-120888, KGNA.

36. Chō Kōhō, *Ima yomigaeru Endō Saburō no hito to shisō: rikugun kōkyū erīto kara hansen heiwashugisha* (Ōbirin daigaku hokutō ajia sōgō kenkyūjo, 2016), 347.

37. Wang Zhendong (Ō Shintō in Japanese), "Taigen senpan kanrishochō to shite," *Chūkiren*, 19gō (Winter 2001): 48.

38. The text of the announcement is available at grips site: *The World and Japan* website, managed by Professor Tanaka Akihiko, National Graduate Institute for Policy Studies (GRIPS), (https://worldjpn.net/indexPC-ENG.html), "Shakaitō hōchūdan to chūgoku jinmim gaikō gakkai no kyōdō komyunike," April 22, 1957.

39. "Confidential British embassy in Peking dispatch, May 9, 1957," in FO 371-127285 "Political relations between China and Japan (1957)," published United Kingdom archives.

40. Kōanchōsachō, *Shisō kaizō to sensō hanzai: chūkyō yokuryūki*, softbound report produced by the Japanese government, May 1957, no. 3419, TBA.

41. Dai 28kai kokkai, shūgiin, gaimuiinkai, dai 20gō, April 9, 1958, JPR; Matsuoka Hajime, *Nicchū rekishi wakai e no michi* (Kōbunken, 2014), 183–185.

42. Nick Kapur, *Japan at the Crossroads: Conflict and Compromise after Anpo* (Cambridge, MA: Harvard University Press, 2018), 7–8.

43. Hei 11nen 4A-21-6654, "Sensō hanzaihōteki kenkyū kankeitsuzuri," the Toyota proposal from March 19, 1964, NAJ.

44. *Taiheiyō sensō e no michi*, 8 volumes, Nihon kokusai seiji gakkai taiheiyō sensō genin kenkyūbu ed (Asahi shinbunsha, 1962-62).

45. Sakano's son-in-law offered a personal glimpse into his father-in-law on his personal blog: "Tōkyō saiban ni tuite, 'jibunshi' kara no bassui," produced November 15, 2005, https://mikasa.exblog.jp/2198881/.

46. Inoki Takenori, *Keizai seichō no kajitsu, 1955–1972* (Chūō kōron shinsha, 2000), 129–131.

47. Helen Hardacre, *Shinto: A History* (Oxford University Press, 2016), 461; Franziska Seraphim, *War Memory and Social Politics in Japan, 1945–2005* (Cambridge, MA: Harvard University Asia Center, 2006).

48. Tokyo saiban kenkyūkai, ed., *Pāru hanketsusho: taiheiyō sensō no kangaekata kyōdō kenkyū*, 2 vols. (Tokyo saiban kankōkai, 1966).

49. Hei 11nen 4A-21-6654, "Sensō hanzaihōteki kenkyū kankeitsuzuri," the Toyota proposal from March 19, 1964, NAJ.

50. Emeritus professor Yamamoto Taketoshi gave the first lecture of a twenty-first-century university study group, which follows similar lines. "Tokyo saiban to kenetsu taisei," in the Kyokutō kokusai gunji saiban kenkyū purojekkuto, *Hikaku hōsei kenkyū* (Kokushikan daigaku), dai 38gō, (2015): 87–100.

51. Fukuma Yoshiaki, *Sensō taiken no sengoshi* (Chūkō shinsho, 2009), 3–5.

52. There is a museum in Tokyo dedicated to this, Wadatsumi no koe kinenkan, http://www.wadatsuminokoe.org (accessed July 30, 2022).

53. Hosaka Masayasu, *'Kike wadatsumi no koe' no sengoshi* (Bunshun bunko, 2002).

54. "Senbotsu gakusei ni koe araba shasetsu," *Asahi shimbun*, May 21, 1969, Tokyo morning edition.

55. Julia Strauss, *State Formation in China and Taiwan Bureaucracy, Campaign, and Performance* (Cambridge: Cambridge University Press, 2020), 98–99.

56. Brad R. Roth, "Human Rights and Transitional Justice: Taiwan's Adoption of the ICCPR and the Redress of 2/28 and Martial-Law-Era Injustices," in *Taiwan and International Human Rights: A Story of Transformation*, ed. Jerome A. Cohen, William P. Alford, and Chang-fa Lo (Singapore: Springer, 2019), 54.

57. Chihyun Chang, ed., *The Chinese Journals of L. L. Little, 1943–1954: An Eyewitness Account of War and Revolution*, vol. 3, *The Financial Advisor, 1950–1954* (London: Routledge, 2018), 237. In 2001, the Taiwanese government found that the charges against Sun Li-jen were unjustified.

58. Jerome Cohen, "Taiwan's Political-Legal Progress: Memories of the K Dictatorship," in *Taiwan and International Human Rights: A Story of Transformation*, ed. Jerome A. Cohen, William P. Alford, and Chang-fa Lo (Singapore: Springer, 2019), 20.

59. Chen Tsui-lian, "Lishi zhengyi de kunjing: zuqun yiti yu ererba lunshu," *Guoshiguan xueshu jikan*, (16) (June 2008): 195.

60. Ka Girin (He Yilin in Chinese), *Taiwan gendaishi: ni ni hachi jiken o meguru rekishi no saikioku* (Heibonsha, 2014), 218–220; Wu Chun-Ying, "'Fuchen zhuanan' yu guomindang danju dui ererba shijian quanshi de xueshu zhuanxiang," *Taiwanshi yanjiu*, di 29juan di 4qi, (December 2022): 173–230.

61. Su Seng and Guo Jiancheng, *Fuqu lishi mingjingzhong de chenai* (Alhambra, CA: Meiguo nanhua wenkhua shiye goingsi, 1986); Chen, "Lishi zhengyi de kunjing," 196; Chen Tsui-lian, *Chonggou ererba: zhanhou meizhong tizhi, zhongguo tongzhi moshi yu Taiwan* (Xinbeishi, Taiwan: Weicheng chuban, 2017), 13.

62. Michael Berry, *A History of Pain: Trauma in Modern Chinese Literature and Film* (New York: Columbia University Press, 2008), 218.

63. Chun-Hung Chen and Hung-Ling Yeh, "The Battlefield of Transitional Justice in Taiwan: A Relational View," in *Taiwan and International Human Rights: A Story of Transformation*, ed. Jerome A. Cohen, William P. Alford, and Chang-fa Lo (Singapore: Springer,

2019), 71; Thomas J. Shattuck, "Transitional Justice in Taiwan: A Belated Reckoning with the White Terror," Foreign Policy Research Institute, 2019, https://www.fpri.org/article/2019/11/transitional-justice-in-taiwan-a-belated-reckoning-with-the-white-terror/.

11. Evaporating Legal Memory and KMT War Criminals

1. "Shanghai sifajie renshi zhankai fanyoupai douzheng, yaoqiu faxuehui lishihui biaoming taidu, zhichu Wang Zaoshi Yang Zhaolong wenti yanzhong bixu renzhen gaoqing," June 26, 1957, CARMD.

2. "Wufa keyi shi huairen gandao wusuo guji, haoren gandao quefa baozhang," original was from May 7, 1957), *Xinwen ribao* and titled "Yang Zhaolong 'Woguo zhongyao fadian heyi chichi bubanbu'"; it was included in proceedings against Yang as "Youpai fenzi Yang Zhaolong de yanlun fudan daxue Yang Zhaolong fudan daxue xiaokan bianjishi, August 1957," CARMD.

3. "Quanti sifa ganbu tuanjie zaidang de zhouwei chedi dakua youpai fenzi de changkuang jingong: Shi Liang zai diyijie quanguo renmin daibiao dahui disici huiyishang de fayan," Shi Liang, July 12, 1957, CARMD.

4. Shen Guansheng, "Rang fachui qiaoxiang lishi de jingzhong," *Renmin fayuanbao*, September 3, 2014.

5. "Zhonggong zuigao renmin fayuan xingting zhibu guanyu kaichu youpai fenzi Jia Qian dangji de jueding (Jia Qian)," February 15, 1958, CARMD.

6. "Zhonggong zuigao renmin fayuan xingting zhibu guanyu kaichu youpai fenzi Zhu Yaotang dangji de jueding," February 15, 1958, CARMD.

7. "Zhonggong zuigao renmin fayuan xingting zhibu guanyu kaichu youpai fenzi Yang Xianzhi dangji de jueding (Yang Xianzhi)," February 15, 1958, CARMD.

8. "(Hao Shaoan) zhonggong zuigao renmin fayuan xingting zhibu guanyu kaichu youpai fenzi Hao Shaoan dangji de jueding," February 15, 1958, CARMD.

9. Yuan Guang, *Cong hongjun zhanshi dao junfa jiangjun* (Jiangxi renmin chubanshe, 1998), 149–170.

10. "Zhonggong zuigao renmin fayuan xingting zhibu guanyu kaichu youpai fenzi Zhang Xiangqian dangji de jueding (Zhang Xiangqian)," April 24, 1958, CARMD.

11. Dangdai zhongguo congshu bianji weiyuanhui, ed., *Dangdai zhongguo de gongan gongzuo* (Beijing: Dangdai zhongguo chubanshe, 1992), 126. For more on the fate of Chinese "war criminals" the CCP pursued postwar, see Barak Kushner, "The Real Manchurian Candidates: Chinese War Criminals in the Postwar, Prisoners of History," *International Journal of Asian Studies* 20, no. 1 (January 2023): 19–37.

12. Quanguo zhengxie wenshi he xuexi weiyuanhui, ed., *Huiyi gaizao zhanfan*, 2 vols. (Beijing: Zhongguo wenshi chubanshe, 2013). See also Dangdai zhongguo congshu bianji weiyuanhui, ed., *Dangdai zhongguo de gongan gongzuo*, 126–128.

13. Xia Jicheng, "Guomindang tewu touzi Kang Ze cong beifu dao teshe," *Yanhuang chunqiu*, originally published June 2018 (see online article: http://www.yhcqw.com/30/12657.html).

14. Lei Hao, "Jinjing qianhou canyu guanjiao guomindang zhanfan jishi," in *Huiyi gaizao zhanfan*, xiace, ed. Quanguo zhengxie wenshi he xuexi weiyuanhui (Beijing: Zhongguo wenshi chubanshe, 2013), 417.

15. Mao Zedong, "Lun shida guanxi," April 25, 1956. The full Chinese text is available on the Chinese communist material storehouse, the Zhongwen Makesizhuyi wenku at: https://www.marxists.org/chinese/maozedong/marxist.org-chinese-mao-19560425.htm.

16. This is the name of the region that encompasses Shanxi, Hebei, and Chahar Provinces. In 1948, Chahar was combined with other areas to form the Inner Mongolian Autonomous Region.

17. Lei, "Jinjing qianhou canyu guanjiao guomindang zhanfan jishi," 409.

18. "Shokei hōshin, moto Shū Onrai shushō ga tekkai meirei kyū nihongun senpan kanrijo moto kanbu ga kataru," *Asahi shimbun*, April 10, 1998, evening edition.

19. Liu Jiachang and Liu Renyuan, *Zuihou de xuanze guomindang mingjiang Huang Wei teshe qianhou* (Beijing: Jiefangjun chubanshe, 1999), 205.

20. Jin Luxian, *The Memoirs of Jin Luxian*, vol. 1, *Learning and Relearning, 1916–1982*, trans. Willam Hanbury-Tenison (Hong Kong University Press, 2012), 245.

21. Jin Yuan, "You yici weida de lishi shijian," in *Huiyi gaizao zhanfan*, xiace, ed. Quanguo zhengxie wenshi he xuexi weiyuanhui (Beijing: Zhongguo wenshi chubanshe, 2013), 448.

22. J. A. Fyfield, *Re-educating Chinese Anti-Communists* (London: St. Martin's Press, 1982), 54.

23. Duan Kewen, *Zhanfan zishu*, vol. 1 (Taipei: Shijie ribaoshe, 1978), 4.

24. Duan, *Zhanfan zishu*, vol. 1, 19.

25. Fyfield, *Re-educating Chinese Anti-Communists*, 52; Duan, *Zhanfan zishu*, vol. 1, 26.

26. Jin, "You yici weida de lishi shijian," 448.

27. Jin, "You yici weida de lishi shijian," 449.

28. Liu and Liu, *Zuihou de xuanze guomindang mingjiang Huang Wei teshe qianhou*, 57.

29. "The Ambassador in China (Stuart) to the Department of State," Nanking, December 30, 1948, FRUS, 1948, The Far East: China, Volume VII, Document 591.

30. Ryan Grauer, *Commanding Military Power: Organizing for Victory and Defeat on the Battlefield* (Cambridge: Cambridge University Press, 2016), 107.

31. Huang Wei, "Wo zai gongdelin de gaizao shenghuo," *Wenshi jinghua*, 2qi, (1995): 5. Huang's longer original memoir of this era, "Gongdelin gaizao shenghuo jishi," was first published in a collection of KMT former war criminal recollections in Zhongguo renmin zhengzhi xieshanghuiyi quanguo weiyuanhui wenshi ziliao yanjiu weiyuanhui 'cong zhanfan dao gongmin' bianji, ed., *Cong zhanfan dao gongmin: yuan guomindang jiangling gaizao shenghuo de huiyi* (Beijing: Zhongguo wenshi chubanshe, 1987), 113–136.

32. Liu and Liu, *Zuihou de xuanze guomindang mingjiang Huang Wei teshe qianhou*, 65–66.

33. Huang, "Wo zai gongdelin de gaizao shenghuo," 8.

34. Lei, "Jinjing qianhou canyu guanjiao guomindang zhanfan jishi," 415–416.

35. Liu and Liu, *Zuihou de xuanze guomindang mingjiang Huang Wei teshe qianhou*, 131.

36. Liu and Liu, *Zuihou de xuanze guomindang mingjiang Huang Wei teshe qianhou*, 189–190.

37. Lei, "Jinjing qianhou canyu guanjiao guomindang zhanfan jishi," 416.

38. Fyfield, *Re-educating Chinese Anti-Communists*, 33. See also Huang's daughter's interview: Huang Huinan and Zhou Haibing, "Yige guomindang zhongjiang de gaizao lichen," *Jianghuai wenshi*, (September 2014): 75–87.

39. "Gai'e congshan qiantu guangming," *Renmin ribao*, September 18, 1959.

40. Ji Min, "1959: Gongheguo zhuxifachu tesheling," *Zongheng*, 10qi, (1998): 39.

41. Huang, "Gongdelin gaizao shenghuo jishi," 131.

42. Frederick Wakeman, *Spymaster Dai Li and the Chinese Secret Service* (Berkeley: University of California Press, 2003), 4.

43. Fyfield, *Re-educating Chinese Anti-Communists*, 11.

44. Shen Zui, *Zhanfan gaizao suojianwen* (shang) (Beijing: Qunzhong chubanshe, 1990), 39–40; Philip F. Williams and Yenna Wu, *The Great Wall of Confinement: The Chinese Prison Camp through Contemporary Fiction and Reportage* (Berkeley: University of California Press, 2004), 161.

45. Fyfield, *Re-educating Chinese Anti-Communists*, 31–33. See also Julia Lovell, "The Uses of Foreigners in Mao-Era China: 'Techniques of Hospitality' and International Image-Building in the People's Republic, 1949–1976," *Transactions of the RHS* 25 (2015): 135–158.

46. Tom Buchanan, *East Wind: China and the British Left, 1925–1976* (Oxford: Oxford University Press, 2012), 164.

47. R. K. S. Ghandhi, "Mao Tse-Tung: His Military Writings and Philosophy," *Naval War College Review* 17, no. 7 (March 1965): 19.

48. Felix Greene, *China: The Country Americans Are Not Allowed to Know* (New York: Ballantine Books, 1961). See also "[Mao Zedong's] Conversation with [Bernard] Montgomery, [British Viscount of Alamein]," May 27, 1960, History and Public Policy Program Digital Archive, Gang er si Wuhan daxue zongbu et al., eds., *Mao Zedong sixiang wansui* [Long live Mao Zedong thought], vol. 4 (1958–1960) (Wuhan, internal circulation, May 1968): 281–291, https://digitalarchive.wilsoncenter.org/document/230144

49. Buchanan, *East Wind*, 164.

50. Dangdai zhongguo congshu bianji weiyuanhui, *Dangdai zhongguo de gongan gongzuo*, 115–126.

51. Zhang Jicheng, ed., *Fushun zhanfan guanlisuo jiuzhi chenlieguan gushi* (Nanjing: Nanjing chubanshe, 2014), 143–146.

52. Fyfield, *Re-educating Chinese Anti-Communists*, 31

53. Ning Wang, *Banished to the Great Northern Wilderness: Political Exile and Reeducation in Mao's China* (Ithaca, NY: Cornell University Press, 2017), 82–83.

54. Liu Binyan, "Murder at Nenjiang Camp," in *Seeds of Fire: Chinese Voices of Conscience*, ed. Geremie Barmé and John Minford (New York: Noonday Press, 1989), 65–67.

55. Fyfield, *Re-educating Chinese Anti-Communists*, 75.

56. Robert Jay Lifton, *Thought Reform and the Psychology of Totalism: A Study of Brainwashing in China* (New York: W. W. Norton, 1963); Monica Kim, *The Interrogation Rooms of the Korean War: The Untold History* (Princeton, NJ: Princeton University Press, 2019).

57. Christian Sorace, "Extracting Affect: Televised Cadre Confessions in China," *Public Culture* 31, no. 1 (January 2019): 147–148.

58. Ji Min, "Teshe zhanfan shenqing qu taiwan shouzu neimu," in *Shengsi lunhui: gaizao zhanfan midang quan gongkai*, ed. Ji Min (Beijing: Zhongguowenshi chubanshe, 2011), 56–57.

59. Dangdai zhongguo congshu bianji weiyuanhui, *Dangdai zhongguo de gongan gongzuo*, 132. Other sources cite this amnesty as the work of Deng Xiaoping.

60. Ji Min, "Zhou Enlai linzhong dui taiwan wenti de pishi," *Yanhuang chunqiu*, (June 2002): 7–14; Li Haiwen, "1975nian Mao Zedong juece shifang guomindang zhanfan de neiqing," *Wanxia*, (24), (2011): 42–46.

61. Sugano Atsushi, *Taiwan no kokka to bunka: datsu nihonka chūgokuka hondoka* (Keisōsha, 2011), 289–292.

62. Jay Taylor, *The Generalissimo: Chiang Ching-kuo and the Revolutions in China and Taiwan* (Cambridge, MA: Harvard University Press, 2000), 320.

63. Denny Roy, *Taiwan: A Political History* (Ithaca, NY: Cornell University Press, 2003), 147; Li Zhanheng, *Teshe huitaibei: cong zhanfan dao zuojia* (Beijing: Jiefangjun chubanshe, 1999).

64. "Moto kokumintō senpan ni taiwan tōku," *Asahi shimbun*, September 3, 1975, Tokyo morning edition.

65. Ren Haisheng, *Bubi shashen chengren: guomindang zhongyao jiangling gaizao jishi* (Beijing: Jiefangjun chubanshe, 1999), 317–345.

66. Andrew Morris, "'Praising Righteous Fan': PLA Air Force Commander Fan Yuanyan's 1977 Defection to Taiwan," *International Journal of Taiwan Studies* 2 (2019): 57–84; Andrew Morris, *Defectors from the PRC to Taiwan, 1960–1989: The Anti-communist Righteous Warriors* (London: Routledge, 2022).

67. Morris, "'Praising Righteous Fan,'" 59; "Chinese Mig-19 Pilot Defects: Almost Draws Taiwan into Dogfight," *Washington Post*, July 8, 1977.

68. Mark Bowden, "The Dark Art of Interrogation," *Atlantic Monthly*, (October 2003): 56.

69. As quoted from the 1946 US Strategic Bombing Survey in Jeremy A. Yellen, "The Specter of Revolution: Reconsidering Japan's Decision to Surrender," *International History Review* 35, no. 1 (February 2013): 206.

70. Ali Soufan, *The Black Banners, Declassified, How Torture Derailed the War on Terror after 9/11* (New York: Norton, 2020), 424.

71. The *New York Times* maintains an updated interactive website that follows the situation with prisoners detained at Guantanamo in "The Guantanamo Docket." As of the end of 2021 its website tabulated these statistics. See: https://www.nytimes.com/interactive/2021/us/guantanamo-bay-detainees.html.

12. Owning the War

1. UN General Assembly Resolution No. 2758.

2. Asahi Shimbun Company, *Media, Propaganda and Politics in 20th-Century Japan*, trans. and abridged by Barak Kushner (London: Bloomsbury, 2015), 235–236.

3. "Shū shushō, nijikan amari no netsuben Gotō henshūkyokuchō to no kaiken," *Asahi shimbun*, November 6, 1971, morning edition.

4. Kissinger's secret memo to the White House, November 1971, https://www.cia.gov/library/readingroom/docs/LOC-HAK-460-9-16-4.pdf.

5. Samuel S. Kim, "The People's Republic of China in the United Nations: A Preliminary Analysis," *World Politics* 26, no. 3 (April 1974): 307; Samuel S. Kim, *China, the United Nations and World Order* (Princeton, NJ: Princeton University Press, 1979), 106–107.

6. Margaret Macmillan, *Seize the Hour: When Nixon Met Mao* (London: John Murray Publishers, 2007), 146.

7. "Preface, and "Introduction," in Alexander C. Cook, ed., *Mao's Little Red Book: A Global History* (Cambridge: Cambridge University Press, 2014), xiii, 1. The official title of the book was *Quotations from Chairman Mao Zedong*.

8. Geremie Barmé, *Shades of Mao: The Posthumous Cult of the Great Leader* (London: M. E. Sharpe, 1996), 5–7.

9. Antony Best, "Japan and the Cold War: An Overview," in *The Oxford Handbook of the Cold War*, ed. Richard H. Immerman and Petra Goedde (Oxford: Oxford University Press, 2013), 293.

10. Takashi Shiraishi and Caroline Sy Hau, "Only Yesterday: China, Japan, and the Transformation of East Asia," in *The Cold War in Asia: The Battle for Hearts and Minds*, ed. Yangwen Zheng, Hong Liu, and Michael Szonyi (Leiden: Brill, 2010), 29.

11. "Dai 1kai Takeiru Yoshikatsu Shū Onrai kaidan kiroku," July 27, 1972, accessed from The World and Japan website, managed by Professor Tanaka Akihiko, National Graduate Institute for Policy Studies (GRIPS), https://worldjpn.net/indexPC-ENG.html. See also: Nakasone Yasuhiro, *Jiseiroku: rekishi-hōtei no hikoku toshite* (Shinchōsha, 2004), 99–100.

12. H. H. King, "The Boxer Indemnity: 'Nothing but Bad,'" *Modern Asian Studies* 40, no. 3 (July 2006): 663–689.

13. "Record of the First Meeting between Takeiri Yoshikatsu and Zhou Enlai," July 27, 1972, History and Public Policy Program Digital Archive, 2001–298, Act on Access to Information Held by Administrative Organs. Also available at the Diplomatic Archives of the Ministry of Foreign Affairs of Japan. Obtained by Yutaka Kanda and translated by Ryo C. Kato. http://digitalarchive wilsoncenter.org/document/118833.

14. "Record of the Second Meeting between Takeiri Yoshikatsu and Zhou Enlai," July 28, 1972, History and Public Policy Program Digital Archive, 2001–298, Act on Access to Information Held by Administrative Organs. Also available at the Diplomatic Archives of the Ministry of Foreign Affairs of Japan. Obtained by Yutaka Kanda and translated by Ryo C. Kato. http://digitalarchive.wilsoncenter.org/document/118834; Zhai Xin, "Zhou Enlai he Songcun Qiansan de wuci fanghua," *Zhonggong dangshi yanjiu*, di 11qi, (2015): 89–98.

15. Rana Mitter, "China and the Cold War," in *The Oxford Handbook of the Cold War*, ed. Richard Immerman and Petra Goedde (Oxford: Oxford University Press, 2013), 136.

16. Inoue Masaya, "Kokkō seijōka, 1972," in *Nicchū kankeishi, 1972–2012*, vol. 1, seiji, ed. Takahara Akio and Hattori Ryūji (Tokyo daigaku shuppankai, 2012), 41.

17. NHK shuzaihan, *Shū Onrai no ketsudan: nicchū kokkō seijōka wa kōshite jitugen shita* (Nihon hōsō shuppan kyōkai, 1993), 128–136; *Jianguo yilai Mao Zedong wengao*, vol. 13 (Beijing: Zhongyang wenxian chubanshe, 1998), 316.

18. Gao Wenqian, *Zhou Enlai: The Last Perfect Revolutionary* (New York: Public Affairs, 2007), 235–236.

19. Ezra Vogel, *Deng Xiaoping and the Transformation of China* (Cambridge, MA: Harvard University Press, 2011), 184; Robert Weatherley, *Mao's Forgotten Successor: The Political Career of Hua Guofeng* (Basingstoke: Palgrave Macmillan, 2010).

20. Robert Suettinger, *Negotiating History: The Chinese Communist Party's 1981* (Project 2049 Institute, July 2017), available as a PDF paper at the institute's website (https://project2049.net).

21. Suettinger, *Negotiating History*, 7. See also Dai Huang, *Hu Yaobang yu pingfan yuanjia cuoan* (Beijing: Xinhua chubanshe, 1998); Xu Lizhi, "Beyond 'Destruction' and 'Lawlessness': The Legal System during the Cultural Revolution," in *Victims, Perpetrators, and the Role of Law in Maoist China*, ed. Daniel Leese and Puck Engman (Berlin: Walter de Gruyter, 2018), 25–51.

22. Vogel, *Deng Xiaoping and the Transformation of China*, 189.

23. Vogel, *Deng Xiaoping and the Transformation of China*, 2.

24. Richard Baum, *Burying Mao: Chinese Politics in the Age of Deng Xiaoping*, updated ed. (Princeton, NJ: Princeton University Press, 1994), 76.

25. "Yanzheng de shenpan—beijingshi zhongji renmin fayuan shenpan Wei Jingsheng fangemingan pangtingji," *Renmin ribao*, October 17, 1979.

26. Excerpts from "Qincheng: A Twentieth Century Bastille," published in *Exploration* (March 1979), on the Wei Jingsheng Foundation website (http://www.weijingsheng.org/doc/en/Excerpts%20from%20Qincheng.htm).

27. Mu Xin, *Ban guangming ribao, shinian zishu, 1957-1967* (Beijing: Zhonggong dangshi chubanshe, 1994), 373; Roderick MacFarquhar and Michael Schoenhals, *Mao's Last Revolution* (Cambridge, MA: Belknap Press of Harvard University Press, 2006), 342.

28. Itō Ritsu, *Itō Ritsu kaisōroku: pekin yūhei nijūshichinen*, 269–270.

29. Itō, *Itō Ritsu kaisōroku*, 303.

30. This correspondence was conducted through the Chinese embassy in Tokyo and coordinated by Miyoshi Hajime, deputy head of the Japan-China Friendship Association. "Shinu mae ni shōgen ketsudan, Itō Ritsushi," *Asahi shimbun*, December 21, 1980, Tokyo morning edition.

31. Itō, *Itō Ritsu kaisōroku*, 326.

32. Dai 93kai kokkai, hōmuiinkai, dai7gō, November 26, 1980, JPR. See also the story of a Japanese spy who was detained longer than Itō: Fukatani Toshio, *Nihonkoku saigo no kikanhei, Fukatani Yoshiharu to sono kazoku* (Shūeisha, 2014).

33. "Renda changweihui zhuoshou yanjiu jianquan fazhi," *Renmin ribao*, February 15, 1979.

34. Huang Jiayang, "Deng Xiaoping, 'Lishi jueyi' qicao shou shiju suoxian," accessed September 13, 2019, http://www.hybsl.cn/beijingcankao/beijingfenxi/2012-03-15/28976.html (online site: Hu Yaobang shiliao xinxiwang).

35. Guoguang Wu, *The Anatomy of Political Power in China* (EAI, National University of Singapore, Marshall Cavendish Academic Press, 2005), 116–118.

36. Roderick MacFarquhar, "The Succession to Mao and the End of Maoism, 1969–1982," in *The Politics of China: Sixty Years of the People's Republic of China*, 3rd ed., ed. Roderick MacFarquhar (Cambridge: Cambridge University Press, 2011), 330. See also Richard Baum, "Modernization and Legal Reform in Post-Mao China: The Rebirth of Socialist Legality," *Studies in Comparative Communism* 19, no. 2 (Summer 1986): 69–103.

37. Guoguang, *Anatomy of Political Power in China*, 147.

38. Xiao Donglian, *Lishi de zhuangui: cong boluanfanzheng dao gaigekaifang, 1979–1981*, vol. 10 of series Zhonghua remin gongheguoshi (Hong Kong: Xianggang zhongwen daxue dangdai zhongguo wenhua yanjiu zhongxin, 2008), 127; "Shishi qiushi de jiejuehao silei fenzi zhaimao wenti, gonganbu buzhang Zhao Cangbi tongzhi da benbao jizhewen," *Renmin ribao*, January 30, 1979.

39. Xiao, *Lishi de zhuangui*, vol. 10, 89.

40. Xiao, *Lishi de zhuangui*, vol. 10, 104.

41. Alexander C. Cook, *The Cultural Revolution on Trial: Mao and the Gang of Four* (Cambridge: Cambridge University Press, 2016), 2.

42. "Zhengyi de panjue," *Renmin ribao*, January 26, 1981.

43. Cook, *Cultural Revolution on Trial*, 25.

44. Fei Xiaotong, "Yige shenpanyuan de ganshou," *Renmin ribao*, January 30, 1981.

45. *A Great Trial in Chinese History: The Trial of Lin Biao and Jiang Qiang Counter-Revolutionary Cliques, Nov. 1980–Jan. 1981* (Honolulu: University Press of the Pacific, 2004; reprint of the 1981 version), 3.

46. *Great Trial in Chinese History*, 7.

47. Alexander Cook, "'Settling Accounts': Law as History in the Trial of the Gang of Four," in Andrew Lewis and Michael Lobban, eds., *Law and History: Current Legal Issues* 6 (2003): 413.

48. Cook, *Cultural Revolution on Trial*, 8.

49. Cook, *Cultural Revolution on Trial*, 28.

50. Cook, *Cultural Revolution on Trial*, 113.

51. You Chenjun, Fan Zhongxin, and Gong Xiangzhai, *Weishenme yao chongjian zhongguo faxi: Ju Zheng fazheng wenxuan* (Beijingshi: Zhongguo zhengfa daxue chubanshe, 2009), 24–47.

52. Gu Nianzu, ed., *Dongwu chunqiu: dongwu daxue jianxiao baishi zhounian jinian* (Suzhou: Suzhou daxue chubanshe, 2010), 141–142.

53. Cook, *Cultural Revolution on Trial*, 68–69; Ma Lingguo, "Tebie fating de falu guwen Qiu Shaoheng," *Shiji*, 5qi, (1995): 18–21.

54. Ma, "Tebie fating de falu guwen Qiu Shaoheng," 20.

55. Zheng Shanlong, "Qiu Shaoheng: cong dongjing shenpan dao shenpan sirenbang," *Shiji*, 3qi, (2007): 56.

56. *Great Trial in Chinese History*, 147.

57. "Qiu Shaoheng: rushan tiezheng jianzhi rijun baoxing," September 3, 2015, in *Zhengyi de shenpan zhi xinzhongguo shenpan shenyang* (Beijing: Renmin fayuanbao tekan, 2015).

58. Guoguang, *Anatomy of Political Power in China*, 101.

59. Guoguang, *Anatomy of Political Power in China*, 102.

60. Xiao, *Lishi de zhuangui*, vol. 10, 267–270.

61. "Guanyu jianguo yilai dangde ruogan lishi wenti de jueyi (June 27, 1981, passed unanimously at the sixth session of the CCP's 11th Central Committee Meeting)." The original was reposted on a Xinhua news site, which is currently no longer available, but it was archived on the Internet Archive Wayback Machine: https://web.archive.org/web/20151123222207/http://news.xinhuanet.com/ziliao/2002-03/04/content_2543544.htm. A full text of the English version can be found at https://www.marxists.org/subject/china/documents/cpc/history/01.htm. The first historical resolution was in the 1945 CCP's "Resolution on Certain Historical Questions" (Guanyu ruogan lishi wenti de jueyi). The full Chinese text of the 1945 proclamation on history is found on the party education website, https://xcb.cdtc.edu.cn/info/1089/2011.htm.

62. Xiao, *Lishi de zhuangui*, vol. 10, 272–275.

63. "Xi Jinping tan fandui lishi xuwuzhuyi," on the Shanghai CCP party history website, http://www.ccphistory.org.cn/node2/shds/n218/n514/u1ai14999.html (accessed October 6, 2019).

64. Ji Zhengju, "Cong lishi xuwuzhuyi de weihai kan sugong kuatai de jiaoxun," http://www.dswxyjy.org.cn/n1/2017/1219/c398751-29716651.html; and an English version by Peter Moody at his website: https://sites.nd.edu/peter-moody/2019/06/21/historical-nihilism/. See also Christopher Vassallo, "China Eyes the Soviet Demise: CCP Perspectives on the Collapse of the Soviet Union, 1989–2021" (master's dissertation at Schwarzman College, Tsinghua University, August 2021); and Jude Blanchette, *China's New Red Guards: The Return of Radicalism and the Rebirth of Mao Zedong* (Oxford: Oxford University Press, 2019), 127–147.

65. Gotelind Mueller, *Documentary, World History, and National Power in the PRC: Global Rise in Chinese Eyes* (London: Routledge, 2013), 133–165.

66. Zhonggong zhongyang bangongting, guowuyuan bangongting, zhongyang junwei bangongting yinfa, "Guanyu jinyibu jiaqiang lieshi jinian gongzuo de yijian," on website of The Central People's Government of the People's Republic of China, published July 3, 2013, http://www.gov.cn/jrzg/2013-07/03/content_2439984.htm.

67. The full text, at least as of October 2019, was viewable at the PKU Law site: http://www.pkulaw.cn/fulltext_form.aspx?Db=chl&Gid=313960#.

68. Law of the People's Republic of China on the Protection of Heroes and Martyrs, on the PKU law website, produced May 1, 2018, "Disantiao, yingxiong lieshi shiji he jingshen shi zhonghua minzu de gongtong lishi jiyi he shehuizhuyi hexin jiazhiguan de zhongyao tixian," "Diwutiao, meinian 9yue 30ri wei lishi jinianri, guojia zai shoudu beijing tiananmen guangchang renmin yingxiong jinianbei qian juxing jinianyishi, mianhuai yingxiong lieshi." See http://www.pkulaw.cn/fulltext_form.aspx?Db=chl&Gid=313960#.

69. Sebastian Veg, "The 'Restructuring' of Hong Kong and the Rise of Neostatism," June 2020, https://tocqueville21.com/le-club/the-restructuring-of-hong-kong-and-the-rise-of-neostatism/.

70. Sebastian Veg, "The Rise of China's Statist Intellectuals: Law, Sovereignty, and 'Repoliticization,'" *China Journal* 82 (July 2019): 33–37.

71. Veg, "Rise of China's Statist Intellectuals," 37.

72. "Iperitto nado no dokugasu, nihongun ga tsukatte ita chūgoku sensen de tairyō ni 56reizu iri de kijutsu beikōbunshokan ni hozon," *Asahi shimbun*, June 14, 1984, Tokyo morning edition.

73. 101-shū-gaimuiinkai-16gō, June 20, 1984, JPR. Abe Shintarō was the father of Japan's longest-serving prime minister, Abe Shinzō.

74. Matsuno Seiya, *Nihongun no dokugasu heiki* (Gaifūsha, 2005), 311; Dai134kai kokkai, sangiin, gaimuiinkai, dai 9gō, November 30, 1995, JPR; Yoshiko Nozaki, *War Memory, Nationalism and Education in Postwar Japan, 1945–2007* (London: Routledge, 2008), 94–105.

75. Michael J. Green and Igata Akira, "The Gulf War and Japan's National Security Identity," in *Examining Japan's Lost Decades*, ed. Funabashi Yoichi and Barak Kushner (London: Routledge, 2015), 158–175.

76. Nakasone Yasuhiro, *Jiseiroku: rekishi hōtei no hikoku to shite* (Shinchōsha, 2004), 32.

77. "Nakasone Yasuhiro, Miyazawa Kiichishi (tokubetsu taidan kenpō 50nen:1)," *Asahi shimbun*, April 22, 1997.

78. Fifth installment of this Miyazawa-Nakasone conversation, *Asahi shimbun*, April 26, 1997.

13. Afterlives of the Damned

1. Fushunshi zhengxie wenshi weiyuanhui, ed., *Weiman huangdi Pu Yi ji riben zhanfan gaizao jishi* (Zhongguo wenshi chubanshe, 1990), 196.

2. Fushunshi zhengxie wenshi weiyuanhui, *Weiman huangdi Pu Yi ji riben zhanfan gaizao jishi*, 199.

3. Zhao Yuying, "Senpan mo kawari, watashitachi mo kawatta," in *Chūgoku bujun senpan kanrijo shokuin no shōgen*, ed. Arai Toshio shiryō hozonkai (Nashi no kisha, 2003), 334–347; Zhao Yuying, "Gaizao riben zhanfan zhong de yihu gongzuo," in *Huiyi gaizao zhanfan*, shangce (vol. 1), ed. Quanguo zhengxie wenshi he xuexi weiyuanhui (Beijing: Zhongguo wenshi chubanshe, 2013), 122–134; Zhao Yuyin, interview in Fushun, China, June 2, 2019, in Shanghai guangbo dianshitai jilupian zhongxin Chen Yinan gongzuoshi, ed., *Yatai zhanzheng shenpan* (Shanghai: Shanghai jiaotong daxuechubanshe, 2021), 223–225.

4. Hou Jiahua, interview, Fushun, China, June 2, 2019.

5. "Wuwang zhanzheng zhi tong, heping yongzai renxin," *Renmin gonganbao*, October 19, 2015.

6. Yoshihisa Amae, "Pro-colonial or Postcolonial? Appropriation of Japanese Colonial Heritage in Present-Day Taiwan," *Journal of Current Chinese Affairs* 40, no. 1 (2011): 19–62.

7. Tsai Chin-Tang, "Taiwan de zhonglieci yu riben huguo shenshe, jingguo shenshe zhi bijiao yanjiu," *Shida taiwanshi xuebao*, (3) (2010): 7. See also Dong Nian, "Taoyuanxian zhonglieci—zhongguo wenhua yuantouxia de riben shenshe jianzhu he sixiang," *Lishi yuekan*, (219), (2006): 10–14; Lu Pan, *Image, Imagination and Imaginarium: Remapping World War II Monuments in Greater China* (Singapore: Palgrave Macmillan, 2020), 190–201.

8. Paul Williams, *Memorial Museums: The Global Rush to Commemorate Atrocities* (New York: Berg Publishers, 2007), 5.

9. This idea is originally from David Lowenthal but persuasively argued in Shu-Mei Huang and Hyun Kyung Lee, *Heritage, Memory, and Punishment: Remembering Colonial Prisons in East Asia* (London: Routledge, 2020), xiii.

10. Williams, *Memorial Museums*, 4.

11. This event took place under Taiwan president Ma Ying-jeou, a KMT loyalist who still identified with the ROC. The current government under Tsai Ing-wen and the DPP takes a different stand.

12. Lu Junsheng and Zeng Xiaowen, eds., *Nanyang yinglie: erzhan qijian babuyaniujineiya jingnei guojun jiangshi jilu* (Taibei: Guofangbu shizheng bianyishi, 2009), 144–146.

13. Williams, *Memorial Museums*, 177.

14. Linh D. Vu, "Bones of Contention: China's World War II Military Graves in India, Burma, and Papua New Guinea," *Journal of Chinese Military History* 8 (2019): 96.

15. Joseph R. Allen, *Taipei: City of Displacements* (Seattle: University of Washington Press, 2012), 152.

16. Julia Ross, "Taiwan's Statue Wars," *Time*, May 24, 2007; Jeremy E. Taylor, "Qujianghua: Disposing of and Re-appraising the Remnants of Chiang Kai-shek's Reign on

Taiwan," *Journal of Contemporary History* 45, no. 1 (2010): 181–196. See also Kirk A. Denton, *The Landscape of Historical Memory: The Politics of Museums and Memorial Culture in Post-martial Law Taiwan* (Hong Kong: Hong Kong University Press, 2021), 153–161.

17. One of the official websites of the 228 Foundation websites, https://www.228.org.tw (accessed December 1, 2022).

18. Eric N. Danielson, "Revisiting Chongqing: China's Second World War Temporary National Capital," *Journal of the Royal Asiatic Society Hong Kong Branch* 45 (2005): 177; Lu, *Image, Imagination and Imaginarium*, 358–367; Kevin Paul Landdeck, "Under the Gun: Nationalist Military Service and Society in Wartime Sichuan, 1938–1945" (PhD diss., University of California, Berkeley, 2011), 431–432; Kirk A. Denton, *Exhibiting the Past: Historical Memory and the Politics of Museums in Postsocialist China* (Honolulu: University of Hawaii Press, 2013).

19. Tony Brooks, "Angry States: Chinese Views of Japan as Seen through the Unit 731 War Museum since 1949," in *Remembering Asia's World War Two*, ed. Mark R. Frost, Daniel Schumacher, and Edward Vickers (New York: Routledge, 2019), 27.

20. Sanitized Copy Approved for Release 2011/02/24: CIA-RDP91B00135R000500980010-0.

21. Robert Weatherley and Qiang Zhang, *History and Nationalist Legitimacy in Contemporary China* (London: Palgrave Macmillan, 2017), 127–128; Lu, *Image, Imagination and Imaginarium*, 35–37.

22. Weatherley and Qiang, *History and Nationalist Legitimacy in Contemporary China*, 141.

23. https://www.theguardian.com/world/2019/jun/27/chinese-war-film-the-eight-hundred-premiere-cancelled-in-apparent-censorship.

24. "Rana Mitter Reviews a Revisionist New Book and TV Series on China's WWII," November 4, 2020, https://chinachannel.org/author/rana-mitter/); Patrick Frater, "'The Eight Hundred' Controversial War Film Finally Given China Release Date," *Variety*, https://variety.com/2020/film/asia/eight-hundred-film-finally-given-china-release-date-1234723185/.

25. The park's website is http://ki43.on.coocan.jp.

26. *Kannon no iware*, http://www.koakannon.org/page03.html. These recollections are from the head priest of Rising Asia Kannon Temple, Inami Ninrei, 8–10.

27. Takazawa Hiroaki, "Amerika kokuritus kōbunshokan ga shozō suru tōkyō saiban hishikeisha no itai shogū kankei shiryō," *Nihon daigaku seisangakubu kenkyū hōkoku B*, 6gatsu, 55kan, (2022): 11.

28. "Gokuhi de okonowareta A kyū senpan no ikotsu dakkan sakusen! sono zenbō o chōsa shita," vol. 2, *Yokohama no Kuboyama hōmon*, https://chinobouken.com/atypebone2/.

29. Renmin fayuanbaoshe, ed., *Zhengyi de shenpan: jinian zhongguo renmin kangri zhanzheng shengli qishi zhounian* (Renmin fayuanchubanshe, 2016), 404.

30. "Tanaka Masaaki kōa kannon o mamorukai kaichō kōa kannon o kataru," *Kōa kannon no kaihō*, inaugural issue, autumn 1994. The web page for the Buddhist Temple has a digital backlist of all of its internal pamphlets. See http://www.history.gr.jp/koa_kan_non/backnumber.html. Itami Ninrei, "Kōa kannon no iware," http://www.koakannon.org/box4/a01.pdf. See also Sendai dōmori Itami Ninrei (jutsu), "Junkoku shichishi no hi kōa kannon ni sono haka no aru wake," dai16gō, October 18, 2002; this is an explanatory essay written by the head cleric, http://www.koakannon.org/box4/a01.pdf.

31. "Kōa kannon kaiki rokujūnen, kōa kannon o mamorukai sōritsu roku shūnen no atatte," *Kōa kannon*, dai 12gō, October 18, 2000; Michael Lucken, *The Japanese and the War: From Expectation to Memory*, trans. Karen Grimwade (New York: Columbia University Press, 2017), 251–256.

32. Tokutomi Tasaburō, "Kōa kannon o kangaeru kōa kannon o mamorukai riji," *Kōa kannon no kaihō*, inaugural issue, Autumn 1994.

33. Sejima Ryūzō, "Watakushidomo no tsutome," *Kōa kannon*, dai 3gō, April 18, 1996.

34. Webpage of the Rising Asia Kannon Temple, http://www.asahi-net.or.jp/~un3k-mn/0815-3izuyama.htm (accessed July 30, 2022).

35. Webpage of the Rising Asia Kannon Temple, http://www.asahi-net.or.jp/~un3k-mn/0815-3izuyama.htm (accessed July 30, 2022). Michael Lucken, "Autour de quelques os: La mémorialisation des criminels de guerre de catégorie A," *Cipango* 15 (2008): 1–17, http://ki43.on.coocan.jp/junkoku/7.03.html.

36. "Watashi to gikyoku 'kami to hito no aida' bōkyaku ni tsuit," *Asahi shimbun*, October 12, 1970, Tokyo morning edition; Lucken, *Japanese and the War*, 219–228.

37. Eric J. Gangloff, introduction to *Between God and Man*, by Kinoshita Junji (London: University of Tokyo Press, 1979), 12.

38. 91-san-kensetsuiinkai-3gō, February 21, 1980, JPR; Kaya Okinori, *Senzen/sengo hachijūnen* (Keizai ōraisha, 1976), 194. See also Barak Kushner, "Heroes, Victims, and the Quest for Peace: War Monuments and the Contradictions of Japan's Post-imperial Commemoration," in *Sites of Imperial Memory: Commemorating Colonial Rule in the Nineteenth and Twentieth Centuries*, ed. Dominik Geppert and Frank Mueller (Manchester: Manchester University Press, 2015), 70–91.

39. The Kōmyō Temple website, special page for the war martyrs, http://tokyowanyosai.com/sub/ibutu/sekihi/irei-232.html (accessed August 23, 2021).

40. Odamura Shirō, "Sensō no koshō o tadasō," *Kōa kannon no kaihō*, Daiyongō, October 18, 1996.

41. Wanglai Gao, "Unearthing Poison: Disposal of Abandoned Chemical Weapons in China," *Bulletin of the Atomic Scientists* 73, no. 6 (2017): 404–410.

42. "Japan, China at Odds over Compensation Payments for Mustard Gas Incident," *BBC Monitoring Asia Pacific*, September 14, 2003; Yoshimi Yoshiaki, *Dokugasusen to nihongun* (Iwanami shoten, 2004), 284–290.

43. Yoshimi, *Dokugasusen to nihongun*, 280.

44. Funabashi Yōichi, *Genpatsu haisen: kiki no rīdāshippu to wa* (Bungei shunjū, 2014), 255.

45. "Abe shushō, Akyū senpanra hōyō ni sokoku no ishizue, shigatsu jimin sōsaimei de aitō messēji," *Asahi shimbun*, August 27, 2014, Tokyo morning edition. However, we must also be cautious in overextending too conservative of a label on Abe, as Hosoya Yūichi noted in an article after Abe's assassination. See Hosoya Yūichi, "Saishō Abe Shinzōron," *Chūō kōron* (September 2022): 48–55.

46. Fuji Seiji, *Riron kingendai shigaku: hontō no nihon no rekishi*, expanded ed. (Fusōsha, 2017).

47. Park Yu-ha, *Teikoku no ianfu: shokuminchi shihai to kioku no tatakai* (Asahi shimbusha, 2015); Tomomi Yamaguchi, "Revisionism, Ultranationalism, Sexism: Relations between the Far Right and the Establishment over the 'Comfort Women' Issue," *Social Science Japan Journal* 21, no. 2 (2018): 193–212.

48. Ministry of Foreign Affairs of Japan website, "Announcement by Foreign Ministers of Japan and the Republic of Korea at the Joint Press Occasion," December 28, 2015, https://www.mofa.go.jp/a_o/na/kr/page4e_000364.html.

49. Todd Hall, "German Lessons for Sino-Japanese Relations?" (talk at East Asian Seminar Series, University of Cambridge, February 23, 2015).

50. Yi Yong-hun, ed., *Hannichi shuzoku shugi—nikkan kiki no kongen* (Bungei shunjū, 2019).

51. Lon L. Fuller and Kenneth I. Winston, "The Forms and Limits of Adjudication," *Harvard Law Review* 92, no. 2 (December 1978): 366.

52. Martti Koskenniemi, "Between Impunity and Show Trials," in *Max Planck Yearbook of United Nations Law*, vol. 6, ed. J. A. Frowein and R. Wolfrum (Leiden: Brill, 2002), 34.

Conclusion

1. Jelena Subotic, *Hijacked Justice: Dealing with the Past in the Balkans* (Ithaca, NY: Cornell University Press, 2010), 5.

2. Philip Gourevitc, *We Wish to Inform You That Tomorrow We Will Be Killed with Our Families: Stories from Rwanda* (New York: Farrar, Straus and Giroux, 1998).

3. "75th anniversary of the end of the 2nd World War, May 8, 2020, Federal Germany presidential webpage: www.bundespraesident.de/SharedDocs/Reden/EN/Frank-Walter-Steinmeier/Reden/2020/05/200508-75th-anniversary-World-War-II.html.

4. "Statement by Prime Minister Shinzo Abe," August 14, 2015, on the Prime Minister of Japan and His Cabinet website, https://japan.kantei.go.jp/97_abe/statement/201508/0814statement.html. I am indebted to Cavin Yeo for pointing out the discrepancy between these two statements. Lily Gardner Feldman, "Commemoration in Comparison Germany's Comprehensive and Complex Culture of Remembrance," in *Memory, Identity, and Commemorations of World War II: Anniversary Politics in Asia Pacific*, ed. Daqing Yang and Mike M. Mochizuki (Lanham, MD: Lexington Books, 2018), 141–155.

5. Her poem was put up in full on the CNN website after the event. See: "READ: Youth Poet Laureate Amanda Gorman's Inaugural Poem," January 20, 2021, https://edition.cnn.com/2021/01/20/politics/amanda-gorman-inaugural-poem-transcript/index.html.

6. Lionel Babicz, "Japan–Korea, France–Algeria: Colonialism and Post-colonialism," *Japanese Studies* 33, no. 2, (2013): 202.

7. Benjamin Stora, *Les Passions Douloureuses* (Paris: Albin Michel, 2021).

8. The full text of the original Chinese article was republished online for the East South West North website, in December 2006, Yuan Weishi, "Xiandaihua yu lishi jiaokeshu," http://www.zonaeuropa.com/20060126_2.htm. Yuan Weishi, *Chūgoku no rekishi kyōkasho mondai—hyōten jiken no kiroku to hansei* (Nihon kyōhōsha, 2006); Li Datong, *Hyōten teikan no butaiura* (Nihon kyōhōsha, 2006).

9. Barak Kushner, "Nationality and Nostalgia: The Manipulation of Memory in Japan, Taiwan, and China since 1990," *International History Review* 29, no. 4 (December 2007): 793–820.

10. Liu Jie, *Chūgoku no kyōkoku kōsō: nisshin sensō kara gendai made* (Chikuma shobō, 2013), 41–42; Liu Jie and Nakamura Motoya, eds., *Chōtaikoku chūgoku no yukue*, vol. 1, *bunmeikan to rekishininshiki* (Tokyo daigaku shuppankai, 2022).

11. Wang Yi, "Bringing the East and West Together in Shared Commitment to Multilateralism" (speech, 56th Munich Security Conference, February 15, 2020), https://www.fmprc.gov.cn/mfa_eng/wjdt_665385/zyjh_665391/t1745384.shtml.

12. Rana Mitter, "The World China Wants," *Foreign Affairs*, published online on December 8, 2020, https://www.foreignaffairs.com/articles/china/2020-12-08/world-china-wants?utm_medium=social&fbclid=IwAR3WCzHJw_2UWrJOStbscWWH38GH04TZ6WRDJLy49_zH74TGeMFGo9Cfst0.

13. Martti Koskenniemi, *The Politics of International Law* (Oxford: Hart Publishing, 2011), 242.

14. Koskenniemi, *Politics of International Law*, 243.

15. Cheng Zhaoqi, *Dongjing shenpan weile shijie heping* (Shanghai: Shanghai jiaotong daxue chubanshe, 2017).

16. A. T. Williams, *A Passing Fury: Searching for Justice at the End of World War II* (London: Penguin, 2016), 432.

17. Karina Korostelina, "Understanding Values of Cultural Heritage within the Framework of Social Identity Conflicts," in *Values in Heritage Management: Emerging Approaches and Research Directions*, ed. Erica Avrami, Susan Macdonald, Randall Mason, and David Myers, online publication of the Getty Foundation, 2019, https://www.getty.edu/publications/heritagemanagement/.

18. Renée Diresta, Carly Miller, Vanessa Molter, John Pomfret, and Glenn Tiffert, *Telling China's Story: The Chinese Communist Party's Campaign to Shape Global Narratives* (Hoover Institution: Stanford Internet Observatory, 2020), 9–11.

19. The group's name in Japanese is: *Nihon no zento to rekishi kyōiku o kangaeru wakate giin no kai*. "Seiji no genba, anteishugi, 5, monkashō to ichiji no kyōchō," *Yomiuri shimbun*, October 26, 2006, Tokyo morning edition.

20. This blog post is no longer on his site, but it was archived on the Internet Archive Wayback Machine. Nihon no zento to rekishi kyōiku o kangaeru wakate giin no kai, ed., *Rekishi kyōkasho e no gimon—wakate kokkai giin ni yoru rekishi kyōkasho mondai no sōkatsu* (Nihon no zento to rekishi kyōiku o kangaeru wakate giin no kai publishers, 2008).

21. The original report was a thirty-page investigation with the title "Nankin mondai shōiinkai no chōsa kenshō no sōkatsu" that was used in media events beginning June 19, 2007. This was then published as a book: Nihon no zento to rekishi kyōiku o kangaeru giin no kai, ed., *Nankin no jissō: kokusai renmei wa 'nanking 2mannin gyakusatsu' sura mitomenakatta* (Nisshin hōdō, 2008).

22. James Baldwin's speech is available in full on the internet: https://www.youtube.com/watch?v=7_1ZEYgtijk.

Archival Sources

Australia

Australia War Memorial
National Archives of Australia

China

Beijing Municipal Archives (北京檔案館)
Chinese Ministry of Foreign Affairs Archives (外交部檔案館)

Great Britain

Kew Garden, National Archives

Hong Kong

China's anti-rightist movement database (中國反右運動數據庫, 1957). This database is collated by Song Yongyi and housed at the University Services Center for China Studies Collection, Chinese University Hong Kong.

China's mid-1950s political movement database (中國五十年代初中期的政治運動數據庫：從土地改革到公私合營, 1949–1956). This database is collated by Song Yongyi and housed at the University Services Center for China Studies Collection, Chinese University Hong Kong.

Chinese Communist Party Internal Reference Reports Collection (內部參考資料), the University Services Center for China Studies Collection, Chinese University Hong Kong

Israel

Knesset Debates

Japan

Japan's Parliamentary Record (国会会議録)

Ministry of Defense Archives (防衛研究所), Ichigaya, Tokyo. This archive used to be housed in Ebisu.

Ministry of Foreign Affairs Archives (外交資料館)
Modern Japanese Political History Materials Room (憲政資料室) in the National Diet Library, Tokyo
National Archives of Japan (国立公文書館), Tokyo
Shōwa tennō jitsuroku (昭和天皇実録) (Actual Record of the Showa Emperor)
Tōyō Bunko Archives (東洋文庫), Tokyo
Yasukuni Shrine Archives (靖国偕行文庫), Tokyo

Switzerland

International Red Cross Archives, Geneva

Taiwan

Academia Historica (國史館)
KMT Archives (中國國民黨黨史館)
Ministry of Foreign Affairs Archives housed in Academia Sinica (外交部檔案, 中研院近史所檔案館)
National Archives Administration of Taiwan (國家發展委員會檔案管理局)

United States

Columbia University Oral History Archives
Columbia University papers of Qin Dehuai, Wellington Koo
Declassified CIA reports
Digital National Security Archive collection: China and U.S. Intelligence, 1945–2010 section
Foreign Relations of the United States
Hoover Institute Archives, Stanford, California
National Archives, College Park, Maryland
Philip J. Jaffe Papers at Stuart A. Rose Manuscript, Archives, and Rare Book Library, Emory University
Roscoe Pound Papers at Harvard University Law Library, Cambridge, MA
Sir Leon Radzinowicz Archive, Florida State University, Tallahassee, FL
United States Relations with China: With Special Reference to the Period 1944-1949, published by Department of State, United States. Division of Publications, 1949
University of California at Los Angeles Archives
Wilson Center Cold War Archives, online

Museums Visited as Reference Sites

9.18 Museum, Liaoning Province
Beituan Village Martyrs site
Bridge Street Prison, Shanghai
Cixi Sculpture Garden, Taiwan

Fushun War Criminals Management Center, Liaoning Province
Lijixiang Comfort Women Museum in Nanjing
Nanjing Civilian War of Resistance Against Japan Museum, Jiangsu Province
Nanjing Massacre Museum, Jiangsu Province
National Human Rights Museum in Taipei, Taiwan
Shenyang Trial Museum, Liaoning Province
Taiyuan Prison Camp, Shanxi Province
Unit 731 Museum, Heilongjiang Province

Index

www.ingramcontent.com/pod-product-compliance
Lightning Source LLC
Chambersburg PA
CBHW020742170726
48298CB00016BA/272/J
9781501774010